# Table of Contents

# Why an All-Digital Solution?

We decided to move our Public Speaking course to an all-digital textbook in Fall 2013. We run an eight-week course that requires our students to have instant access to course materials. Most of our students are using e-readers, tablets, and access ancillary course materials online already. The fact that the digital textbooks provide us with a free trial allows all students to have instant access to the correct textbook the first day of class. We are excited because we love *McGraw-Hill's LearnSmart™*. *LearnSmart* gives the instructor insights into what concepts students are learning and what concepts they need assistance with. We now can catch students before they fall behind and provide the proper assistance to help them achieve.

—Kenisha Burke, Public Speaking Coordinator and Communication Instructor, Department of Communications, Austin Peay State University

If you are anything like the thousands of communication instructors we have worked with, your most pressing goal is to help your students communicate effectively, the gateway to academic and professional success. When you assign **Connect Communication** you can be confident—and have data to demonstrate—that your students, however diverse, are acquiring the baseline skills, principles, and critical processes that constitute effective communication. This leaves you to focus on your highest course expectations.

**TAILORED TO YOU. Connect Communication** offers on-demand, single sign-on access to learners—wherever they are and whenever they have time. With a single, one-time registration, learners receive access to McGraw-Hill's trusted content. **Learners also have access to a three-week *Free Trial* period during registration.**

**EASY TO USE. Connect Communication** seamlessly supports all major learning management systems with content, assignments, performance data, and LearnSmart, the leading adaptive learning system. With these tools you can quickly make assignments, produce reports, focus discussions, intervene on problem topics, and help at-risk learners—as you need to and when you need to.

**PROVEN EFFECTIVE. Connect Communication** can be used in a variety of ways to establish course consistency and assessment transparency, and to verify that program outcomes are being sought and met. **Connect** can track the progress of individual learners or whole sections toward course goals. **Connect** generates professional, easy-to-read reports suitable for program evaluation and accreditation.

# Connect Communication Makes Assigning Online Easier

McGraw-Hill is firmly committed to the success and professional growth of our customers as they use our digital course solutions. We understand that incorporating new systems and technologies into your programs can feel daunting, but we know it can also be transformative. **Connect Communication** supports instructors of all proficiencies, with the goal of helping every one of our customers exceed their expectations.

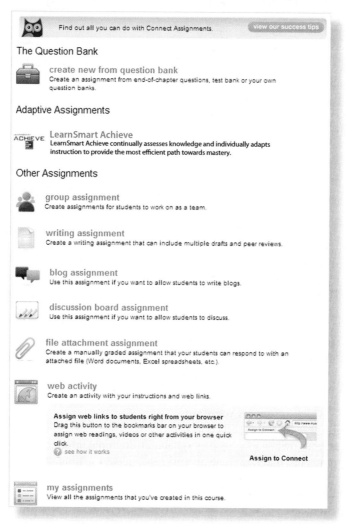

When you draw upon **Connect Communication** to implement your curriculum, you use digital tools developed by communication experts to create a state-of-the-art teaching and learning environment that engages your learners with their course assignments.

The flexible content and powerful tools found in **Connect Communication** work well in traditional course settings as well as in online or hybrid courses.

# Tailoring Your Course Materials

## McGraw-Hill Create™
### Create your own *Experience Communication*.

We understand that not
every school wants to
approach Public Speaking
in the same way, and so
McGraw-Hill offers several
ways for you to customize
a solution to meet your
program's needs:

- Easily arrange and
  rearrange material
  from a variety of
  sources, including your
  own.
- Select content by
  discipline or collection, including 4,000 textbooks, 5,500 articles, 25,000 cases,
  and 11,000 readings.
- Use a McGraw-Hill Express Book in CREATE as a starting point to build your
  custom text.
- When you build a CREATE book, you will receive a complimentary print review
  copy in 3 to 5 business days or a complimentary electronic review copy (eComp)
  via e-mail in about one hour. Go to mcgrawhillcreate.com and register today.

### With CREATE you can
- **choose which chapters you want from *Experience Communication* [or *Public
  Speaking Matters*]**
- **choose which resources you want**
  - ✓ from other McGraw-Hill collections
  - ✓ from your own works, such as syllabi, institutional information, study guides,
    assignments, diagrams, and artwork; and student writing, art, and photos
- **choose which format you want**
  - ✓ print
  - ✓ electronic

## McGraw-Hill's Learning Solutions Consultants

Our Learning Solutions Consultants will collaborate with you to build courses and
materials for communication that suit the content, delivery, and platform needs of
your department or institution.

# LearnSmart

No two students are alike. Why should their learning paths be? LearnSmart uses revolutionary adaptive technology to build a learning experience unique to each student's individual needs. It starts by identifying the topics a student knows and does not know. As the student progresses, LearnSmart adapts and adjusts the content based on his or her individual strengths, weaknesses, and confidence. LearnSmart also takes into account that everyone will forget a certain amount of material. LearnSmart pinpoints areas that a student is most likely to forget and encourages periodic review to ensure that the knowledge is truly learned and retained.

**WANT PROOF?** Students who use LearnSmart are 35% more likely to complete their class; are 13% more likely to pass their class; and have been proven to improve their performance by a full letter grade.

## How It Works

LearnSmart guides students to an understanding of core concepts by helping them identify knowledge gaps and by providing key content at specific intervals to ensure mastery and long-term knowledge retention. LearnSmart continuously adapts as students answer questions, building an optimal learning path, so that students spend less time on concepts they already know and more time focused on those they don't. Here's how:

- **Establish Baseline Understanding**—Students begin by answering a series of questions in their LearnSmart Assignment related to core concepts and key themes from the modules you have selected.

- **Identify Confidence Level**—Students assign a confidence rating to each question they answer, acknowledging how aware they are of their level of knowledge. LearnSmart uses this information, in tandem with the answer itself, to improve the individual learning path by adjusting which questions to present, as well as the difficulty of these questions.

- **Review and Compare**—Students can compare their performance with that of others, or they can choose to focus solely on their own progress by viewing a series of detailed performance reports.

- **Revisit Core Concepts**—LearnSmart directs students to revisit core content in the eBook to reinforce materials they should study and ensure that knowledge is transferred to long-term memory.

- **Informative Reports**—Reports provide valuable information about individual and class performance, allowing you to identify students who need additional instruction or topics that the class is struggling with in aggregate.

» *For more on reports, see pages 11–13.*

# SmartBook

As the first and only adaptive reading experience, SmartBook is changing the way students read and learn. SmartBook creates a personalized reading experience by highlighting the most important concepts a student needs to learn at that moment in time. As a student engages with SmartBook, the reading experience continuously adapts by highlighting content based on what each student knows and doesn't know. This ensures that he or she is focused on the content needed to close specific knowledge gaps while it simultaneously promotes long-term learning.

## How It Works

Built off of the proven LearnSmart engine that identifies what a student does or does not know and adapts in real time to maximize each minute of time spent studying, each SmartBook contains four stages, which transform student reading from a linear activity into a dynamic learning experience: Preview, Read, Practice, Recharge.

- **Preview**—Students start with a preview of each chapter and the corresponding key learning objectives. This preview establishes a framework of the material in a student's brain to help retain knowledge over time.
- **Read**—While students read the material, they are guided to core topics where they should spend the most time studying.
- **Practice**—As students read the material, SmartBook presents them with questions to help them identify what content they know and what they don't know.
- **Recharge**—To ensure concept mastery and retention, students complete the Read and Practice steps until SmartBook directs them to Recharge the important material they're likely to forget.

Green highlights indicate student mastery of the topic in this section.

Dimmed text indicates content that is less relevant for students at the time based on their progress, but the text can be revealed with one click.

Yellow highlights indicate important topics for students to study based on their progress.

# LearnSmart Achieve

Fueled by McGraw-Hill's LearnSmart, the most widely used and intelligent adaptive learning resource, LearnSmart Achieve is designed to help students improve learning with rich, dynamic learning resources; retain more knowledge; and get better grades. As a student progresses through LearnSmart Achieve, the program's continuously adaptive learning path adjusts to deliver just-in-time resources—instructional videos, simulations, and more—catered to each student's needs. This model is designed to accelerate learning and strengthen memory recall.

## How It Works

LearnSmart Achieve consists of three key phases—Tune In, Focus, Practice—which add up to a highly personalized, constantly adapting learning plan that leads to true concept mastery:

- **Tune In**—Students are asked a sample series of questions related to a specific learning objective to assess their baseline understanding of the content.
- **Focus**—Based on their responses to the Tune In questions, Achieve presents students with a variety of learning resources (videos, detailed artwork, a narrative coach reading, and more) to reinforce the concepts they are struggling with most.
- **Practice**—After the Focus phase, students are asked a more in-depth series of questions to confirm their understanding of key objectives. Achieve then adjusts the learning plan to provide suggested learning resources to assist students in mastering all core concepts.

- **Recharge**—After a student completes a module, LearnSmart Achieve encourages retention of the materials by identifying what concepts a student is most likely to forget and brings those concepts back for review before the student forgets them.

# Speech Capture and Speech Preparation Tools

Designed for use in face-to-face, real-time classrooms, as well as online courses, Connect Speech Capture allows you to evaluate your students' speeches using fully customizable rubrics. You can also create and manage peer review assignments and upload videos on behalf of students for optimal flexibility.

In preparing self-reviews and peer reviews, students can leave rubric comments (if a rubric is provided by the instructor), post comments, and leave time-stamped comments. Students can upload a video of their speech from their hard drive or use Connect's built-in video recorder. They can even attach and upload additional files or documents like a works cited page or PowerPoint.

## Peer Review

Peer review assignments are easier than ever. Create and manage peer review assignments and customize privacy settings.

## Speech Assessment

Connect Speech Capture lets you customize the assignments, including self-reviews and peer reviews.

Connect saves your frequently used comments, simplifying your efforts to provide feedback.

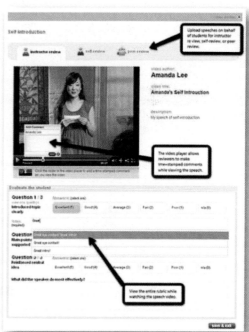

# Speech Preparation Tools

This suite of tools aids students with all facets of speech preparation, from selecting a topic and outlining their speeches to creating audience analysis questionnaires and properly citing sources. Connect also includes a customizable outline tool that lets you define an outline format for your students that is consistent with your course. You can also decide which tools—or combination of tools—to make available for your students.

- **Topic Helper**—Provides students with an alphabetized list of topics to help them prepare for speech assignments. Students can filter through the Topic Helper to discover new and exciting ideas.

- **Outline Tool**—Guides students systematically through the process of organizing and outlining their speeches. Instructors can customize parts of the outliner, as well as turn it off if they don't want their students to use it.

Connect provides links to these two web-based tools for ease of student access.

- **EasyBib**—Automates the formatting of citations and bibliographies.

- **Survey Monkey**—Helps students and instructors create and manage audience-analysis questionnaires and dynamic reports.

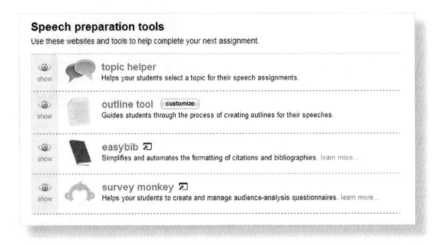

# Connect Communication Reports

Connect generates a number of powerful reports and charts, which let you quickly review the performance of a specific learner or an entire section. It also allows you to run reports that span multiple sections.

The **Assignment Results report** shows your entire class's performance across all of your assignments. Each learner's attempt appears alongside the score, organized by columns or each assignment. You can look closely at a particular learner's work by selecting the learner's name and choosing an individual assignment attempt.

The **Student Performance report** focuses on a specific learner's progress across your assignments. You can view submitted and in-progress assignments, so that you can provide guidance or feedback during or after an assignment.

The **Assignment Statistics reports** give you quick data on each assignment, including the mean score, high score, and low scores, as well as the number of times it was submitted.

The **Item Analysis report** is the best way to get a bird's-eye view of a single assignment. You can tell if learners are improving or identify concepts on which you want to spend additional time.

The **Category Analysis report** provides data on performance relative to the categories that have been tagged to questions assigned from the Connect Communication question bank.

The **At-Risk Student report** identifies learners who are at risk of not persisting in a course due to low engagement levels,

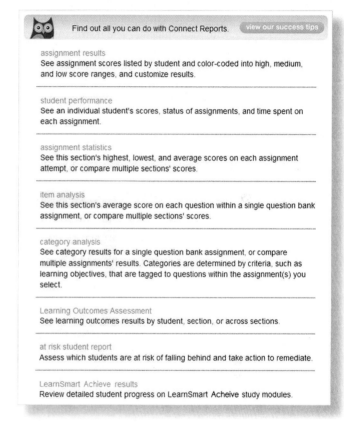

Find out all you can do with Connect Reports. view our success tips

**assignment results**
See assignment scores listed by student and color-coded into high, medium, and low score ranges, and customize results.

**student performance**
See an individual student's scores, status of assignments, and time spent on each assignment.

**assignment statistics**
See this section's highest, lowest, and average scores on each assignment attempt, or compare multiple sections' scores.

**item analysis**
See this section's average score on each question within a single question bank assignment, or compare multiple sections' scores.

**category analysis**
See category results for a single question bank assignment, or compare multiple assignments' results. Categories are determined by criteria, such as learning objectives, that are tagged to questions within the assignment(s) you select.

**Learning Outcomes Assessment**
See learning outcomes results by student, section, or across sections.

**at risk student report**
Assess which students are at risk of falling behind and take action to remediate.

**LearnSmart Achieve results**
Review detailed student progress on LearnSmart Acheive study modules.

based on patterns such as the frequency of logins and assignment submissions.

The **LearnSmart reports** focus on student usage and progress in LearnSmart, Connect Communication's highly personalized, adaptive learning resource.

## Grade Book Syncing

The raw data from the Assignment Results report synchronizes directly with programs like Blackboard, Canvas, Desire2Learn (D2L), and many other learning management systems, allowing for scores to flow automatically from Connect Communication into school-specific grade book centers.

# LearnSmart Reports

## Reports for LearnSmart, SmartBook, and Achieve

The LearnSmart Instructor Reports are part of why LearnSmart allows instructors to spend less time remediating and more time having rich conceptual discussions with their students. The Instructor Reports allow instructors to quickly monitor student activity, making it easy to identify which students are struggling and provide immediate help to ensure that those students stay enrolled in the course and improve their performance. LearnSmart Instructor Reports also highlight the concepts and learning objectives that the class as a whole is having difficulty grasping. This essential information lets you know exactly which areas to target for review during your limited class time.

Some key LearnSmart reports include

- **Progress Overview report**—View student progress for all LearnSmart modules, including how long students have spent working in the module, which modules they have used outside of any that were assigned, and individual student progress through LearnSmart.
- **Missed Questions report**—Identify specific LearnSmart probes, organized by chapter, that are problematic for students.

- **Most Challenging Learning Objectives report**—Also organized by chapter, this report identifies the specific topic areas that are challenging for your students, including specific page references. Use this information to tailor your lecture time and assignments to cover areas that require additional remediation and practice.

- **Metacognitive Skills report**—View statistics on how knowledgeable your students are about their own comprehension and learning.

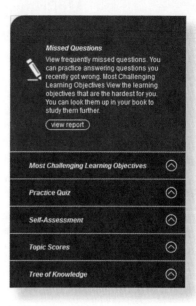

Similarly, the Student Reports break down the time the student spends studying and tracks his or her progress to identify what the student knows and doesn't know. The reports make it clear to each student where he or she should focus valuable study time to achieve maximum results.

*Students may access the self-assessment report to view how aware they were of whether they knew the answers. This metacognitive awareness will help them study more effectively.*

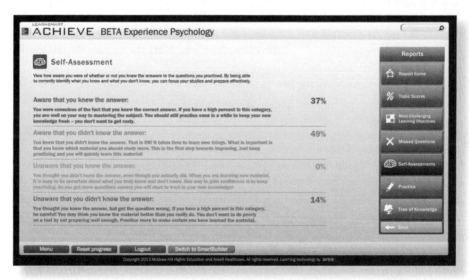

# McGraw-Hill's Digital Faculty Consultants for Connect Communication Offer Insight Based on Experience

LearnSmart has revolutionized how I do assessment in my courses. Instead of traditional quizzes I now assign the LearnSmart for each chapter. My students absolutely love this new technology. They tell me that they feel like this tool allows them to learn as they're being tested. They quickly get credit for what they know and the technology helps them to review the information that they need to spend more time with. LearnSmart has been an incredible hit with my students.

I love using Speech Capture to grade speeches. The electronic rubrics and the banked comments have allowed me to give the most comprehensive feedback of my career.

Speech Capture allows me to make comments at a time stamped moment on each student's video. My students have been thrilled as they rewatch their video and comments from myself and their classmates pop-up at the exact moment the feedback is referring to.

**Jeff Przybylo, Speech & Debate Team Director, Harper College**

Connect has transformed the way I teach my class. LearnSmart tells me quickly what students know and don't know so it transforms my lecturing time. Speech Capture provides a FERPA-safe way to record and upload student speeches so that only the students who need to view the speech can access it. I like the different ways to customize an assignment, especially the peer assessment where I can move students around to avoid potential student conflicts or to make sure that students who gave speeches are also able to complete the peer assessment. Now there's SmartBook! I can already see how this tool will transform how students approach material and learn in a way that is truly adaptable to their learning abilities.

**Tim Pierce, Coordinator, COMS 100, Northern Illinois University**

As a requirement of our university, I just finished "flagging" students who are "at risk" academically in my class. Students are able to see that they are at risk, in what ways, and hopefully they respond. I use LearnSmart's Progress and Metacognitive reports as well as Connect's "at risk" report to help me "flag" my students. It is so exciting to have a quantitative way to measure student progress or lack thereof.

**Jennifer Chochrane, Senior Lecturer Emerita, Dept. of Communication Studies, Indiana University–Purdue University Indianapolis**

Engaging students is changing! Learning is breaking away from just brick-and-mortar classrooms and is happening on student schedules, on their time, with crazy-cool and ready tools. ConnectPlus does that. Do I still use a text? Yes, but it's great that it's on-the-go available as an etext on digi devices for the students and me 24/7 in an easy-to-read layout. Compelled to cover identifiable competencies by your school? No problem. ConnectPlus lets me select the specific competencies/material from chapters, highlights them for students in their etext, and lets them know when they've mastered them—specifically! Students love the fun of LearnSmart, accessibility, and ability to review their own progress—all on their schedule. Speech capture is easy using Connect. And the peer review option for speeches is an impressive tool which helps create a feeling of real community in online Speech classes; it's uncomplicated and super easy for instructors and students to use.

**Rhonda Rye, Associate Professor, Speech Communication, Eastern Florida State College**

# Support To Ensure Your Success

- **Digital Success Academy**—The Digital Success Academy on Connect offers a wealth of training and course creation guidance for instructors. Presented in easy-to-navigate, easy-to-complete sections, it includes the popular *Connect* video shorts, step-by-step *Click through Guides*, and *First Day of Class* materials that explain how to use both the Connect platform and its course-specific tools and features. http://create.mcgraw-hill .com/wordpress-mu/success-academy

- **Digital Success Team**—The Digital Success Team is a group of specialists dedicated to working online with instructors—one-on-one—to demonstrate how the Connect platform works and to help incorporate Connect into a customer's specific course design and syllabus. http://mpss.mhhe.com/orientation.php

- **Digital Learning Consultants**—Digital Learning Consultants are local resources who work closely with your McGraw-Hill learning technology consultants. They can provide face-to-face faculty support and training. http://catalogs.mhhe.com/mhhe/findRep.do

- **Digital Faculty Consultants**—Digital Faculty Consultants are experienced instructors who use Connect in their classroom. These instructors are available to offer suggestions, advice, and training about how best to use Connect in your class. To request a Digital Faculty Consultant to speak with, please e-mail your McGraw-Hill learning technology consultant. http://connect.customer.mcgraw-hill.com/dfc/

- **National Training Webinars**—McGraw-Hill offers an ongoing series of webinars for instructors to learn and master the Connect platform as well as its course-specific tools and features. We hope you will refer to our online schedule of national training webinars and sign up to learn more about Connect! http://webinars.mhhe.com/

## Contact Our Customer Support Team

McGraw-Hill is dedicated to supporting instructors and students. To contact our customer support team, please call us at 800-331-5094 or visit us online at http://mpss.mhhe.com/contact.php.

# How Do I Set Up a Course?

## How do instructors access Connect Communication?

**For more details** and videos on how to set up your course, visit
http://connect.mcgraw-hill.com/help.

### Instructor Quick Tips

Use this instructor Quick Tips guide for a quick and easy start with McGraw-Hill
Connect. You'll get valuable tips on assignment creation and management, as well as
information about support center hours.

### Setting Up Your Course

**TIP:** To get started in Connect, you will need these items:

- Following your course creation, Connect will generate your customizable
  section Web Address via a "Boarding Pass," which you should print and share
  with your students.
- Please ensure you use the course designation and term in the course name field
  when creating an account (e.g., COMM 101 Fall13).

Sample of unique Connect Web Address:
http://connectmcgrawhill.com/class/ COMP101 Fall13

**REMINDER:** In order for your learners to register for your Connect course, you need to
provide them with the unique section Web Address. Your learners will also need the
Connect access code. If they do not have that code, they can purchase ConnectPlus
from your unique section Web Address.

- Connect offers trial access (typically, three weeks) for learners who do not have
  an access code or have not yet secured tuition funds to purchase access via the
  "Free Trial" links.

## Assignments

### Naming an Assignment

When creating a new assignment, it is best to use a descriptive title for the chapter
and type of assignment (e.g., Thesis Homework). Please refrain from including
dates in the assignment title, as it will be easier to recycle your assignments in future
courses or sections. It is best not to change assignment names during the semester to
avoid student confusion.

## Grouping Assignments (Optional)

Group your assignments to organize them by week, chapter, type, etc. To use groups, click "add/edit groups" from your Connect homepage.

## Choosing Questions from the Question Bank

To maximize student learning, it is best to select a small group of McGraw-Hill Question Bank items (5–8 questions) for each assignment to help learners complete their assignments and facilitate greater learning opportunities. If you choose to create an assignment with an abundance of questions (e.g., 50 questions), you may want to focus on True/False and/or Multiple Choice so you do not get overwhelmed with a lot of manual grading.

## Active Assignment Editing

Once your learners begin working on an assignment, certain options are locked from editing, such as adding or removing questions, decreasing the number of attempts, adjusting the due date, and deactivating the timer. This prevents any adverse effects to reports and student data collected for assignments.

To avoid having an assignment become active before you are ready for students to access it, immediately after you create the assignment, click the Show/Hide eye icon to the right of each assignment on the assignment list on your Home Page. When you see a line through the eye icon, it means the assignment cannot be seen by the student. Click the eye icon again and the assignment will be visible to students.

An alternate process would be to set the start date as a future date, so that the assignment cannot be accessed by your learners until that time.

## Best Practices for Using Speech Capture

- Preparing and uploading a video online is not easy for all students to learn to do. To give your students a chance to practice this new skill, at the start of each term, set up a speech assignment with self-review, peer review, and instructor review all turned **off**; be sure, however, to assign a point value, to encourage students to complete this practice upload. In this way, you can require your students to practice preparing and uploading a video to Connect, so that so they are better prepared for the real speech assignments later on.
- Be sure to give your students instructions on preparing, compressing, and uploading speech videos to Connect. You can find our Guide to Preparing Speeches for Connect at www.mhhe.com/videoupload.

## Library

**TIP:** The library section within your Connect course/section will provide shortcuts to various resources:

- You can access an electronic version of your textbook by clicking on the *eBook* button on the *Library* tab. The eBook can also be accessed from the section information widget of the *Home* tab.
- Tegrity Campus will allow you to capture your lectures and share them with your learners so they can search and review through Connect when needed. To get started with Tegrity Campus, click on *Lectures* from the Library tab.
- To access additional instructional materials to assist you in your course, visit the *Instructor Resource* page available on the Library tab. Instructor materials include resources such as test banks, presentations, and resource manuals.
- The Library section is also where you and your students will find Speech Preparation Tools and a Video Bank of sample speeches.

## Student Experience

- Preview Connect assignments that are currently available to your learners by clicking on *"Switch to Student Home View"* when viewing your assignment list. Only the assignments that appear in this list are seen by your learners. By switching to the student view, you can also take some assignments as a student.

**NOTE:** Any scores you generate in "student view" mode will not appear under the Reports tab, as "student view" is for demonstrative purposes only.

- Encourage your learners to click *"Save & Exit"* if they are unable to finish any assignment in one sitting.

## Need More Help?

**TIP:** When working inside Connect, be aware that contextual help is available.

| CONTACT US ONLINE | GIVE US A CALL |
| --- | --- |
| Visit us at: www.mcgrawhillconnect.com/support | Call us at: 1-800-331-5094 |
| Browse our support materials, including tutorial videos and our searchable Connect knowledge base. | Our live support is available: Mon–Thurs: 8 am–11 pm CT Friday: 8 am–6 pm CT Sunday: 6 pm–11 pm CT |
| If you cannot find an answer to your question, click the "Contact Us" button to send us an email. | |

# Integrating Connect into Your Course Syllabus

## Introduce Learners to Connect at the Start of Your Course

Integrating Connect into your syllabus helps learners build familiarity and confidence to maximize their experience. We recommend that you introduce Connect to your learners at the very start of your course and include the following information in your syllabus:

- A brief description of Connect and how it's being used in the course
- How learners can obtain a Connect access code
- Registration instructions
- How Connect fits into your overall course grade
- Expectations and/or policies related to your course assignments
- McGraw-Hill's CARE Support information
- Reference to "Student Quick Tips" included in your Connect Welcome Kit

# Suggested Wording to Use in Your Syllabus

## Overview and Setting Expectations

McGraw-Hill's Connect is a web-based assignment and assessment solution required for this course. Connect is designed to assist you with your coursework based on your needs. As outlined in this syllabus, assignments will make up a significant portion of your overall course grade.

## Access

To receive a Connect access code at the lowest price, contact your sales representative. You can also purchase a Connect access code at the college bookstore.

**NOTE:** You can register in Connect and have access without a code for a limited time period (typically, three weeks).

## Support and Tips

If you have any issues while registering or using Connect, please contact McGraw-Hill's CARE team through http://www.mhhe.com/support. To avoid problems related to unexpected technical issues, you are advised not to wait until the last moment to complete assignments. Please review your "Student Quick Tips" for further support.

# How Do Learners Access Connect Communication?

**For more details** and videos on how to set up your course, visit http://connect.mcgraw-hill.com/help.

## Student Quick Tips

Use this Student Quick Tips guide for a quick and easy start with McGraw-Hill Connect. You'll get valuable tips on registering, doing assignments, and accessing resources, as well as information about the support center hours.

## Getting Started

**TIP:** To get started in Connect, you will need the following:
- Your instructor's Connect Web Address
  Sample of Connect Web Address:
  http://www.mcgrawhillconnect.com/class/instructorname_section_name
- Connect Access Code

**TIP:** If you do not have an access code or have not yet secured your tuition funds, you can click *"Free Trial"* during registration. This trial will provide temporary Connect access (typically, three weeks) and will remind you to purchase online access before the end of your trial.

## Registration and Sign In

1. Go to the Connect Web Address provided by your instructor.
2. Click on **Register Now**.
3. Enter your email address.

**TIP:** If you already have a McGraw-Hill account, you will be asked for your password and will not be required to create a new account.

4. Enter a registration code or choose **Buy Online** to purchase access online.
5. Follow the on-screen directions.

**TIP:** Please choose your Security Question and Answer carefully. We will ask you this information if you forget your password.

6. When registration is complete, click on **Go to Connect Now**.
7. You are now ready to use Connect.

## Trouble Logging In?

- Ensure you are using the same email address you used during registration.
- If you have forgotten your password, click on the *"Forgot Password?"* link at your Instructor's Connect Course Web Address.
- When logged into Connect, you can update your account information (e.g., email address, password, and security question/answer) by clicking on the *"My Account"* link located at the top-right corner.

## Home (Assignments)

**TIP:** *If you are unable to begin an assignment, verify the following:*

- The assignment available date has passed.
- The assignment due date has not passed.
- You have not completed the maximum number of attempts.

**TIP:** *Based on the assignment policy settings established by your Instructor, you may encounter the following limitations when working on your assignment(s):*

- Ability to Print Assignment
- Timed assignments—once you begin a *"timed assignment,"* the timer will not stop by design

**TIP:** *"Save & Exit"* vs. *"Submit"* button

- If you are unable to complete your assignment in one sitting, click the *"Save & Exit"* button to save your work and complete it at a later time.
- Once you have completed your assignment, use the *"Submit"* button in order for your assignment to be graded.

**TIP:** *Speech Assignments*

- Before recording your speech, run a test in the environment where you will be speaking to make sure your video will be clear. Stand so that light is shining on you, not behind you. In addition, eliminate unwanted ambient sound; for example, if you are in someone's home, turn off the television.
- Dress professionally when you deliver your speech.
- If you encounter any difficulties uploading a video to Connect, please be sure to click HELP to read the troubleshooting tips provided.
- If your video upload does not complete within 10–15 minutes, your file is probably either very large or there is an issue with your Internet bandwidth. Compress files that are larger than 100 MB, following the instructions in HELP. Also be sure to turn off any other streaming activity that may be using up your Internet bandwidth (Internet radio, YouTube, etc.).

- If you continue to have difficulties, contact our Customer Support team for HELP. Phone number and hours are listed below.
- Be sure to complete all reviews (self-review and peer reviews) if your instructor has included them with your speech assignment.

## Library

**TIP:** *The Library section of your Connect account provides shortcuts to various resources.*

- If you purchased ConnectPlus, you will see an *eBook* link, which can also be accessed from the section information widget on the *Home tab.*
- *Recorded Lectures* can be accessed if your instructor is using *Tegrity Campus* to capture lectures. You may also access recorded lectures when taking an assignment by clicking on the projector icon in the navigation bar.
- Check the *Media Library* for sample speeches provided as examples of high-quality student work.

## Reports

**TIP:** *Once you submit your assignment, you can view your available results in the Reports tab.*

- If you see a dash (-) as your score, your instructor has either delayed or restricted your ability to see the assignment feedback.
- Your instructor has the ability to limit the amount of information (e.g., questions, answers, scores) you can view for each submitted assignment.
- Any questions that require manual grading by your instructor (including Writing Assignments) will display an incomplete score until the instructor submits a grade. These assignments display with a special flag icon in your reports.

| CONTACT US ONLINE | GIVE US A CALL |
|---|---|
| Visit us at:<br>www.mcgrawhillconnect.com/support | Call us at:<br>1-800-331-5094 |
| Browse our support materials, including tutorial videos and our searchable Connect knowledge base. | Our live support is available:<br>Mon–Thurs: 8 am–11 pm CT<br>Friday: 8 am–6 pm CT<br>Sunday: 6 pm–11 pm CT |
| If you cannot find an answer to your question, click the "Contact Us" button to send us an email. | |

# Notes

# Communication

Experience

Mc
Graw
Hill
Education

EXPERIENCE COMMUNICATION WITH INSTRUCTOR'S GUIDE TO CONNECT

Published by McGraw-Hill Education, 2 Penn Plaza, New York, NY 10121. Copyright © 2015 by McGraw-Hill Education. All rights reserved. Printed in the United States of America. No part of this publication may be reproduced or distributed in any form or by any means, or stored in a database or retrieval system, without the prior written consent of McGraw-Hill Education, including, but not limited to, in any network or other electronic storage or transmission, or broadcast for distance learning.

Some ancillaries, including electronic and print components, may not be available to customers outside the United States.

This book is printed on acid-free paper.

1 2 3 4 5 6 7 8 9 0 DOC/DOC 1 0 9 8 7 6 5 4

ISBN 978-1-25-918049-1
MHID 1-25-918049-2

Senior Vice President, Products & Markets: *Kurt L. Strand*
Vice President, General Manager, Products & Markets: *Michael J. Ryan*
Vice President, Content Production & Technology Services: *Kimberly Meriwether David*
Managing Director: *David S. Patterson*
Director: *Susan Gouijnstook*
Executive Director of Development: *Lisa Pinto*
Editorial Coordinator: *Jamie Daron*
Lead Digital Content Editor: *Scott Harris*
Digital Product Analyst: *Janet Smith*
Marketing Manager: *Laura Kennedy*
Director, Content Production: *Terri Schiesl*
Content Project Manager: *Dana M. Pauley*
Senior Buyer: *Sandy Ludovissy*
Design: *Debra Kubiak*
Cover Image: © *Dragan Grkic/Getty Images*
Content Licensing Specialist: *Shawntel Schmitt*
Typeface: *Palatino LT Std 9.75/12.5*
Compositor: *Lachina Publishing Services*
Printer: *R. R. Donnelley*

**Library of Congress Cataloging-in-Publication Data**
Child, Jeff.
   Experience communication with instructor's guide to Connect / Jeff Child, Kent State University, Judy Pearson, Paul Nelson. – First edition.
      pages cm
   Includes bibliographical references and index.
   ISBN 978-1-25-918049-1 (alk. paper)—ISBN 1-25-918049-2 (alk. paper)
   1. Communication—Study and teaching (Higher) 2. Communication in education. I. Title.
P91.3.C45 2015
302.2′0711—dc23
                                                                                                2013035474

The Internet addresses listed in the text were accurate at the time of publication. The inclusion of a website does not indicate an endorsement by the authors or McGraw-Hill Education, and McGraw-Hill Education does not guarantee the accuracy of the information presented at these sites.

www.mhhe.com

# Experience Communication

Strong communication skills have never been more important than in today's digitally driven and global environment. *Experience Communication* teaches a diverse student population the fundamentals of successful communication and motivates them to confidently use digital tools to meet their communication and course challenges. These challenges include:

- Reading and applying course content
- Finding meaningful and rewarding work
- Presenting themselves effectively in person and online
- Engaging responsibly in mediated communication
- Understanding the communication needs of a global workplace

The *Experience Communication* program offers McGraw-Hill's adaptive learning system, Smartbook, which continually assesses student understanding, and adapts itself to help students achieve academic success and meet these challenges.

Using this program, instructors can feel confident that their students will meet course objectives. Instructors will also find an array of digital tools to help them manage the time they spend covering a wide range of course content, and focusing on those areas in which students need remediation.

See what *Experience Communication* has to offer you and your students!

**Connect Communication** provides a wealth of resources to help students improve their communication skills. With engaging activities and powerful public speaking tools, Connect Communication addresses key course challenges to help boost student performance.

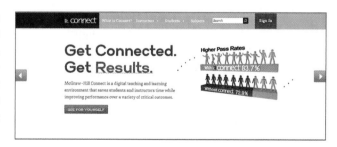

# PROVIDES AN ADAPTIVE READING AND LEARNING EXPERIENCE

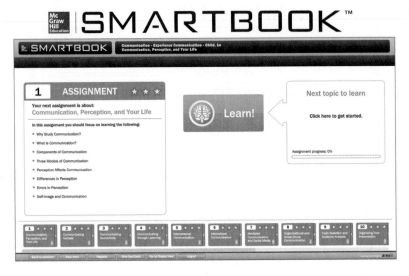

SmartBook, McGraw-Hill's adaptive ebook, facilitates the reading process by identifying what content a student knows and doesn't know, highlighting the concepts that are most important to that study session. As a student reads, the material continuously adapts to ensure the student is focused on the content he or she needs the most to close specific knowledge gaps. SmartBook helps students master core concepts and apply communication skills to all aspects of their lives. Students are more engaged with course content, can better prioritize their time, and come to class ready to participate in thoughtful discourse.

SmartBook for *Experience Communication* contains four stages—Preview, Read, Practice, Recharge—that transform student reading from a linear activity into a dynamic learning experience.

- **Preview**—Students start with a preview of each chapter and the corresponding key learning objectives. This preview establishes a framework of the material in a student's brain to help retain knowledge over time.
- **Read**—While students read the material, they are guided to core topics where they should spend the most time studying.
- **Practice**—As students read the material, SmartBook presents them with questions to help identify what content they know and what they don't know.
- **Recharge**—To ensure concept mastery and retention, students complete the Read and Practice steps until SmartBook directs them to Recharge and review the important material they're likely to forget.

**SmartBook Reports** provide students and instructors with real-time information about individual and class performance and understanding, keeping students and instructors fully up to date on course progress.

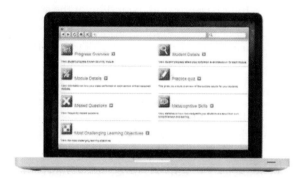

## LearnSmart Achieve

Taking learning one step beyond SmartBook, *Experience Communication* offers a digital learning environment that teaches students to apply the skills of the communication course. LearnSmart Achieve focuses on crucial study skills, such as time management, and creates a personalized learning experience tailored to students' skill levels. Using questions to identify what students don't know, LearnSmart Achieve provides on-the-spot tutoring utilizing learning resources, such as videos, detailed artwork, a narrative coach, other visual aids, supplemental reading, or a combination of all these tools.

Similar to SmartBook, LearnSmart Achieve contains four stages—Tune In, Focus, Practice, Recharge—that transform student reading from a linear activity into a dynamic learning experience.

- **Tune In**—Students are asked a sample series of questions related to a specific learning objective to assess their baseline understanding of the content.

- **Focus**—Based on their responses to the Tune In questions, Achieve presents students with a variety of learning resources (videos, detailed artwork, a narrative coach, supplemental reading, and more) to reinforce the concepts they are struggling with most.

- **Practice**—After the Focus phase, students are asked a more in-depth series of questions to confirm their understanding of key objectives. Achieve then adjusts the learning plan to provide suggested learning resources to assist students in mastering all core concepts.

- **Recharge**—After a student completes a module, LearnSmart Achieve encourages retention of the materials by identifying what concepts a student is most likely to forget and brings those concepts back for review before the student forgets them.

## DEVELOPS THE KEY SKILLS EMPLOYERS SEEK IN EMPLOYEES

As students prepare to enter their chosen careers, effective communication skills will become all the more relevant. From the cover letter to the job interview, students' professional success hinges on their ability to *inform* potential employers of their skills, and to *persuade* others to consider their candidacy seriously. In its detailed coverage of workplace communication, organizational and small group communication, and public speaking, *Experience Communication* emphasizes the practical applications of effective communication skills—such as evaluating information, speaking in front of others, and working productively and ethically as part of a team—skills identified by the recent survey conducted by the National Association of Colleges and Employers.

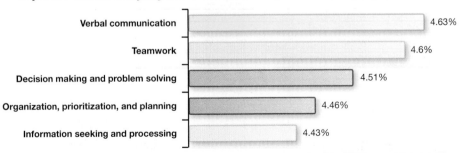

**Top Five Skills Employers Seek in Prospective Employees\***

| Skill | Percentage |
|---|---|
| Verbal communication | 4.63% |
| Teamwork | 4.6% |
| Decision making and problem solving | 4.51% |
| Organization, prioritization, and planning | 4.46% |
| Information seeking and processing | 4.43% |

\*National Association of Colleges and Employers, Job Outlook 2012.

**Skill Builder boxes** reinforce communication skills by encouraging students to put them into practice. Topics include decreasing defensiveness, improving language skills, and practicing proper self-disclosure.

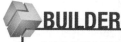

**BUILDER**

### LEARN HOW TO DECREASE DEFENSIVENESS

Rewrite the following statements in a way that would decrease defensiveness. Use the categories generated by Jack Gibb. For example, replace *evaluation* statements with *description* statements.

- "What's wrong with you, anyway?"
- "Who's responsible for the mess in the library?"
- "I don't really care what you do."
- "We're not leaving here until I say we're leaving."
- "We don't need to meet. I know how to solve the problem."
- "I don't need your help."

## HELPS STUDENTS PRACTICE AND BECOME MORE EFFECTIVE PUBLIC SPEAKERS

*Connect Experience Communication* offers **a suite of 9 full sample speech videos, sixty speech video clips, and speech tools,** making it easier for students to observe and practice effective communication.

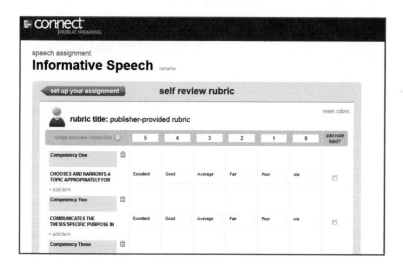

Additionally, the **Speech Capture** assignment in Connect gives instructors the ability to evaluate speeches live, using a fully customizable rubric. Instructors can also upload speech videos on behalf of students, as well as create and manage peer review assignments. In addition, students can upload their own videos for self-review and/or peer review.

# UNDERSCORES THE EXPANDING ROLE OF TECHNOLOGY IN STUDENTS' LIVES

With more and more interactions taking place online and over text messages, mediated communication has become a critical component of students' daily routines. Using the most up-to-date research and scholarship, *Experience Communication* provides a foundation for exploring the opportunities and challenges advanced by communication technologies.

*Experience Communication* devotes **a full chapter to computer-mediated communication and social media.** Rich and up-to-date, this coverage demonstrates to students the most effective ways to convey messages over all computer-mediated platforms, as well as tips for presenting and protecting themselves online. Additionally, **a full chapter on workplace communication** includes best practices for using digital technologies to communicate with colleagues and prospective employers—across the globe.

## PREPARES STUDENTS FOR COMMUNICATING GLOBALLY

**Communicating Globally boxes** provide contemporary examples of real-life scenarios, emphasizing the most common challenges of global communication as well as the opportunities globalization can afford.

 **GLOBALLY**

### COMMUNICATING

### SOCIAL MEDIA USE AROUND THE GLOBE

Although Facebook, YouTube, and Twitter are enormously popular in the United States and Europe, in China, where free speech is not encouraged, these sites are not accessible. To maintain control of the messages that are made public, the Chinese government has banned the use of certain social media sites and closely monitors those that are allowed.

Much like the users in the United States and Europe, Chinese citizens use social media to interact with family and friends; to meet new people; to engage in citizen journalism; and to organize protests. For example, in July 2011, when a large train accident occurred in western China, the government tried to downplay the damage and limit mainstream media coverage. However, information on the crash was immediately available to the Chinese public on the social media site Weibo.

Although the Chinese government makes great efforts to regulate social media use, it has been more successful at censoring traditional media, including newspapers, television, and radio. Meanwhile, Chinese social media sites like Weibo, Renren, and YouKu have only grown in popularity. Weibo, China's version of Twitter, now boasts 300 million registered users.[1]

# For Instructors

A comprehensive **Instructor's Manual** provides a range of tools for each chapter to help structure the course, including chapter outlines, objectives, teaching tips, and suggestions for Connect integration.

The **Test Bank** offers multiple-choice questions, true/false questions, fill-in-the-blank questions and essay questions for each chapter.

**PowerPoints and Prezis** are available for each chapter through Connect, as well as on the Online Learning Center (OLC) (www.mhhe.com /experiencecommunication). Please contact your McGraw-Hill representative for access information to the OLC.

**Instructor Reports** in SmartBook allow instructors to spend less time remediating and more time having rich conceptual discussions with their students. Reports allow instructors to quickly monitor student activity, making it easy to identify which students are struggling and provide immediate help to ensure that those students stay enrolled in the course and improve their performance. Instructor Reports also highlight the concepts and learning objectives that the class as a whole is having difficulty grasping. This essential information lets you know exactly which areas to target for review during your limited class time.

**An Instructor Edition of Experience Communication with the Connect Quick Guide** will guide instructors through setup and implementation of McGraw-Hill's Connect.

## A FLEXIBLE PROGRAM FOR YOUR COURSE NEEDS AND YOUR STUDENTS' LEARNING NEEDS

With McGraw-Hill Create, instructors may choose from *Experience Communication*'s chapters to custom design a Table of Contents that serves individual needs. Create also allows easy upload of course content, including course syllabus, teaching notes, or other material. Create even allows instructors to personalize their book's appearance by selecting the cover and adding name, school, and course information. Instructors who order a Create book will receive a complimentary print review copy in 3 to 5 business days, or a complimentary electronic review copy (eComp) via e-mail in about one hour.

**Begin creating now at** www.mcgrawhillcreate.com.

# ACKNOWLEDGMENTS

We thank the many instructors across the country who offered insights and suggestions to improve the quality of the instructional material and student experience throughout the entire *Experience Communication* program:

Lawerence Albert *Morehead State University*

Ashley Alfaro *Tarrant County College Southeast*

Ennis Allen *Prince Georges Community College*

Emily Anzicek *Bowling Green State University*

Len Assante *Volunteer State Community College*

Rachelle Biderman *Hawkeye Community College*

Tonya Blivens *Tarrant County College Southeast*

Derek Bolen *Angelo State University*

Kathy Brady *University of Wisconsin Whitewater*

Ellen Bremen *Highline Community College*

Guy Bruno *Edison Community College*

Christy Burns *Jacksonville State University*

Aaron Burtch *Lipscomb University*

Michael Caudill *Western Carolina University*

Jason Chapa *South Texas College*

Virginia Chapman *Anderson University*

John (Shiao-Yun) Chiang *State University College-Oneonta*

Sarah Clements *Pulaski Technical College*

Preston Coleman *University of North Georgia-Gainesville*

Julie Copp *Saint Louis Community College-Flors Valley*

Kelly Crue *Saint Cloud Technical and Community College*

Shirley Crum *Coastal Carolina Community College*

Phil Dalton *Hofstra University*

William Davis *Westchester Community College*

Jethro De Lisle *Tacoma Community College*

Allison DeStefano *Waubonsee Community College*

Allen Dutch *Georgia Highlands College*

Dawn Esser *Southwestern Iowa Community College*

Emilie Falc *Winona State University*

Robert Fussell *Guilford Technical Community College Jamestown*

Angela Gibson *Shelton State Community College*

Jessica Gleason *Gateway Technical-Kenosha*

Luke Green *Saint Cloud Technical and Community College*

Douglas Hoehn *Bergen Community College*

Cheryl Hunter *NHTI Concord Community College*

Linda Kalfayan *Westchester Community College*

Brian Kline *University of North Georgia-Gainesville*

Charles Korn *Nova Community College-Manassas*

Benjamin Krueger *Winona State University*

Amy Lenoce *Naugatuck Valley Community College*

Darren Linvill *Clemson University*

Martin Machover *Rockland Community College*

Lucas Messer *Scottsdale Community College*

Shellie Michael *Volunteer State Community College*

Robert Mild *Fairmont State University*

Yolanda Mitchell *Pulaski Technical College*

Lauren Morgan *College of Dupage*

Lee Ann Nelson *Saint Charles County Community College*

Thomas Notton *University of Wisconsin Superior*

Travice Baldwin Obas *Georgia Highlands College*

Tami Olds *Nova Community College-Loudoun*

Darren Osburn *Saint Charles County Community College*

Lisa Packard *Gateway Technical-Kenosha*

Danielle Parsons *University of Rhode Island-Kingston*

Lisa Pavia-Higel *East Central College*

Andrea Pearman *Tidewater Community College Virginia Beach*

Richard Pineda *University of Texas at El Paso*

Tom Preston *University of North Georgia-Gainesville*

Marlene Preston *Virginia Technical*

Deborah Prickett *Jacksonville State University*

Shannon Proctor  *Highline Community College*
David Schrader  *Oklahoma State University–Stillwater Campus*
Natalie Shubert  *Ohio University Athens*
Karen Solliday  *Gateway Technical-Kenosha*
Don Spitler  *Pulaski Technical College*
Steve Stuglin  *Georgia Highlands College*

Charlotte Toguchi  *Kapiolani Community College*
Curt Vangeison  *Saint Charles Co Community College*
James Wilson  *Shelton State Community College*
Emily Workman  *Guilford Technical Community College Jamestown*

# Brief Contents

# Contents

**4   Communicating Through
Listening   51**

**PART 2   Communication
Contexts**

**5   Interpersonal
Communication   64**

**6   Intercultural Communication   85**

**7   Mediated Communication
and Social Media   103**

## PART 3 Public Speaking Basics

# Communication Basics

**Why study communication? Throughout these chapters, we will examine some compelling reasons. We'll begin with the basics of communication and the factors that affect the ways we communicate. You will also see that listening is an important, and often overlooked, communication skill.**

CHAPTER 1

## Communication, Perception, and Your Life

Why Study Communication?
What Is Communication?
The Components of Communication
Three Models of Communication
Perception Affects Communication
Differences in Perception
Errors in Perception
Self-Image and Communication
Chapter Review

CHAPTER 2

## Communicating Verbally

The Functions of Verbal Communication
How Words Communicate
The Rules of Verbal Communication
Words to Avoid
Words to Use Carefully
Strategies for Improving Your Verbal Communication
Chapter Review

CHAPTER 3

## Communicating Nonverbally

What Is Nonverbal Communication?
How Are Verbal and Nonverbal Communication Related?
What Are Nonverbal Codes?
Why Are Nonverbal Codes Difficult to Interpret?
How Can You Improve Your Nonverbal Communication?
Chapter Review

CHAPTER 4

## Communicating Through Listening

The Importance of Listening
Types of Listening
Attention and Listening
Barriers to Listening
Chapter Review

# Communication, Perception, and Your Life

In this chapter we will take a look at why studying communication is so important. We will also describe the process of perception and explore the concepts of self-image and identity management, all powerful influences on communication.

## LEARNING OBJECTIVES

*After reading this chapter, you should be able to:*

- List the benefits of studying communication.
- Define communication and explain the roles that meaning and context play in it.
- Name and describe the components of communication.
- Name and describe the three models of communication.
- Describe the process of perception and its impact on communication.
- Explain the factors that affect and shape people's perceptions.
- Explain how and why errors in perception occur.
- Describe the ways in which self-image and identity management affect communication.

## WHY STUDY COMMUNICATION?

Communication is our link to others at home, at work, and on the street. And although communication isn't always easy, the good news is that you can improve your communication skills with study and practice. You can start that improvement by understanding why the study of communication is important.

1. *Studying communication can improve the way others see you.* Compare a person who stumbles over words, falls silent, interrupts, and uses inappropriate language with someone who has a good vocabulary, listens when you speak, and smoothly exchanges ideas with you. The second type of person is what we call a competent communicator, and most of us prefer to relate to him or her. As you become increasingly competent, you will find that others will seek you out for conversations, assistance, and advice.

2. *Studying communication can make you more sensitive in your relationships.* By studying communication, you can learn specific ways to improve your relationships. A good example relates to listening. Men in our culture are rarely praised for being empathic or even considerate listeners. Women are widely perceived as talkers but also as better listeners. In fact, an Indiana University School of Medicine study indicated that men used only half of the brain when listening, whereas women used the entire brain.[1] When one partner in a relationship does not think the other really cares because of poor listening skills, that relationship may be doomed. Both men and women can learn to be effective listeners by following the practical advice on listening in Chapter 4.

3. *Studying communication can teach you important thinking skills.* Whether you are learning how to gather and evaluate information or to present an argument using evidence, you are working to hone your skills as a critical thinker,[2] problem solver, and decision maker. By studying communication and becoming more aware of the ways in which you communicate with others, you'll also become better at defining your own position on important issues, discerning which arguments and evidence are strong or weak, and analyzing which arguments and evidence your audience is likely to accept as proof.

4. *Studying communication can help you learn how to resolve conflicts at home, at work, and on the street.* Conflict is often resolved through communication, whether in person, on the telephone, or by e-mail. You have also likely experienced conflicts that have gone unresolved and friendships have been lost or relationships put on hold. In such cases, a meaningful exchange is often the key to finding a resolution. John Gottman, a social psychologist, and his fellow researchers even predicted which marriages would end in divorce by observing couples' inability to resolve conflict.[3] Good communication principles and practices can resolve disputes

between individuals, as well as between organizations, political parties, and nations.

5. *Studying communication can boost your confidence by helping you learn how to communicate in pairs, groups, and large audience contexts.* In a study based on the responses from 344 students at a large public university, those who had completed a communication course were more likely than those who hadn't to feel confident, comfortable with how others perceived them, satisfied with their ability to reason with others, and able to use language appropriately in a variety of communication situations.[4]

6. *Studying communication will encourage you to expand your comfort zone in communicating with others.* As you stroll through a mall, deposit money in a bank, go to a movie, or work at your job, about one in every five people you come in contact with will speak English as a second language. According to the 2007 American Community Survey, conducted by the U.S. Census Bureau, over 55 million Americans speak a language other than English in their home, and of that number, 67% speak Spanish in the home.[5] Learning how to communicate in today's world, whether English is your first language or not, requires an understanding of communication and culture and how those two concepts are related.

7. *Studying communication can help you succeed professionally.* A look at job postings online will give you an immediate understanding of the importance of improving your knowledge and practice of communication. What communication skills are employers seeking? The ability to speak clearly, succinctly, and persuasively is crucial to many jobs, including sales positions,[6] as are public speaking skills.[7] Employers also value strong interpersonal skills[8] and an ability to work in teams or groups.[9] Professionals in fields as diverse as accounting, auditing, banking, counseling, engineering, information science, public relations, and sales have all noted the importance of oral communication skills.[10] The variety of these careers suggests that communication skills are important across the board.

## WHAT IS COMMUNICATION?

*Communication* comes from the Latin word *communicare*, which means "to make common" or "to share." The root definition is consistent with our definition of **communication**—*the process of using messages to generate meaning.*

Communication is considered a process because it consists of a series of actions, activities, or behaviors we engage in to achieve a particular result. In communication, the result of this process is, ideally, the conveyance and interpretation of meaning through messages. In other words, communication is not an unchanging product; nor is it an object you can hold in your hand; it is an activity in which you participate.

When you smile at another person, you send a message—that you are friendly or that you are interested in that person. When a radio announcer chooses particular words—for example, *emergency*, *crisis*, or *disaster*—to describe an event, she creates a particular kind of message. Because of the importance of word choice, a public speaker might spend days choosing just the right words, as well as considering his bodily movements, gestures, and facial expression to get across the desired message. In each of these examples, the person hopes to generate common meanings through the messages he or she provides.

Meaning, also covered in Chapter 2, is an understanding of the message as the speaker intended. People are not always successful in generating meaning. For example, a college professor may be very knowledgeable about a subject but has a hard time putting this knowledge in terms that students can relate to or understand. Understanding the meaning of another person's message cannot occur unless the two communicators have common meanings for words, phrases, and even movements and gestures. When you use language, common meanings facilitate a response that indicates that the message has been understood. For example, suppose you ask a friend for a ride home. She says nothing but walks with you to her car. You and your friend share the same meaning of the message exchanged.

But a message can be interpreted in more than one way, especially if the people involved have little shared experience. Let's say you ask a new friend to "meet at a restaurant for lunch around noon." You may assume that means he'll arrive at noon, no more than 5 to 10 minutes late, but he thinks "around noon" means that the arrangement is loose. You arrive at the restaurant a few minutes before noon, but he does not appear until 12:30. You end up waiting, but you are not happy when he arrives so terribly late, by your understanding of the situation. In such a case, you could have determined more accurately what he was planning or thinking by *negotiating*. So, for example, if your new friend had said, "Would 12:30 or 12:45 be OK?" you might have responded, "No, that would be too late for me." Or you might have provided additional information to him—for example, by saying, "I have a class at 1:30, and I don't want our meal to be rushed, so it would be great if you could be there by noon." And if he said, "But you said 'around noon,'" you would explain, "Oh, I'm sorry. I really meant *at* noon."

Although we do not include this concept in our formal definition of communication, it is important to note that all communication happens in a **context,** meaning it occurs within *a set of circumstances or a situation.* Contexts for communication include two friends talking on the way to class, five business acquaintances in a small-group setting, and a lecturer and an audience filling an auditorium. At many colleges and universities, the material covered in communication courses is defined by context: interpersonal, global and intercultural, mediated, and organizational or small-group. In other words, communication occurs in a variety of contexts. Part 2 looks at a number of these contexts in depth.

## THE COMPONENTS OF COMMUNICATION

In this section you will see how communication in action really works by learning about its components: people, messages, channels, feedback, code, encoding and decoding, and noise. Then in the next section, by looking at three models of communication, you will see how each component has a part to play in the process of generating, as well as potentially obstructing, the meaning of a message.

### People

People are involved in the human communication process in two roles—as both the sources and the receivers of messages. A **source** *initiates a message*, and a **receiver** is *the intended target of the message*. Individuals do not perform these two roles independently. Instead, they are the sources and the receivers of messages simultaneously and continually.

People may vary in the way they respond to the same message; they may also vary in the way they convey the same message. An individual's characteristics, including race, sex, age, culture, values, and attitudes, affect the way he or she sends and receives messages. A teenager, for example, uses slang expressions that an older person is less likely to use or perhaps even to understand. An acquaintance might use Facebook to maintain contact with you; your parents perhaps use text messages; and your grandparents probably use the telephone. In addition to the channels being different, the words that each communicator chooses will likely differ.

### The Message

The **message** is *the verbal and nonverbal expression of the idea, thought, or feeling that one person (the source) wishes to communicate to another person or group of people (the receivers)*. As noted, the message includes the verbal symbols (words and phrases) you use to communicate your ideas, as well as the nonverbal ones—that is, your facial expressions, bodily movements, gestures, use of physical contact, and tone of voice. The message may be relatively brief and easy to understand or long and complex.

Communication can take the form of either intentional or unintentional messages. For example, if you wave to your friend when she enters a shopping center where you agreed to meet, that is intentional communication; you want her to see you and walk over to you. But if you just happen to have your hand in the air when she comes in (perhaps you are scratching your head) and she thinks you are waving to her, that is unintentional. Nevertheless, you still have communicated, and she may come toward you and begin to carry on a conversation, whether you wanted her to or not.

### The Channel

The **channel** is *the means by which a message moves from the source to the receiver of the message*. Airwaves, sound waves, twisted copper wires, glass fibers, and cable are all communication channels. So are phone calls, e-mails, text messages, face-to-face conversations, and so on. The channel used to convey a message can have great significance. Does anyone think that breaking off a serious relationship with someone by e-mail is the right way? When the spouse of an active-duty soldier sees an armed forces car in front of the house, with two uniformed officers on their way to the door, that spouse can be pretty sure that this personal attention is not good news. Yes, the channel, the means of delivering a message, makes a serious difference. A delivery of flowers, an electronic get-well card, a surprise birthday cake—all of these are channels used to deliver a message, sometimes with words and sometimes with acts or items.

### Feedback

**Feedback** is *the receiver's verbal and nonverbal response to the source's message*. Ideally, you respond to another person's messages by providing feedback, so that

## YOURSELF

### Why Do I Need to Take a Communication Course When I Have Been Communicating All My Life?

Students taking an introductory communication course often ask themselves this question. Although it may be true that you have been communicating all your life, it may also be true that you have not always communicated with success. The aim of this course is to give you the opportunity to learn how to communicate more effectively, competently, and efficiently. With practice, you will find that not only will your communication improve but so will your relationships.

One challenge we all face is having the sensitivity and foresight to choose the channel and form of interaction appropriate for the relationship and the interaction goals at hand. It is very likely that most of your interactions happen over mediated channels of communication—over cell phones, text messages, and social media, to name a few. However, it is all too common that social media use and text messaging interfere with relationships and cause friction in and outside the work environment.

To head off such friction, think about the unintended messages you might send when you reach to answer your cell phone, respond to a text message, or snap a photo you want to post to your social media site while you are with someone else:

1. Will the person I am with feel less important if I text others while we are together?
2. Will my date think I am not enjoying our time together if I interrupt to provide a status update post?
3. Do I really need to disrupt my conversation to attend to a form of mediated communication?

The proliferation of devices makes it easy to live our lives in a primary relationship with a cell phone, a television screen, or the Internet. Making exclusive time to be in the moment and disconnect from technology can do a great deal to strengthen our connections with others.

the source knows you received the message as intended. Feedback is part of any communication situation. Even no response, or silence, is feedback, as are confused looks and packing away of laptops by students in a lecture hall. Suppose you're looking for a restroom in a building you've never been in before. "Excuse me," you say to a passerby, "can you tell me . . . ," but the person keeps on going without acknowledging you. In this case, the intended receiver did not respond, yet even the lack of a response provides you with some feedback. You may think that the receiver didn't hear you, was in too much of a hurry to stop, or is unfriendly.

### Code

A computer carries messages via binary code on cable, wire, or fiber; similarly, you converse with others by using a code called "language." A **code** is *a systematic arrangement of symbols used to create meanings in the mind of another person or persons*. As you will learn in Chapter 2, words, phrases, and sentences are "symbols" we all use to evoke images, thoughts, and ideas in the minds of others.

If someone yells "Stop!" as you approach the street, the word *stop* is a symbol you are likely to interpret as a warning of danger.

Verbal and nonverbal codes are the two types of code used in communication. Verbal codes are the spoken language we use. "Stop!" in the previous example is a verbal code. Some examples of nonverbal codes, defined and discussed in Chapter 3, are facial expressions (like a smile or a furrowed brow), touch (a handshake), and the clothing and other artifacts you wear (your interview suit, a pair of earrings, a tattoo).

### Encoding and Decoding

Because communication involves the use of codes, the process of communicating can be viewed as one of encoding and decoding. **Encoding** is *the process of translating an idea or a thought into words*. **Decoding** is *the process of assigning meaning to an encoded message*.

For instance, suppose you want to purchase a new car. You are trying to describe

## GLOBALLY

### CODES CARRY MEANING, EVEN IN NAMES

In some African countries, a person's name links him or her to a family, a tribe, a language, a locality, and perhaps even a religion. In the United States, names also carry meaning such that we make certain assumptions about people with a surname like Gonzalez, Patel, or Chen, because we think they are Latino, Indian, or Chinese. Consider what you think when you find on your schedule that your math teacher's name is Mukbir Singh. Does this name evoke stereotypes—for example, that the person is foreign, speaks English with an accent, and may be a math professor with very high standards? Names are often the first fact we learn about other people, and often those names signal a number of messages that may or may not be true.

a compact model to your friend, who wants to help you with your purchase. You might be visualizing your uncle's car with the black interior, sporty design, and silver exterior. Translating this vision into words, or encoding it, you tell your friend only that you are interested in a car that is "small and well designed." Your friend, on hearing this, decodes your words and develops his own mental image. But his love of larger cars and your lack of precision affect this process; as a result, he envisions a sedan rather than the subcompact hatchback you were thinking of.

As you can see, misunderstanding often occurs because of the limitations of language, the inadequacy of descriptions, and a person's own biases. Nonetheless, encoding and decoding are essential to communication, and meanings can be further refined and clarified through negotiation—that is, through asking questions or paraphrasing: "Were you thinking of a sedan?" "No, actually, I prefer the look of a hatchback."

### Noise

In the communication process, **noise** is *any interference in the encoding and decoding processes that reduces the clarity of a message.* Noise can include a variety of distractions—auditory ones, such as loud sounds; visual ones, such as a piece of food between someone's front teeth; and behavioral ones, such as someone standing too close for comfort. Noise can also be psychological, such as daydreams about a loved one or worry about the bills; physical, such as pain from a tooth; or semantic, such as uncertainty about what the other person's words mean. Noise is anything that interferes with receiving, interpreting, or providing feedback about a message. You can find out more about noise and other barriers to listening in Chapter 4.

## THREE MODELS OF COMMUNICATION

Over the years, scholars have developed three basic models of the communication process: the action model, the interaction model, and the transaction model. Each model represents a particular way of understanding the communication process. We'll begin with the model that came first, the action model (Figure 1.1).

**Figure 1.1** The Action Model of Communication

Source
encodes

Channel
Message
Channel

Receiver
decodes

**Figure 1.2** The Interaction Model of Communication

The action model is a one-way process in which a source encodes a message (puts it into language), then sends it through a channel (e.g., a text message or a face-to-face interaction) for the receiver to decode, or interpret. For example, you text a friend to tell her you will be late for your dinner plans. Your friend receives the message and interprets it to mean that she will need to change your reservation at the restaurant, so that you can meet a little later.

The second model is the interaction model, illustrated in Figure 1.2. Although the interaction model includes all the same components as the action model, it differs in two important ways: First, it sees communication as a two-way process; second, it recognizes the role of context and feedback. For instance, you text the same friend about dinner, but this time you take into account that this is her birthday dinner (the context) and that she is likely to be irritated by your change of plans (her feedback). Perhaps you write a text message to explain the reasons for your lag, in hopes that she will understand and not feel that her birthday plans have been ruined.

**Figure 1.3** The Transaction Model of Communication

Finally, the transaction model differs from the other two in that it doesn't distinguish between the source and the receiver and does not see communication as a series of messages that get sent back and forth. Instead, the transaction model, laid out in Figure 1.3, sees communication as an ongoing conversation in which messages are sent in both directions simultaneously. As you begin to send your friend a second text to explain that you are having car trouble, she has already written back to say that she will change the reservation and meet you later that evening. In response to this message, you stop texting and call her to thank her for her understanding and to wish her a happy birthday. In other words, according to the transaction model, even as you are acting as the source of a message, you are also responding to feedback and acting as a receiver, all at the same time.

## PERCEPTION AFFECTS COMMUNICATION

The definition of communication we have provided and the three models we have laid out still do not provide a complete picture of this complex topic. Another very important factor that affects communication is perception.

### What Is Perception?

**Perception** is *the process of using the senses to acquire information about the surrounding environment or situation.*[11] The process of perception involves three stages: selection, organization, and interpretation. **Selection** refers to *the decisions we make to focus on some stimuli—sights, sounds, smells, and other sensations—and neglect others.* We all do this all the time—selecting the messages to which we attend. Perhaps you tend to tune out your nagging roommate but pay close attention to every word of praise from your boss. Selection also occurs when you size up people. Based on your experience with different people, you may treat them with respect, talk to them, or avoid them. Each of these treatments is a response to your perceptions of others.

**Organization** means *grouping stimuli into meaningful units.* In some cases we organize by distinguishing between the figure—or focal point of our attention—and the background against which that figure is set. An employer chooses your name from a list of applicants. For the employer, your name is the figure and all other names have fallen into the background. We also organize using *closure* (the tendency to fill in missing information), *proximity* (perceiving distinct objects as related because of their physical closeness), and *similarity* (grouping objects because they share attributes). You perceive your new boss to be unkind because you overheard him raising his voice (closure); an acquaintance believes you and your best friend to be dating because you are always seen together (proximity); you anticipate getting along with your brother's girlfriend because in a photo she resembles a good friend of yours (similarity).

Finally, perception involves **interpretation,** *the assignment of meaning to stimuli.* Have you ever seen an inkblot test? This well-known test of human psychology relies on the principle of interpretation. Where one person sees a butterfly, another interprets the shapes to be a man's dress coat, a pair of angels, or a human face. Each person's interpretation is the meaning he or she assigns to the shape of the inkblot. Likewise, the way we perceive others—and the way they, in turn, perceive us—involves selection, organization, and interpretation. You can likely already imagine how these processes affect your communication with others.

### What Occurs in Perception?

You meet with your supervisor, thinking she is going to praise you for all the extra work you have done lately, so you approach your meeting perceiving her in a warm and friendly way. When she instead tells you she's reducing your hours because profits are down, your perception of her changes, and the nature of your communication with her (the tone of your voice, the words you choose) are likely to change as well. When this kind of mismatch occurs—between what one expects and what occurs—surprise can turn to anger and disappointment (and no more extra work for that ungrateful supervisor).

Since each person's perceptions are unique, communication is a complicated matter. You will have a better understanding of how complex perception is and how your individual perceptions influence your communication with others once you consider the following two kinds of perception:

- *Active perception.* This is the process by which the mind selects, organizes, and interprets what one senses. You could think of each person you communicate with as having a video camera with a unique lens; as those people aim their camera at different things, they see different colors, degrees of light, and perspectives.

- *Subjective perception.* This is the process by which one attributes meaning to sensed stimuli. To understand this process, consider how much your inner state affects your perceptions. If you have a bad headache, the pain probably will affect the way you feel about your children, the way you respond to the workers at the shop, and even the way you see yourself in a mirror.

## DIFFERENCES IN PERCEPTION

The uniqueness of human experience is based largely on differences in perception. These differences result from physiological features, past experiences, roles, and present feelings.

### Physiological Features

People differ from each other in a multiplicity of physiological ways: for example, sex, height, weight, body type, and acuity of the senses. Each of these features affects the way you see yourself and the way you interact with others. Just imagine if you were a different race and sex or if you had hearing or vision loss how those features would influence your perceptions and, in turn, how you would communicate with others. If you are particularly attractive, you may be accustomed to people looking at you and giving you favored attention. If you are short, the whole world looks very tall. If you have trouble hearing, you might avoid the telephone, especially cell phones, and prefer to text.

## Past Experiences

Your *past experiences lead you to see the world in a way that is difficult to change*. This concept is known as **perceptual constancy.** For example, a bad experience in a given situation may cause you to avoid that situation in the future, just as a good one might encourage you to seek out that situation. In addition, your past experiences affect how you perceive certain categories of people—men, women, professors, police, politicians—whether in a positive or negative way. These perceptions also influence your current and future communication with those categories of people. You may choose never to remarry if you have gone through a difficult divorce. You might not trust women in positions of power if you were fired by a woman who was tactless. You might seek help from a police officer because your father spent his career in policing.

## Roles

A **role** is *a part a person plays in a social context*.[12] The roles we attribute to others affect the way we perceive them, and vice versa. If you play the role of a leader or a loner or a nerd, this will affect the way others perceive you and how receptive they are to your messages. If you label others as athletes, single moms, or beauty queens, that perception will affect your communication with them—the topics you choose to discuss, the vocabulary you use, and the credibility you give to their opinions.

## Present Feelings

How you feel at the moment affects your perceptions—what you see and hear and how it looks and sounds to you—and these perceptions alter your communication. Your child kept you up all night, so you are tired and stressed. When a friend asks how you are, you launch into a torrent of complaints and forget to ask how your friend is. Great news about your mother's health, a brief fight this evening before class, or a disagreeable e-mail from your boss—all these life experiences influence your perceptions and how or whether you communicate with the people around you.

How can you apply this information about perception to your own life? Imagine you are talking to a classmate about an assignment but he looks away and does not respond to you. Your first thought might be that he is distant and disinterested or that he doesn't like you. The truth might be that he is catching a cold and doesn't want to talk because his throat hurts. Or he may be reluctant to get involved because he has helped classmates with their work in the past and gotten no gratitude for his effort. Or it might be something far more basic—that he is hungry and is just trying to get away from you so he can go eat! Clearly, his present circumstances and internal states are influencing his communication with you.

Students of communication who know about the role of perception in communication have a better idea of how to manage such situations. When faced with someone acting unpredictably, they would start by checking their own perceptions and inquiring about the other person's perceptions. They would give the other person a chance to say what is troubling him: "You are not answering me. Am I being unreasonable in asking for your help?" In any case, a person who is knowledgeable about how perception influences communication has an advantage in the exchange.

## ERRORS IN PERCEPTION

Once we understand the active nature of perception and recognize that people hold unique perceptions as a consequence, we can see that we might make errors when we perceive other people. Many types of perceptual errors exist. In Chapter 6, we take a closer look at one of the most common errors, stereotyping. Stereotypes occur when we make a hasty generalization about a group based on a judgment about an individual from that group. Stereotypes often lead to prejudices, a topic also discussed in Chapter 6.

Therefore, an important skill is perceptual checking—a process of describing, interpreting, and verifying that helps you understand another person and his or her message more accurately. The three steps of perceptual checking are

1. Describe to the other person the behavior—including the verbal and non-verbal cues—that you observed.

## BUILDER

### LEARN TO CHECK YOUR PERCEPTIONS

With a partner in class, name a physical feature of yourself that you think affects your communication with others, such as your height, weight, skin color, age, hairstyle, clothing, jewelry, scars, or tattoos.

- First say how you think this feature affects your communication with others.
- Next let the other person say how he or she perceives this feature.
- Then switch roles and repeat.

Each time you practice these steps, you are checking each other's perceptions about a feature that affects your communication.

2. Suggest plausible interpretations of that behavior or feature.

3. Seek verification or rebuttal of your interpretations by asking for clarification, explanation, or amplification.

For example, imagine that you are assigned a group research project in one of your classes. Another member of the group asks you to produce all your primary sources for the project. You presented this source material weeks ago. You respond by saying, "I understand that you want me to give you my primary sources" (describe the behavior or the message). "I might just be acting paranoid, but this makes me feel that you don't trust me" (first interpretation). "Why do you want my primary sources?" (request for clarification).

Perceptual checking can be even more important in personal and romantic relationships. Whatever the relationship, though, you will want to avoid suggesting interpretations that cause the other person to feel defensive. Chapter 5, on interpersonal relationships, offers some very important advice as to how to avoid defensive interactions with the people in your life.

## SELF-IMAGE AND COMMUNICATION

How you see yourself can make a big difference in how you communicate.[13] The great philosopher, sociologist, and psychologist George Herbert Mead said that the self originates in communication.[14] Through verbal and nonverbal symbols, which are the basis of communication, a child comes to accept the expectations of others and, in turn, takes on certain roles. When people are treated as though they are inferior, or intelligent, or gifted, or unattractive, they often act accordingly.

Many communication scholars and social scientists believe that people are products of how others treat them and of the messages others send them. Dominique Moceanu, a successful Olympic gymnast, was influenced quite early in life by what others wanted her to be. Both her parents had been gymnasts, and her father reportedly told her for years that her destiny was to be a world-class gymnast.[15] Most likely she had an inherent physical ability to be a good one, but she may not have become a medal-winning gymnast without the early messages she received from her parents and trainers. Like Moceanu, each of us establishes a self-image based on the messages we receive and the categories others apply to us. Positive, negative, and neutral messages all play a role in forming who we are.

Communication itself is probably best understood as a dialogic process. A **dialogue** is simply *a conversation, discussion, or negotiation*, so communication is a process that occurs in the context of our interactions with other people.[16] A competent communicator considers the other person's needs and expectations when selecting messages to share. Thus, communication begins with the self, as defined largely by others, and involves others, as defined largely by the self.

For example, you can have **intrapersonal communication,** which is *the kind of discussion and decision making that occurs within your own mind.* Consider a situation of importance, such as asking the boss for more responsibilities so that you can earn a larger salary. Before you ever enter the boss's office, you will likely consider what you plan to say, rehearse in your mind how you are going to say it, and even consider what your response is going to be, no matter how the discussion proceeds. Yes, you worry, try out lines, and guess what will be said without uttering a word out loud. You are experiencing intrapersonal communication.

Of course, few of our daily interactions are as rehearsed as the one just described, and as we move from one encounter to the next, we present ourselves to people in a variety of ways, both consciously and unconsciously. Self-presentation can be defined as the way we portray ourselves to others.

A key part of self-presentation is **identity management**—*the control (or lack of control) of what we communicate and what it conveys about us.* Through identity management, we try to present an idealized version of ourselves in order to reach desired ends. Consider a social media profile you update frequently. The identity you project in that profile depends in part on whether you use that site for personal or professional reasons, or a combination of those. If you intend the profile to attract potential dating partners, you might manage your identity by posting photos of you doing things you enjoy or in which you look like a fun or caring person. On a professional site like LinkedIn, your desired end is to find a job or advance your career. You therefore highlight your accomplishments and take care to post information that is accurate and free of grammatical errors. By doing so, you are promoting a professional identity. We all practice identity management in face-to-face interactions as well, presenting the self we want others to see in a particular context.

People manage their identity and the impression they make via three elements of communication: manner, appearance, and setting.[17] Manner is communicated by both verbal and nonverbal codes. A person's manner might be brusque or silly, businesslike or immature, friendly, warm, or gracious. Appearance may be tied to a role an individual plays (administrative assistant as opposed to barista or rock musician), a value one holds (bling as opposed to simplicity), one's personality (easygoing as opposed to extremely tailored and formal), or one's view of the communication setting (unimportant as opposed to crucial). The setting includes the immediate environment (the space in which you are communicating, such as a church as opposed to a coffee shop), as well as other settings in which you display who you are (your home and the way you decorate it, the type of car you drive).

Although communication is complicated, it occurs almost every minute of your life. If you are not communicating with yourself (thinking, planning, reacting to the world around you), you are actively and subjectively

CONSIDERING

## MANAGE YOUR SELF-PRESENTATION ONLINE

Several websites help you actively monitor the information you post online, so that you can make deletions or have someone else do so if you are not the primary content creator.

- Simple Wash (http://simplewa.sh/login): If you are an active social media user, you are likely to have thousands of online posts, pictures, and comments, some of which could negatively impact your reputation. Simple Wash is a website that can access and search your Twitter or Facebook account for questionable content. This application allows you to search for words like *alcohol* or *beer* and find any active posts or pictures about the topic. Then you can delete or hide the identified content. This site may be useful when you start looking for a new job, end a relationship, or go through a major transition and you wish to disassociate yourself from aspects of your former identity.
- Google Alerts (www.google.com/alerts): Sign up for Google Alerts and know when things are published about you online. On this site you can sign up for e-mail alerts about the topics and terms of your choice. You might create alerts for your full name, parts of your name, or your place of employment. If you are alerted to inappropriate content about you, ask those publishing the primary content to remove it from their websites.

perceiving others and responding to their behavior. Even if others did not intend messages for you, you gather observations and draw conclusions. A person yawns and you believe she is bored with your message. A second person looks away and you conclude that he is not listening to you. A third person smiles (perhaps because of a memory of a joke she heard recently) and you believe she is attracted to you. We are continually gleaning meanings from others' behaviors, and we are constantly behaving in ways that have communicative value for them.

## CHAPTER REVIEW

As you are beginning to see, communication is far more than simple information transmission. Communication involves multiple variables—its verbal, nonverbal, and behavioral aspects; the transmission channel used; the characteristics and perceptions of the sender and the receiver; the relationship of the sender to the receiver; and the situation in which the communication occurs. Each of these variables—including the communicator's self-perception and identity-management processes—affects every aspect of communication. Studying communication can heighten your awareness of your business and personal relationships and make you a more competent communicator.

## KEY TERMS

| | |
|---|---|
| channel, 6 | intrapersonal communication, 16 |
| code, 8 | message, 6 |
| communication, 4 | noise, 9 |
| context, 5 | organization, 11 |
| decoding, 8 | perception, 11 |
| dialogue, 15 | perceptual constancy, 13 |
| encoding, 8 | receiver, 6 |
| feedback, 7 | role, 13 |
| identity management, 16 | selection, 11 |
| interpretation, 11 | source, 6 |

## STUDY QUESTIONS

1. List at least 10 ways you use communication in a single day, from the moment something wakes you in the morning until you fall asleep at night. How can you become a more competent communicator with regard to each of the items on your list?

2. Why do we call communication a process? What parts of the process influence meaning, and how exactly do people arrive at shared meanings of a message?

3. Give three specific examples of feedback that college students receive. How does this feedback shape their thinking and behavior?

4. Give examples from your own experience of perceptions organized by closure, proximity, and similarity.

5. Of the four factors that produce differences in perception, which do you think is most powerful? Why? Do you think one can be ranked as more important than the others? Why or why not?

6. Think of a time when perceptual checking would have helped you better understand another person's message. Describe how you would, in that instance, follow the three steps of perceptual checking.

7. List various identities you present in your daily life. How do you manage each via manner, appearance, and setting?

# Communicating Verbally

This chapter will explore the power and importance of verbal communication. We will look at the functions and rules of verbal communication, with three goals in mind: to demonstrate the multiple ways you use verbal communication, to help you avoid errors and offenses, and to guide you in making the best possible impression with your words.

LEARNING OBJECTIVES

*After reading this chapter, you should be able to:*

- Name and explain the four primary functions of verbal communication.

- Explain the meanings and processes by which words communicate.

- Explain the rules that influence and guide verbal communication.

- Recognize the categories of words speakers should avoid to present themselves as thoughtful and balanced verbal communicators.

- Recognize the categories of words speakers should use in moderation to present themselves as thoughtful and balanced verbal communicators.

- List and give examples of strategies that will improve a speaker's verbal communication.

# THE FUNCTIONS OF VERBAL COMMUNICATION

Imagine that today, in one of your classes, a teacher told you that your assignment is due in two weeks; another teacher told you to tell a story in which two characters have a conflict; a third teacher asked you to analyze the school's parking policy; and a fourth stopped you on your way out of class to ask whether you were feeling OK. All four teachers were trying to get messages across to you, mainly with words—with verbal communication.

However, if one of those teachers looked you directly in the eye while speaking, pointed a finger at you, or pounded her fist on a desk, these forms of nonverbal communication would also have meaning and affect your response to the message. We communicate with each other with words, or verbal communication, as well as with eye contact, movement, and gestures (nonverbal communication), and the two forms work together to create a message.

This chapter focuses on **verbal communication,** which is *the use of language to convey meaning.* **Language** is *the code we use to communicate with each other,* a code that follows rules to encourage understanding. **Meaning** is more of a challenge to define, because it refers to *whatever message someone is trying to convey to others, as well as how that message is interpreted.* Although you use verbal communication every day, you may not be aware of the many roles it plays in your relationships. To understand verbal communication, let's look at four of the functions it performs: the instrumental, creative, analytical, and social functions.

## The Instrumental Function

The first teacher mentioned earlier—the one who told you when your assignment was due—was using the **instrumental function** of verbal communication. That is, she was *using language as a directive—a means of getting others to think or do something.* When you use language in an instrumental way, you are using it as a tool or, as the term implies, as an instrument.[1] Instrumental language is unadorned, straightforward, and very descriptive:[2] "The assignment is due in two weeks," "You need to change the oil in your car every 5,000 miles," and "You should vote or quit griping about our leadership." Scientific and technical communication

tends to be instrumental: a chemist's formula, an engineer's instructions for building a robot, and the fix for a computer problem are examples of language used instrumentally.

## The Creative Function

The second teacher—the one who asked you to tell a brief story—was promoting the **creative function** of verbal communication, in which *imagination meets writing or speaking ability.* Called *elocutio* by the Roman rhetorician Quintilian in AD 95,[3] this function was one of the five canons (principles) of rhetoric, which have reigned supreme for many centuries. As an illustration of modern-day creativity with language, social media have spawned inventive acronyms and abbreviations (*lol, sup, idk, omg*) for quick texting and tweeting, in which the message needs to fit within a 140-character limit.[4] When you are asked to use language in an imaginative way, you have a range of rhetorical devices at your disposal—for example, metaphors, similes, hyperbole (exaggeration), and alliteration. These figures of speech allow writers and speakers to play with language and expand its potential.

A **metaphor** (MET-ah-four) *creatively compares two things that do not at first seem alike:* "The morning rainstorm was a crushing blow to his plans," "This economy is a sinking ship," "I'm queen of the house," "Our country is the world's police officer."

A **simile** (SIM-ah-lee) *creatively compares two unlike things, using the word "like" or "as":* "She had a face like an abandoned mining town," "He sweats like a sailor in a sauna," "She worked like an engine, never tiring and rarely resting," "Their team pulls together like huskies in the Iditarod."

**Hyperbole** (high-PURR-baa-lee) *is the use of exaggeration to make a point:* "He looked as if he had been run over by a tank," "My girlfriend is the most beautiful woman in the world," "I plan to be richer than Bill Gates," "That cop is meaner than a pit bull."

**Alliteration** is *the repetition of the initial sound of a word:* "The problem is the price of property," "His tiny, timid eyes looked tired," "She proudly pranced on stage," "The fatty fritters came from the fair." Alliteration is used primarily in poetry and advertising, where it can contribute to rhythm and memorization.

Words targeting the ear (as in speaking) rather than the eye (as in writing) require repetition. Listeners daydream and let their thoughts wander during presentations, so they may need to hear important points several times. To get a message across, then, speakers need to use creative techniques to enhance understanding. One well-known method is to preview by saying what you plan to cover, review by restating in other words what you just said, and summarize to wrap up the message.

Also, effective speakers offer multiple kinds of support for their arguments and ideas. In addition to basic explanations, speakers can incorporate relevant YouTube videos, demonstrations, comparisons, contrasts, and even stories and case studies. The creative use of language can contribute significantly to audience understanding.

## The Analytical Function

When the third teacher asked you to analyze the school's parking policy, he was prompting you to use the **analytical function** of verbal communication, which involves *the use of critical thinking skills to evaluate and critique an issue or idea.* A first step in critical thinking is research. For this assignment, you need to find, read, and understand your school's parking policy and explain it in your own words. Next you need to evaluate it by asking questions such as these: "What is the reasoning behind this policy?" "Is this policy fair to students?" "Is this policy fair to nonstudent residents in the area?" "Should any parts of the policy be changed to reflect conditions that have changed since it was first enacted?" Finally, you can suggest improvements to the current policy. Together, all this work and the paper or presentation that resulted would fulfill the analytical function of verbal communication. Just taking this communication class and learning how to analyze research and prepare speeches will improve your critical thinking skills and your ability to engage in effective use of the analytical function of language.[5]

### The Social Function

When your teacher stopped you on the way out of class to ask whether you were OK, she was demonstrating the **social function** of verbal communication, which refers to *the use of language to build and maintain relationships.* In your case the teacher was letting you know that she had noticed something about you (maybe that you looked down or tired) and that she cared. We also use verbal communication in a social way when we greet friends between classes, chat online, and text or tweet each other. The social function of language can have a positive impact on our emotional health, as in when we turn to social media for support and community with members of our online networks.[6]

One social function of language is achieved through **phatic communication,** *the most casual and often briefest exchanges that are intended to recognize the existence of another person and to demonstrate sociability rather than provide information,* as when you say "hi" in passing. Another social function is achieved through **trouble talk,** *exchanges in which people complain about something without expecting a solution:* "Things are awful at work under that new boss," "My clothes hardly fit anymore," and "I work too hard for too little." A third way in which language functions socially is in **conflict management,** *the use of language to resolve issues between individuals or groups.* Spouses, partners, and friends, as well as union members and management, both create and solve conflicts with verbal communication.

## HOW WORDS COMMUNICATE

Verbal language, of course, is made up of words. But what is a word, and how does it communicate? Let's begin with two definitions.

As Figure 2.1 shows, a **word** is *a symbol that has been assigned meaning.* A **symbol** *represents an idea, a process, or a physical entity.* For instance, the word *car* is a symbol that we have collectively come to agree stands for a vehicle of a certain type. However, over time words and symbols change and new ones are introduced.[7] For example, as some cars became more trucklike and vanlike, we came up with new words to describe them—*SUV*, *wagon*, and *crossover*. The next section explains how we go about interpreting the words and symbols we encounter.

## Two Processes for Interpreting Messages

For words to have meaning, we have to produce and interpret them. To do this, we use the processes of encoding and decoding, as defined in Chapter 1:

- You encode when you translate your thoughts into words. You are wondering if you are doing your job well, so you translate that thought into words to your supervisor: "Did I do that correctly?" You have interpreted the word *correctly* as the one that best communicates your concern. You are saying that you are concerned about whether you are meeting the employer's guidelines for a particular task. If you were concerned specifically with your speed, you could have asked, "Did I do that quickly enough?"

- When you decode, you assign meaning to someone else's verbal communication, translating his words into thoughts of your own. Your supervisor says to you, "Doesn't the cooking area need mopping?" You interpret his words to mean that he wants you to mop the cooking area, but you have to determine from the urgency in his voice whether he means "right now" or "anytime during this shift." The "urgency in his voice" is a nonverbal feature that coordinates with the verbal to make the message. In either case, you assign meaning to the other person's words. If, however, you decode the message to mean that it's OK to wait a few hours before mopping the floor and your supervisor meant "right now," you may make a bad impression. He, of course, could have encoded his message with more precision—for example, "Please mop the kitchen area now."

Because language is an imperfect means of transmission, the thoughts that one person encodes never exactly match what the other decodes, so language often requires further interpretation or clarification, which you achieve when you ask, "Do you mean right now?" or "Can I do the mopping at the end of my shift?"

## Two Kinds of Meaning

Words can carry two kinds of meaning: denotative and connotative. **Denotative meaning** is *the agreed-upon meaning, or the meaning you find in a dictionary.*

**Figure 2.1** What Are Words?

What are words?

**Words** are symbols that have been assigned meanings.

A **symbol** represents an idea, a process, or a physical entity.

We use these symbols, and their intended meanings, to communicate with each other.

The *Webster's New Collegiate Dictionary* says a *cat* is "a carnivorous mammal long domesticated and kept by man as a pet or for catching rats or mice." However, a dictionary meaning fails to capture your feelings for the felines you encounter in your life, which you may either adore or detest. Denotative meanings of words can be fluid, changing over time. For example, a primary meaning for the word *gay* was once *happy,* but now it also means homosexual; the word *troll* once referred to a mythological being, but its meaning has now expanded to include *to search* (as a verb) and *someone who deliberately provokes others on the Internet* (as a noun). The word *bandwidth* went from being a measure related to data transmission to one's ability to handle intellectual or emotional issues.[8]

New words, and new denotative meanings, sometimes enter the language. Such terms are called **neologisms,** *new words or new meanings for old words that are in the process of entering common use.* New technologies create many neologisms, such as *app, tweet cred, hash tag,* and *404.* The last term, meaning clueless, came from the Web's notation for "document not found." Hence, when someone calls a person 404, the message is that the person is clueless.[9]

**Connotative meanings** are *meanings people come to assign because of personal or individual experience.* For example, the word *cat* holds vastly different meanings for people because of their unique experiences with that variety of animal: some fill their homes with cats and pamper them as they would their children, whereas others suffer from serious allergies and swell up and itch at the sight of a cat. Another way to understand the difference between denotative and connotative meanings is to think, for example, of the word *mother.* Everyone knows what a mother is according to the denotative meaning. But each person has his own connotations for that word—laden with emotions that drown the denotative meaning in a flood of remembered experiences. Denotative meanings are general and shared, whereas connotative meanings tend to be individual and personal.

## THE RULES OF VERBAL COMMUNICATION

The way you use words is often determined by the situation you are in. That is, you adapt your speech depending on where you are, whom you are with, and what the context is. Multiple rules and practices guide communication—some that you follow without even being aware of them, others that can benefit you as you gain awareness of them. These are the topics we turn to in this section.

### Rules Regarding Place

You likely already know that where you are affects the way you speak and the words you choose. When you are at home, where people know you well, you can be very informal and make certain assumptions—for example, that people will know what you mean by "the back room" or "that story Dad always tells." When you are out with friends, the formal rules of verbal communication may become extremely relaxed, because friends tend not to be very critical about your language. Among friends you can talk about topics you never would talk about at work, such as your love life, and you may not be so careful about the language you use.

When you are in the more formal setting of a classroom, however, you tend to be more careful with your speech, because you likely want to make a good impression on your professor. You also adapt your speech when you enter a place of worship—a church, synagogue, or mosque—and you speak differently at a funeral than you do in a bar. Certain places—courtrooms, for example—have strict and extensive rules and practices related to verbal communication and appropriate speech, especially related to tone and volume. In other places, the rules may be less clear—if you begin a loud argument in a restaurant, you may be asked to leave, but if you shout in a sports bar during an exciting game, you'll fit right in. Finally, when giving a public speech or when being interviewed for a job, you are under the most pressure of all to follow the formal rules of language and choose your words with care.

### Rules Regarding Conversational Partners

Knowing how and when to adapt your verbal communication based on your relationship with and the status and authority of your conversational partner is part of being an effective communicator. Close relationships with family and friends allow the greatest latitude in terms of the formal rules of grammar and word choice, but even in these close circles, profanity, sex, and various other topics may be taboo. Verbal communication with authority figures—for example, professors, police, and upper-level management—introduces a number of language restrictions and adaptations. Because of the differences in status, you likely know that you want to sound intelligent and well informed with your professor, you don't want to rile a police officer by saying anything that sounds sassy or threatening, and you want to be respectful and emphasize your competence and commitment when speaking to your boss.

These rules don't only apply to face-to-face exchanges. When you communicate with your professor via e-mail, for example, you should use a formal tone. Begin with an appropriate opening (Dear Professor Franklin), put a clear description in the subject line (question about Wednesday's assignment), let your professor know which class you're in, write in complete sentences, avoid the abbreviations you use for texting with your friends, make your message clear and direct, review it for typos, and end with an appropriate salutation (Sincerely, Alison Corsino). Your professor will appreciate the respect you show with your businesslike tone and the care you took to craft a clear message.

### Rules of Engagement

As noted previously, verbal communication comes to us loaded with rules about what can be said to whom, under what circumstances, and how it should be said. In addition, verbal communication comes with **rules of engagement**—*rules about initiating, conducting, and ending a verbal exchange.*

By convention, a public speech begins with an introduction that reveals something about the speaker and the topic. In one-to-one conversation, certain conventions have been established as to who can initiate the exchange—sometimes based on status or gender. For example, at a party or a bar, men are often expected to initiate a conversation with women, although such conventions have loosened up somewhat; in some business contexts, managers initiate meetings with those they supervise, rather than vice versa. In a very formal setting—like a courtroom—the judge is usually the only person who can initiate or permit an exchange, as when he asks questions of lawyers or jurors.

In addition, both public speeches and conversations follow particular organizational patterns. In a public speech the body, or main points, follows the introduction, whereas in a conversation turn taking begins. **Turn taking** means that *one person speaks and the other responds with a certain amount of give and take.* Usually, the signal that one person has said his piece is that he stops talking, so that the other person can respond, but sometimes the speaker is only pausing to collect his thoughts, in which case the conversants may have some awkward moments of speaking over each other as they try to determine whose turn it is or one says, "No, you."

Another aspect of language rules is called **code switching**, which means *shifting from one treatment of language to another based on the audience and place.*[10]

An extreme case of code switching occurs when black Jamaicans speak English to American tourists but speak *patois,* a local language widely understood among local inhabitants but practically never by the hapless tourist, to fellow Jamaicans. A more common case of code switching occurs in the United States when a person from an ethnically concentrated area talks one way in the neighborhood but another way in a workplace full of people from another race or ethnic group. A mild case of code switching occurs when college students talk one way to each other but another way in the presence of their professor. All of us know how to do some code switching depending on the place or audience.

In the context of the rules of engagement, nonverbal indicators can also act as signals between conversational partners. For example, a listener may nod to indicate understanding or encouragement or may look away to indicate distraction or boredom. Conversations can vary considerably in length, but when one person wants to stop the conversation, he signals this message either verbally or nonverbally—for example, saying, "Well, I've got to go now," or getting up to leave and putting on his coat. As with all other phases of a conversation, ending one can have its awkward aspects—as in the case that one person wants to continue talking but the other doesn't. All in all, we have multiple signals—subtle and overt—that we use in starting, continuing, and ending conversations. Moreover, as discussed earlier, we adapt our verbal behavior based on where we are and to whom we're talking.

## WORDS TO AVOID

Another set of rules to make you a more effective communicator focuses on choosing the right words and avoiding the wrong ones. Remember that your word choices affect your credibility. Whether you are at work, at play, or in the classroom, an ill-chosen word can make a difference; for instance, in the spring of 2013, a young man on his first day of work as a broadcast anchor uttered some profanity into a live microphone, only to lose his job minutes after his first broadcast.[11] The following sections describe some categories of words that can get you in trouble with your classmates, work colleagues, and even friends and family.

### Profanity

**Profanity** is *language that is vulgar, abusive, or disrespectful of things sacred*. Many so-called swear words have a religious origin: *hell* and *damn* are examples. Inappropriate use of the words *God* and *Jesus* to express irritation or incredulity can also be considered disrespectful and offensive. Other forms of profanity refer to forbidden statuses or acts: "son of a ___" or "Mother ___." Many people find profanity offensive, so using such words can get you in trouble, especially with people you don't know. Even the Internet has rules about the use of profanity. A note on eBay, for example, says, "We don't allow hateful, offensive, profane, or vulgar language in almost all public areas of the website."

Some people think that profanity is never appropriate, but usage varies by place, age, and sex. Although everyone seems to know that swearing is inappropriate in a place of worship, profanity is fairly common on many college campuses and at athletic events. Also, those in their eighties and nineties seem to have less tolerance for profanity than do middle-aged and younger people. And men tend to cuss more than women. Profanity has become so common that once-forbidden words are so overused that they have lost their impact. You can't be certain what those around you at school, at work, in an audience, or in your social circle really think about such words, and they may judge you harshly if you use them. Think carefully about where you are and who is around before you use words that are potentially offensive.

### Sexist Words

**Sexist language** is *language that excludes individuals on the basis of gender*. The statement "A professor needs to read incessantly to keep up with his field" suggests that all professors are men. A nonsexist way to express this thought is "Professors need to read incessantly to keep up with their fields." People reveal sexism when they assume that all members of any category are all male or all female—for example, that all criminals are male or that all nurses are female. Sexist language also appears in many gender-specific compound words, such as *chairman* and *salesman;* instead, use the term *chair* or *salesperson*.

The use of sexist language varies by sex, with more women than men being victimized by sexist talk. In particular, the vast majority of hostile workplace charges come from women charging men with an offense. Sexism also varies by region. In some parts of the United States a female server might call a man "honey" without meaning anything much, whereas in other parts of the country that word might be seen as flirtatious or at least too personal to use with a stranger. And sexism can vary by age, since younger people have grown up in a time of "political correctness" and are more attuned to the offenses that accompany sexist language. An older generation may use profanity less but exhibit sexist language a bit more. In any case, speakers in conversation or on the stage need to be aware that sexist words can get a person in trouble, sometime career-killing trouble.

Career-killing trouble comes when words create a hostile workplace. The Federal Communications Commission explains the situation this way: "**Hostile work environment harassment** *occurs when unwelcome comments or conduct based on sex, race or other legally protected characteristics unreasonably interferes with an employee's work performance or creates an intimidating, hostile or offensive work environment.*"[12]

### Racist Words

**Racist language** is *language that is insulting because it associates skin color or ethnicity with stereotypical and usually negative characteristics*. The concepts of race and ethnicity—as well as stereotypes and prejudice—are discussed in detail in Chapter 6, on global and intercultural communication. Needless to say, racial and ethnic insults and labels are common in society. Also common is the debate about who is entitled to use certain labels—the "N-word" is one example. The standard rule is that, even though people within a race or an ethnic group may use such words with or about each other, that does not give outsiders permission to use them, and when they do, it can be deeply offensive. Racist language and ethnic slurs are commonly used and well known.

A topic that perhaps is not as commonly discussed or well known is what to do when someone around you uses an offensive racial or ethnic term or makes a racist "joke" in your presence. If you find a comment offensive, an appropriate response is, first, to refrain from laughing at the joke and, second, to tell the speaker that you find the comment offensive and why. These are not easy things to do, however—especially if the person who made the joke has more power than you do (say, it's your boss). Even among friends, it can be difficult to call someone out on bad behavior. The same applies to sexist language and sexist "jokes." Find your way

**Table 2.1**  Common Grammatical Errors[13]

| Incorrect | Correct | Explanation |
|---|---|---|
| "He *don't* care about me anymore." | "He *doesn't* care about me anymore." | Check subject–verb agreement: "don't" is the plural form of the verb "to do," so it should be used only with plural subjects ("They don't care"). "Doesn't" is the singular form of the verb, so it's used with singular subjects (he, she, Joe, Alice, etc.). |
| "I never *would of* thought he would act like that." | "I never *would have* thought he would act like that." | Distinguish spoken from written language: the contraction "would've" sounds like "would of" when spoken but, in fact, stands for "would have." People make this mistake when they confuse the sound of language with its written form. |
| "I'm not speaking to *nobody* in this class." | "I'm not speaking to *anybody* in this class." | Avoid double negatives: instead of "not . . . nobody," say or write "not . . . anybody." |
| "I should *have went* to school yesterday." | "I should *have gone* to school yesterday." | Use verb tenses correctly: "went" is the simple past tense of "go" and is never used with "have." "Have gone" is the present perfect tense, which is formed from the present tense of "to have" + a past participle of another verb—in this case "gone." |

through such difficulties gradually. The more tuned in you are to the damage that such language can do, the better you will become at responding when you hear it.

## Ageist Words

**Ageist language** is *language that denigrates people based on their age, whether young or old.* Classifying every young person as a *child* or a *kid* may be both offensive and inaccurate; referring to someone as a *young person,* an *adolescent,* or a *young adult* is more descriptive and precise. Ageism is also evident in language that infantilizes older persons and diminishes their status as vigorous and vital individuals. Older people may not think of themselves as old and may not appreciate being called senior citizens, golden oldies, or the elderly.[14] The key is to be respectful and thoughtful about applying labels and consider whether you need to refer to people's age at all—or for that matter, their sex, race, or ethnicity—when addressing them or speaking or writing about them. Journalists are trained to describe a subject by race, age, or ethnicity *only* if it is clearly relevant to the story they are presenting.

## Grammatical Errors

**Grammatical errors** are *violations of the formal rules of written and spoken language.* When you use poor grammar in a classroom, a job interview, or a new relationship, you risk making a bad impression. Others may not mention your errors, but they may hold them against you. In Table 2.1, you will find examples of common grammatical mistakes and how to correct them.

## WORDS TO USE CAREFULLY

Because the categories of words discussed in the previous section can offend or insult your listeners, they seriously undermine your ability to communicate. In contrast, the categories of words discussed in this section can have a less serious but still negative impact. In some cases, however, these words or phrases may help you illustrate a point or use language creatively. As always, though, remember the rules regarding place and conversational partners.

### Slang

**Slang** is *informal, casual language used among equals.* It is suitable for use among friends but is not suitable for more formal contexts. Such language may be unacceptable, offensive, or simply incomprehensible to your teacher, your boss, and even your family. Moreover, you may be so used to using some slang terms (*Dude, Bro, gross-out, veg-out*) that you don't even think of them as slang. This is why it's important to reflect on your language use. As you advance through your school and work career, make an effort to eliminate language that may undermine your progress. Table 2.2 offers some examples of American slang. Depending on the communication context, you might be better off using the more formal language listed in the right-hand column.

### Overused Expressions

A **cliché** is *an expression that has lost originality and force through overuse.* Common clichés include "No pain, no gain," "Beauty is only skin deep," and "One for all and all for one." So many clichés exist that avoiding them would be impossible in your conversations, and doing so is unnecessary. But when you want to make a good impression as a competent and original thinker, you will be more successful if you avoid these expressions. Remember that the goal is to be sure your words actually *mean* something and are not empty expressions you repeat without thinking.

### Jargon

**Jargon** is *the language particular to a specific profession, work group, or culture.* In most workplaces the IT support people are infamous for their use of jargon that others may not understand. Because there is now so much of this technology jargon, one website is dedicated to explaining it,

**Table 2.2** Examples of American Slang[15]

| The following expression . . . | is slang for . . . |
| --- | --- |
| "OK, so don't *get bent.*" | "OK, so don't get angry." |
| "He was *decked* in a bar fight." | "He was knocked down hard in a bar fight." |
| "Don't *make waves* at the office if you want a promotion." | "Don't cause trouble at the office if you want a promotion." |
| "Two *big guns* showed up from the head office." | "Two important bosses came from the main office." |

including acronyms, which are abbreviations based on the initial letters of words. Examples include ADSL, AGP, and ALUI.[16] The human relations (HR) officer at your work may also use jargon—also, sometimes, in the form of acronyms. So when your HR person tells you that "your HMO says you used an OON clinic instead of a PPO," you may have no idea what she means. As with slang, the specialized words of your trade or profession may be so familiar to you that you forget you are using them. Outsiders, however, will be frustrated because they cannot understand you. If your goal is to communicate, and it certainly should be, you should use the jargon of your field with care, and if you do, be sure to translate—for example, by explaining that HMO is an acronym for "health maintenance organization" and that OON means "out of network."

### Words That Disguise

A **euphemism** is *a generally harmless word, name, or phrase that replaces an offensive or suggestive one.* Although euphemisms are frequently considered more acceptable than the words for which they are substituted, they distort reality and mask the truth. See examples from the military, business, government, and sports in Table 2.3.

Euphemisms are very common and sometimes unavoidable. We really don't want people talking about bodily functions in stark terms, and there are limited ways to express grief when someone dies or is killed. Perhaps the most

| Table 2.3 | Euphemisms From Various Contexts[17] | |
|-----------|--------------------------------------|---|
| **Context** | **Euphemisms Used** | **What They Mean** |
| Military | Friendly fire | "Killed by soldiers in your own army" (decidedly unfriendly) |
| Business | Pre-owned | "Used" (and possibly a "junker" or a wrecked car) |
| Government | Undocumented worker | A worker who does not have legal citizen status and so can be deported (often referred to as an "illegal alien") |
| Sports | Negative yardage | "Lost ground on the field" (an embarrassing reversal) |

## LEARN FROM PROMINENT SPEAKERS

One way to gain inspiration from the powerful use of words is to read published authors and examine their language use and word choices. The following websites provide examples of effective language use by a range of authors.

- Brainy Quote (www.brainyquote.com): This website lists popular quotations by topic or author. Here you can find a variety of quotations that make effective use of metaphor, simile, and figures of speech. Consider how you might apply the same effective language use choices for a speech on which you are currently working.
- American Rhetoric (www.americanrhetoric.com): Perhaps you want to examine the rhetoric, or language use, of some of the most popular speeches of all time. Here you can examine the transcripts of famous speeches, or even listen to audio clips. These online resources demonstrate how a careful use of language can clarify complex issues and allow you, as a speaker, to connect to people.

unfortunate feature of euphemisms is when they are used to hide grim realities that could be addressed if they were not being masked by the language. Using the term *collateral damage* to refer to the deaths of innocent women, children, and men killed by drones is a good example of euphemism. If we actually referred to such an event as a "multiple murder," perhaps we would be more inclined to recognize these deaths as an offensive result of war technology. Effective communicators need to know when, where, and with whom to use euphemisms, always with a concern about how they affect receivers.

Another way of disguising meaning is by using **ambiguous words,** or *words that can be interpreted in multiple ways*. A politician or university administrator who needs to say something but possibly do little says, "I'll take that under consideration," "I'll get to the bottom of this," or "I'll see what I can do." A slogan like "Do more with less" is vague because what it actually means is that some people are going to lose their job and those who are left will have twice the workload. Many an "education governor" has slashed education budgets across the board. Multiple examples exist of ambiguous words; once you are tuned in to them, you will notice them everywhere.[18]

## STRATEGIES FOR IMPROVING YOUR VERBAL COMMUNICATION

After reading about the many potential problems with words, you must wonder how people ever communicate without offending others. This section offers an array of useful strategies for doing so.

## Ask, "What Did You Mean?"

As defined in Chapter 1, **perception checking** *involves checking in with your conversational partner to ensure you have a common understanding of an event that has occurred or a common definition of a particular phenomenon.* Before an exam, you might ask, "Did you say that you wanted to study together?" Many disagreements occur because people do not stop to make these simple checks on their perception.

## Say It in Your Own Words

**Paraphrasing** is *restating another person's message by rephrasing it in your own words.* Paraphrasing is not simply repeating what you heard. When you say it in your own words, you allow the original speaker to make corrections, in case you misinterpreted what he said. The original speaker must actively listen to your paraphrase to determine whether you understood both the content and the intent of what was said: "So you're saying that we should include others in our study group?"

## Describe Without Judgment

**Description** involves *giving an account of observed behavior or phenomena.* You offer a reasonably neutral description when you say, "I saw two cars run into each other because one car did not stop at the sign." You are judgmental when you say, "I saw that fool run a stop sign and bash that other car." Being descriptive instead of evaluative is difficult, but being descriptive can keep you out of many conflicts. Say what you see; don't judge what you see.

## Define Your Terms

Defining terms is necessary in school and at work as well as in your personal life. When you ask, "Can you explain what you mean by *benefits*?" you have a better chance of avoiding misunderstandings with a potential employer. What, precisely, does an employer mean when she says you may have to work overtime? Major disputes continue to arise over the way human beings define *work hours, gun control, birth control,* and *marriage*.

## Build Your Vocabulary

Building your vocabulary means adding new words to your language. Having a large vocabulary is a sign of intelligence; it means you have many words to choose from and can express yourself with precision. The best way to improve your vocabulary is to read and to look up terms you do not know in a dictionary, as you go. Another fun way to increase the number of words you have at your disposal is to subscribe to a word-of-the-day e-mail, such as the one available on *Merriam-Webster Online* (www.merriam-webster.com/word -of-the-day/). Keep in mind that demonstrating a good vocabulary can help you impress others, but using words incorrectly will likely work against you. Before using a new word, familiarize yourself with its denotative and connotative meanings.

### Paint Pictures With Your Words

Visual imagery helps you communicate complex ideas. For example, a physicist on the national news illustrated the discovery of hundreds of galaxies with the image of a pizza. Earth, he said, is one small dot on a pizza that is our galaxy. Now, he said, imagine hundreds of pizzas surrounding that one, each representing a galaxy like our Milky Way. By referencing an object whose size and shape we all know well, the physicist was better able to communicate the immensity of the known collection of galaxies.

### Make Accurate Observations

**Observations** are *descriptions of what you directly saw, touched, tasted, smelled, or heard.* Even though we put considerable trust in what we observe, research tells us that memory, including in the context of witness identification, is not always reliable.[19] Therefore, be precise in your descriptions, and offer concrete details. Instead of saying, "She drove a nice car," say, "She drove a dark blue 2013 Mazda 6—very sporty." The first observation tells little about what you judge to be a "nice car"; the second demonstrates what style, color, and make you prefer.

### Make Inferences Carefully

Inferences, as defined in Chapter 9, are conclusions we make based on some evidence, such as observations. For example, you can observe that someone took something without paying, but to say that person is a thief is an inference. Inferences, like observations, can be incorrect. The person might have forgotten to pay or might be the nephew of the owner and so has permission to take a candy bar off the shelf. We make observations all the time, and we draw inferences from observations. But we have to be careful about accuracy and error with both observations and inferences.

### Be Specific and Concrete

A person who uses **concrete language** uses *words and statements that are specific rather than abstract or vague.* The statement "You have interrupted me three times since I began to talk. I feel as though you do not consider my point of view as important as yours" is concrete. In contrast, "You never consider my viewpoint" is vague. The first explanation would likely help the person interrupting you to correct his behavior, whereas the second, less specific statement might just make him defensive.

# CHALLENGE YOURSELF

## Does It Really Matter If I Use Correct Grammar, Avoid Profanity, and Avoid Slang?

You don't have to speak correctly, but not doing so can hold you back. Your use of words can mark you as educated, intelligent, and knowledgeable—or not. The worst part about weak language skills is that your partner, your friends, and your boss are unlikely to comment on the way you use words. Instead, they may just make a negative judgment. And even if someone does correct you, you may not, in the moment, feel grateful for the correction.

To improve your language use, speak and listen to others as much as possible. Watching television, reading books, listening to the radio or your professor's lectures, and carrying on conversations are all great ways to study language and to improve your own language use.

Not everyone you speak and listen to will use the strategies and rules discussed in this chapter. However, the more you expose yourself to the different ways people communicate, the better you will be at deciding where, when, and how to speak and doing so with confidence.

## Use Figures of Speech

**Figures of speech** *draw relationships that help listeners remember.* Discussed earlier, in the section "The Creative Function," these figures of speech include metaphors like "you broke my heart," similes like "ugly as sin," and hyperboles like "a dessert to die for." Figures of speech are descriptive and in some cases can clarify a point. For example, describing blockage in a heart valve by specifying its size as a number of millimeters might not be helpful for most patients. Describing the valve's opening as the size of a drinking straw when it should be the size of a water hose is far clearer and more graphic.

## Use the Language of the Locals

**Regionalisms** are *words and phrases specific to a particular region or part of the country.* For example, submarine sandwiches are *hoagies* in Philadelphia, *po' boys* in New Orleans, *grinders* in Boston, *torpedoes* in Los Angeles, *wedgies* in Rhode Island, and *heros* in New York City. Pay attention to the terms used by those around you when you're in a new location. Your mission is to use the correct words for the region.

## CHAPTER REVIEW

In this chapter you learned about verbal communication by first understanding four functions: the instrumental, the creative, the analytical, and the social. You learned how words communicate through denotative and connotative meanings and through two processes for interpreting messages: encoding and decoding. You also learned the importance of several sets of rules of verbal communication. First, rules vary depending on where you are and with whom. Second, rules of engagement—regarding how people start, take turns, switch codes, and end conversations—guide our verbal communication. The next set of rules concerned which words to avoid—those that are profane, sexist, racist, ageist, ambiguous, ungrammatical, and potentially career-killing. To be used only in moderation are slang, clichés, jargon, euphemisms, and ambiguous language. Finally, the list of specific strategies at the end of the chapter can help you improve your verbal communication.

## KEY TERMS

ageist language, 29
alliteration, 21
ambiguous words, 32
analytical function, 21
cliché, 30
code switching, 26
concrete language, 34
conflict management, 22
connotative meanings, 24
creative function, 20
denotative meaning, 23
description, 33
euphemism, 31
figures of speech, 35
grammatical errors, 29
hostile work environment harassment, 28
hyperbole, 21
instrumental function, 20
jargon, 30
language, 20

meaning, 20
metaphor, 21
neologisms, 24
observations, 34
paraphrasing, 33
perception checking, 33
phatic communication, 22
profanity, 27
racist language, 28
regionalisms, 35
rules of engagement, 26
sexist language, 27
simile, 21
slang, 30
social function, 22
symbol, 22
trouble talk, 22
turn taking, 26
verbal communication, 20
word, 22

## STUDY QUESTIONS

1. Provide your own example (not from the book) of the analytical function of verbal communication.

2. What are three words that are loaded with connotative meaning for you?

3. Offer one example of an instance in which you misjudged the importance of place in verbal communication. Examples of places with specific rules regarding communication include the classroom, the office, a job interview, and an event like a wedding or funeral.

4. Tell of one instance where you mistakenly used a word to avoid—for example, profanity—with negative consequences.

5. In the list of strategies for improving language, select one and provide an example of how you could apply that strategy in your daily life.

# 3

# Communicating Nonverbally

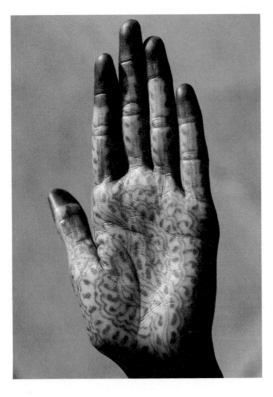

Although everyone knows that the words we use are important, many people forget the importance of nonverbal communication. In this chapter we will define nonverbal communication, explain the relationship between verbal and nonverbal codes, and demonstrate the challenge of interpreting those codes. Finally, we will offer suggestions on how you can improve your nonverbal communication.

## LEARNING OBJECTIVES

*After reading this chapter, you should be able to:*

- Define nonverbal communication.
- Explain the relationship between verbal and nonverbal communication.
- Define and describe the seven nonverbal codes: bodily movement and facial expression, physical attractiveness, space, time, touch, vocal cues, and clothing and other artifacts.
- Explain why nonverbal codes are difficult to interpret.
- Explain how you can improve your nonverbal communication.

## WHAT IS NONVERBAL COMMUNICATION?

**Nonverbal communication** is *the process of using wordless messages to generate meaning.* Nonverbal communication includes nonword vocalizations, such as inflection, and nonword sounds, such as "ah" and "hmm." When you raise your hand in class or furrow your brow when concentrating on what your professor is saying, you are communicating nonverbally.

Some people believe that nonverbal communication may be more important than the words we use. It is difficult to determine how much meaning comes from words and how much comes from the nonverbal cues we offer. However, we know that nonverbal messages often provide much more meaning than people realize.[1] Indeed, when we are not certain about another person's feelings, or about our feelings for him or her, we may rely far more on nonverbal cues—a smile, a touch on the arm, the clothes worn on a date—and less on the words that are used.[2]

## HOW ARE VERBAL AND NONVERBAL COMMUNICATION RELATED?

Both verbal and nonverbal communication are essential for effective interactions with others. But how are the two related? A recent study examined the role of verbal and nonverbal elements of communication to determine which is most important in a persuasive message. The results showed that the content (the verbal portion of the speech) was most important in determining the effect of the speech. Emphasis and gestures, however, can make a speech seem lively and powerful.[3] In other words, both the verbal and the nonverbal elements of a speech play an important role in the outcome of communication.

Nonverbal communication works in conjunction with the words we use in six ways: to repeat, to emphasize, to complement, to contradict, to substitute, and to regulate. **Repetition** *occurs when the same message is sent verbally and nonverbally.* When we use **emphasis,** we are *using nonverbal cues to strengthen a message.* **Complementing** *goes beyond duplication of the message in two channels; the verbal and nonverbal codes add meaning to each other and expand the meaning of either message alone.* In contrast, **contradiction** is *when verbal and nonverbal messages conflict.* **Substitution** *occurs when nonverbal codes are used in place of verbal codes.* Finally, **regulation** is *the use of nonverbal codes to monitor and control interactions with others.* Table 3.1 demonstrates each of these relationships between nonverbal and verbal communication and offers examples of each.

## WHAT ARE NONVERBAL CODES?

**Nonverbal codes** are *nonword symbols, gestures, or vocalizations that communicate meaning.* Have you ever shrugged your shoulders in answer to a question, moved away from someone who was becoming too friendly, or worn a particularly

| Table 3.1 | Relationships Between Nonverbal and Verbal Cues | |
|---|---|---|
| | **Description** | **Example** |
| **Repetition** | When the same message is sent verbally and nonverbally | You frown at a speaker while asking what she means. |
| **Emphasis** | The use of nonverbal cues to strengthen your message | You hug a friend while telling him how much you care about him. |
| **Complementing** | Goes beyond duplication of the message in two channels; the verbal and nonverbal codes add meaning to each other and expand the meaning of either message alone | You point to your favorite dessert in the bakery case as you describe to your friend how delicious it is. |
| **Contradiction** | Occurs when your verbal and nonverbal messages conflict | You sarcastically state that you are fine about something that has happened when you are not. |
| **Substitution** | Occurs when nonverbal codes are used instead of verbal codes | You roll your eyes, shrug your shoulders, or stick out your tongue instead of saying out loud how you feel. |
| **Regulation** | Occurs when nonverbal codes are used to monitor and control interactions with others | You walk away from someone who isn't finished talking to you. |

professional outfit when interviewing for a job? All of these represent nonverbal codes, and they fall into several categories, discussed in the following paragraphs.

### Bodily Movement and Facial Expression

**Kinesics** is *the way we interpret nonverbal behavior related to movement, such as body language and facial expression.* Psychology professor Albert Mehrabian studied nonverbal communication by examining the concepts of liking, status, and responsiveness among the participants in communication situations.[4] Mehrabian explained these concepts in the following way:

- *Liking* is expressed by forward leaning, a direct body orientation (such as standing face-to-face), proximity, increased touching, a relaxed posture, open arms and body, a positive facial expression, and direct eye contact.

- *Status,* especially high status, is communicated nonverbally by bigger gestures, a relaxed posture, and less eye contact.
- *Responsiveness* is exhibited by movement toward the other person, spontaneous gestures, shifts in posture and position, and facial expressiveness.

Other researchers have categorized movement on the basis of its functions, origins, and meanings.[5] The categories they have identified—emblems, illustrators, affect displays, regulators, and adaptors—are described in Table 3.2.

You may be far more adept at reading bodily movement and facial expressions than you realize. Psychologists recently determined that people are even perfectly capable of reading their dogs' facial expressions. Two researchers have concluded that humans and dogs have a natural empathy for each other, because they have evolved side-by-side for the past 100,000 years. As they observed, this is not news for anyone who has a pet.[6]

### Physical Attractiveness

Some characteristics—bright eyes, symmetrical features, and thin or medium build—are generally associated with physical attractiveness.[7] Moreover, such characteristics may not be limited to one culture but may be universal.[8]

**Table 3.2** Categories of Movement Based on Functions, Origins, and Meanings

| | Description | Example |
|---|---|---|
| **Emblems** | Nonverbal movements that substitute for words and phrases | ■ A curved index finger meaning "come here"<br>■ An open hand held up meaning "stop" |
| **Illustrators** | Nonverbal movements that accompany or reinforce verbal messages | ■ Nodding or shaking your head when you say yes or no |
| **Affect displays** | Nonverbal movements to express emotion | ■ Showing joy for the winning team<br>■ Slamming a door in anger |
| **Regulators** | Nonverbal movements that control the flow or pace of communication | ■ Moving away when you want the conversation to stop<br>■ Looking away when you are not interested |
| **Adaptors** | Nonverbal movements that you might perform fully in private but only partially in public | ■ Gently scratching or touching an insect bite in public but rubbing it vigorously in private |

Physical attractiveness affects many aspects of our lives. Generally, people who are physically attractive are privileged over those who are not.[9] This bias is stronger for women than for men.[10] Further, people are more likely to accurately describe the traits of those who are attractive over those whom they perceive to be unattractive. They may take more care in getting to know the attractive individuals, or they may value the information they receive from them more than they value it from those whom they deem less attractive.

The influence of physical appearance begins as early as age four. Children are treated differently by their daycare teachers based on their physical appearance.[11] Moreover, children's misbehaviors are viewed as isolated events if they are attractive, but as a chronic tendency to be bad if they are not. These patterns continue throughout one's life.[12]

Physical attractiveness affects both credibility and the ability to persuade others. Attractive people receive higher initial credibility ratings than do those who are viewed as unattractive.[13] Attractive women have more success in persuading the opposite sex than do attractive men, but less so as they grow older.[14]

### Space

Anthropologist Edward T. Hall introduced the concept of **proxemics**—*the study of the human use of space and distance*—in his book *The Hidden Dimension*.[15] Two concepts considered essential to the study of the use of space are territoriality and personal space.

- **Territoriality** refers to *your need to establish and maintain certain spaces as your own*. In a shared dormitory room, the items on the common desk area mark the territory. For example, you might place your notebook, pens and pencils, and iPad or tablet on the right side of the desk, and your roommate might place books, a cell phone, and a laptop on the left side. Although the desk is shared, you are each claiming part of the area.

- **Personal space** is the personal "bubble" that moves around with you. It is *the distance you maintain between yourself and others; the amount of space you claim as your own*. Large people usually claim more space because of their size, and men often take more space than women.

Figure 3.1 shows how people regularly use four distances when they communicate.[16] Beginning with the closest contact and the least personal space and moving to the greatest distance, they are intimate distance, personal distance, social distance, and public distance.

- **Intimate distance** *extends from your body outward to 18 inches; it is used by people who are relationally close*. This distance is employed to show affection, to give comfort, and to protect,

**Figure 3.1** The Four Distances

and it usually elicits a positive response. This is because individuals tend to stand and sit close to people they are attracted to.[17] However, occasionally people overestimate how close another person feels to them and they sit or stand too close for the comfort of the second person. Communication researcher Judee K. Burgoon labeled this behavior as a personal space violation.

- **Personal distance** *ranges from 18 inches to 4 feet, and it is the distance most Americans use for conversation and other nonintimate exchanges.*

- **Social distance** *ranges from 4 to 12 feet, and it is used most often to carry out business in the workplace.* The higher the status of one person, the greater the distance.

- **Public distance** *exceeds 12 feet and is used most often in public speaking in such settings as lecture halls, churches, mosques, and synagogues.*

## Time

Temporal communication, or **chronemics,** *refers to the way people organize, relate to, and use time and the messages that result.* Some people particularly value the past and collect photographs and souvenirs to remind themselves of times gone by. Others focus more intensely on the future and are always chasing dreams or planning future events. Still others live in the present and savor the current time. They try to live each day to its fullest and neither lament the past nor show concern for the future.

What kinds of messages relate to the way we use time? People who are perennially late might send the message that their time is more important than that of those around them, whereas those who tend to be early might be understood as being responsible and conscientious. People in different cultures view time differently, a topic we will cover in greater depth in Chapter 6, on global and intercultural communication.[18]

## Touch

**Tactile communication,** also known as haptics, is *the use of touch in communication.* Because touch always involves invasion of another's personal space, it commands attention. It can be welcome, as when a parent holds a crying child, or unwelcome, as in an instance of sexual harassment.

Our need for, and appreciation of, tactile communication starts early in life.[19] Insufficient touching can lead to health disorders, such as allergies and eczema, speech problems, and even death. Untouched babies and small children, for example, can grow increasingly ill and die.[20] For adults, touch is a powerful means of communication,[21] and touch is usually perceived as positive, pleasurable, and reinforcing. People who are extroverts, or highly sociable, are more likely to engage in touching.[22] The association of touch with the warmth and caring that began in infancy carries over into adulthood.

The use of touch varies by gender:[23]

- Women value touch more than men do.[24]
- Women are touched more than men, beginning when they are six months old.[25]
- Women touch female children more often than they touch male children.[26]
- Men and their sons touch each other the least.[27]

Touch sends such a powerful message that it has to be handled with responsibility. Some people may welcome it in work or clinical settings, but it is equally likely to be undesirable or annoying. Certainly, touch can be misunderstood in such settings.[28] When the right to touch is abused, it can result in a breach of trust, anxiety, and hostility. When touch is used to communicate concern, caring, and affection, it is often welcomed, desired, and appreciated.

## Vocal Cues

Nonverbal communication includes some sounds, as long as they are not words. We call them **paralinguistic features**—*the nonword sounds and nonword characteristics of language, such as pitch, volume, rate, and quality.* The prefix *para* means "alongside" or "parallel to," so *paralinguistic* means "alongside the words or language."

The paralinguistic feature examined in this section is **vocal cues**—*all of the oral aspects of sound except words themselves.* Vocal cues include those outlined in Table 3.3.

These vocal cues are important because they are linked in our minds with a speaker's physical characteristics, emotional state, personality characteristics, gender characteristics, and even credibility. Vocal cues may convey information about the speaker's age, height, appearance, and body type.[29] For example, when you talk to strangers on the telephone, you form an impression of how they look and how their personalities might be described.

Vocal cues are not only important in interpersonal settings but also essential to successful public speakers. Vocal cues can help a public speaker establish credibility with an audience and can clarify the message:

- Pitch and inflection can be used to make the speech sound aesthetically pleasing, accomplish subtle changes in meaning, and tell an audience whether you are asking a question or making a statement, being sincere or sarcastic, or being doubtful or assertive.

- A rapid speaking rate may indicate you are confident about speaking in public or that you are nervously attempting to conclude your speech.

| Table 3.3 | Vocal Cues |
|---|---|
| Pitch | ■ The highness or lowness of your voice |
| Rate | ■ How rapidly or slowly you speak |
| Inflection | ■ The variety or changes in pitch |
| Volume | ■ The loudness or softness of your voice |
| Quality | ■ The unique resonance of your voice, such as huskiness, nasality, raspiness, or whininess |
| Nonword sounds | ■ Using "mmh," "huh," "ahh," and the like, as well as pauses or the absence of sound for effect in speaking |
| Pronunciation | ■ Saying a word correctly |
| Articulation | ■ Coordinating your mouth, tongue, and teeth to make a word understandable to others |
| Enunciation | ■ Combining pronunciation and articulation to produce a word with clarity and distinction, so that it can be understood. A person who mumbles has an enunciation problem. |
| Silence | ■ The lack of sound |

- Variations in volume can be used to add emphasis or create suspense.

- Enunciation is especially important in public speaking because of the increased size of the audience and the fewer opportunities for direct feedback.

- Pauses can be used to create dramatic effect and arouse audience interest. Vocalized pauses—"ah," "uh-huh," "um," and so on—are not desirable in public speaking and may distract the audience.

## Clothing and Other Artifacts

**Objectics,** or object language, refers to *the study of the human use of clothing and other artifacts as nonverbal codes.* **Artifacts** are *ornaments or adornments you display that hold communicative potential,* including jewelry, hairstyles, cosmetics, automobiles, canes, watches, shoes, portfolios, hats, glasses, tattoos, body piercings, and even the fillings in teeth. Your clothing and other adornments might communicate your age, gender, status, role, socio-economic class, group memberships, and personality.

Conformity occurs when one tries to go along with the norms of a group in attitudes, clothing, language, or other behaviors. Conforming to current styles is correlated with an individual's desire to be accepted and liked.[30] People can also choose to deviate from the norms of a group, in which case clothing and other adornments may be used as a form of creative self-expression.[31]

Cultural and religious differences can often be apparent in the clothing people wear. For example, the dress of Muslim

# CHALLENGE YOURSELF

### What Should I Know About Body Language, Clothing, and Accessories, so I Don't Make a Fool of Myself When It Comes to Socializing or Looking for a Job?

As you've learned throughout this chapter, nonverbal communication includes many cues: bodily movement and facial expression, physical attractiveness, use of space, time orientation, use of touch, vocal cues, clothing, and other artifacts.

- Think about how much attention you pay to each set of cues. Are you aware of the nonverbal messages you might be sending? Are they the messages you want to be sending?
- Let's focus on clothing and other accessories. How would you dress for an interview? You would probably wear fairly conservative clothes. You could wear a suit or a matching outfit in dark colors. You would not forget a belt or socks. Your jewelry—whether male or female—should be minimal and conservative. Good hygiene is essential.
- A different set of standards applies to going for coffee or going clubbing with friends. You can be more expressive on a social occasion than when you interview for a job.
- Can you add other suggestions about appropriate clothing and adornments? Have you ever erred in how you dressed? Have you observed others who have? What advice would you offer a younger sibling or a student new to your school about how to fit in or stand out?

After considering clothing, think about the other kinds of nonverbal codes. If you feel confident about your own sensitivity to them, ask a trusted friend to provide feedback to you about your clothing, about your use of space and touch, and about your use of time in social or casual situations. If you are seeking a job, you might ask someone whose opinion you trust about how you might manage the same sets of cues in a formal setting. You might also find ways to improve by paying attention to the nonverbal behavior of others. All of us make mistakes from time to time with complex nonverbal cues, but by being both more thoughtful and more reflective, you may experience more success.

women, which tends to be modest and consist of loose and fairly heavy materials, is distinctive. Some Muslim women cover their entire body, including their face and/or hands, whereas others wear a simple Hijab, or head covering, with long sleeves and long skirts. Like Muslim women, Orthodox Jewish women tend to dress modestly. Generally, they wear dark-colored, loose clothing and cover their elbows and knees. Married Orthodox Jewish women usually cover their hair as well. Some women from India who are Hindu may wear dhotis and saris, at least for formal occasions. Although the skirts are long, frequently the midriff can be glimpsed in these outfits.

Body modifications, such as tattoos and piercings, are a type of artifact. Although they can be removed, the procedures may be both costly and time intensive. What do tattoos signal to others? Most people who adorn themselves with tattoos and piercings probably do so because they believe it adds to their overall attractiveness. A recent study, however, presented findings on how others perceive people with tattoos. Men with tattoos were viewed as more dominant than nontattooed men, and women with tattoos were seen as less healthy than women without tattoos.[32]

## WHY ARE NONVERBAL CODES DIFFICULT TO INTERPRET?

Perhaps you have been in a situation where you misinterpreted someone's nonverbal cues. You thought that a touch on your arm communicated liking, that a frown meant someone disapproved of what you said, or someone looking elsewhere while you were talking suggested a lack of interest, but you later found out you were wrong. If you have had these experiences, you know that nonverbal codes are difficult to interpret. In this section, we talk about two reasons this is so.

### One Code Communicates a Variety of Meanings

The ambiguity of nonverbal codes occurs in part because one code may communicate several meanings. For example, the nonverbal code of raising your right hand

## GLOBALLY

### GREETINGS

When greeting, Chinese, Japanese, and Koreans bow and Thais bow their heads while holding their hands in a prayerlike position. The bumi putra, or Muslim Malaysians, have a greeting of their own: they shake hands as Westerners do, but they follow up by touching their heart with their right hand to indicate that they are greeting you "from the heart." In the Philippines, a limp handshake is a proper greeting, whereas in the United States, a firm handshake is considered appropriate and even preferable.

Within the United States, various groups have unique ways of greeting each other. Colleagues might shake hands, while close friends might hug, kiss on the cheek, or bump fists. How do you greet your friends? What about those you work with? And finally, how would you greet a grandparent, or other family member you love and respect? Sensitivity, and perhaps adaptability, in the greetings you exchange may allow you to communicate more smoothly.

COMMUNICATING

may mean that you are taking an oath, you are demonstrating for a cause, you are indicating to an instructor that you would like to answer a question, a physician is examining your right side, or you want a taxi to stop for you.

Although people in laboratory experiments have demonstrated some success in decoding nonverbal behavior accurately,[33] in actual situations receivers of nonverbal cues can only guess about the meaning.[34] Several lay authors have been successful in selling books suggesting that observers can learn to easily and accurately interpret specific nonverbal cues. Unfortunately, these authors have not been able to demonstrate any significant improvement among their readers.

### A Variety of Codes Communicate the Same Meaning

Nonverbal communication is not a science: any number of codes may be used to communicate the same meaning. Consider the many nonverbal ways that adults communicate love or affection. You may sit or stand close to someone you love. You might speak softly, use a certain vocal intonation, or alter how quickly you speak.

Cultural differences are especially relevant in this context. How do you show respect to a speaker? In some cultures, listeners show respect by averting their eyes; in other cultures, listeners show respect and attention by looking directly at the speaker. Depending on her own culture, a speaker who is not familiar with the cultural practices of others might feel that people who look away are inattentive or people who look directly are overstepping the boundaries of privacy.

### HOW CAN YOU IMPROVE YOUR NONVERBAL COMMUNICATION?

You can improve your nonverbal communication by being sensitive to context, audience, and feedback. The **context** includes *the physical setting, the occasion, and the situation.*

In conversation your vocal cues are rarely a problem unless you stutter, stammer, lisp, or suffer from some speech pathology. Vocal cues are perhaps most important in public speaking, because you have to be highly attuned to your volume and rate, you have to enunciate very clearly, and you have to introduce

## BUILDER

### LEARN TO IMPROVE YOUR NONVERBAL SENSITIVITY

You can improve your nonverbal sensitivity by paying attention to the context, by adapting to your audience, and by providing feedback to others.

- Consider the context: ask yourself if the physical setting, the occasion, and the situation require changes in your behavior. For example, does the occasion or the lack of air conditioning in the room signal to you that you should keep your presentation brief?
- Adapt to your audience: does the audience seem bored or uninterested in your message? If so, add gestures and bodily movement to encourage their attention and increase their curiosity.
- Give and receive feedback: observe your audience. Are they telling you nonverbally that they would like to continue the conversation? Are you providing nonverbal feedback that lets them know that their needs and interests matter to you?

more vocal variety to keep the audience's attention. The strategic use of pauses and silence is also more important in public speaking than in conversations or small-group discussions.

The occasion and physical setting also affect the potential meaning of a nonverbal cue. For example, you may stand farther away from people in formal situations when space allows but closer to family members or strangers in an elevator.

You also have to adapt to the audience. When speaking to children, you must use careful enunciation, articulation, and pronunciation. With an older audience—or with younger audiences whose hearing has been impaired by too much loud music—you must adapt your volume. Generally, children and older people in both interpersonal and public speaking situations appreciate slower speech. Adaptation to an audience may also determine your choice of clothing, hairstyle, and jewelry.

Your attention to audience feedback can be very important in helping others interpret your nonverbal cues. If your listeners give quizzical looks, stare, or nod, you can interpret these as signals to talk louder, introduce variety into your pace or pitch, restate your points, or clarify your message. If your conversational partner or audience does not provide you with feedback, ask questions and check on their perceptions.

## CHAPTER REVIEW

In this chapter you explored nonverbal communication first by learning what it means to communicate without words. You also learned about the relationship between verbal and nonverbal communication—that it can function to repeat, emphasize, complement, contradict, substitute, or regulate your verbal communication. Understanding this relationship can mean the difference between communicating effectively and obscuring your meaning with cues that are too easily misunderstood. The last section of this chapter therefore focused on how you can improve your nonverbal communication, no matter the context—whether you are on a date, speaking in front of your peers, or interviewing for a job.

## KEY TERMS

artifacts, 45
chronemics, 43
complementing, 39
context, 48
contradiction, 39
emphasis, 39
intimate distance, 42
kinesics, 40
nonverbal codes, 39
nonverbal communication, 39
objectics, 45
paralinguistic features, 44

personal distance, 43
personal space, 42
proxemics, 42
public distance, 43
regulation, 39
repetition, 39
social distance, 43
substitution, 39
tactile communication, 44
territoriality, 42
vocal cues, 44

## STUDY QUESTIONS

1. How much does nonverbal communication contribute to a message? Under what circumstances is it especially important?
2. Name two ways in which verbal and nonverbal communication work together, and give examples of each.
3. List two kinds of nonverbal codes, and explain how each contributes to a message. Describe scenarios from your own experience that illustrate each of the two codes.
4. Name two reasons people sometimes misinterpret nonverbal messages. Describe an experience you had or witnessed (including in a book or movie) when a message was misinterpreted for one of these reasons.
5. What are the three areas to focus on when working to improve your nonverbal communication? Give an example from your own experience to illustrate each.

# Communicating Through Listening

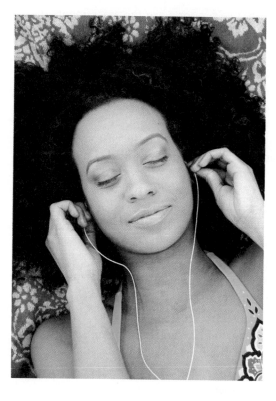

Listening is your most used communication skill. In fact, research shows that, as a college student, you spend roughly 51% of your time listening to others, including those in the mass media—on talk shows, news programs, podcasts, and the radio.[1] In this chapter you will learn why listening is such an important communication skill, which kinds of listening require the most effort, what factors affect your attention and focus, and the many barriers to effective listening, which you can overcome.

## LEARNING OBJECTIVES

*After reading this chapter, you should be able to:*

- Explain the difference between hearing and listening.
- Describe the different types of listening.
- Understand the factors that affect attention.
- Know how to overcome barriers to listening.

# THE IMPORTANCE OF LISTENING

Although listening is your most used communication skill, it is also very likely your least studied. You learned reading and writing from grade school through high school, and even into college, but did you ever study listening? As you transition into a career, listening will remain an important skill and one worth practicing.

## Why Listen?

Consider the data in Figure 4.1, which shows the average amount of time that working professionals spend listening, speaking, writing, and reading. According to this chart, as well as other sources referenced in this chapter, listening is likely to play a vital role in your work life, whatever career you choose. It's possible that, on the job, you will even spend more time listening (33%) than speaking (25%)!

- According to an article in *Training & Development*, 80% of the corporate executives who were surveyed rated listening as the most important skill in the workforce.
- Nearly 30% of those executives said that listening was the communication skill most lacking among their employees.[2]
- Underscoring the significance of these self-reports are the assessments of those in upper management, like the CEO of Best Buy, who asserts that, because customer interests rapidly evolve, not listening guarantees failure.[3]

Try to think of a job you've had where your communication skills made no difference. If you work in entry-level retail—from fast food to clothing—customers will care how you treat them. The following points taken from customer-service questionnaires at retail chains across the country demonstrate the impact your listening skills can have on the customers with whom you interact and very likely on the outcome of your job. In almost any customer-service position, your performance will be measured in large part by your ability to:

- Get to know the customer base by listening when they ask questions or make requests.
- Ask questions about customers' lifestyles—and listen to their answers—to better understand their needs.
- Interact with customers, which includes receiving orders and preparing products according to those orders.
- Listen and respond appropriately to customer issues.

**Figure 4.1** Listening in the Workforce: Average Time Spent Listening, Speaking, Writing, and Reading

■ Listening  ■ Speaking  ▢ Writing  ■ Reading

The importance of listening extends to all levels and all fields. In health-related fields, from personal care specialists to dental hygienists and licensed practical nurses, communication is vital to the experiences of the patients being treated. Receptionists, secretaries, administrative assistants, service managers, cashiers, telemarketers, and truckers are expected to communicate well with visitors, customers, and clients. A friendly FedEx or UPS driver can spread goodwill to 50 people each day simply by having good communication skills. Everyone in the world of business—at every level—needs to know how to listen and speak in ways that maintain positive relationships.

Your ability to listen affects your personal life, too. Consider the following situations that invite good listening skills:

- Your partner asks you to pick up three items on the way home from work. You not only listen but remember to bring home all three items. Your partner thinks you are wonderful.

- You meet several new people at a friend's party; you remember their names and use them during the party and later. You listened, remembered, and impressed the guests.

- You listened and remembered that your mother makes a big deal out of Mother's Day, so you arrange to be with her on her special day. She communicated; you listened, remembered, and acted appropriately.

In other words, listening to people—those you've just met and those you love—pays off in more positive relationships.

### Hearing vs. Listening

How many times have you sat in class with words flowing in your ears only to forget, later on, what your teacher and peers were saying? In situations like this, the reason for your difficulty recalling information lies in the difference between hearing and listening, as illustrated in Figure 4.2. **Hearing** is *the act of receiving*

**Figure 4.2** The Difference Between Hearing and Listening

| Hearing | Listening |
| --- | --- |
| ■ **Hearing** is sound entering your ears, something you cannot prevent. <br> ■ Unless you have earbuds or earplugs in your ears, you cannot keep the sounds from entering. | ■ **Listening** is the act of interpreting those sounds in your brain. <br> ■ This occurs when you are paying attention but does not occur if you are busy texting when you are supposed to be listening. |

*sound*; you cannot stop sound from entering your ears. **Listening** is *the act of interpreting the sounds you hear, to determine their meaning.*

As you can see, you can be present in class and absent at the same time. Although your body may be present—and you may even appear to be listening—your mind can easily become engaged in other matters, like texting a friend, updating your Facebook page, or admiring the person two rows ahead.

Noise, as defined in Chapter 1, is any physical or psychological interference that reduces the clarity of a message. Consider some everyday examples of noise that interferes with listening and their potential effects:

- Texting while driving is worse than drunk driving, because you are not watching traffic or listening for dangers, such as sirens or screeching brakes.[4]

- Listening to loud, fast music significantly diminishes your ability to comprehend things you read or hear.[5]

- Checking devices may also reduce your ability to listen. An article in *Advertising Age* reported that smartphones and other personal communication devices might be diminishing face-to-face communication skills, such as listening.[6]

- Using Facebook and texting while studying can be blamed for lower grades.[7]

# COMMUNICATING GLOBALLY

## SOME CULTURES VALUE LESS TALK

North American culture places more value on talking than on listening, but some cultures here and abroad value silence, listening, and observation. Many Native American tribes, like the western Apache, quietly listen to and observe other people in an effort to understand them. Similarly, in many Pacific Rim countries—Japan, for example—people allow for much more silence. As Thomas Nakayama, co-author of *Experiencing Intercultural Communication*, says, "silence in Japan is not simply the absence of sound or a pause in the conversation that must be filled."[8] So in conversation and team meetings, you may encounter individuals whose culture does not value a quick verbal response, an immediate jump into the business at hand, or a winning argument; instead, people from some cultures want quiet time to assess the person who is speaking.

Now you know why listening is so important, can differentiate between hearing and listening, and can identify the noise that often gets in the way. But knowing about listening and learning to become an effective listener are two different things. In the next section, you will see that there are several types of listening, and each requires a different kind of attention. As you will learn in the remainder of this chapter, practicing your listening skills, and adapting to the kind of listening required, can advance your opportunities both professionally and personally.

## TYPES OF LISTENING

Your purpose in listening largely determines how actively you try to process information. If you are just listening to music to relax, you do not have to work very hard to listen; in fact, listening is more pleasure than work. But if you are listening in a class and your purpose is to learn, understand, and remember, that listening takes sustained effort. Anyone who sits through college lectures understands how hard one has to focus to sustain attention in a class.

### Listening to Discern Content and Intent

"Isn't it warm in here?" says an elderly woman, one of many at a crowded meeting. The content of her words indicates only that she is seeking agreement from others about the temperature. But very likely the intent of her message is to have someone open a window, turn on a fan, or start the air conditioning. "Where is the salt?" says a father, a man of few words. On the content level, his inquiry is simply about location, but the intent is to have someone pass the salt. **Content** is *the literal meaning of a message,* whereas **intent** is *what the speaker really wants.* Notice in both examples that an active listener has to be prepared to interpret another person's message, because the content often only suggests what the person wants. When your boss says, "Is it closing time already?" as you prepare to leave your job a little early, you understand that he isn't really just inquiring about the time. In other words, you know how to read the intent behind his content.

### Listening for Learning

One important reason for learning to listen well is that communication skills will help you to succeed in school, as well as to gain and keep a job. When your professor is explaining what will be covered in the next class session, when your

## BUILDER

### LEARN TO LISTEN IN CONVERSATION

Sometimes listening during conversation can be a challenge all its own. Follow these practical tips to show others you are listening:

- Face the other person. Don't act as if you are trying to get away.
- Make eye contact. Keep your eyes on the other person instead of looking around for other opportunities.
- Occasionally agree, disagree, or make a noise to indicate that you are receiving the message.
- "Play back" a piece of the message in your own words (paraphrase) or repeat the other person's words back to her (repetition).
- Respond in some way consistent with what the other person is saying: add to what he is saying, provide an example, bring up another line of argument, or provide evidence, for example.

supervisor is describing what she wants in an oral report to be delivered to the CEO, when you are listening to your supervisor evaluate your job performance, and when you are listening to customers' complaints and compliments about service in the workplace, your listening requires focus. When listening to learn, you may have to write down what you hear to remember the messages. This kind of listening requires the most effort and can reap the greatest rewards. Those who listen well and remember are those who advance inside and outside the classroom.

### Listening for Relating

**Empathic listening** is *the attempt to understand another person.* You engage in empathic listening by trying so hard to understand the other person that you put yourself in that person's shoes. For instance, Nicole tells her friend between classes that she could hardly focus because of a fatigue headache from a sleepless night. Her friend listens empathically and says, "I feel so sorry for you. Those headaches not only hurt your head but are so distracting. I'll share my notes from class with you in case you missed something." The ability to listen empathically is often the foundation on which close relationships are built.

### Listening for Pleasure

*Listening to relaxing, fun, or emotionally stimulating information*—like music on an iPod, audio books, or albums—is known as **listening for pleasure.** Listening can be as involving and exciting as attending a live concert or as mellow as putting yourself to sleep listening to your favorite artist. We listen to make ourselves happy.

## ATTENTION AND LISTENING

The ability to listen changes, depending on how much and how long we attend to what we hear. Some sounds prompt an immediate reaction, whereas others require more effort and attention. The key is that we engage in different kinds of attention, which affects how we choose what to listen to and what to remember.

### Attending and Focusing

You respond to what you hear in one of two ways: automatically or selectively. With **automatic attention,** *we listen in spite of ourselves, without effort.* A siren, a loud noise, or your name shouted from across the room can capture your automatic attention. We respond immediately and automatically to sharp sounds, dangerous sounds, and warning sounds. If you are walking alone down a dark street late at night and a police car hits the siren just a few yards away, you can be sure it will get your automatic attention.

**Selective attention,** in contrast, is *the sustained focus we choose to give to things that are important to us.* Your favorite music, conversation with your spouse, statements made by your dinner companion, and your professor at the front of the class all can draw a person's selective attention. The trouble with selective attention is that it's difficult to sustain over time. The classroom, especially in a lecture, is a great example of a place where listening takes effort, even if you choose to listen. Experts agree that, except for listening for pleasure, listening takes effort, focus, and purpose to sustain.

## Scanning and Choosing

Listening involves **scanning and choosing**—*a process of taking in stimuli and choosing what to listen to and how.* A useful analogy can be seen in the use of social media sites. When on these sites, we quickly scan our surroundings and analyze them, assessing the importance of several items of interest and noting how they relate to one another.[9] Think about the timeline in a Twitter feed. You would not open Twitter and focus on only one tweet; rather, you would quickly scan hours' worth of tweets to see what is trending. In other words, you would quickly give selective attention to each tweet and then determine what trends are present, which

you'd like to follow, and so on. Similarly, as you walk across campus, you hear traffic, people talking, and wind blowing, but you scan that environment for sounds that have meaning for you. When you hear someone call your name, all the other sounds fade into the background and you choose where to focus.

## Listening and Remembering

We listen, but how much do we actually remember? Your psychological sticky note, **short-term memory**—*where you temporarily store information*—is limited in both the quantity of information it can store and the length of time it can retain it.[10] Specifically, short-term memory can retain only seven simple items, plus or minus two. Here's an easy way to remember this: telephone numbers have nine digits because that is about all most people can remember. You might notice that most speeches are limited to three main points—your average audience is lucky to remember that many![11]

Your **long-term memory** is *reserved for facts, figures, and concepts that you know you have to remember,* at least until the next test. To move input gleaned from listening to long-term memory takes excitement, rehearsal, or extraordinary effort. Most of us are so thin-skinned that we remember many of the

CONSIDERING

## LISTEN TO EXPAND YOUR PERSPECTIVES

Ted.com hosts a wide selection of dynamic content. Its recorded speeches address topics that range from technology to entertainment and design—including thousands of short speeches.

- Watch any of the following four talks:
  - Ethan Zuckerman, *Listening to Global Voices*
  - Evan Williams, *Listening to Twitter Users*
  - Julian Treasure, *5 Ways to Listen Better*
  - Evelyn Glennie, *How to Truly Listen*
- Next think about how you might incorporate one of these into a speech about the topic of this chapter, listening.

negative things that are said to us. However, to remember the name of a person we've just met, we have to repeat it in our minds over and over until it earns a place in our long-term memory.

## BARRIERS TO LISTENING

Although you might agree that listening is important, you might not be properly prepared for effective listening. Perhaps the best way to help you become an effective listener is to know what stands in the way.

The barriers to listening are common. But as our cultural listening habits change, these barriers evolve and new ones crop up. Noise takes a toll on both adults and children. And the noise we create—from cars and airplanes to iPods and videogames—can have serious consequences.

With so much in front of us, and so much to do, many of us feel the urge to multitask. **Multitasking** is *trying to do two or more tasks at once,* sometimes with very negative results. Driving while texting can cause fatal accidents, for example. Physical and mental distractions, too, can keep you from focusing on a message or can cause your mind to wander. As adults we constantly struggle to tune out these distractions. Even children are affected. The sheer number of audible distractions in a child's environment can lead to lower levels of achievement.[12] To better understand the various types of barriers to listening, consider the examples in Table 4.1.

As you can see, barriers to listening include not only the noises around you but also your perceptions of others and yourself. Your perceptions of others are influenced by factors such as status, stereotypes, and the sights and sounds that surround you. When **status** affects your listening, you are *devoting attention to someone you think is particularly important.*

When you **stereotype,** you *treat individuals as if they were the same as others in a given category.* The way someone looks, or the sound of that person's voice, can also affect the degree to which you listen.

Finally, you play an important role in the kinds of listening in which you engage. Much like stereotyping, when you are listening with a **personal bias,** you are *letting your*

**Table 4.1** Barriers to Listening

| Type of Barrier | Explanation and Example |
| --- | --- |
| **Noise** | |
| Physical distractions | All the distractions in the environment that keep you from focusing on the message<br>Example: loud music at a party |
| Mental distractions | The wandering of the mind when you are supposed to be focusing on something<br>Example: thinking about lunch while listening to a teacher |
| Multitasking | Trying to do two or more tasks simultaneously<br>Example: talking on your cell phone while reading Facebook updates |
| Factual distractions | Focusing so intently on details that you miss the main point<br>Example: focusing on the name of a character in a book your friend mentions but missing the name of the book and the reason your friend told you about it |
| Semantic distractions | Overresponding to an emotion-laden word or concept<br>Example: not listening to a teacher when she mentions "Feminist Theory" |
| **Perception of Others** | |
| Status | Devoting attention to someone you think is particularly important<br>Example: not listening to a first-year student in a group activity full of more senior students |
| Stereotypes | Treating individuals—especially negatively—as if they were the same as others in a given category<br>Example: assuming all young people are unemployable and want to live at home with their parents |
| Sights and sounds | Letting appearances or voice qualities affect your listening<br>Example: not listening to a person with a screechy voice |
| **Yourself** | |
| Egocentrism | Seeing yourself on stage and in the spotlight in every conversation<br>Example: changing the topic of conversations to your own problems |
| Defensiveness | Acting threatened and feeling that you must defend what you have said or done<br>Example: assuming others' comments are criticisms of you |
| Experiential superiority | Looking down on others as if their experience with life were not as good as yours<br>Example: not listening to those with less experience |
| Personal bias | Letting your own prejudices interfere with your ability to interpret information accurately<br>Example: assuming that people are generally truthful (or deceitful) |
| Pseudolistening | Pretending to listen but letting your mind or attention wander to something else<br>Example: daydreaming while your professor is lecturing |

# YOURSELF

CHALLENGE

### What Do I Need to Know About Effective Listening? I Spend Much of My Time in College Listening to Others, but My Grades Show That I'm Not Getting Much Out of All That Talk.

On average, we remember most of what we listen to for about 20 seconds, only 50% of a message immediately after listening to it, and only 25% after a short delay. Simply learning how to sharpen your memory can make you a more effective listener.

- Taking notes on your laptop or notebook is a method of helping you remember what you hear. The act of writing the words embeds them in your mind and allows you to review later.
- Linking what you hear to something else you know can help you remember what you have learned by listening. You might remember the four modes of speech delivery (discussed in Chapter 12) by recalling the phrase "I'm me," whose acronym (IMME) stands for impromptu, memorized, manuscript, and extemporaneous.
- Linking new information to what you already know and believe aids your memory. If someone tells you something bad about a politician you already dislike, you can easily store that information along with all the negative things you already believe.
- In conversation you can lengthen your listening capacity by paraphrasing what you think the person said.
- You can communicate by using comparisons, contrasts, and figurative language to help others remember what you say.

Listening, writing down, and linking to something you know better are three ways to enhance your listening by helping you remember longer.

own prejudices interfere with your ability to interpret information accurately. Perhaps the most common barrier to listening, however, is **pseudolistening,** *pretending to listen but letting your mind or attention wander to something else.* In today's noisy world, listeners of all skill levels can struggle to keep their minds—and their listening—focused. When a good listener catches his mind wandering to other things, or feels the urge to multitask, he puts in the effort to refocus and listen.

## CHAPTER REVIEW

In this chapter you learned what listening is; how it differs from hearing; why it is important in school, at home, and in the workplace; why and how we listen; how attention and memory relate to listening; and the many barriers to listening that an effective listener needs to overcome. Because listening is not taught the way that reading and writing are, we might assume that listening is not so important. But listening is a skill that is useful to everyone, from an entry-level server to the CEO of a company.

## KEY TERMS

automatic attention, 56
content, 55
empathic listening, 56
hearing, 53
intent, 55
listening, 54
listening for pleasure, 56
long-term memory, 57

multitasking, 58
personal bias, 58
pseudolistening, 60
scanning and choosing, 57
selective attention, 57
short-term memory, 57
status, 58
stereotypes, 58

## STUDY QUESTIONS

1. Describe a situation in which you were at your best as a listener. What factors of the situation contributed to your good listening? Now describe a situation in which you did not listen as well as you could have. What factors interfered with your listening?

2. Provide examples from the past couple days of when you engaged in each of the four types of listening. How well did you do in each case? Where were you, and whom were you with? What, if anything, interfered with your ability to listen well?

3. Explain the difference between automatic attention and selective attention. Give examples of each from your recent experience.

4. Which barriers listed in the chapter tend to interfere most often with your ability to listen well? Give an example. Which barriers tend not to bother you much at all? Why don't they?

# Interpersonal Communication

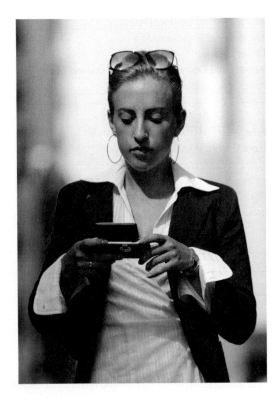

You know that interpersonal relationships can be complicated, and they sometimes require a lot of work. You also know how important and satisfying those relationships can be—especially if you have strong communication skills. In this chapter you will learn some of the basic elements of interpersonal relationships and interpersonal communication, including the stages of relational development, maintenance, and deterioration.

## LEARNING OBJECTIVES

*After reading this chapter, you should be able to:*

- Define interpersonal relationships and interpersonal communication.
- Describe the changing nature of interpersonal relationships.
- Name and explain the three stages of interpersonal relationships.
- Explain the dark side of relationships.
- Name strategies for improving your interpersonal communication behaviors.
- Describe the components of a healthy interpersonal relationship.

## WHAT IS INTERPERSONAL COMMUNICATION?

**Interpersonal communication** is broadly defined as *the process of exchanging meaning in interpersonal relationships.* It is a *process* because it is characterized by change or action. Your communication with your parents is not the same today as it was when you were five years old. Your communication with a romantic partner does not stay at the same level or intensity as the day you met. It is an *exchange* because the people interacting change roles—sometimes acting as the speaker and other times as the listener, jointly giving and taking, exchanging *meaning*, not simply messages.

As noted, interpersonal communication occurs in **interpersonal relationships,** which may be defined as *associations between at least two people who are interdependent, who use consistent patterns of interaction, and who have interacted for an extended period of time.* Consider the elements of this definition in more detail.

- *Interpersonal relationships include two or more people.* Often, interpersonal relationships consist of just two people—a dating couple, a single parent and a child, a married couple, two close friends, or two co-workers. But interpersonal relationships can also involve more than two people—a family unit, a group of friends, or a social group.

- *Interpersonal relationships involve people who are interdependent.* **Interdependence** refers to *a situation in which people are mutually dependent and have an impact on each other.*

- *Individuals in interpersonal relationships use some consistent patterns of interaction.* These patterns may include behaviors generally understood across a variety of situations, as well as behaviors unique to the relationship.

- *Individuals in interpersonal relationships generally have interacted for some time.* Although interpersonal relationships might last for a lifetime, they vary in duration. However, one-time interactions do not count as interpersonal relationships.

Five characteristics of interpersonal communication help us narrow this broad definition further (Table 5.1). First, interpersonal communication begins with you, including who you are and what you have experienced. Your culture, language, attitudes, and experiences all come into play in your interpersonal exchanges.

| **Table 5.1** Characteristics of Interpersonal Communication |
| --- |
| 1. It begins with the self. |
| 2. It is transactional. |
| 3. It has both content and relationship dimensions. |
| 4. It generally requires that communicators share physical proximity. |
| 5. It is irreversible and unrepeatable. |

Second, interpersonal communication is transactional. This means that it is far more than an interaction in which one person serves as the speaker and, when he or she is finished, the other person "catches the ball" and takes a turn. Generally, our conversations move quickly, and the participants serve simultaneously as listeners and speakers. We observe nonverbal cues from our partner while we are speaking and while we are listening, and these observations continuously shape our message.

Third, interpersonal communication has two dimensions—a content dimension and a relationship dimension, as described in Chapter 1. If you are interacting in a fairly impersonal setting—say, purchasing a ticket from a bus driver, asking a stranger for directions, or buying a loaf of bread at a new convenience store—you generally limit yourself to the content of your brief interaction.

In contrast, if you are trying to convince your partner to go out to dinner, to change his or her job, or to quit working for the evening and watch television with you, you have both content and a relationship to consider. Perhaps your partner likes to please you and generally follows your lead and your suggestions. Or perhaps you changed jobs in the past to follow him or her, and it is your turn to take the lead. All these factors are as important as the content of your message and will therefore influence how you present it.

Fourth, interpersonal communicators generally share physical proximity. That is, they are in a position that they can both hear and see their conversational partner. Developments in technology, of course, have altered this feature somewhat, enhancing our ability to communicate intimately and accurately even when we do not share physical proximity. Consider all the tools you have to create a physically proximate space, even when you are across the country or around the world.

Fifth, interpersonal communication is irreversible and unrepeatable. We have all been angry at one time or another and made hurtful statements to our family members or friends. Or we have been careless in our use of language or in our listening habits. You might say that you did not mean what you said, but you cannot really take it back. Both you and your partner will recall the event—sometimes for a good long time.

Consider the opposite situation—that is, when you have shared your feelings and truly touched your partner. Your touch, your posture, and your words were all coordinated to tell him or her how much you care about your relationship. You might attempt to repeat that situation, but no other time will be quite the same. As with a special evening out, you can go to the same restaurant a second time, order the same menu items, and enact similar behaviors, but you cannot perfectly duplicate the original experience.

## THE CHANGING NATURE OF INTERPERSONAL RELATIONSHIPS

Who is a friend? This question was not so difficult to answer in the past, but today it is more complicated, with social networking sites such as Facebook,

Twitter, and LinkedIn. In the past, a friend was a person with whom we had face-to-face conversations and shared the details of our lives. Today our definitions have shifted. People may count dozens, or even hundreds, of people as their "friends."

One of the advantages of these new relationships is the ease with which they can be begun or ended. The disadvantage is that these relationships may be shallow or unfulfilling. Why do people form online relationships? How do you know whom you can trust with personal information? How can you move between online and offline friendships?

If friendships have changed in definition, romantic relationships have been transformed. In the past, romantic relationships that included a sexual element occurred between people who had a long-term, exclusive commitment to each other. Friends with benefits relationships (FWBRs) include two good friends who share sex but have no long-term emotional commitment. FWBRs have rules just as more traditional sexual romantic relationships do. The partners need to agree on how attentive they will be and whether the sexual relationship is secret; they need to clarify that the relationship is temporary; and they must negotiate the rules for emotion and communication in the relationship.[1] Clearly, these relationships can be as complicated as traditional romantic relationships.

College students may be the group most likely to experiment with new friendships and new romantic relationships. In addition to engaging in FWBRs, some students are also experimenting with online relationships. Two psychologists determined that 36% of college students have formed online friendships. Of those friendships, 22% were identified as romantic relationships. Respondents rated their online romantic relationships as superior to, or similar to, those they established off-line in satisfaction, strength, and ease of communication.[2]

Most likely, gay and lesbian romantic relationships have existed since people began to couple. However, they are more prevalent in the news today because of the evolving rights of gay and lesbian people to marry and parent children. The 2000 U.S. Census reported that 601,209 gay and lesbian families existed, and they lived in 99.3% of all of the counties in the United States. The Human Rights Campaign estimates that the number of such families may be undercounted by as much as 62%.[3]

At the same time, heterosexual unions are decreasing. The rate of marriages in 2000 was 8.2 per 1,000 people in the United States, whereas the rate fell to 6.8 per 1,000 in 2011. At the same time, the divorce rate also decreased—from 4 per 1,000 in 2000 to 3.6 per 1,000 in 2011.[4] Although many people have the impression that the divorce rate has been increasing in recent times, that was true only in the first part of the twentieth century, and the rate peaked in the 1970s. Since that time, the overall rate has been continually decreasing.[5] However, this decline applies only to people in middle- or upper-income brackets; the divorce

# MEDIA

## ANALYZING YOUR ONLINE INTERACTIONS

You can increase your understanding of your Facebook friendships by using Internet applications that analyze your activity and provide information on user trends. For example, the WolframAlpha website offers one such application.

- Visit www.wolframalpha.com and type the phrase "Facebook report" into the search box. You will be asked to sign in to your Facebook account so the application can gather information about your friendship network.
- If you are concerned about allowing the application to access your data, limit the application to post information for you exclusively. You then can remove the application after you run the report.
- Here is what you can learn by skimming your own Facebook friendship network report:
- What type of content do you tend to share with your online friends (photos, status updates, website links, or videos)?
- What times of the day do you tend to interact and post content?
- How long is your average post?
- What words do you use most often when interacting with friends?
- Who shares your posts or comments on them most often?
- What are the demographic trends of your Facebook network?

This information can help you judge the appropriateness of the information you share. Much as in a public speaking situation, you can benefit from analyzing your audience and selecting your topics accordingly, a subject covered in greater depth in Chapter 9.

rate for the poor and those from racially and ethnically diverse populations has increased.[6]

The one family type that has increased over the past four decades is the single-parent family. Nearly all of these are single-mother families. Recent estimates suggest that 25% of children, or one in four, are raised in a single-parent household in the United States. This figure is higher than for all other developed countries. The single-mother family leads to a number of problems, including higher rates of poverty. In addition, more of the children drop out of school, become disconnected from the labor force, and become teen parents. Both the public and policymakers view these issues as significant, with lasting effects.[7]

As societal and technological changes alter the nature of relationships, you need to consider the options that are right for you. Whatever you choose—online relationships or face-to-face, FWBR or the more traditional approach to romance, cohabiting or marrying—good communication skills will play a crucial role. All successful relationships rely on clear, open communication.

Communication and relationship development are symbiotic; that is, communication affects the growth of relationships, and the growth of relationships affects communicative behavior.[8] When you become closer to another person, you are likely to communicate more often and more intimately, and the communication is likely to be more satisfying. Similarly, when you experience positive interactions with another person, you are more likely to feel close to him or her.

### Relational Development

Communication theorist and researcher Mark Knapp created a model that has been useful in considering how people come together in relationships, as well as how they split apart.[9] Each has five stages. The coming together phase includes initiating, experimenting, intensifying, integrating, and bonding, as illustrated in Figure 5.1.

The **initiating stage** *begins with the first impressions you have of a potential partner.* Why do we begin relationships with some people, but not others? Five factors affect our relational development:

- **Proximity**—*the location, distance, or range between persons and things*— is the first factor. You are more likely to have a relationship with someone who is physically, emotionally, or attitudinally close to you.

- **Attractiveness** *includes physical attractiveness, how desirable a person is to work with, and how much "social value" the person has for others.*[10] Sharing similar standards for how to interact with others in a given group or community, also known as social values, can greatly increase the attraction between two people.

- **Responsiveness,** *the idea that we tend to develop relationships with people who demonstrate positive interest in us,* is another factor. For example, when you are interested in someone, you respond to his or her text messages quickly, or perhaps even immediately.

- **Similarity,** *the idea that our relational partners usually like or dislike the same things we do,* is another feature of relational development. You might have friends in common or enjoy the same movies. Similarity can be a powerful factor in the initiating stage.

- Finally, **complementarity** is *the idea that we sometimes bond with people who provide something we do not have; in turn we may have qualities or characteristics*

**Figure 5.1** Knapp's Relational Model for the Stages of Coming Together

| Initiating | Experimenting | Intensifying | Integrating | Bonding |

*they lack.* Whereas you may be slightly shy, your friend may be assertive. In situations that call for assertiveness, your friend may play that role for you.

A couple who appears to exemplify many of these factors is Brad Pitt and Angelina Jolie. The two met on the set of *Mr. and Mrs. Smith* (proximity), and they found each other to be irresistible (attractiveness and responsiveness), even though Pitt was married at the time to Jennifer Aniston, of *Friends* fame. They are clearly similar in that they have followed similar career paths and have been adventurous in both adopting children and having children of their own (six in all).

The second stage is the **experimentation stage.** People in this stage *make an effort to find some common ground, including background, interests, attitudes, or values.* This stage is also referred to as the probing stage, because the individuals probe each other for information that would allow them to further the social connection between them. Some relationships end here, never developing into more than a mere acquaintance.

Relationships that do move forward go to the **intensifying stage,** *when the communication between two people changes and deepens.* At this point people begin to self-disclose. **Self-disclosure** is *the process of making intentional revelations about yourself that others would be unlikely to know and that generally constitute private, sensitive, or confidential information.* Although such self-disclosures are intentional, people can use disclosed information about themselves inappropriately. Here are three guidelines for appropriate self-disclosure:

- *Disclosure generally increases as relational intimacy increases.* Do not provide your life story to people you have just met.
- *Disclosure tends to be reciprocal.* When others offer you information about themselves, it is appropriate to reveal information to them.
- *Negative disclosure is directly related to the intimacy of the relationship.* As you become closer to another person, you can increasingly reveal negative information about yourself.

These guidelines become even more important as you establish relationships online. In online situations, you know far less about the other person. Too much disclosure early in a relationship could render you vulnerable to a predator, a poser, or someone with other malicious intent. Be careful in online situations. Negative information you share online may have a greater impact than it does in face-to-face communication, because you have far fewer clues about the receiver.

People stimulate relational development in many ways besides self-disclosure. They might offer gifts, ask for a romantic relationship commitment, or express affection verbally and nonverbally. Partners in some relationships may "test the waters" to see if particular advances are welcomed or frowned upon. These "secret" tests are intended to test the intensity of a relationship. They can include presenting the other person as a girlfriend or boyfriend (presentation) or seeing if the relationship lasts when a temporary physical separation occurs.

The fourth stage is the **integration stage,** and here the *two people begin to merge their lives.* Their status as a couple becomes obvious. The couple may engage in a sexual relationship at this stage, and they are more likely to disclose very personal information. Friends and family reinforce the relationship by including both of them, rather than just one of them, at social occasions.

The final stage is referred to as the **bonding stage,** when *the couple communicate their relationship to others.* They might marry or celebrate their love through a commitment ceremony. This stage may last indefinitely, until death divides them.

## Relational Maintenance

Once individuals have bonded, they enter a stage of **relational maintenance** in which they begin *establishing strategies for keeping the relationship together.* Although people in this stage reach stability and level off their relationship, the process is probably not best represented as a flat line. Instead, people become more intimate or closer at some periods and more distant at other times.

Communication theorists Barbara Montgomery and Leslie Baxter coined the **dialectic theory,** which suggests that *relationships include contrary tendencies or opposing values* like those described earlier.[11] These opposing values include **autonomy and connectedness,** meaning that we have *an interest in being close to others, but we also need to maintain a separate identity.* We also move between the need to be open and the need to be closed; we wish to *self-disclose and provide information about ourselves as well as to be private and keep secrets.* Most relational partners also experience **novelty and predictability;** that is, they wish to be able to *predict events in their relationship, and they yearn for the original and new.* In other words, our relationships in the maintenance stage are actually dynamic, moving forward and back; they are not stagnant or stable.

Another way of understanding the changes that occur in relationships is through the identification and discussion of "turning points."[12] A **turning point** is *a transformative event that alters the relationship in some way.*[13] Researchers have asked couples to reflect on changes in their relationships and to graph those changes. The turning points can propel the relationship toward more or less commitment. They might include outside events that occurred (the loss of a job or the offer of a new one in a different location), decisions the couple made (to buy a new house, have a child), a change in their social network (someone moving in or out), or circumstances beyond their control. Partners usually agree about half the time on the importance of the turning points they recall, but the extent of their agreement is not related to their satisfaction with the relationship.[14]

Although we initially develop relationships on the basis of factors like attractiveness and similarity, we maintain

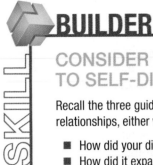

# BUILDER

## CONSIDER YOUR OWN APPROACH TO SELF-DISCLOSURE

Recall the three guidelines for disclosure discussed in this chapter. Next consider one of your newer relationships, either with a friend or romantic partner, and answer the following questions.

- How did your disclosure develop in the first few minutes of your time together?
- How did it expand as you became better acquainted?
- Did you both disclose, and were you aware of the mutual disclosure at the time?
- How long did it take before you both began to disclose negative information?
- Do you believe you followed the three guidelines suggested here? If not, were the effects damaging to the relationship?

them for different reasons. After you have gotten to know someone, why do you choose to maintain the relationship? One reason is that maintained relationships invite certain levels of predictability, or certainty.[15] In this stage of the relationship, we are interested in our partner's ability to focus on us through empathic, caring, and concerned involvement.[16] Indeed, one of the key features of relationships during maintenance is that partners not only become more empathic but also begin to mirror each other's behavior.

Some couples achieve satisfying and long-term relationships. One study looked at couples who had been happily married for more than 40 years. Many of these marriages were characterized by stubbornness ("This marriage will succeed no matter what"), positive distortion ("She is the most beautiful woman in the world"), unconditional acceptance (regardless of faults), and the continuous push and pull of autonomy or independence versus unity or interdependence.[17]

Maintaining positive, satisfying relationships is not easy, but the people who are the most satisfied with their relationships are probably those who have worked hardest at maintaining them. Communicatively, people in long-term, satisfied relationships are distinctive from those in short-term or unhappy relationships. For example, people in long-term and satisfied relationships are more likely to use joint rather than individual identity pronouns ("we" and "us" rather than "I" or "me").[18]

### Relational Deterioration

Not all relationships last. Some deteriorate and others end. About half of all marriages end in divorce; in second and third marriages, the failure rate is even higher. Why do interpersonal relationships end? Several factors encourage people to seek the conclusion, rather than the continuation, of a relationship. We consider a few of these factors here.

**Hurtful messages** *create emotional pain or upset, and they can encourage the end of a relationship.* Hurtful messages occur in most relationships; however, if they become a pattern or are so intense that one partner cannot forget them, they can be disruptive.

**Deceptive communication**—*the practice of deliberately making somebody believe things that are untrue*—can also lead to relational dissatisfaction and termination. All relational partners likely engage in some level of deception from time to time. Telling a "little white lie," avoiding telling the "whole truth," and omitting some details of an event are commonplace. In contrast, deliberate and regular deception can lead to the destruction of trust and the end of the relationship.

**Aggressiveness** *occurs when people stand up for their rights at the expense of others' and care about their own needs but no one else's.* Aggressiveness might help you get your way a few times, but ultimately others will avoid you and let their resentment show. People who engage in aggressive behavior may do so because they have formed negative self-concepts or because they learned this pattern of behavior growing up.

Aggressiveness is not the same as argumentativeness. **Argumentativeness** is defined as *a predisposition to recognize controversial issues, advocate positions, and refute opposing positions.*[19] Indeed, argumentative people may value argument as a normal social communicative activity. Argumentativeness may actually be a positive behavior for some cultures, whereas it may be negative for others.

**Defensiveness** *occurs when a person feels attacked.* Trust is essential to healthy relationships.[20] But trust must be established between individuals, and not be based on roles, positions, or status. In other words, people should come to relationships without all the trappings of the roles they play outside the relationship. Can you imagine how unsuccessful the relationships would be between President Obama and his wife, Michelle; between Prince William and his wife, Kate; and between Matt Damon and his former-bartender wife, Luciana, if the men entered, or tried to maintain, their relationships proud and boastful of their roles as world leader, royalty, or successful actor? Most likely their marriages would not survive. You might not ever be in a relationship with someone who is quite so well known, but people sometimes get stuck in their roles as professor, pastor, or residence hall advisor. These roles can lead to defensiveness on the part of the "lower-status" partner. Reducing defensiveness is essential to building trust.

As mentioned earlier, Knapp's relational model includes stages of coming together and stages of coming apart. Here we consider the five stages of coming apart, as illustrated in Figure 5.2. First is the **differentiating stage.** During this time, *differences are emphasized, as opposed to commonalities.* The momentum

**Figure 5.2** Knapp's Relational Model for the Stages of Coming Apart of togetherness shifts to independent and individualist directions. People may complain of being held back by the commitment to their partner. Temporary separations may occur.

Next is the **circumscribing stage.** The primary focus now is on *setting limits and boundaries on communication between the two people.* The couple no longer share intimate and private communication. Their interactions become shallow, and the range of topics significantly decline. The two may fear discussing deep topics because they lead to conflict.

If the decline of the relationship continues, it enters the third stage, stagnation, which builds on many of the problems of the circumscribing stage. Communication is even more limited and less frequent. In the **stagnation stage,** relationships are *sluggish and do not grow or progress.* The **avoidance stage** may follow. Now the *partners avoid each other, desiring separation.* Physical separation often occurs at this point. Finally, **termination** can occur as *the relationship stops completely.* Although it is possible to save a relationship from this stage of development, it is relatively rare.

Communication theorist Jack Gibb distinguished between behaviors that encourage defensiveness and those that reduce it. He identified evaluation, control, neutrality, superiority, certainty, and strategy—outlined and defined in Figure 5.3—as promoting defensive behaviors in others.[21]

**Figure 5.3** Behaviors That Encourage Defensiveness

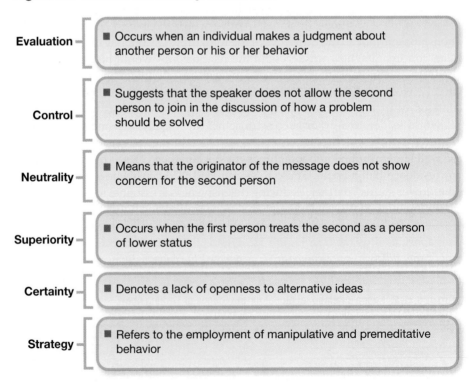

Evaluation
- Occurs when an individual makes a judgment about another person or his or her behavior

Control
- Suggests that the speaker does not allow the second person to join in the discussion of how a problem should be solved

Neutrality
- Means that the originator of the message does not show concern for the second person

Superiority
- Occurs when the first person treats the second as a person of lower status

Certainty
- Denotes a lack of openness to alternative ideas

Strategy
- Refers to the employment of manipulative and premeditative behavior

In contrast, behaviors for reducing defensiveness include description, problem orientation, empathy, equality, provisionalism, and spontaneity. People who use *description* report their observations, rather than making judgments or evaluations. People with a *problem orientation* do not act as though they have the solution but are eager to discuss multiple ideas. People who exhibit *empathy* demonstrate concern for others, as shown through careful listening for both content—what the other person states—and intent— what the other person actually means. *Equality* means that the communicator demonstrates that she is neither superior nor inferior to the other person. *Provisionalism* suggests that the communicator is open to other ideas. *Spontaneity* implies naturalness and a lack of premeditation. To decrease the likelihood of ending a relationship, replace behaviors that create defensiveness with those that reduce it, as demonstrated in Table 5.2.

| Table 5.2  Creating and Reducing Defensiveness | |
| --- | --- |
| **Create Defensiveness** | **Reduce Defensiveness** |
| Evaluation | Description |
| Control | Problem orientation |
| Neutrality | Empathy |
| Superiority | Equality |
| Certainty | Provisionalism |
| Strategy | Spontaneity |

## THE DARK SIDE OF INTERPERSONAL RELATIONSHIPS

Although your interpersonal relationships may generally be pleasurable and positive, you might also have experienced painful and negative effects of relationships. What are some of the qualities of negative relationships? Obsession that includes jealousy certainly creates negative outcomes.[22] Similarly, misunderstanding, gossip, conflict, and **codependency,** or *the tendency to depend on the needs of, or the control by, another,* can lead to harmful results. Abuse, which can be sexual, physical, mental, and emotional, characterizes the most harmful and destructive of relationships.[23]

For many people, the thought of staying in a relationship that is abusive or violent seems absurd. Since relationships are ideally positive, generally focused on helping each other, and imbued with shared memories, why do some people maintain agonizing or distressing relationships? Two examples in the news illustrate the dark side of relationships.

Thirteen-year-old Megan Meier took her own life by hanging after being cyber-bullied. According to news reports, Meier communicated over time with a 16-year-old she knew as "Josh Evans" on MySpace. "Josh" was actually created by three people: a former friend, the mother of this former friend, and a co-worker of the mother. The former friend felt wronged by Megan and chose this communication path to punish her. At first the messages "Josh" sent Megan were positive and Megan was exuberant, but over time the messages changed.

## BUILDER

### LEARN HOW TO DECREASE DEFENSIVENESS

Rewrite the following statements in a way that would decrease defensiveness. Use the categories generated by Jack Gibb. For example, replace *evaluation* statements with *description* statements.

- "What's wrong with you, anyway?"
- "Who's responsible for the mess in the library?"
- "I don't really care what you do."
- "We're not leaving here until I say we're leaving."
- "We don't need to meet. I know how to solve the problem."
- "I don't need your help."

They began to suggest that Megan was a bad person, that everyone hated her, and that the world would be a better place without her. Megan maintained this negative relationship but finally chose to take her own life.

More recently, singers Rihanna and Chris Brown have been in the news. Their on-again, off-again relationship was highlighted in 2009 when Brown assaulted Rihanna on the night before the Grammy Awards. Brown was arrested for domestic assault. Rather than going to jail, he pleaded guilty to the assault, plea bargained to do community service, and promised that he would undergo counseling. On several occasions before the assault, Rihanna had been seen with injuries and mysterious marks on her body that could have been the result of Brown's physical attacks. Nonetheless, the couple spent Thanksgiving together in 2012, and shortly thereafter it was reported that they were together again.

Most couples are optimistic when they initiate a relationship. Few people would enter a new relationship they believed was doomed to failure or that could cause them harm. Often the negative behaviors develop gradually. They may begin with harsh words, verbal aggression, or "playful" blows. The person who receives this treatment may rationalize that he deserves it. However, the violence generally escalates, and excuses can no longer be made.

Many options exist if you are in an abusive relationship. Consider counseling if you believe your partner is willing and motivated to change. If not, you may want to leave the relationship. Ending an abusive relationship is not a simple matter, however. You need to determine a plan that allows you to leave safely. You may need to enlist the help of family, friends, a social agency such as a crisis center, or the police. You can find help at the National Domestic Violence Hotline at (800) 799-SAFE.

## IMPROVE YOUR INTERPERSONAL COMMUNICATION BEHAVIORS

Many of the communication behaviors discussed earlier in this text are important in interpersonal communication. For example, you need to (1) be aware of the role perception plays in relationships, (2) cultivate a good self-concept, (3) provide clear verbal and nonverbal cues to others, and (4) listen attentively and empathically as others provide messages to you.

Some additional behaviors are associated with effective interpersonal communication. For example, in interpersonal relationships you should show affection and support, learn how to influence others, understand how to bargain, and develop behavioral flexibility. Let's consider each of these.

### Using Affectionate and Supportive Communication

Affection, the holding of fond or tender feelings toward another person, is essential in interpersonal relationships. You express your affectionate feelings for others nonverbally with touch, hugging, kissing, or caressing. You engage in verbal statements of affection, such as "I care about you," "I really like being with you," or "I love you."

A number of variables affect the appropriateness of statements of affection. Therefore, affectionate communication may be viewed as risk-laden. Among the factors you will consider when you choose to offer affectionate statements are your own and your partner's biological sex, the kind of relationship you have (platonic or romantic), the privacy and emotional intensity of the situation, and your predispositions.[24] Telling another person that you love him or her, for example, may hold significantly different meanings depending on your sex, your partner's sex, your past relationships, the degree of privacy of the situation in which you choose to share your feelings, and the other person's feelings about you.

Although generally positive, the expression of affection may not always be so.[25] If the receiver of the affectionate message does not respond similarly, the sender may be embarrassed or feel a loss of face. Recall a time when you expressed affection toward another person but that person did not return the same warmth. How did you feel? In general, when people have particular expectations about communicative behavior and those expectations are not met, both trouble and change may follow.[26]

Supportive communication is also important in interpersonal relationships. Support may include giving advice, expressing concern, and offering assistance. Although people generally respond well to supportive communication, the type of support they prefer may vary with the receiver's age[27] and the support provider's goals.[28] In times of distress, comforting messages (suggesting a diversion, offering assistance, expressing empathy, and expressing optimism, for example) may encourage people to feel less upset. At the same time, the recipients of such messages may also feel humiliated or humbled. The distressed person is less likely to be upset about comforting messages when those messages are offered by a close friend rather than an acquaintance.[29] Comfort, then, is viewed as most positive in close interpersonal relationships, rather than in more distant ones.

## Influencing Others

You might think that influencing others is generally a goal of public speaking or the mass media. However, influence is important in interpersonal communication as well. In general, **influence** is *the power a person has to affect other people's thinking or actions.* In interpersonal communication, influence has been studied widely. Two forms of influence are especially relevant: compliance-gaining and compliance-resisting.

**Compliance-gaining** may be defined as *attempts to persuade another person to do something he or she might not ordinarily do.*[30] Compliance-gaining occurs frequently in interpersonal communication. We ask a parent for financial assistance, or we encourage a relational partner to feel more committed. Children become more skillful at identifying situational and personal cues in possible compliance-gaining as they develop, with girls showing more sensitivity than boys.[31]

**Compliance-resisting** *occurs when targets of influence messages refuse to conform to requests.* When resisting requests, people often offer reasons for their refusal.[32] People who are more sensitive to others and more adaptive are more likely to engage in further attempts to influence, despite the resistance.[33] Indeed, they may address some anticipated obstacles when making their original request, later adapting their attempts to influence by offering counterarguments.

For example, if you are asking a friend to borrow his car, you can consider some of the reasons he might refuse. He might state that he needs his car at the same time you do, that the last time you borrowed his car you returned it with no gas, or that the only time he ever hears from you is when you want something from him. In your initial message, you might suggest to him that you believe you have been neglecting him, that you want to spend some time together, and that you have not been as considerate as you could have been with him. When he suggests that he needs his car at the same time you do, you might offer to use his car at a different time.

## Bargaining

Often we engage in bargaining in our interpersonal relationships. **Bargaining** *occurs when two or more parties attempt to reach an agreement on what each should give and receive in the relationship.* Bargains may be explicit and formal, such as the kinds of agreements you reach with others to share tasks, to attend a particular event, or to behave in a specified way. Bargains may also be implicit and informal. For example, in exchange for receiving compliments from your relational partner, you help him or her with math homework. One member of the couple might make delicious evening meals in exchange for the partner's doing all the laundry. You may not even be aware of some of the unstated agreements you have with others.

A study on interpersonal bargaining identified three essential features of a bargaining situation:

1. All parties perceive the possibility of reaching an agreement in which each party would be better off, or no worse off, than if no agreement were reached.
2. All parties perceive more than one such agreement that could be reached.[34]
3. Each party perceives the others as having conflicting preferences or opposed interests.

What are some examples of bargaining situations? You may want to go out with friends when your partner would prefer a quiet evening at home. One member of the couple might prefer to go hiking, whereas the partner is more eager to take a cruise. In each of these instances, the disagreement can be resolved through bargaining.

## Maintaining Behavioral Flexibility

Finally, interpersonal communication may be improved through behavioral flexibility. **Behavioral flexibility** is *the ability to adapt to new situations and relate in new ways when necessary.*[35] Behavioral flexibility allows you to relax when you are with friends or to be formal and professional while interviewing for a job. The key to behavioral flexibility may be self-monitoring, or awareness of the effect of your words on the audience in a particular context.

Flexibility is important in a variety of ways. Psychologists have suggested that women and men who are **androgynous**—who *possess both stereotypically male and stereotypically female traits*—are more successful in their interactions than are people who are unyieldingly masculine or absolutely feminine. Flexibility in gender roles is more useful than a static notion of what being a man or woman means in our culture. For instance, if you are a single parent, you may be called on to behave in a loving and nurturing way to your child, regardless of your sex. If your goal is to be a successful manager in a large corporation, you may have to exhibit competitiveness, assertiveness, and a task orientation, regardless of your sex. As you move from interactions with co-workers to interactions with family and friends, you may need to change from traditionally "masculine" behaviors to those that have been considered "feminine."

Behavioral flexibility is especially important in interpersonal communication, because relationships between people are in constant flux. For example, the family structure has gone through sharp changes in recent years. In addition, the United States has an increasingly older population. Changes in the labor force also require new skills and different ways of interacting with others. People travel more often and move more frequently. Finally, social media require enormous changes in how we communicate.

What kinds of changes can you expect in your own life that will affect your relationships with others? You may change your job 10 or more times. You may move your place of residence even more frequently than you change your job. You probably will be married at least once, possibly two or three times. You might have one child or more. You will experience loss of family members through death and dissolution of relationships. You may have a partner whose needs conflict with your own. You may find that social media both help and hinder your interactions with others. Last, other family members may view the world differently than you and challenge your perceptions. When your life appears to be most stable and calm, unexpected changes will occur.

How can behavioral flexibility assist you through life's changes? A flexible person draws on a large repertoire of behaviors. Such an individual is confident about sharing messages with others and about understanding the messages others provide. The flexible person self-discloses only when appropriate. The flexible person can demonstrate listening skills but is not always the one who is listening. The flexible person can show concern for a child who needs assistance, can be assertive on the job, can be yielding when another person needs to exercise control, and can be independent when called on to stand alone.

## THE HEALTHY INTERPERSONAL RELATIONSHIP

Can we paint a portrait of a healthy interpersonal relationship? Actually, the material in this chapter gives us some broad brush strokes. First, by definition, and by practice, healthy relationships include people who are mutually dependent on each other. Psychological research demonstrates that healthy dependency includes perceptions of oneself as competent and of others as trustworthy. Healthy dependency results in security in intimacy and confidence in autonomy. Motivationally, a healthy person has a desire for closeness in a relationship, as well as autonomy and self-reliance. Behaviorally, the person functions autonomously but couples this with situation-appropriate help seeking.[36]

Second, individuals in healthy interpersonal relationships are consistent in their patterns of interaction. They do not behave randomly with no explanation. They do not switch from enthusiasm to despair. In general, their partners can predict how they will react to circumstances and to others.

Third, individuals in healthy relationships understand that their relationships will probably last for some time. A parent expects to have a relationship with a child long after the child has moved away from home. Romantic partners are not pursuing a "one night stand"; they want a relationship that can last for a long time, even a lifetime.

Fourth, individuals in healthy relationships understand that their interpersonal communication begins with themselves, and they take responsibility for their role in the relationship. They do not place blame on their partners; rather, they recognize that sometimes they are to blame. Similarly, they share in the positive outcomes of their relationship.

Thus, interpersonal relationships that work operate on the principle that they are transactional. Partners do not blame each other for "starting the battle." Instead, they know that both communicators are continually sending and receiving messages—from each other as well as from other people. A woman who blames her mother-in-law for interfering may not recognize that the mother-in-law seeks a closer relationship with her grandchild. The daughter-in-law and mother-in-law with a healthy relationship talk openly about their needs and how they can both be fulfilled.

In addition, healthy relationships include people who know that their communication includes both content and relationship dimensions. Perhaps your partner calls you by a nickname she's given you, when you are alone together or at home. "Sweetheart" and "dear" have a content dimension—that is, they both refer to you, as does your given name. On the other hand, the relationship dimension of these terms of endearment is also meaningful. Your partner understands this well if she knows that you do or do not appreciate being called "sweetheart" at dinner with friends or in line at the grocery store.

Although healthy relationships do not require that communicators share physical proximity all the time, some time together is likely part of the relationship. Couples today live apart for days, weeks, or even months at a time due to work or other obligations. Generally, though, they plan time to be together. Others begin their relationship online, but most eventually meet and spend time face-to-face. Most likely, although the jury is not in, healthy relationships include some sharing of physical proximity.

Healthy relational partners know they cannot "delete" or "erase" a careless remark, a hurtful statement, or the admission of caring more for another person. Thus, they are probably somewhat careful in their statements and disclosures. They recognize that communication is irreversible. They also know that, no matter how many times they attempt to "replay" a special day, evening, or even moment, it will not be the same.

Healthy relationships contain some levels of predictability—the knowledge that your friend or partner will help you out when you need it, will respond to your messages, will do what he or she has agreed to do. And partners in healthy relationships are empathic and caring; they demonstrate concerned involvement. They listen without judging. They attempt to put themselves in your shoes. They do not disregard your feelings or experiences. As these relationships develop, the partners are likely to use words like "we" and "us."

Healthy partners avoid hurtful messages. They do not try to create emotional pain or upset, and they do not signal that they want to end the relationship. They do not talk about past relationships, past sexual behavior, or past errors, including breaking the law in order to provoke or upset their partners.[37] They also avoid deceptive communication. They are not aggressive—standing up for their own rights at the expense of their partner's.[38]

Violent behavior, abusive statements, and bullying are all off-limits. Do not hesitate to seek help if you encounter these behaviors.[39] More education in building and maintaining healthy relationships—whether from a short course, from continuing education, or online—may be helpful. In addition, many online resources have been created to help couples learn to communicate better in their intimate relationships.[40] Finally, the suggestions listed earlier—using affectionate and supportive communication, learning to influence others in sensitive ways, learning to bargain successfully, and maintaining behavioral flexibility—are all keys to healthy relationships, whether among friends, family members, or lovers.

# YOURSELF

## CHALLENGE

### What Can Social Science Tell Me About How People Meet, Mate, and Procreate in an Era of Social Media?

Fairy tales about "happily ever after" have been replaced with stories about tabloid breakups, casual sex, and relationships that begin online through social media or online dating sites. And "friends with benefits" may be more common than permanent sexual partners or fiancés. A recent article in the *New York Times* suggests that dating as we once knew it is obsolete. In addition, people in their twenties have begun to coin new words for "hooking up" and use old words ("date") in new ways—for perhaps meeting online or with a group, not for a two-person face-to-face encounter.[41]

Even though sexual relationships with no ties are widespread, some people may not be emotionally prepared for casual hookups. In the past, when an individual did not want to date another person or wanted to initiate a breakup, he or she would conveniently "lose the person's number." Today you "unfriend" the partner, and you need to inform your family and friends to do the same. Social media may play a role in terminating relationships in other ways as well—for example, when people are not wary about privacy settings and a partner learns too much information about a partner's flirting and infidelities. Social skills appear to be on the decline as technology is on the incline.

- Your attitudes about dating are important. If you are an optimistic person, people will be drawn to you in face-to-face interactions as well as online. And if you are single—and comfortable with the fact that you have not yet found the right person—this will make you far more desirable to a potential partner than obsessing over the importance of hooking up.
- Be honest with others, whether online or in person. Make disclosures that are appropriate for the stage in the relationship, gradually increasing disclosure as your relationship develops. Reveal information to others as they reveal information to you. Finally, do not disclose negative information until your relationship is established, but do not misrepresent yourself, either. Being honest is essential to finding the right person.
- Most important of all, know who and what you are looking for in a potential partner. Do not settle for someone who has 2 of the 10 qualities most important to you. At the same time, be realistic in your expectations. Remember the roles of proximity, attractiveness, responsiveness, similarity, and complementarity as you consider potential partners.

# CHAPTER REVIEW

In this chapter you learned that the difference between a failed relationship and a healthy one frequently depends on the partners' communication skills. Relationships include three stages: development, maintenance, and deterioration. And some relationships hold a dark side. The good news is that you can improve your interpersonal communication and the health of your relationships by reducing defensiveness and by knowing the difference between a healthy relationship and an unhealthy or abusive one. Countless social scientific investigations provide insight into the components of a healthy relationship.

## KEY TERMS

aggressiveness, 73
androgynous, 79
argumentativeness, 73
attractiveness, 69
autonomy and connectedness, 71
avoidance stage, 74
bargaining, 78
behavioral flexibility, 79
bonding stage, 71
circumscribing stage, 74
codependency, 75
complementarity, 69
compliance-gaining, 78
compliance-resisting, 78
deceptive communication, 73
defensiveness, 73
dialectic theory, 71
differentiating stage, 73

experimentation stage, 70
hurtful messages, 73
influence, 78
initiating stage, 69
integration stage, 71
intensifying stage, 70
interdependence, 65
interpersonal communication, 65
interpersonal relationships, 65
novelty and predictability, 71
proximity, 69
relational maintenance, 71
responsiveness, 69
self-disclosure, 70
similarity, 69
stagnation stage, 74
termination, 74
turning point, 71

## STUDY QUESTIONS

1. Define interpersonal communication and interpersonal relationships. What is the connection between the two?

2. How do your interpersonal relationships differ from those of your parents and grandparents? What are some factors that account for these differences?

3. Describe the stages of relational development, maintenance, and deterioration.

4. What are the characteristics of a dark relationship? Why do people sometimes become entangled in such relationships?

5. How can you improve your interpersonal behaviors?

6. Describe some of the components of a healthy relationship. Are any of these components reflected in your own relationships?

# Intercultural Communication

As technology extends both the ability and the need to interact with people around the globe, we all must learn to communicate with people from various racial, ethnic, and cultural backgrounds. The goal of this chapter is to increase your confidence in your ability to do so.

LEARNING OBJECTIVES

*After reading this chapter, you should be able to:*

- Define and explain the differences among culture, race, ethnicity, and co-culture.
- Explain why the study of intercultural communication is important.
- Explain the three most common reasons for intercultural communication problems.
- Identify four broad characteristics that distinguish cultures from each other.
- Name strategies for improving communication with people from other cultures.

## DEFINING INTERCULTURAL COMMUNICATION

**Intercultural communication** refers to *interactions between people from different cultural backgrounds.* This kind of communication occurs, for example, when a businessperson raised in the United States works with a Japanese businessperson on a mutually beneficial project. It also occurs when a U.S. student works on a school project with a student raised in Somalia, Pakistan, Mexico, or China. To accomplish mutual goals, they must adapt to their differences in language, attitudes about work, and culture-based customs.

A **culture** is *a unique combination of traditions and customs that is transmitted through learning and that shapes the beliefs and behavior of the people who live within it.* Cuba is a country, but we also regard the Cuban people as having a culture, because they speak Spanish, most are Roman Catholic, and they live under a Communist political system, eat particular foods, have close-knit families, and have a sense of a shared culture.

Cultures develop in countries, or nation-states, over time such that the people who live there share similarities that come to characterize them. Language is a significant unifying feature of a culture. Japan has a single language, which dominates and therefore unifies the people who speak it. Religion, too, can be a significant unifying cultural feature, as Buddhism is in Thailand and Islam is in Saudi Arabia. Thus, a combination of features, such as language, religion, customs related to family, and dietary practices, creates a culture.

Two closely related terms that sometimes overlap and cause confusion are *race* and *ethnicity.* The concept of **race** generally refers to biological characteristics—in this sense, it refers to *a category of people distinguished by inherited features, such as skin color, facial features, or quality of hair.* But scientific evidence for racial distinctions is very weak.

On close examination, the concept of race is vague, and it can be difficult to determine what the categories should be. For example, should "Hispanic" be considered a race? For one approach to this question, see Figure 6.1.

It can also be difficult to determine who belongs in which category and where the boundaries are between them. For example, we think of President Barack Obama as African American; however, his father was African and his mother was Caucasian. He is only one among many Americans whose ancestors came from all corners of the world, bearing multiple variations of skin color, facial features, and hair qualities. As you can see in Figure 6.1, the Census Bureau acknowledges this fact by allowing people to check more than one box. Even more problematic than who fits where is the fact that, in the early nineteenth century, so-called racial differences came to be associated with differences in health, intelligence, and personality. Many societal ills, including stereotyping and prejudice (discussed later in the chapter), have flowed from such ideas, but there is no scientific evidence to support them.

**Figure 6.1** Reproduction of the Questions on Hispanic Origin and Race Form From the 2010 Census

Reproduction of the Questions on Hispanic Origin and Race From the 2010 Census

→ NOTE: Please answer BOTH Question 5 about Hispanic origin and Question 6 about race. For this census, Hispanic origins are not races.

5. Is this person of Hispanic, Latino, or Spanish origin?
☐ No, not of Hispanic, Latino, or Spanish origin
☐ Yes, Mexican, Mexican Am., Chicano
☐ Yes, Puerto Rican
☐ Yes, Cuban
☐ Yes, another Hispanic, Latino, or Spanish origin — *Print origin, for example, Argentinean, Colombian, Dominican, Nicaraguan, Salvadoran, Spaniard, and so on.* ↗

6. What is this person's race? *Mark* ☒ *one or more boxes.*
☐ White
☐ Black, African Am., or Negro
☐ American Indian or Alaska Native — *Print name of enrolled or principal tribe.* ↗

☐ Asian Indian  ☐ Japanese  ☐ Native Hawaiian
☐ Chinese  ☐ Korean  ☐ Guamanian or Chamorro
☐ Filipino  ☐ Vietnamese  ☐ Samoan
☐ Other Asian — *Print race, for example, Hmong, Laotian, Thai, Pakistani, Cambodian, and so on.* ↗  ☐ Other Pacific Islander — *Print race, for example, Fijian, Tongan, and so on.* ↗

☐ Some other race— *Print race.* ↗

*Source:* U.S. Census Bureau, 2010 Census questionnaire.

In contrast to race, which is associated with physical features, the concept of ethnicity is related to cultural ones. An **ethnic group** *consists of people who share common cultural elements—for example, language or religion—as well as a common history.* The Jews, Irish, Poles, and Greeks are often referred to as ethnic groups. Within the category "Asian," which was once considered a single race, there are multiple, diverse cultures and ethnicities: Japanese, Chinese, Vietnamese, Thai, Korean, and so on (Figure 6.1). As you can see, the terms *race, ethnicity,* and *culture* can overlap, and there are no simple rules for sorting all this out. Some people identify their race or ethnicity by where their parents or grandparents came from, but many of us don't know all the threads of ancestry that produced us—for example, that somewhere three, four, or five generations back we had an ancestor who was Native American, Turkish, or Irish.

In all societies, we encounter the concept of a **dominant culture,** *the group that has the most power, influence, and rights.* In the United States, the dominant culture is composed of white, educated males who are employed, usually in managerial or professional occupations. The dominant group tends to make rules that work to its advantage, whether in the context of business, government, school, or the family.

Nondominant, or **co-cultural, groups** *include but are not limited to women, ethnic minorities, gay and lesbian individuals, immigrants and refugees, persons who are physically or mentally challenged, and even neighborhood gangs and political groups that have formed to promote a cause.* Those who are outside the dominant culture often are subjected to unequal treatment.

Women are an unusual "co-culture" in the United States, because they outnumber men; yet women are classified as a co-culture because they have not been equal to men in terms of power, influence, and earning ability. Unlike many third-world countries, such as India, Pakistan, and Brazil, the United States has never had a female president. The Senate and House of Representatives have fewer women than do the parliaments of other countries, and large corporations and their boards of directors are very heavily male. Last but not least, women have never received equal pay (Table 6.1). Feminist scholar Cheris Kramarae, a communication professor, noted long ago that women are a "muted group," largely ignored in the workplace and often unheard even in group discussions.[1]

The Amish in America are also a co-culture and might be considered an ethnic group. The Amish people share religious beliefs, are relatively isolated from the dominant culture, have strict practices related to their dress and work, and have common German origins.

Gays and lesbians in the United States can also be considered a co-culture, as their sexuality unifies them, although contrasting with the heterosexuality of the dominant culture. Although this group is gaining rights, its members have faced extensive discrimination and have not yet achieved equal rights under the law.

What is the point of tuning into co-cultures? First, democratic societies like ours are enriched by their contributions. Once banned by law, homosexuality has become increasingly accepted in American culture. Celebrities such as Jodi Foster in film and Wanda Sykes in comedy have come out about their lesbian relationships. On TV, Anderson Cooper on CNN, Jim Parsons on *The Big Bang Theory*, Neil Patrick Harris[2] on *How I Met Your Mother*, and Ellen DeGeneres are among the many openly gay or lesbian celebrities who educate and entertain us. In 2013, NBA player Jason Collins, too, disclosed that he is gay, a first for an athlete in one of the four major pro sports in the United States. If we do not learn to accept and appreciate those who differ from us, we limit our opportunities to advance, both personally and professionally.

| **Table 6.1**   Women as a Co-Culture in the United States |
| --- |
| ■ The United States has more women than men (157 million vs. 152 million males). |
| ■ Women have more high school diplomas, bachelor's degrees, and master's degrees than men (31 million vs. 29 million for males), but males earn more doctorates and professional degrees. |
| ■ Women earn 79% of male salaries, a difference of more than 20%. |
| ■ Women's entry-level pay is about the same as men's, but college-educated women start to fall behind at 30 years of age. |
| ■ College-educated women hit a glass ceiling salary level of $60,000 per year at age 39, whereas men's salaries don't peak until 48 years of age, at an average of $95,000. |

*Sources:* Retrieved from www.cleveland.com/business/index.ssf/2010/04/salary_gap_between_men_and_wom.html; retrieved from www.businessinsider.com/salary-growth-between-men-and-women-2012-5

## WHY STUDY INTERCULTURAL COMMUNICATION?

Not long ago, only select groups concerned themselves with intercultural communication—missionaries, jet-setting business executives, foreign correspondents, and political figures. Now, however, developments in technology have made intercultural and co-cultural communication more possible and more likely than ever before. Around the world, people can cheaply communicate with each other on the Internet. Phone, video, and audio merge into a system that can allow for sight and sound. Cell phones, pagers, and handheld computers bring communication technology to our fingertips. Shifts in demographics, too, have created a world in which almost everyone engages in intercultural communication in their daily lives.

In short, we have increasingly been introduced to a variety of ethnic, national, and political groups. And this has occurred because of advancing technology, transnational jobs, international conflicts, military and humanitarian service, and the presence of immigrants, refugees, and new citizens in our communities. The national events on September 11, 2001, in particular, changed our perceptions of the world. Americans discovered that they knew little about the Islamic religion or the people of Afghanistan, Iraq, and Saudi Arabia and realized that they needed to educate themselves. Moreover, the composition of the U.S. population is shifting. As you can see in Figure 6.2, the percentage of Hispanics as compared with non-Hispanics has been increasing since 2000 and is projected to continue to increase.

Today chances are excellent that you will at least occasionally encounter individuals from unfamiliar groups—not just in the news but in your everyday life. Thus, you will need to know the basics of intercultural communication. In metropolitan Washington, DC, your server may be from Colombia, South America; your bus driver may be from Ethiopia; the student sitting next to you may be from the Sudan; and the cashier at the grocery store may have come from Vietnam. The story is similar in Miami, New York City, Detroit, and Chicago. America is now (and always was) an exotic salad with many cultures contributing to its overall flavor. The first reason, then, for studying intercultural communication is that communication with people from other cultures and co-cultures is becoming increasingly common.

A second reason to study intercultural communication relates to the economy. The United States sells corn, wheat, and cars in Asia and buys coffee from

**Figure 6.2** Hispanics and Non-Hispanics as a Percentage of the U.S. Population: 2000–2050

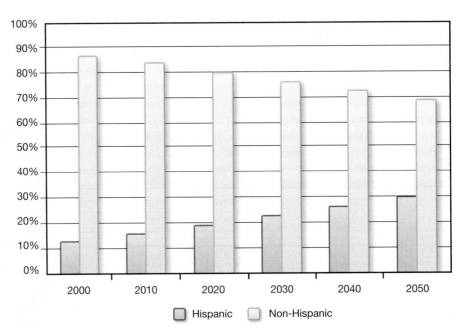

*Source: Congressional Research Service Report for Congress.* (2011). Retrieved from www .fas.org/sgp/crs/misc/RL32701.pdf

Colombia, bananas from Costa Rica, and oil from Africa, the Middle East, and South America. Much of our clothing comes from China and Panama, our shoes from Mexico, and our cars from Germany, Hungary, or Canada. Business is increasingly global, which means that you will almost certainly find yourself working with people from many cultures.

A third reason to study intercultural communication is, simply, curiosity about others. What does it mean to wear a turban or a headscarf? Why don't some people eat meat? Why do people from some cultures bow, whereas others shake hands or kiss? People from some cultures stand close when they converse; others maintain more physical distance. People from some cultures respect silence, whereas others avoid it. Learning about intercultural communication means that we can become better informed about our world.

## BIASES THAT AFFECT INTERCULTURAL COMMUNICATION

We all have biases related to those who differ from ourselves. In this section, we will review some of the most common forms those biases take in intercultural communication: ethnocentrism, stereotyping, and prejudice.

 **GLOBALLY**

COMMUNICATING

### LATINO OR HISPANIC?

The question of how to label various ethnic or racial groups has long been a matter of debate for social scientists and statisticians, people in the media, and the rest of us: people who simply want to be respectful and do what's "right."

The people who have come to the United States from Mexico, Central and South America, Spain, Cuba, and Puerto Rico make up our nation's largest minority. As shown in Figure 6.1, the U.S. Census Bureau refers to the people in this group as *Hispanic*. Moreover, *Diversity Journal*[3] reports that a significant majority of the members of this co-culture prefer that term over *Latino*, the other term that has been commonly used. The term *Hispanic* refers to a person's place of origin rather than to a race, because people from the countries named can be of any race.

The term *Latino* originally referred to places that had been conquered by the Romans, where the language was based on Latin—for example, France, Italy, and Spain. Now, however, the word *Latino* has come to mean the people of South America, where the language is Spanish. But it also includes Brazil, where the primary language is Portuguese; by the original definition, *Latino* is the more inclusive term, applying to all people who were dominated by the colonial powers that brought Latin-based languages to the New World, thus including South America's largest and most populated country, Brazil.

This is an enormously diverse group of people, and individuals differ in their feelings about these words, much as some people do about the term *African American* versus *black*. There's no harm in asking people what they prefer, and why.

### Ethnocentrism

The most common problem that occurs during intercultural communication is **ethnocentrism,** *the belief that your own group or culture is superior to all other groups or cultures.* Common examples include the attitude that everyone in the world should speak English and the related idea that people in the United States should not have to learn languages other than English; that foods eaten in other cultures are disgusting rather than practical, nutritious, or even delicious; and that the Asian custom of bowing is odd, rather than something to try to understand.[4]

We cannot avoid operating to some extent from an ethnocentric perspective, but problems arise when we judge other cultures as inferior, rather than simply different. Generally, a lack of interaction with people from other cultures fosters high levels of ethnocentrism and encourages the notion of cultural superiority, which in turn creates defensiveness and barriers between communication partners.

In contrast to ethnocentrism, in which we use our own culture as the measure that others are expected to meet, **cultural relativism** involves *viewing other cultures as objectively as possible, without judgment.* It's a standard set by anthropologists and other social scientists as they work to describe a culture from the point of view of someone living within it. The foods of another culture; the style of dress; and the beliefs and practices regarding the family, the role of

## BUILDER

### REFLECT ON YOUR OWN CULTURAL IDENTITY

Each of us is a product of our own culture, and we have multiple identities within that culture. These identities shape how we see others who differ from us. To better understand your cultural self, complete the following exercise.

- Draw a circle in the middle of a piece of paper and write your name in it.
- Radiating out from this circle, draw other circles. In each of those, list aspects of yourself that define who you are. Examples are your sex, your country of origin or ancestry, your marital status, your religion (or lack of one), your role in your family (mother, father, daughter, etc.), and your race or ethnicity.
- Reflect on why these aspects of yourself are important to you and how they shape you.
- Reflect on whether each aspect affects the way you view the world. For example, if you are a mother, does that identity affect your religious beliefs or your ideas about family? If you are biracial, how does that identity affect your view of race?
- How do you feel if someone ignores or disrespects one of your identities?

The point of this exercise is to increase your understanding of your own complex cultural identity, so that you can become more sensitive to the complex cultural identities of others.

women, and punishment and criminal behavior are all cultural elements that social scientists attempt to view objectively, without judgment, in order to understand them in the context of that culture.

On the other hand, social scientists may strive to meet the standard of cultural relativism in their work, but they can still take moral stands or make moral judgments about another culture's beliefs or practices. For example, no social scientist needs to view violence against women or children as acceptable just because it occurs in someone else's culture. Ethnocentrism and cultural relativism are two ends of a spectrum. The ideal for intercultural communication lies somewhere between, in the acknowledgment that other people's values and norms may differ from your own but that, with respectful curiosity, people can work toward understanding.

### Stereotyping

Ethnocentrism is not the only bias people bring to intercultural communication. Equally dangerous is the tendency to stereotype, or generalize, to all individuals in a group from the characteristics of a few. The result of stereotyping is that all members of the group are viewed in a limited way; especially if the stereotype is negative, they may be treated negatively or disrespectfully. A particularly negative set of stereotypes is currently circulating about Muslims and people from the Middle East as being violent extremists. However, with 1.6 billion Muslims in the world as of 2010,[5] we intuitively understand (or should) that not every one of them could be a violent extremist. Still, because of fear and lack of familiarity, such stereotypes persist.

Stereotypes are most often negative. However, even "positive" stereotypes can be insulting or limiting. For example, not all Jews are wealthy, not all Asians are gifted at math, and not all black Americans are great athletes. As you would expect, most people resent negative comments being made about them, whether as individuals or as members of a social group. In one study, however, participants also responded negatively to positive comments about their social group, if the comments reflected a stereotype.[6] People do not like being robbed of their individuality and being diminished to only one aspect of their identity.

If you feel that you are being stereotyped, what can you do? In one study, confrontation was a helpful strategy for both parties. Perhaps simply stating directly that the language being used or the assumptions being made make you uncomfortable or simply do not hold true in your experience. Confrontations of this kind should always be carried out with respect, never with aggressive words or actions. Although the person making a stereotyping comment may initially respond negatively to the person doing the confronting, he or she may be more hesitant to make such comments in the future.[7]

### Prejudice

Whereas ethnocentrism involves thinking that your culture is better than others and stereotyping is viewing all members of a group as alike, the closely related concept of **prejudice** is *a negative attitude toward a group of people just because they belong to that group.* Often the people on the receiving end of prejudice belong to marginalized minority groups—people in poverty, people of color, people who speak a language other than English, gay men and lesbian women—but sometimes the group being discriminated against is larger than the group that exhibits the prejudice.

For example, as discussed earlier, in many countries, including the United States, women are subject to prejudicial treatment in the form of lower pay and fewer opportunities for corporate advancement, even though they are a majority. Much more so than men, women are also subject to demeaning and degrading comments related to their gender, as well as sexual objectification in the media, and women experience depression, anger, and lower self-esteem because of such prejudices.[8]

As with ethnocentrism and stereotyping, prejudice is often based in ignorance. That is, the person expressing the prejudice simply does not know much about the target of the prejudice, or the person simply dismisses the target group as deserving of its inferior status. Women and African Americans have made some headway against prejudice, but stereotypical attitudes and assumptions are hard to eliminate: you can see this when someone assumes that a man—not a woman—is the manager or owner of a business, that an African American man standing beside a luxury car is someone's driver, or that a Mexican man on a street corner must be a day laborer.

## SKILL BUILDER

### LEARN ABOUT YOUR OWN BIASES

We all have biases when it comes to the race or ethnicity, religion, gender, skin color, and age of others. But by identifying these biases, we can learn to improve our interactions with people of all kinds.

- To test your biases and social attitudes, visit Harvard's Project Implicit at https://implicit.harvard.edu/implicit/.
- Choose one or several of the tests available there, and see what you can learn about your attitudes toward others.
  - Were you aware of the biases that the tests revealed?
  - What can you learn from your results?

## CHARACTERISTICS THAT DISTINGUISH ONE CULTURE FROM ANOTHER

Accepting that your own culture is not superior to, just different from, another person's culture is one way to improve your intercultural communication. Another way is to understand some of the values and norms of other cultures.

Suppose you are an American teaching in Japan. Your students' first assignment is to give a speech before the class. Even though you don't tell them to do so, they form groups and each group selects a spokesperson to give the speech. In contrast, in the United States, students would be unlikely to turn a public speaking assignment into a small-group activity unless specifically directed to do so. Neither behavior pattern is right or wrong; both are rooted in the culture of the country. If you didn't know anything about the norms and customs of the Japanese culture, you could be baffled by your students' behavior.

In this section you will learn about four characteristics that distinguish cultures from each other: individualism versus collectivism, uncertainty-accepting versus uncertainty-rejecting, implicit rulemaking versus explicit rulemaking, and M-time versus P-time orientations. Keep in mind that these characteristics are general tendencies; they are not always true of a culture and are not true of everyone in a culture.

## Individualistic vs. Collectivist Cultures

Much of what is known about individualistic and collectivist cultures comes from a study in 1980 of more than 100,000 managers from 40 countries.[9] Although neither China nor Africa was included, the study is a classic in its comprehensiveness.

**Individualistic cultures** *value individual freedom, choice, uniqueness, and independence.* These cultures place "I" before "we" and value competition over cooperation, private property over public or state-owned property, individual achievement over group accomplishments, and individual opinion over what anyone else might think. In an individualistic society, people are likely to leave the family home or geographic area in which they were raised to pursue their dreams, they have only limited loyalty to organizations, they are unafraid of moving for advancement, and they may leave religious institutions that no longer meet their needs.

Loyalty to other people also has limits. Individualistic cultures have high rates of divorce and unmarried parents. Individualistic cultures have sayings like "God helps those who help themselves" and "The squeaky wheel gets the grease," both of which favor individual action over group cooperation. According to this 1980 study, the top-ranking individualistic cultures are those of the United States, Australia, Great Britain, Canada, and the Netherlands.[10]

**Collectivist cultures,** in contrast, *value the group over the individual.* These cultures place "we" before "I" and value commitment to family, tribe, and clan; people in collectivist cultures tend to be loyal to their spouse, employer, community, and country. They value cooperation over competition, as well as group-defined social norms and duties over personal opinions.[11] Illustrating collectivist cultures are the Ethiopian proverb "When spider webs unite, they can tie up a lion" and the Asian saying "The nail that sticks up gets hit by the hammer." The Ethiopian proverb enforces the idea that collective action brings surprisingly powerful results, and the Asian saying discourages individual action over that of the group. The highest-ranking collectivist cultures in the 1980 study were those of Venezuela, Pakistan, Peru, Taiwan, and Thailand.[12]

### Uncertainty-Accepting vs. Uncertainty-Rejecting Cultures

**Uncertainty-accepting cultures** *tend to be tolerant of ambiguity and diversity, and they are more often democracies than dictatorships or countries led by powerful royalties.* The populations of uncertainty-accepting cultures tend to be diverse in ethnicity, religion, and race. In addition, they are more likely to accept political refugees and immigrants.

The United States, Canada, and the United Kingdom are democratic countries that have attracted some of the most diverse populations in the world. They embrace general principles related to tolerance, as in England, which accepts immigrants from over 50 British Commonwealth countries that were once British colonies.[13] Other countries that ranked high in uncertainty-acceptance in the 1980 study were Denmark, Sweden, Singapore, Hong Kong, Ireland, and India.[14]

**Uncertainty-rejecting cultures** *have difficulty with ambiguity and diversity.* Most are not democracies. These cultures are more likely to have many rules regarding behavior, and they are more likely to reject outsiders, such as immigrants, refugees, and migrants, especially if they look different from and act differently than the majority population. South Korea and Japan, for example, do not welcome diversity, except for the uneasy presence of U.S. soldiers. Other countries that ranked high on the study's uncertainty-rejecting scale were France, Spain, Greece, Portugal, Belgium, Peru, Chile, Russia, China, and Argentina.[15]

Cultures' tendency to be uncertainty-accepting or -rejecting can have a powerful effect on intercultural communication. Those in uncertainty-accepting cultures tend to welcome outsiders, including offering citizenship. However, today, we are seeing that acceptance of outsiders can erode, even in uncertainty-accepting cultures, when the outsiders become numerous, refuse to integrate into the dominant culture, or come from cultures that are viewed with suspicion or prejudice. Countries like Germany and France have become less tolerant of outsiders because of an influx of Muslim immigrants, and the United States has a controversial relationship with Mexicans who have entered the country illegally. Nonetheless, some countries absolutely reject outsiders, whereas others grapple with these issues, as the United States is doing as it formulates a new immigration policy and path to citizenship for immigrants.

### Implicit-Rule vs. Explicit-Rule Cultures

An **implicit-rule culture** is one in which *cultural rules are embedded in tradition and followed faithfully.* For example, a traditional Arab woman knows that one rule of her culture is that she is to walk a few paces behind her husband. Individuals in such cultures are unlikely to question societal rules. People from implicit-rule cultures tend to be more polite, less aggressive, and more accommodating than those from explicit-rule cultures. Implicit-rule cultures are typically found in the Middle East, Africa, and Latin America.[16]

An **explicit-rule culture** is one in which *policies, procedures, and expectations are more likely to be discussed or negotiated.* For example, American parents negotiate with their children: "You can stay up late if you help with the dishes and clean your room." Compared with people from implicit-rule cultures, people from explicit-rule cultures tend to be more combative, less willing to please, and less concerned about offending others. Explicit-rule cultures are typically found in northern and western Europe and the United States.[17]

You might think about the differences in this way: in an implicit-rule culture, the social rules are part of who and what people are. The rules are ancient and unquestioned. Sex, status, and seniority dictate where each person sits around the decision-making table, and those at the table are unlikely to question their placement. In contrast, in an explicit-rule culture, rules are more likely to be developed, discussed, and negotiated. At dinner parties and even at decision-making meetings, people's placement around the table may largely be determined by who gets there first.

## M-Time vs. P-Time Cultures

The fourth distinguishing characteristic relates to perceptions of time. Cultures associated with **M-time,** or *a monochronic time schedule, compartmentalize time to meet personal needs, and they separate tasks from social activities.*[18] M-time is dominant in Canada, the United States, and northern Europe.

People in M-time cultures see time as something that can be wasted or saved. Americans, for example, tend to schedule times for working out, going to the doctor, holding meetings, and taking the family out to dinner. Time is segmented, dedicated to work or social life (but usually not both), and thought of in terms of future events and activities. Within this scheme, getting to any appointment on time is treated with considerable importance.

Cultures associated with **P-time,** or *polychronic time schedules, view time as "contextually based and relationally oriented."*[19] What does this mean? For those in P-time cultures, time is not saved or wasted; it is only one factor in a much larger and more complicated social context. Someone in a P-time culture would wonder, Why halt a conversation with an old friend to hurry off to an appointment on a relatively unimportant issue?

In other words, relationships trump time considerations in some contexts. Inhabitants of P-time cultures orchestrate their relational and task obligations with the fluid movements of jazz, whereas those in M-time cultures treat life as a march, in which people strive mainly to stay on schedule and be efficient, valuing tasks over relationships. Typical P-time cultures are found in Latin America, the Middle East, Asia, France, Africa, and Greece. North America is predominantly M-time because of the strong European influence, but some co-cultures in the United States exhibit P-time tendencies.

Businesspeople in P-time cultures do conduct business, but they do it very differently than those in M-time cultures. For example, a businessperson in a P-time culture might have a large waiting room outside her office, and the people in that waiting room may use the space and time to meet with each other and resolve issues. In other words, a great deal of business in P-time cultures is conducted in public rather than in a series of private meetings, as it would be in M-time cultures. In an M-time culture, the waiting room at a place of business is often silent, with everyone occupied with his paperwork or smartphone, each waiting for a turn to be heard.

If you live in an M-time culture and you travel to other parts of the world, including most countries in Latin America and the Middle East, you will probably experience a disconnect or disorientation. You may feel psychologically stressed, as others always seem to be late. On the other hand, you may note that, once your P-time associates arrive, they focus exclusively on you. They are not distracted by schedules or other commitments.

Notice in Table 6.2 how these cultural characteristics tend to cluster. In the left-hand column, you will see that the same cultures cluster under individualistic, uncertainty-accepting, explicit-rule, and M-time usage. The cultures that share these characteristics are northern European or Commonwealth countries (for example, Australia and the United States) that were strongly influenced by Great Britain. Much of the rest of the world tends to be collectivist, uncertainty-rejecting, implicit-rule, and P-time-oriented, including China, the South American continent, and much of Africa. However, the world is not so simple to explain. Western influence has pushed those who engage in global business toward the column on the left, such that, in a predominantly Chinese culture, as in Hong Kong and Singapore, people now conduct business in a very Western manner. Moreover, American businesspeople have learned the importance of establishing relationships with people in the Middle East, Africa, and South America before proposing business deals. The good news is that, driven by global economics, people in different cultures are strongly encouraged to learn more about each other.

## STRATEGIES FOR IMPROVING INTERCULTURAL AND CO-CULTURAL COMMUNICATION

Effective intercultural communication can take considerable time, energy, and commitment. Although some people would like "10 easy steps," no foolproof plan is available. However, the following strategies should give you some ways to increase your comfort and competence in intercultural contexts and help you avoid potential problems.

1. *Conduct a self-assessment.* What are your attitudes toward other cultures and co-cultures? Be specific about your own discomforts and lack of information. Those attitudes likely influence your communication with others, so an honest assessment of your communication style, beliefs, and prejudices is a good first step toward more open and respectful communication.
2. *Practice supportive communication behaviors.* Supportive behaviors, such as empathizing with the situation of the other person, encourage success in intercultural and co-cultural exchanges.

**Table 6.2** Cultural Characteristics

| Individualistic Cultures Tend To . . . | Collectivist Cultures Tend To . . . |
|---|---|
| ■ Value individual freedom; place "I" before "we" | ■ Value the group over the individual; place "we" before "I" |
| ■ Value independence | ■ Value commitment to family, tribe, and clan |
| ■ Value directness and clarity | ■ Value cooperation over competition |
| ■ *Examples:* United States, Australia, Great Britain | ■ *Examples:* Venezuela, Pakistan, Taiwan, Thailand |
| **Uncertainty-Accepting Cultures Tend To . . .** | **Uncertainty-Rejecting Cultures Tend To . . .** |
| ■ Be willing to take risks | ■ Be threatened by ideas and people from outside |
| ■ Avoid rules; seek flexibility; reject hierarchy | ■ Establish formal rules for behavior; prefer stability, hierarchy, and structure |
| ■ Value individual opinion, general principles, and common sense | ■ Embrace written rules, regulation, and rituals |
| ■ *Examples:* United States, Great Britain, Denmark | ■ *Examples:* Japan, France, Spain, Greece, Argentina |
| **Explicit-Rule Cultures Tend To . . .** | **Implicit-Rule Cultures Tend To . . .** |
| ■ See cultural rules as explicit; explain and discuss procedures | ■ See cultural rules as set and not to be questioned |
| ■ Be straightforward, and people have to cope with embarrassment or insult | ■ Prefer "saving face" to soothing an insulted person |
| ■ *Examples*: Northern and western Europe, United States | ■ *Examples*: Middle East, Africa, Latin America |
| **M-Time Cultures Tend To . . .** | **P-Time Cultures Tend To . . .** |
| ■ Compartmentalize time, separating work from social time and task time from relational time | ■ Factor in time as one element of a larger context, which includes family, social responsibilities, and tasks |
| ■ View time as something that can be wasted or saved | ■ Value social relationships and time considerations together |
| ■ *Examples:* North America, northern Europe | ■ *Examples:* Latin America, Middle East, Asia, France, Africa |

*Source*: Adapted from Dodd, C. H. (1998). *Dynamics of intercultural communication* (5th ed.). New York: McGraw-Hill.

3. *Develop sensitivity toward diversity.* Recognize that you can learn something from people from other countries and cultures. Don't be afraid to ask respectful questions; you may be surprised by what you learn.

4. *Avoid stereotypes.* Don't make assumptions about another's culture; get to know individuals for themselves.

5. *Avoid ethnocentrism.* You may know your own culture the best, but that familiarity does not make your culture superior to all others. You will learn more about the strengths and weaknesses of your own culture by becoming more familiar with other cultures.

6. *Develop code sensitivity.* **Code sensitivity** is *the ability to adapt to the verbal and nonverbal language of the individual with whom you are communicating, regardless of cultural or co-cultural differences.* The more you know about another's culture, the better you will be at adapting. Be open-minded about your differences. Can you patiently wait in silence when communicating with someone who is Native American or Japanese, who might be comfortable with quiet gaps in the conversation as she thoughtfully sizes you up?

7. *Use and encourage descriptive feedback.* Providing and receiving feedback are crucial in intercultural communication, so that people make sure their messages are clear and understood. Feedback should be immediate, honest, specific, and clear. Say, "I don't understand. Could you repeat that?" or "What time do you mean when you say 'I'm coming over tomorrow'?" or "Are you saying that you'd prefer not to see the movie?"

8. *Make time to open communication channels.* Intercultural communication can be frustrating. Misunderstandings are likely because of all the differences between people, so everyone involved in intercultural communication may need to spend time negotiating the meanings of messages. Many cultures encourage tea or coffee time together as a way to connect and get to know one another in a relaxed atmosphere. Sometimes conversational partners can clarify their meanings by writing down words that are difficult to communicate. Patience is key to mutual understanding.

9. *Manage conflicts that arise over beliefs and practices.* Think ahead about how you might handle minor and major differences. Minor differences include very different conceptions of time and different ideas about touching or appropriate ways of dressing. Major conflicts can arise over beliefs, such as the appropriate role of women or acceptable behavior for children. We all need to exercise caution about judging other cultures and cultural practices, as no culture is above criticism.

10. *Be reflexive.* **Reflexivity** means *being self-aware and learning from interactions with the intent of improving future interactions.* When being reflexive, you assess an interaction, identify what went well and what could have gone better, and then learn from those observations.

Through reflexivity you not only will improve your intercultural communication skills but will also become a more effective communicator in nearly every situation.

11. *Practice intercultural communication competence.* Of course, the most effective strategy for improving your intercultural communication competence is practice. Fortunately, the increasing diversity of our own culture means that such practice can take place with the people at the corner market, those at your place of employment, and even others in class.

 **CHAPTER REVIEW**

In this chapter we explored the increasing importance of intercultural communications skills. You learned about the concepts of culture, race, ethnicity, and co-culture. Because people from various cultures differ in their communication styles and behaviors, problems can arise; some of the attitudes that can lead to these problems are ethnocentrism, stereotyping, and prejudice. There are four main ways in which cultures differ from each other, and by using such strategies as being reflexive and providing feedback, you can improve your skills in communicating with people from different cultures.

## KEY TERMS

co-cultural groups, 88
code sensitivity, 100
collectivist cultures, 95
cultural relativism, 92
culture, 86
dominant culture, 88
ethnic group, 88
ethnocentrism, 92
explicit-rule culture, 97
implicit-rule culture, 96

individualistic cultures, 95
intercultural communication, 86
M-time, 97
prejudice, 94
P-time, 97
race, 86
reflexivity, 100
uncertainty-accepting cultures, 96
uncertainty-rejecting cultures, 96

## STUDY QUESTIONS

1. What is the difference between a race and an ethnicity? What are some of the problems surrounding the concept of race?

2. What are some reasons that students in the United States should learn about other cultures and co-cultures?

3. Explain the relationships among ethnocentrism, stereotyping, and prejudice.

4. The United States is regarded as an individualistic nation, but this is a broad generalization. Think of experiences from your life that show collectivist characteristics in this individualistic culture.

5. Explain at least one strategy for relating to people from other cultures and co-cultures that would improve relationships in your school. Give an example from your own experience.

# Mediated Communication and Social Media

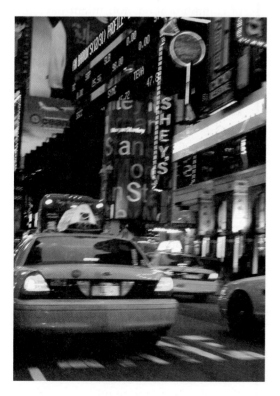

Although you use it every day and it saturates the world in almost uncountable ways, you might not be familiar with its name, *mediated communication.* In this chapter we will explore its most popular form, social media, in depth and will examine the various features and uses of social media, as well as some of the most important skills relevant to you as a user.

LEARNING OBJECTIVES

*After reading this chapter, you should be able to:*

- Identify the reasons for studying mediated communication.

- Describe how mass media influence behavior and shape culture.

- Demonstrate an understanding of various types of computer-mediated communication and how they affect interactions and relationships.

- Understand how to become a responsible and critical consumer of mass media.

- Know how to protect and present yourself on social media.

## UNDERSTANDING MEDIATED COMMUNICATION

**Mediated communication** refers to *messages that are transmitted not directly from person to person but through some other communication tool, such as print, electronic, or digital communication devices.* Some mediated messages are generated for masses of people to consume (such as television programs); others are targeted to individuals or smaller groups (such as e-mail and text messages).

Mediated communication includes messages conveyed through television, radio, and print (like newspapers and magazines), as well as through computer- and Internet-based means (such as e-mail messages, text messages, websites, discussion boards, and social media sites). Given the prevalence of social media in our lives, this chapter will focus on these forms of mediated communication.

## COMMUNICATING GLOBALLY

### SOCIAL MEDIA USE AROUND THE GLOBE

Although Facebook, YouTube, and Twitter are enormously popular in the United States and Europe, in China, where free speech is not encouraged, these sites are not accessible. To maintain control of the messages that are made public, the Chinese government has banned the use of certain social media sites and closely monitors those that are allowed.

Much like the users in the United States and Europe, Chinese citizens use social media to interact with family and friends; to meet new people; to engage in citizen journalism; and to organize protests. For example, in July 2011, when a large train accident occurred in western China, the government tried to downplay the damage and limit mainstream media coverage. However, information on the crash was immediately available to the Chinese public on the social media site Weibo.

Although the Chinese government makes great efforts to regulate social media use, it has been more successful at censoring traditional media, including newspapers, television, and radio. Meanwhile, Chinese social media sites like Weibo, Renren, and YouKu have only grown in popularity. Weibo, China's version of Twitter, now boasts 300 million registered users.[1]

### Why Study Mediated Communication?

Imagine trying to get through an entire day without consuming, or making reference to, mediated forms of communication. You might have trouble distinguishing the sugar from the salt, because you would have to cover all product labels at home, and you might have trouble preparing a presentation at work, because you wouldn't have access to your research materials. You could not turn on the television, computer, or cell phone; check your Facebook account or e-mail; or look at newspapers, billboards, and magazines. Possibly the only way you could avoid all forms of mediated communication would be to go to a national park, leaving all your electronic devices at home, and take a walk in the wilderness.

One reason for studying mediated communication is to better understand how the messages that surround us influence behavior and shape culture. To understand the media's influence on your own behavior, do some self-reflection. Answer the following questions based on your behavior today:

- How frequently did you check your e-mail or Facebook account?
- Did you leave the television or music on while doing other things?
- How much time did you spend reading a newspaper?
- Finally, did anything you read, saw, or heard in any of those media change what you thought or talked about with others?

Your answers to these questions will help you understand the impact of mediated communication in your life.

The second reason is to help you become a more critical consumer of the mediated messages you encounter. For example, have you ever thought about how the actors and models in advertisements influence your own body image? The magazines you read and the movies and television shows you watch are filled with advertisements intended to impact your self-image and to encourage you to buy products and services that promise to improve that self-image. Research indicates that media influence on self-image,[2] and body image in particular, is powerful.[3] We will discuss this power in greater detail later in this chapter, as well as strategies for turning a more critical eye on the media you encounter.

The third important reason to study mediated communication is that doing so will improve your own mediated interactions. As you consider the many means through which you communicate electronically, you will learn ways to ensure that your mediated interactions are effective in conveying the messages you intend and are appropriate for the context. For example, you do not e-mail your instructor or employer with the same casual style and abbreviations you use with your friends and peers. Understanding these differences, and shaping your messages accordingly, will greatly improve your mediated interactions and their outcomes.

## The Forms of Mediated Communication

Mediated communication can be broken down into two broad categories: mass communication and computer-mediated communication. **Mass communication** *involves the use of print and electronic technology by professional communicators to share messages over great distances for large audiences.*[4] **Mass media,** then, include *the specific means by which we use print and electronic technology to communicate.* **Computer-mediated communication** (CMC) is *human-to-human interaction using networked computer environments.*[5]

Even if you are not familiar with the term *CMC,* you are likely to use examples of it, such as Facebook, e-mail, chat, or instant messaging, on a daily basis. Figure 7.1 demonstrates one way to understand mass communication and CMC by breaking them down into the components of the traditional communication model (sender-message-receiver-feedback), discussed in Chapter 1.

Mass communication and CMC seem to be converging, or coming together. Broadly speaking, **media convergence** refers to *the ways in which different technologies have evolved to perform similar outcomes or tasks.* For example, mass media sources like the *New York Times* are becoming interactive and can be accessed in print or online. Reporters now post stories in written and video format, and readers interact with reporters and other readers by posting comments to stories. Media convergence applies to other media as well: For instance, viewers can vote for their choices on competitive TV shows. Today everyone is a consumer of mediated messages.

## MASS COMMUNICATION AND MASS MEDIA

Researchers who study our motivations for consuming media consistently find a variety of reasons for our behaviors.[6] For example, we use media for information ("I need to know how to keep myself healthy"), entertainment ("This show

**Figure 7.1** Mass Communication, CMC, and the Communication Model

### Mass Communication and the Communication Model

- **Sources/Senders:** Mass communication sources include the television, a newspaper reporter, an author, an announcer, and a studio production team.
- **Messages/Channels:** Common channels for transmitting mass communication messages include cable and satellite systems, printing presses, computers, and the Internet.
- **Receivers:** In mass communication, large groups are the intended recipients of the messages disseminated.
- **Feedback:** With modern technology, mass communication provides a channel for feedback from intended receivers. Take, for example, much of reality television, where viewers are asked to call in and vote for their favorite contestants. On blogs and websites, readers can leave comments.

### CMC and the Communication Model

- **Sources/Senders:** CMC sources include e-mails, social media, instant messages, and texts.
- **Messages/Channels:** Common channels for transmitting mass communication messages include cell phones, computers, and the Internet.
- **Receivers:** In CMC, receivers can be individuals (as in an instant message exchange) or large groups (as when you post a message to a Facebook group).
- **Feedback:** Possible feedback to a social media post includes silence from an online community (no response), "likes" for your posts, and online commentary that either reinforces or changes how you think about what you posted.

always makes me laugh"), relaxation ("This show always helps me unwind at the end of the day"), escape[7] ("I sometimes use YouTube to distract myself when I need a break from my paper"), habit/addiction fulfillment ("I can't end my day without checking my apps for any notifications"), companionship ("When I watch *Ellen* I don't feel so alone"), excitement ("I wonder what trouble the characters on *Revenge* will get into this week"), social interaction ("I browse through the *New York Times* each day, so that I can have something to talk about with my friends"), and co-viewing experiences ("I watch the football game because it's what I do with the guys").[8]

Think of the last time you turned on the television or sought out information on the Internet. What motivated you to do so? How do your motivations differ from those of important people in your life? Perhaps you watch a particular program to be entertained, whereas your partner watches as a co-viewing experience—that is, to find common ground with you. Reflecting on these questions may help you more critically evaluate why you turn to mass communication and what you gain from it.

### The Influence of Mass Media on Behavior

A recent Nielsen report tracked television viewing patterns during the first half of 2012. The report showed that the typical American spends 34 hours a week watching live television and an additional 6 hours a week watching recorded programs.[9] Put otherwise, average Americans devote as much time to television viewing as they do to their full-time jobs.

How does media consumption affect our beliefs, perceptions, and behaviors? Media-effects researchers explore this question by focusing primarily on violence and body image, as illustrated in Figure 7.2.

**Figure 7.2** Effects of Mass Media on Behavior and Culture

**Media Violence**  As we all know, violence is prevalent in the mass media. But did you know that, by the time a child gets through high school, she has seen nearly 200,000 violent acts and 16,000 murders?[10] When considering the influence of mass media consumption on behavior, media-effects scholars focus primarily on the link between viewers' exposure to violence in movies, television, and videogames and violent or aggressive behaviors.

Research consistently demonstrates a relationship between the consumption of media violence and aggressive[11] or violent behavior.[12] One hypothesis offered by researchers is that such programming desensitizes us to violence, making us more tolerant of it and more likely to respond to aggression and hostility with violent acts.[13] Many factors, of course, contribute to violent behavior. For example, mental illness is believed to have played a role in the tragic mass killings in Tucson, Arizona, and Newtown, Connecticut. Nevertheless, the prevalence of media violence and its potential effects on viewers will continue to be a focus as the discussion of violence and gun control in the United States continues.

**Media and Body Image**  A second area of research focuses on how media consumption affects body image. Using extensive air-brushing and photo editing, the media project the impression that there is one ideal body for women (thin and young) and another for men (thin with developed muscles). Researchers found that, the more media that men and women consumed, the more likely they were to be dissatisfied with their bodies and to demonstrate symptoms associated with eating disorders.[14]

Based on the findings on violence and body image in the media, you might conclude that the media's influence on our behaviors is entirely negative. But the media can be a positive force for both adults and children. Adults who watch a variety of programs can gain a greater appreciation and understanding of other cultures. Children's media consumption can help them acquire language and interpersonal skills, like empathy and conflict resolution.[15] However, to fully understand mass media's potential to positively impact our lives, we must also understand its relationship to the culture we live in.

### The Relationship Between Mass Media and Culture

Whereas some scholars focus on the ways in which mass media influence our behaviors and cultural values, others examine the ways that media affect and shape our culture. Both perspectives are worth considering; media both reflect our culture and help shape it.

Consider the prevalence of sporting events in the media. Some might argue that the ubiquity of these events on television, radio, and even videogames intensifies the degree to which Americans value competition, individualism, and winning. However, others would say that the reason there are so many sporting events on television is because we value competition and individualism so much. In other words, if we didn't embrace these values in the first place, our media might reflect different programming altogether. To further explore how this relationship between cultural values and media works, let's look at four ways in which media can shape culture.

**Gatekeeping** Gatekeeping is *the process of determining what news, information, or entertainment will reach a mass audience.*[16] To see how gatekeeping works, consider what happens when a new shopping complex opens in a community. Gatekeeping first occurs when newspaper editors determine whether the store's opening is important enough to justify sending reporters to the scene. If a story is written, it goes to a copy editor, who acts as a gatekeeper by deciding how the story will be framed, how the sentences will be written, and so on. Next the story goes to the city editor, who acts as a gatekeeper by judging the importance of the story and thus determining its placement—on the front page or way in the back, above the fold or below. Front-page stories attract the attention of more readers and are therefore more likely to be the subject of broader discussion than are those buried in the middle of a paper.

Bloggers and individuals who actively post on social media also act as gatekeepers. When people comment on news stories and post links back to the site that originally reported on them, they drive even more traffic to the newspaper or magazine, or to the store that is opening. In some cases, coverage from a blogger, tweeter, or Facebook friend becomes even more popular or trusted than the original source.

A news director at a television station, an acquisitions editor at a book publishing company, and other kinds of gatekeepers make similar decisions about what will be presented to the public and how. Every day a number of people control what you will see and hear when you consume mass media; in doing so, they help shape the cultural dialogue.

**Agenda-Setting** Agenda-setting is *the process of shaping what topics are considered critical for discussion by society.*[17] According to research, media officials and journalists may not explicitly tell us what to think, but they do tell us what topics we should be thinking about. Whereas gatekeeping determines what issues are critical to pass on to the public, agenda-setting involves more active promotion and discussion of particular issues. For example, CNN's multipart investigative TV series *Diversity in America* elevated the issue of diversity to a matter of universal public concern. In the age of the Internet, other forces also shape agendas, such as political bloggers and citizen journalists.

**Perpetuating Stereotypes and Challenging Norms** The media shape culture by perpetuating stereotypes while challenging societal norms. For instance, when the television show *Will and Grace* first aired in 1998, many considered it to be groundbreaking for placing gay characters in prominent roles at a time when most prime-time television avoided gay issues altogether. In other words, the show exposed viewers to perspectives they were not used to encountering. Now that television has introduced a diverse array of gay characters and lifestyles in shows like *Glee*, *The New Normal*, and *Six Feet Under*, the once radical depictions of gay life on *Will and Grace* have been criticized for relying on stereotypes of gay culture. Newer programs, like *Archer*, represent a less rigid structure of sexuality in which characters are often depicted in gay and bisexual relationships.

The media are notoriously full of stereotypes. Many television programs cast minority race characters in secondary roles, with white, middle-class men and women taking center stage. These depictions do little to challenge the norms about whose voices our society values most, thus helping perpetuate stereotypes. Although the characters we see on television are developed based on extensive marketing research and therefore reflect, to a large extent, what viewers want to see, the characters and situations presented also have the potential to alter our expectations and open (or close) our minds. In other words, television is shaped by our culture as much as it in turn shapes us.

**Cultivating Perceptions** Mass media also affect culture because of its **cultivation effect.** This means that *heavy television and media use leads people to perceive reality as consistent with media portrayals*.[18] Cultivation theory is often applied to the issue of media violence, with research indicating that those who view too much violence on television and other media come to perceive the world as a dangerous place.[19] Cultivation theory provides a potentially powerful analysis of how media affect us and has been applied to topics ranging from violence to mediated discussions about sex.

*The Secret Life of the American Teenager* is a popular TV program, as well as a focus for cultivation theory research. The show depicts teenage dialogues about sex and sexuality, revealing that few teenagers go to parents or medical officials for trusted advice about sex. Instead, they turn to their peers to discuss the possible consequences of sex, such as unwanted pregnancy or diseases. Cultivation scholars who have done research on this topic argue that these depictions are likely to cultivate fear and avoidance among teenage viewers about openly discussing sex with adults.[20]

As you can see, the relationship between mass media and culture is complex. Media gatekeepers, like editors, producers, traditional journalists, bloggers, and citizen journalists, decide what information is passed on to us and in what forms. Our attitudes and perspectives are affected by which media we choose to consume and in what quantities. Mass media—from prime-time news to weekly sitcoms—likewise reflect our society's ideals and trends. As such, the media both shape and are shaped by culture.

### Thinking Critically About Mass Media Messages

Mass media sometimes blur the distinction between news and entertainment, making it particularly important to critically evaluate and cautiously interpret mediated messages. To help you engage in more critical evaluation of the media, this section provides recommendations for increasing your overall media literacy skills and offers ways to counter some of the negative media effects.

**Media literacy** refers to *the ability to think critically about mediated messages and how they influence us.*[21] Sometimes when we turn on the television, the last thing we want to do is critically evaluate what we're watching. Nevertheless, media literacy experts prescribe a healthy dose of skepticism.[22]

Many media literacy efforts focus on increasing our understanding of how mass media messages are framed and created. Because the technology used to produce such messages has become less expensive, almost anyone can produce mass media content. The large volume of messages disseminated on YouTube, Facebook, Twitter, and other message boards makes the task of finding accurate, unbiased information all the more challenging.[23]

Citizen journalists produce some of the most popular Internet videos, accessed by thousands of people each day on YouTube and Vimeo. As with other forms of media, this content must be carefully evaluated. In Chapter 11 we discuss the process of gathering information and offer a list of questions to ask yourself with regard to every new source you evaluate.

## COMPUTER-MEDIATED COMMUNICATION AND SOCIAL MEDIA

CMC can be categorized according to two prominent characteristics: the degree to which an interaction is synchronous or asynchronous. **Synchronous communication** *occurs when the people involved interact with one another at the same time as both senders and receivers of information.* **Asynchronous communication** *occurs when the people involved experience a delay in interacting with one another and take turns being senders and receivers of information.* Figure 7.3 identifies the types of CMC associated with each type of interaction.

**Figure 7.3** Synchronous vs. Asynchronous Communication

| Synchronous Communication | Asynchronous Communication |
|---|---|
| ■ *The people involved interact with one another at the same time as both senders and receivers of information.* Examples:<br>• Face-to-face communication<br>• Skype or Facetime video chat sessions<br>• Cell phone conversations<br>• Instant messaging<br>• Online chat sessions | ■ *The people involved experience a delay in interacting with one another and take turns being senders and receivers of information.* Examples:<br>• E-mail<br>• Discussion boards<br>• Online support groups<br>• Social media websites |

**Social media** are *a variety of websites that allow users to connect and interact with acquaintances, friends, family members, organizations, colleagues, and customers all over the world through the exchange of user-generated content.* You may have noticed that the word *media* is used with a plural verb, such as "media are." That's because there are so many types, especially in the case of social media. Let's begin by looking at who is using social media websites, also referred to as platforms, and why.

Once known as the interaction domain of the millennial generation (those born roughly between 1980 and 2000), today social media attract users of all ages, as shown in Figure 7.4. In the early 2000s, the first type of social media to attract users was diary-based blogs, like MySpace, Blogger, and LiveJournal. In 2004, Facebook launched and quickly grew in popularity, among college students at first and then more broadly when the site opened its registration to anyone in 2006. In the later 2000s, sites like Twitter and YouTube established and expanded their user base as well.

**Figure 7.4** Who Is Using Social Media?

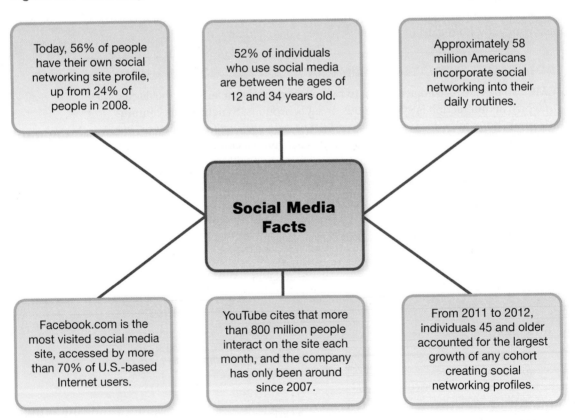

*Sources:* YouTube. (2012). YouTube statistics. Retrieved from http://youtube.com/t/press_statistics; Nielsen. (2011). State of the media: Social media report q3. New York: Author; Edison Research. (2012, June). The social habit. Retrieved from http://socialhabit.com/research/

Since 2009, Facebook has been the most popular social media website worldwide, but a growing number of platforms accommodate a variety of users. Having expanded beyond their use as a social networking tool, social media now play a much broader role in how we communicate. Later in this chapter, we will examine the effects of social media use across various contexts.

## The Features and Uses of Social Media

Social media include a range of platforms, the four most common of which are blogs, microblogs, vlogs, and social networking websites (Figure 7.5). Much debate surrounds the question of whether the widespread use of social media is "good" or "bad." Have you ever asked yourself any of the following questions?

- Do social media make me feel more, or less, connected with others?
- Am I better off meeting my friends at a local coffee shop, or does the convenience of the computer or smart phone trump an in-person meeting?
- Do I waste time when I check my Facebook page or Twitter feeds, or are these important ways of staying connected?

**Figure 7.5** Types of Social Media Platforms

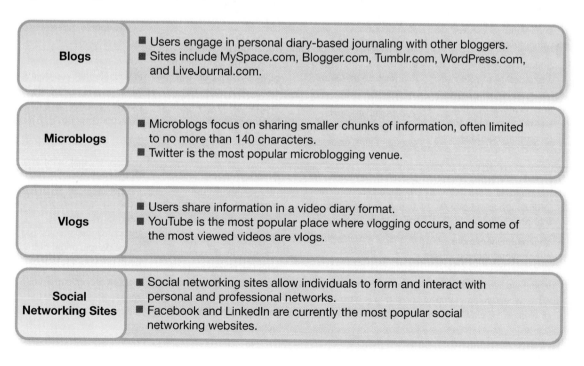

| Blogs | ■ Users engage in personal diary-based journaling with other bloggers.<br>■ Sites include MySpace.com, Blogger.com, Tumblr.com, WordPress.com, and LiveJournal.com. |
|---|---|
| Microblogs | ■ Microblogs focus on sharing smaller chunks of information, often limited to no more than 140 characters.<br>■ Twitter is the most popular microblogging venue. |
| Vlogs | ■ Users share information in a video diary format.<br>■ YouTube is the most popular place where vlogging occurs, and some of the most viewed videos are vlogs. |
| Social Networking Sites | ■ Social networking sites allow individuals to form and interact with personal and professional networks.<br>■ Facebook and LinkedIn are currently the most popular social networking websites. |

Social media are neither entirely good nor entirely bad; the uses and applications of social media have both benefits and drawbacks. Table 7.1 highlights some of the advantages and disadvantages of the most prominent features of social media.

**Table 7.1**  Important Characteristics of Social Media

### Social Media . . .

| Enable Ease of Communication | Accommodate a Variety of Devices | Allow Access to a Range of Individuals | Provide a Rich Interaction Medium |
|---|---|---|---|
| Users exchange and share photos, status updates, videos, and Global Positioning System (GPS) location information. | Users contribute content from a host of devices, including smartphones, tablets, iPads, laptops, and desktop computers. | Users connect with known and unknown audiences, personal and professional contacts, strong and weak relational ties, and geographically close and distant relations. | Users achieve several interaction goals, including expediting, enhancing, or avoiding face-to-face interactions with others. |
| **Advantages:** A great deal of information can be communicated easily. | **Advantages:** Real-time updates can be provided from anywhere. | **Advantages:** It is easy to build a diverse communication network. | **Advantages:** You can observe interactions with friends or family members without needing to use a telephone. |
| You can upload a photo that reflects a fond memory with someone, provide a brief caption, tag the friend, and rekindle a connection without saying much at all. | You can quickly include people in what you are doing by posting a status update or sharing a thought about your day. | You can keep in contact with people despite major life transitions, like taking new jobs or moving to new places. | You can contribute your thoughts and ideas to the public sphere and see how others respond. |
| Social media allow you to share details of your daily life in ways that you might not otherwise do—for example, posting a silly picture of your dog. | You can share your digital photos, accompanying images with text and reflection.<br><br>You can share news quickly, such as you might during natural disasters. | You might interact with others who share different political, racial, or religious identities that are not characteristic of your face-to-face network. | When something happens in your life that you do not wish to retell to multiple people, you can post it to everyone at once. |
| **Disadvantages:** You may inadvertently share information about others that upsets them. | **Disadvantages:** Social media can take up more time than you anticipate, or you may over disclose because devices are so readily available. | **Disadvantages:** You may accidentally share a message to a broader audience than you intended. | **Disadvantages:** Some people might be offended if the primary way you interact with them is through social media, and some people might not even get your messages. |
| You might share more information than you intend to (information such as where we live, what we drive, when we are home, or when we are away from home). | You might also put something in writing on a post that is hard to take back and that you regret. | You may trust someone who lies to you and pretends to be something he or she is not (like an adult posing as a high school student). | People may misinterpret a message because of the lack of nonverbal cues. |

Communication scholars describe social media as a **boundary-crossing medium** because it is *a communication channel whose personal and professional uses span communication contexts.*[24] Social media allow people to express their opinions, attitudes, values, beliefs, judgments, and evaluations on any topic and to share them with anyone—friends, colleagues, classmates, family members, and even strangers.

One challenge associated with a boundary-crossing medium of interaction has to do with norms, the general patterns of behaviors we uphold. We tend to establish different norms for communicating with different groups, like our family, our co-workers, and our friends. At work you are likely to engage in more professional interactions, perhaps not sharing your political beliefs with co-workers. Your friends, on the other hand, will know more about your political and personal beliefs but perhaps not as much about your workplace identity. Imagine a party where all your co-workers and friends are in attendance. How would you behave? Which norms would you use to interact? On social media sites, where users often mix their social networks, these questions present a relevant challenge.

One way to meet this challenge is to be explicit. Tell people when you approve them as friends how you would like them to interact with you in the social media environment you have created. Alternatively, think about the interaction norms you uphold with different groups; then simply deny requests to individuals whose norms are likely to clash with the norms of others in your established network. For example, many teachers do not like their students to be a part of their social media networks, because they worry about violating boundaries, causing conflicts, or encouraging the perception of favoritism. You should give thought to the types of relationships you allow to comingle.

## Uses and Gratifications Theory

One theory that is particularly useful for studying social media is the **uses and gratifications (U&G) theory,** which *suggests that people use social media to satisfy their own needs and desires.* U&G theorists do not view the effects of social media use as either positive or negative.[25] Instead, they argue that the impacts of social media use (such as isolation, engagement, or boredom), whether negative, positive, or neutral, are tied to the personality traits of the individual users, not the platform itself.

U&G theorists would explain the social media use of an extrovert, a person who thrives on social interaction with others, as satisfying his need to socialize. In contrast, according to U&G theorists, the lack of social media use by an introvert, a person who thrives in a quieter environment, satisfies her need for individual reflection. In other words, social media satisfy a range of needs. Moreover, a U&G theorist would be cautious in making statements such as "Social media isolate people," "Social media engage people," or "Social media create boredom," because they recognize the platform's flexibility, the variety of needs that people have, and the multiple ways such needs can be gratified via communication.

Researchers exploring the characteristics of those who use the various types of social media have come to the following conclusions:

- *Some personality traits correlate with social media use.*
  - Extroverts use social media more frequently than do introverts.[26] Introverts gain strength from having more reflective moments, so they do not turn to social media as frequently as do extroverts. Extroverts, on the other hand, gain strength from interacting with people, a trait that can be easily expressed through social media.
  - Users who experience more social anxiety tend to use social media more frequently than do people who are less socially anxious.[27] For example, if you are concerned about saying the right thing in a given situation, you are more likely to want to test your message on a social media audience first. Less socially anxious people do not require as much feedback about the impressions they convey to others.
  - Communication-based personality characteristics affect how people manage their privacy on social media. High self-monitors, people who think a lot about what they say before speaking, protect their privacy more when they use social media than do low self-monitors, people who think very little about what they say before speaking.[28]
- *People choose particular social media experiences based on their unique personality characteristics.*
  - *Facebook users:* People with a greater need for entertainment and outlets for self-expression tend to interact frequently on Facebook.[29]
  - *YouTube users:* Individuals who are motivated to interact socially, to be entertained, or to share viewing experiences gravitate to this platform.[30]
  - *Social media users in general:* People who interact through social media can be divided into six general categories, as laid out in Figure 7.6.[31]

The unique profiles in Figure 7.6 demonstrate how people use social media in different ways and for different reasons. Consider the characteristics of your social media use. Do you tend to hold back pictures from a party, because you are concerned that a future employer might evaluate you negatively? If so, your behavior fits the utilitarian profile. Do you avoid posting phone numbers or specific meet-up location details? If you do, your behavior fits the protective orientation. And if you often know exactly what you are going to say through social media and have clear reasons for posting what you do, your behavior reflects a planning orientation.

You will identify with several of these user profiles at different stages of your life. When you are young, you might identify with the sharing profile,

**Figure 7.6** Social Media User Profiles

**Utilitarian users** try to anticipate and think about all possible consequences before posting anything, to minimize problems.

**Planners** have a purpose for everything they post. They might discuss something controversial that has potentially adverse consequences if they feel there is a clear purpose for relaying the information.

**Self-centered users** present themselves clearly and do not necessarily care about the reactions of others when they post. Such a user is most driven by personal gain.

**Unworried users** don't give much extended thought to what they do when they interact through social media. They tend to engage in more mindless use of social media.

**Sharing users** freely share information through social media as a means of connecting with others. These users are likely to want to share everything they know through social media without much discrimination.

**Protective users** use caution not to reveal too much about themselves. These protective users of social media are often not concerned about violating other users' privacy expectations.

because you care about expanding your friendship network and finding potential dating partners. When you finish college and enter the job market, you might reflect the utilitarian, or consequence-driven, profile, because you realize that your social media interactions can affect your employment opportunities. Once you have a steady career, you might be an unworried user, especially if social media use is not as important to you as networking face-to-face within your company. Whatever your current perspective on social media use, you are likely to experience more rewarding interactions if you take into consideration your goals as a user.

## Evaluating Your CMC Interactions

A big difference between mass media and CMC is that CMC is interactive, meaning that it offers the potential for many to communicate. Using the Internet, romantic partners in long-distance relationships can maintain contact; members of the U.S. armed forces stationed overseas can communicate with family and friends; business can be conducted from almost any distance; videogame enthusiasts can compete with each other in virtually simulated worlds, forming friendships in the process. Some relationships exist entirely online.

Despite the evolving potential of CMC interactions, an important question remains: can these interactions truly replace the intimacy of face-to-face interaction? One group of theorists, describing what they call the **hyperpersonal perspective,** contend that, *in certain circumstances, CMC can be beneficial and rewarding, and perhaps even preferable to face-to-face interactions.*[32]

Developed in the 1990s by communication scholar Joseph Walther, the hyperpersonal perspective debunked much of the research suggesting that CMC was an impersonal and unrewarding way to carry out relationships. Because CMC lacked the dimension of nonverbal communication, many people considered it an extremely limited medium for interaction. Not only did Walther's work debunk the notion that CMC is merely impersonal communication but his propositions went on to suggest the circumstances under which CMC might be characterized as superior to face-to-face communication—or, as he calls it, a type of hyperpersonal interaction.

A hyperpersonal interaction can occur when a CMC user takes into account the following three factors when interacting online: (1) the ability to control one's self-presentation (i.e., the desire to edit and review messages before sending them), (2) the ability to control what cues one sends out (i.e., denying access to one's real name, identity, or images), and (3) the expectation that interaction partners may never actually meet face-to-face (i.e., the CMC relationship can exist in an entirely online space and place).[33]

If you prefer online dating, perhaps you are familiar with one or more of the features of hyperpersonal interaction. Some online daters hide what they believe to be negative aspects of their identity (such as being a smoker or being overweight) in order to test how limiting the knowledge of this information, and in some instances engaging in positive distortions of the facts, changes the way people interact with them. These people may not be able to hide these facts as easily in face-to-face conversations.[34]

CMC relationships sometimes evolve more quickly than face-to-face relationships. This happens in part because individuals tend to ask more direct questions through CMC, often as a way to make up for the lack of nonverbal cues.[35] This rapid disclosure can be highly rewarding, especially if, after you meet in person, you feel satisfied with the match. On the other hand, participants who construct a misleading online identity may appear to be more promising candidates than they actually are.

Many people continue to characterize CMC interaction as impersonal rather than hyperpersonal because they find interacting synchronously, or face-to-face, to be more rewarding. After all, face-to-face interaction allows for a far fuller range of both verbal and nonverbal messages. Nevertheless, Walther's research has changed the way communication theorists think about CMC and therefore remains crucial to any discussion of its value and applications.

### Thinking Critically About CMC Messages

One of the most critical differences between face-to-face communication and CMC rests on content-level messages. As discussed earlier, this is because some forms of CMC (e-mail and text messages) lack nonverbal cues, such as tone. People using CMC have found some ways to try to convey tone and intent by using emoticons, capitalization, and boldface.

Although CMC expedites communication between people (think of the difference between sending a letter and sending an e-mail), the absence of nonverbal cues can result in misunderstandings. Consider the use of capitalization in CMC. A sender can use capitalization to emphasize part of a content-level message, such as "I DO NOT AGREE WITH THIS DECISION" or "PLEASE RESPOND BY THE END OF THE DAY." However, capitalization can also convey a range of relational-level meanings. If you use capitalization to highlight a sentence or two in a message, as in the previous examples, a receiver might think you are asserting that he is not intelligent enough to figure out what is critical. Moreover, many people don't like all caps because they feel they are being shouted at.

When deciding whether to use a CMC or face-to-face communication channel, always consider the verbal and nonverbal indicators that will be available to you. Research shows that people tend to interpret e-mail messages more negatively than senders intend,[36] because e-mails do not provide full access to nonverbal cues.

With all of this in mind, if you are upset about a grade and wish to convey your frustrations to your professor, you might best manage this conversation in a medium that allows for the full range of both verbal and nonverbal expression. In face-to-face communication, nonverbal communication could help you convey the proper tone of respect with your content-level messages. Finally, there are circumstances in which sending an e-mail is more appropriate than engaging in face-to-face communication; you might introduce yourself to a new professional contact through an e-mail, as opposed to cold-calling or simply showing up at the place of business and risk interrupting.

## SOCIAL MEDIA USE ACROSS CONTEXTS

Why do you use social media? Do you use them mostly to stay in touch with friends and family? Do you keep your personal network distinct from your work or school network? Perhaps you use one platform for socializing and another, like LinkedIn, for networking with others in your field. Of course, there are no right answers to these questions. Your use of social media most likely corresponds to your personal and professional goals. To illustrate,

Figure 7.7 lists common personal and professional uses of social media across communication contexts.

Each context presents unique challenges and opportunities for social media users. As the following examples illustrate, social media provide unique opportunities to share information, but they also require careful management.

### Interpersonal Communication

Although many people use CMC to seek out new relationships, most people tend to use it to maintain existing ties.[37] Facebook is typically thought of as a

**Figure 7.7** Examples of Social Media Uses Across Communication Contexts

| | |
|---|---|
| **Interpersonal Communication** | ■ Staying in touch with family while at college<br>■ Checking out a blind date on Facebook<br>■ Networking through family and friends for future career options |
| **Organizational Communication** | ■ Connecting to company pages where you frequently shop for updates and coupons<br>■ Interacting with co-workers about work priorities |
| **Public Relations and Crisis Communication** | ■ Producing potentially viral messages for dissemination as part of your job<br>■ Providing information after a crisis, as BP did after the Gulf Coast oil spill<br>■ Cultivating your own online reputation on Twitter |
| **Journalism and News Reporting** | ■ Sharing a story from an online newspaper that you think your network friends will find interesting<br>■ Turning to bloggers for the most up-to-date information |
| **Political Communication** | ■ As a citizen, providing a YouTube link and discussing your favorite speech from a recent political convention on your social media page<br>■ As a politician, using social media to inform, persuade, or mobilize your constituencies |
| **Health Communication** | ■ As one who is suffering with a particular medical condition, blogging about it and supporting others<br>■ As a doctor, looking up a patient's social media page for insights into healthcare quality |
| **Global Communication** | ■ As an individual, forming and maintaining friendships around the globe<br>■ As a representative of a multinational corporation, connecting with organizational partners around the world about practices, policies, and issues |

way for individuals to connect with their peer networks.[38] But recent evidence suggests that many young adults also connect with their parents through social media.[39] And the trend does not stop there:

- Compared with individuals from families with open communication, individuals from families that tend toward secretiveness are more likely to reject parental requests for Facebook site access.[40]

- Facebook trends reveal that new mothers are more likely than new fathers to turn to social media to share the experience of transitioning to parenthood, and parents who use Facebook are more satisfied in their parental roles than are parents who choose to not use Facebook.[41]

Just as familial networks benefit from the use of social media, so do friendship networks. For example, social media help us maintain existing friendships as we age and encounter new experiences. Social media help maintain both strong ties and weak ties. **Strong ties** are *relationships that we are highly committed to and that we devote substantial energy to maintaining, regardless of individual circumstances that may occur.* With strong ties, such as those with your best friends, you are likely to interact face-to-face and over the phone, as well as through social media. In other words, social media provide yet another platform for strengthening your most vital relationships.

Social media are unique in that they offer significant opportunities for maintaining weak ties as well. **Weak ties** are *personal relationships to which we are not as committed overall and in which we would not invest as much time and energy to maintain.* Social media provide a great platform for maintaining relationships with people whom we might otherwise lose contact with, such as friends from high school or people who live far away. Instead of losing these friends, we may choose to maintain these relationships by uploading images and videos, posting status updates, and reading about one another's lives through blog posts.

### Organizational Communication

The use of social media is also changing the workplace, or organizational communication, a topic we will address in more detail in Chapter 8. Companies and organizations use Facebook to seek and confirm the information that prospective employees share during interviews and, ultimately, to make employment decisions.[42] As a result, employees have been fired for casual comments made to their social networks about their personal lives or their companies.[43] If an employer discovers information about you that conflicts with what is available through more formal organizational channels, you could lose your job, or you might not be hired in the first place.

Organizations also use social media to facilitate more effective internal and external organizational functioning. For example, some companies use social media so that members of the organization can work together on group projects or blog about pertinent workplace issues. Social media provide a venue for asking questions related to administrative matters or new work priorities and help facilitate external organizational communication practices, such as marketing, public relations, and crisis communication. Businesses use social media to connect with customers, respond to complaints, and interact with critical stakeholders.

If you are using social media to communicate on behalf of your organization, either internally or externally, use good judgment about whom you choose to welcome into your network. A recent study shows that most professionals who receive Facebook friend requests from co-workers accept the requests. However, some companies require employees to be more private about business matters; individuals at these companies tend to deny or ignore friend requests from co-workers.[44] Always be sure you understand your company's disclosure policies before you post messages that concern the company or are addressed to your fellow employees.

### Public Relations and Crisis Communication

Over the past 10 years, public relations officers and crisis communication experts have increasingly used social media in their jobs. More and more companies are employing people whose primary responsibility is to craft messages that have the potential to "go viral." **Viral social media campaigns** are *video messages created with the intentions that people will forward and discuss them through social media and that the messages will be widely seen.*

Do you remember how you heard updates about Hurricane Sandy or how you followed the results of the presidential election? When it comes to natural disasters and breaking news, public relations representatives rely on all kinds of media outlets, including traditional media and social media, to keep people updated. Although social media allow companies to respond immediately to developing concerns—say, about a product recall—and to convey urgent messages, traditional media, such as news reports and press releases, also remain important sources of information.[45] Individuals, too, can be sources of messages that go viral during crises, such as those who helped spark the uprisings in Egypt, Libya, and Syria.

### Journalism and News Reporting

Many news agencies have developed a strong digital presence, allowing individual users to read and respond to messages online or share commentary about events with their own audiences. Watching the nightly news, you have probably noticed the inclusion of social media messages or Twitter feeds, some created by professionals but also some by average television viewers who are social media users. The *New York Times* has adapted particularly well to media convergence by making subscriptions available in both print and digital formats. The electronic version of the daily *Times* includes written stories, video clips from its correspondents, links to YouTube videos, slide shows, citizen journalist or blog content, and a social media format that makes interacting, posting comments, and sharing content easy.

## Political Communication

Social media, in all their forms, play a prominent role in political election cycles. When individuals and groups discuss their views on sites like Twitter, they inform our views on issues of policy, for instance. Interactive political discussions on social media can better our understanding of political activity on both a small and large scale.[46]  For example, social media sites let a political speechwriter study trends in an opponent's rhetoric and allow undecided voters to access information that will help decide their vote or party affiliation.

As with face-to-face communication, political discussions through social media can highlight deeply rooted differences. Unfortunately, social media users do not always share their political views in thoughtful ways, sometimes violating the rules of courteous dialogue. Anonymity and physical distance over social media embolden some people to be more direct and forceful in their political opinions than they would be face-to-face. Moreover, research shows that, unless someone is identified as an **opinion leader,** meaning that *a range of people consistently turn to that person for advice and informed perspectives on issues,* that person's views are unlikely to change the opinions of others.[47] Nonetheless, political messaging over social media signifies political involvement in the same way that placing a candidate sign in your front yard or a bumper sticker on your car has long served a similar purpose. Political engagement is important in a democratic society; to the extent that social media encourage engagement, they can be a positive force.

## Health Communication

Increasingly, healthcare providers are struggling with the unique challenges social media present to their field. The Health Insurance Portability and Accountability Act (HIPAA), a series of regulations governing healthcare practices, requires healthcare providers to exercise extreme caution in protecting the privacy and security of patients' health information. In keeping with HIPAA regulations, most doctors do not allow patients to connect with them through social media in which patients reveal their identity.[48] However, when it comes to seeking support for healthcare issues, people frequently turn to social media networks, websites, or blogs to find people who also suffer from the same conditions.

Whereas most doctors deny Facebook friend requests from patients, some turn to social media to learn more about the patients they are treating. A social worker or therapist might want to observe what a patient is disclosing to an online social network, for example.[49] However, all it takes is one Facebook friend request to a primary physician to trigger a privacy breach that can affect the patient, the doctor, and the medical facility.

### Global Communication

The term **global communication** refers to *exchanges between people whose communication practices, patterns, and understandings differ because they come from distinct cultures.* Global communication can occur in a person's own neighborhood, where people from many parts of the world live and work; on a college campus, where students of diverse backgrounds gather; on the Internet, which connects people all over the world; or in the more formal venues of international business, politics, and diplomacy.

Through advances in communication technology and social media, individuals around the globe can make contact with one another. Global communication therefore has become a prominent area of study. As never before, we can gain insights into cultural differences, share experiences, and connect as a global village. Just consider the number of important social movements that have been fueled and supported by social media, such as the Occupy movements and the

## CONSIDERING MEDIA

### GET THE PULSE ON SOCIAL MEDIA TRENDS

Although most search engines pull information from social media sites, not all are designed to do so. The following websites provide some of the most useful information about trends, issues, and topics discussed on social media.

- Social Networking Watch (www.socialnetworkingwatch.com):
  - This site reveals how people are using social media, emphasizing changes in the social media landscape.
  - Subscribe to a free daily e-mail summarizing social media trends.
- Social Mention (www.google.com/alerts):
  - This website identifies the top issues being discussed through social media and allows you to specify your own search terms.
  - When you run a social media analysis, this site provides top mentions for the search; tells you when the topic was last mentioned; reveals top sources, hashtags, and users; and shows how many authors are contributing to topic discussions.

By staying on top of social media user trends, you can make smart decisions about how to reach your audience with your own messages.

Arab Spring revolutions. Indeed, amid the chaos and violence of the Libyan revolution, social media became an important news source for people around the world, as well as a coordinating tool for those directly involved.

Organizations, too, are adjusting to this new global world by practicing outsourcing and establishing offices in countries with different legal and cultural practices. You may end up working for a global company where you will need to interact with people at times that don't correspond with the traditional workday. Social media, for example, can be a useful way to share information about different practices, policies, and issues with offices around the globe.

## PROTECTING AND PRESENTING YOURSELF ON SOCIAL MEDIA

As we explored in Chapter 1, on perception, impression management is the careful control of the information provided (in this case, through social media) when supporting desired viewpoints and impressions. One important way to do this is to give careful consideration to the ways you manage your privacy online.

### Managing Your Privacy Online

**Communication privacy management (CPM) theory** *focuses on the processes people use to decide whether to reveal or conceal private information and how to manage the private information they share with others.*[50] CPM theory is particularly relevant when it comes to studying social media, privacy, and disclosure practices, because so many people around the globe use some type of social media. As a way of analyzing how people manage their privacy, CPM theory sets out three categories of rules that people adhere to: privacy co-ownership rules, privacy linkage rules, and privacy permeability rules.[51]

- **Co-ownership rules** *clarify your expectations for how others will treat your disclosures.* For example, you might ask the members of you social media network not to share information about your health with people outside the network; you tell them that you are open, however, to discussing it fully within the network. By establishing this rule, you clarify their responsibilities as co-owners of that private information.

- **Linkage rules** *clarify your need to have others exercise caution about sharing information with certain individuals.* Thus, if you were seeking advice from your network about how to handle a disagreement with a relational partner, you could stipulate that they not share your concerns with the partner in question.

- **Permeability rules** *clarify how much private information you are comfortable with others sharing about specific topics.* Users of social media might navigate permeability rules by clearly establishing with their network which topics they can talk about online and which topics are off limits.

In addition to discussing, negotiating, and clarifying privacy rules, users of social media can also use privacy settings to ensure the protection of information. But even when you clearly lay out privacy-management parameters, **privacy turbulence** can occur, meaning that *those allowed to access your private information have not upheld the stipulated obligations.*

Research shows that most users of social media examine their posted information, photos, and content and make deletions.[52] This is a healthy sign. However, a smaller group of users never make deletions. This group views doing so as unnecessary, either because they practice caution before posting or because they simply do not care how others see them. The top seven reasons motivating deletions among social media users are described in Table 7.2.

Perhaps the most effective way to practice good privacy-management habits is to learn from the mistakes of others. The news is full of stories about people who did not believe they would be held accountable for what they communicated through social media. Consider these recent examples:

- In Texas, after a deputy sheriff lost an election, he posted angry, frustrated rants on Facebook and was fired for his unprofessional comments about other governmental officials.[53]

## CHALLENGE YOURSELF

### How Should I Manage Social Media to Gain and Maintain Friendships Without Getting in Trouble With Others, Including Employers?

Keep in mind that social media companies are not concerned about your privacy. In fact, the default privacy settings provided by most sites are not designed to protect your privacy. This is because they profit from selling your information to others. Changing the default settings can prevent your posts from potentially popping up in online search engines. It can also ensure that your information is available only to the people you have designated as friends.

Take some time to explore your privacy options on each site you use. For example, you may decide to establish different groups and then sort people into these groups according to the privacy norms you use in those groups. When you establish a group, you can usually provide the group unique access to part of your social media site. Each time you want to post something, consider which group or groups will have access to the content. You might even post similar content separately for each unique group. For instance, you may not want members across groups to be able to discuss your posts with one another.

Finally, periodically return to the content you have posted and make deletions. Also, return to your friend list and defriend individuals who have no reason to be on your site. If you haven't interacted with someone in a year, chances are you won't miss having that person as a social media friend. Some people only want to be your friend so that they can passively observe what you post and seek out information about you.

**Table 7.2** Top Motivators for Deleting Social Media Content

**Social media users most frequently make decisions in order to:**

1. **Manage conflict:** Deleting a post that creates tension or friction in an important relationship

2. **Ensure safety:** Removing an image that makes it too easy for people to know exactly where you live

3. **Prevent getting sued or ridiculed:** Removing rants that friends make about their jobs on your site

4. **Minimize job-related problems:** Removing posts that show you doing things away from home—for instance, when you took a sick day from work and your coworkers expected you to be at home

5. **Control impressions:** Removing a post that possibly portrays you to be interpreted as insensitive or immature

6. **Regulate emotions:** Removing posts that demonstrate an emotional reaction rather than a clear and rational thought, such as someone who verbally attacks another on your site

7. **Remove any indicators of sour relationships:** Deleting every picture and post of an ex-boyfriend or girlfriend and defriending that person

*Source:* Child, J. T., Haridakis, P. M., & Petronio, S. (2012). Blogging privacy rule orientations, privacy management, and content deletion practices: The variability of online privacy management activity at different stages of social media use. *Computers in Human Behavior, 28,* 1859–1872.

- Former New England Patriots cheerleader Caitlin Davis was fired in 2008 because she posted a photo on Facebook showing an obscene picture she drew on the face of someone who had passed out at a party.[54]
- Former Rutgers student Dharun Ravi was found guilty of hate crimes after posting video and text that revealed his roommate, Tyler Clementi, making out with a man. After learning of the posts, Clementi committed suicide.[55]

It is easy to misjudge the way a post will be taken by others. Just as face-to-face communication cannot be reversed, it can often be difficult to withdraw a written record, like a post. Because you can be held accountable for anything you say through social media, it is important to think before you post.

## Presenting Yourself Online

A useful framework for understanding your interactions on social media is the concept of self-presentation.[56] Sociologist Erving Goffman used the metaphor of actors in a play to explain the ways we present ourselves in different social contexts. According to Goffman, the various situations in which you find yourself require that you act certain parts. For example, when you are in the classroom, you take on the role of student. At home, you are a son or daughter, a parent or spouse, a sibling or roommate. Some of these roles, like those you adopt at work or school, are more public—they take place "onstage." Others, like those you adopt at home or in private, are considered "backstage" roles.

In the context of social media, the internal dialogues, values, attitudes, and perspectives you do not share can be placed in the category of backstage. The images, messages, links, videos, and even friendships you post or make public are onstage. Just as the clothes you wear to an interview communicate a certain message about you and your attitude toward the job, the content you share over social media acts as a sort of costume, conveying your social media identity to the personal and professional contacts in your network. Be certain that you present yourself in a manner that will best serve your goals.

# BUILDER

## LEARN TO ANALYZE YOUR SOCIAL MEDIA PRESENCE

Choose one of your social media sites to analyze. Reflect on the following questions to better understand the impressions your site gives to others, including potential employers.

- What kinds of topics do you post or discuss often, and what do these topics say about you?
- In photos or videos of you, what locations appear most frequently?
- Who tends to comment and interact with you, and what does this say about the company you keep?
- What organizations, causes, and groups have you connected to through social media?
- Are there impressions on the front stage of your social media site that you need to rethink?
- How might you alter the impressions you cultivate through social media?

 **CHAPTER REVIEW**

On a daily basis, mediated communication facilitates flexibility, efficiency, and variety in how we access information. Moreover, mediated communication will continue to be a pivotal area for study, because technology continues to advance and to change the way we interact. This chapter identified the most common sources of mediated communication and discussed some of its most relevant features. We also examined the many aspects of interacting over social media, the ways you use social media across a variety of contexts, and how you can best present and protect yourself online.

## KEY TERMS

agenda-setting, 109
asynchronous communication, 111
boundary-crossing medium, 115
communication privacy management
   (CPM) theory, 125
computer-mediated communication
   (CMC), 105
co-ownership rules, 125
cultivation effect, 110
gatekeeping, 109
global communication, 124
hyperpersonal perspective, 118
linkage rules, 125
mass communication, 105

mass media, 105
media convergence, 106
media literacy, 111
mediated communication, 104
opinion leader, 123
permeability rules, 125
privacy turbulence, 126
social media, 112
strong ties, 121
synchronous communication, 111
uses and gratifications (U&G)
   theory, 115
viral social media campaigns, 122
weak ties, 121


## STUDY QUESTIONS

1. How do the components of the traditional communication model (sender-message-receiver-feedback) apply to mass communication sources of information?

2. Analyze a television program by describing how it challenges a societal norm or perpetuates a stereotype.

3. Explain the difference between synchronous and asynchronous communication channels. Then make two lists: in one, list all the circumstances in which you would prefer to communicate synchronously; in the other, list those in which you would choose an asynchronous communication channel. Explain your reasons for your choices.

4. Identify the seven contexts of social media use discussed in the text. Think of one example, not described in this text, of social media use in each context.

5. State one example of a co-ownership rule, a linkage rule, and a permeability rule that you have practiced.

# Organizational and Small-Group Communication

As in every other sphere of life, communication is central to your success in the workplace. In fact, many people consider their work identity and relationships to be an important part of who they are.[1] To help you succeed in college and in your future career, this chapter will examine concepts and practices that will help you function effectively in organizations and groups. To begin, we will take a look at organizational culture.

## LEARNING OBJECTIVES

*After reading this chapter, you should be able to:*

- Define organizational culture and discuss the proper methods for assessing the culture of an organization.
- Explain how small groups and teams function within organizations and the role communication plays.
- Describe leadership as a process of communication.
- Name and explain strategies for cultivating positive relationships in organizations.

## WHAT IS ORGANIZATIONAL CULTURE?

Understanding an organization's culture means understanding the "right way to do things in the eyes of an organization or company."[2] In some organizations, it's clear that employee interactions should focus exclusively on work issues and that employees should leave their personal lives at home. In others, the culture is more open to what is known as work-life balance. **Organizational culture** refers to *the attitudes, values, and beliefs that are common among and that characterize the interactions of organizational members and the way they work and behave.* Learning to quickly assess culture will help you adapt your behavior and communication practices.

Often people are so immersed in their organization's culture that they are not even aware that it is a culture with a unique set of characteristics. In contrast, outsiders or newcomers, with their fresh eyes, are in a better position to become cultural detectives—that is, they can observe many behaviors and interactions that illuminate the workplace culture and beliefs.[3]

### Investigating Organizational Culture

Organizations communicate their cultural values in several ways: (1) the way employees use language and the stories they tell, (2) the rituals and routines they adhere to, and (3) the symbols and artifacts on display in the environment. Table 8.1 provides a set of questions to consider for each of these three realms as you attempt to investigate an organization's overall culture. Table 8.2 will help you determine what your findings may reveal.

Keep in mind that all three areas (language and storytelling, rituals and routines, and cultural markers) are critical to understanding organizational culture. Furthermore, employees will not always directly communicate aspects of their culture—sometimes because they are too used to them to perceive them. Nonetheless, it is important for you to understand and consider culture when evaluating whether you would be comfortable and effective working for a particular company.

However, you might have to depend on your own sleuthing abilities to extract information about organizational practices related to difference, diversity, and advancement. No human resources professional would say, "We do not promote women in this organization," but your observations may lead you to this conclusion. Still, be cautious in putting too much interpretation into any single marker of organizational culture. You should be looking for themes supported across multiple indicators of organizational culture. You are not likely to find an organization that is completely congruent with your own preferences. Weigh the benefits and drawbacks of a company's organizational culture in relation to your own preferences. You might not take a job with an organization that stresses high productivity and extensive time commitments if you know you need weekends to unplug completely from work.

**Table 8.1** Questions for Investigating an Organization's Culture

| Language Use and Storytelling | Established Rituals and Routines | Prominent Cultural Markers (symbols and artifacts) |
|---|---|---|
| ■ What terms do people commonly use?<br>■ How do people refer to one another (e.g., co-worker, colleague, associate, friend)?<br>■ Who is frequently discussed as a hero or role model?<br>■ Who, if anyone, is considered a villain? What stories are shared about this person?<br>■ How frequently do people communicate as a group formally (e.g., meetings) versus informally (coffee breaks, lunch, or after work)?<br>■ How do people communicate or prefer to communicate with one another?<br>  ● By e-mail?<br>  ● Face-to-face?<br>■ Do people openly and respectfully engage in conflict?<br>■ Which, if any, topics and issues do people avoid talking about at work?<br>■ Are there certain people that individuals avoid or go out of their way to talk to in the organization? | ■ What procedures are followed for evaluating work?<br>■ Who makes decisions and how many people are involved in decision making?<br>■ How do people get disciplined or rewarded?<br>  ● What procedures or activities are in place for rewarding people for exemplary work?<br>  ● When someone does not meet expectations, what procedures are followed?<br>■ What are some of the prominent rules in the handbook and policy manual?<br>  ● Does the company have anti-fraternization or dating policies?<br>  ● Is every aspect of work spelled out or are policies flexible regarding the completion of work?<br>■ What types of celebrations are in place to bring people together?<br>  ● How, if at all, does the organization formally acknowledge its heroes?<br>    ● How, if at all, does the organization bring people together in casual ways, such as picnics or after-work social gatherings?<br>      ■ What routines are in place that either encourage or discourage people from interacting with one another? | ■ Do offices differ in size based on the position of an individual within the organization?<br>■ Do all offices look the same?<br>■ Do people ever bring their children or pets to work?<br>■ Does one have to pass a security station and/or receptionists to get access to other people in the organization?<br>■ How do people dress? Are they dressed formally or casually? Do they have earrings (men and women)? Tattoos? Unusual hair colors?<br>■ Are executives or managers separated from general employees?<br>■ What is the level and function of technology?<br>  ● Do people have access to and use computers, cell phones, or Internet-based technologies?<br>  ● Are people free to listen to music while they work?<br>■ How diverse are the people in each level of the organization?<br>  ● What is the proportion of men and women in entry level versus management positions?<br>  ● Are the facilities accessible to those with disabilities, both as workers and as customers? |

As you evaluate the aspects of an organization's culture, keep in mind that who you are and where you come from will impact the conclusions you draw. For example, if you are a member of a dominant culture (as discussed in Chapter 6), your perspective on a particular organization's culture will

**Table 8.2** Using Findings to Understand an Organization

| Language Use and Storytelling | Established Rituals and Routines | Prominent Cultural Markers (symbols and artifacts) |
|---|---|---|
| ▪ When heroes are described as assertive in seeking out new opportunities, it may suggest that the organization values people who push themselves and are self-starters.<br>▪ When people frequently laugh and refer to one another on a first-name basis, it may suggest that the organization has a relaxed culture where employees enjoy one another's company.<br>▪ When groups meet frequently, it may suggest a culture that places a high value on group participation and collaboration versus independent decision making.<br>▪ Understanding whom people turn to for answers or avoid may suggest where power lies within the organization. | ▪ If an organization focuses rewards, such as monthly bonuses, on the top performers in each unit, it suggests that productivity is an important value. Rewards for other aspects of performance, such as mentoring newcomers or making charitable contributions, indicate other kinds of values.<br>▪ If an organization has few events that bring people together—picnics or a monthly potluck meal—it suggests a more formal culture that does not encourage the mingling of the personal and the professional.<br>▪ An organization where few people are consulted before important decisions are made suggests a culture where power is centralized.<br>▪ If an organization holds a yearly award celebration for employees, it suggests a supportive and appreciative culture. | ▪ When managers are segregated on their own floor or wing, with offices that are larger than those of general employees, it suggests that management voices are more important than employee voices.<br>▪ Organizations where employees display personal pictures and artifacts may suggest that organizational members are valued as people beyond their formal roles in the workplace.<br>▪ An organization with many gatekeepers suggests a more formal organization with a strict hierarchy.<br>▪ Organizations with less gender, racial, or age diversity in upper management may avoid advancing members who represent those groups.<br>▪ An organization that goes out of its way to be accessible to all people demonstrates that diversity matters. |

differ in important ways from that of someone from a nondominant culture, or co-culture. A fully able-bodied individual may claim that her organizational culture is tolerant of diversity; however, if you speak to a member with a disability from the same organization, you might get a different answer. This is similarly true of gender inequalities. Asking a white, middle-class man whether women have equal opportunities within his company would gain you less insight than talking directly with women in the organization.

## Understanding Organizational Structure

In addition to organizational culture, an organization's structure affects communication. Among the primary structural features that impact communication are hierarchy, differentiation and specialization, and formalization.

**Hierarchy** comprises *the levels of responsibility and relationships within an organization.* Some organizations stress hierarchy more than others. Those that are strongly hierarchical lay out clear procedures for whom employees report to up the entire chain of command. Moreover, individuals further up the chain of command rarely communicate directly with those in the lowest levels. Messages go through the hierarchy to reach appropriate audiences.[4] The military is a strongly hierarchical organization. Each person has a clearly defined rank, and a clear structure exists for who is in charge of decision making at each level of the organization. Although not as rigid as the military, colleges and universities also have hierarchies; students who have an issue with their instructor must take the matter to the instructor before other administrators. Organizations vary in the degree to which they depend on hierarchy. Organizations that place less stress on hierarchy empower multiple individuals to have a say in decision making.

**Differentiation and specialization** refers to *the division of labor in an organization and the degree to which each individual has a unique role and responsibility.*[5] Many fast-food and service industry jobs incorporate a high degree of differentiation and specialization of tasks to reduce uncertainty in the work environment. Each person knows precisely what he needs to do: one person takes the orders, another fills the drink orders, and another fries the hamburgers. Of course, in some settings this kind of specialization can make work mindlessly repetitive, but in other settings it can create a strong team of experts who can respond collectively to a wide range of concerns—more so than could one individual trying to manage multiple tasks.

The emergency room of a hospital is an example of an organizational team that has members with a high degree of specialization and the ability to respond to a range of problems. General medical doctors and nurses work in shifts. If a

# BUILDER

## USE METAPHORS TO UNDERSTAND ORGANIZATIONAL STRUCTURES

Three metaphors are commonly used to describe organizational structure:

- *The machine metaphor:* The organization is like a car, with separate parts that all work together.
- *The family metaphor:* The organization has loyal members who are all necessary and important to its functioning and who care for and support each other beyond their formal roles.
- *The organism metaphor:* The organization has interdependent systems and organs, like the human body, and its organs regulate proper functioning and homeostasis.[6]
  1. What might these metaphors suggest about hierarchy, differentiation and specialization, and formalization?
  2. Which of these metaphors describes an organization that you would most like to work for?
  3. What does each metaphor suggest about communication styles?
  4. If you had to create your own metaphor to describe effective organizational functioning, what would it be and why?

patient arrives at the hospital needing more specialized expertise, on-call doctors are consulted and brought into the hospital.

Not every organization has highly specialized and differentiated roles. Some organizations incorporate **strategic ambiguity,** or *intentional uncertainty and vagueness,* so that they can adapt more easily to changing circumstances.[7] In either case, communication flows from the organization's approach to division of labor and specialization.

**Formalization** refers to *the rules, procedures, and norms that exist for carrying out work practices.* Highly formalized organizations have extensive rules and manuals in place to specify what people do and how they do it. Organizations with less formalization allow individuals a great deal of flexibility in how they carry out their work. For example, many student groups elect leaders (e.g., president and vice president) who fulfill their duties for their organizational groups with few formalized structures from the student body government. However, the same groups usually have handbooks that are shared within the group and that help provide formalization to carrying out leadership roles. An organization can incorporate both formalized and less formalized structures. A highly formalized organization can reduce creativity and innovation, whereas an organization with little formalization can be more chaotic.

## Analyzing Organizational Communication Practices

The culture and structure of an organization affect its communication practices. In general, communication in organizations can be broken down into two types: formal and informal. **Formal communication** consists of *messages that follow prescribed channels of communication throughout the organization.* The most common way of depicting formal communication networks is with organizational charts, as in Figure 8.1.

**Figure 8.1** Example of an Organizational Chart

**CHALLENGE**

**What Can I Learn About Workplace Communication, so That I Can Attract an Employer's Attention, Interview Well, and Keep a Good Job?**

Chapter 15 of this text provides a lot of information that can help you get a job—for example, fine-tuning your résumé and thinking about how you might answer interview questions. The most important advice, useful throughout your career, is to be proactive, positive, and persistent.

- People who look for ways to do their job more effectively always stand out in the eyes of leaders. Proactive people make themselves indispensable to organizational functioning. When you have become skilled with your assigned tasks, ask what else you can do to contribute rather than being satisfied with the skills you have already mastered. For example, when Hillary Clinton did not get the democratic nomination for president, she did not disengage from politics. She became secretary of state and continued her learning about international issues and concerns. Similarly, Thomas Edison failed over 1,000 times in inventing the lightbulb. When asked about these failures, he is quoted to have said something like "I have not failed 1,000 times. Rather, I have discovered over 1,000 ways not to make a lightbulb." These people exemplify what it means to be proactive, to get up and try again.
- Be a person whom others seek out because of your positive attitude and your interest in new opportunities. For example, while pursuing your studies, you might approach an instructor who teaches something you find very interesting. You could ask to be involved in her teaching or research practices. Many opportunities pass people by, because they do not express an interest and create an opportunity to be more involved.
- Finally, do not stop challenging yourself. Even if your ideas are shot down, continue to exert creative energy in the organization. In doing so, you will show your commitment, which can open many doors for you.

Organizational charts clearly indicate who is responsible for a given task and which employees are responsible for others' performance. Communication in formal networks typically flows in one of three ways:

- *Downward communication* occurs whenever superiors initiate messages to subordinates. Downward communication includes job instructions, job rationales, policies and procedures, performance feedback, and motivational appeals.
- *Upward communication* occurs when messages flow from subordinates to superiors. Upward communication includes monthly reports, scheduling issues, and feedback to supervisors about things like the effectiveness of policies and procedures.
- *Horizontal communication* flows between people who are at the same level of the organizational hierarchy. Horizontal communication includes task coordination, problem solving, information sharing, and conflict resolution.

Employees must know the official and formal chain of command, so that they know where to take their issues and concerns. However, research demonstrates that bad news does not typically travel up to higher levels of management as frequently and clearly as it moves down the hierarchy.[8]

One prominent recent example of this is the Jerry Sandusky sex scandal at Penn State University. Although the first assault occurred in 1994, university leaders did not take action until 2012, when Sandusky was convicted of abusing 10 boys while using university facilities.[9] At the trial, janitors reported seeing Sandusky abusing the boys during those years but agreed to pretend they did not see anything. Why? People do not report bad news upward because they fear the negative repercussions of conveying bad news to a superior. They also worry about how bad news, if shared, could severely damage important relationships in the workplace.[10] Clearly, people in leadership positions need to respond appropriately to bad news, so that subordinates can feel safe conveying it to them.

**Informal communication** is *any interaction that emerges out of social interactions among organization members rather than following the rules of the formal chain of command.* Much information in organizations goes through informal channels, not through memos, meetings, or organization wide announcements.[11] Examples of informal communication include hearing things from co-workers like "Hey, did you hear that Sandra is going to quit?" or "Louis told me that he gets really defensive when people suggest new strategies that involve his department."

Informal communication is important because it allows the transmission of information that may be critical to know to be successful in an organization but that may never come through formal organizational channels.[12] Informal communication can also help you understand important aspects of organizational culture. Informal networks, sometimes referred to as "grapevine communication," are typically very accurate, with between 80% and 90% of the information being correct.[13] An understanding of formal and informal networks in organizations is critical as you join and try to fit into a new organization.

Everything you have learned thus far in the chapter about evaluating organizational culture and understanding organizational structure will help you as you launch an effective job search. We explore this topic further in Chapter 15.

## COMMUNICATING IN SMALL GROUPS AND TEAMS

Many workplace projects are put into the hands of small groups, and your ability to understand and work well in them will serve you throughout your career. Small groups drive and invigorate nearly all facets of our lives: our families, classrooms, clubs, sports teams, and community organizations. In this section we will examine small-group functioning from a communication perspective, exploring the types of small groups, norms and roles in groups, and group climate. Let's begin by defining the central concept.

**Small-group communication** is *the interaction among three to nine people who are working together to achieve an interdependent goal.*[14] This definition implies several things:

- Groups must be small enough for members to be aware of the collective entity of the group. For example, people who post comments on a particular blog are less likely to have a sense of group identity than are people who meet regularly, whether in an online forum or face-to-face, to address a particular issue, such as campus safety. Groups typically contain between three and nine people but may be larger if members perceive the group as an entity. Research shows that groups of three or four people are more productive than groups with five or more people.[15] If given a choice, working with a smaller group may produce better results.

- Interaction between members is the substance that creates and holds the group together. Communication practices and styles shape each group in unique ways and allow the group to function. As with all human communication, small-group communication involves sending verbal and nonverbal signals, which other people perceive, interpret, and respond to.

- Group members are **interdependent,** which means they *cannot achieve their goals without the help of one another.* If you watch reality television shows like *Survivor,* you have seen examples of how groups of people must work as interdependent units to achieve success. Business consulting firms are now using a reality-show approach to teach the importance of interdependence for corporate work teams. Corporations pay $75,000 to have their team members locked in a house over some period of time to develop interdependent skills.[16]

### Types of Small Groups

Think about the groups to which you belong. You may regularly study with other students from your accounting class, belong to a club on campus, and have a regular group of friends with whom you socialize. What are the key differences among these groups? In answering that question, first consider how you came to be a member. In this context, there are two types of groups:

- *Assigned groups* occur when individuals are appointed to be members. A student union advisory board is one example. Members are assigned to such groups, for example, by being elected as a leader of a student organization, with the goal of making the university better for students overall. Wanting to be a member is not sufficient to become one.

- *Emergent groups* occur when individuals decide to form a cohesive group out of personal need or desire. A group of friends who meet at college and decide to work together to get a better grade in a class is an example of an emergent group.

We can also classify groups according to the function they serve:

- *Task-oriented groups* are formed for the purpose of completing tasks such as solving a problem or making a decision. A community task force convened to come up with novel solutions for combatting underage drinking is an example of a task-oriented group.

- *Relationship-oriented groups* are long-term groups that exist to meet individual needs. A family is a relationship-oriented group that provides emotional and other kinds of support for its members.

Classifying groups according to whether they are task-oriented, relationship-oriented, assigned, or emergent risks oversimplifying how groups actually work in your life. Because people form groups, and because groups can grow and change through communication, lines between types and functions can easily blur. For example, members of relationship-oriented groups, such as families, may start a business together, in which case they need to make strategic decisions and cooperate to complete work tasks.

Members of task-oriented groups may forge strong personal bonds and continue their relationships even after completing their assigned task. In fact, task-oriented groups can benefit from strong relational bonds that allow members to feel appreciated and valued. Also, if members of an assigned group establish positive relationships, the group can start to look and feel like an emergent group, in the sense that a relationship-oriented social group may emerge. Much as in our personal relationships, the quality of our group membership is constantly in flux.

### Norms and Roles in Small Groups

Beginning with their very first interactions, group members establish the group's **norms,** which are *the beliefs about how individual members should interact and behave in a particular context*. Norms often develop naturally based on how members structure tasks and allow work to progress. However, norms can also be developed explicitly, as when group members openly discuss expectations for group members. Some groups even create a group contract.

Norms can make a group effective, as when the norm is for everybody to arrive on time, be well prepared, and get to work. Or they can make a group ineffective, as when the norms are for people to be casual about arrival time, to socialize instead of getting to work, or to take cell phone calls or return text messages while others are speaking. To ensure a productive set of norms, consider having a discussion about members' expectations for group functioning. The following questions may help in this discussion:

- What are the purpose and function of the group?
  - What does each member identify as the group goal?
  - What do members view as the mission statement?
- What will constitute ethical and unethical group interactions?
- What expectations do members hold for group functioning and behavior?
  - How will the group handle violations of group expectations, such as the following?
  - What about arriving to a meeting late or failing to show up?
  - What if members fail to uphold individual obligations or complete work in a timely manner?
- How will the group make decisions when differences of opinion arise?
- How can members get in touch with one another for input or further assistance?
- How frequently should the group meet?
- What can the group do so that everyone gets the opportunity to contribute to ideas?
- How can the group ensure that everyone contributes to the output or final products?

The intent is to spend time making explicit what is implicit in group members' minds. If one member thinks that all decisions should run through the group but another member expects more flexibility, the group is likely to experience conflict. A discussion of decision-making procedures can lead to clarity. In addition, clarifying the roles that group members might fulfill will ease group functioning.

Every group member enacts a unique **role,** *a consistent pattern of interaction or behavior exhibited over time.* In movies, characters enact roles to drive the story; in small groups, members enact roles to drive the interaction of the group. Whereas

actors learn their roles from scripts, group members create their roles spontaneously during interactions with others and while drawing on their unique skills and attitudes. Just as an actor plays different roles in different scripts, individuals enact diverse roles in the groups to which they belong.

Group roles are either formal or informal. A **formal role** (sometimes called a **positional role**) is *an assigned role based on an individual's position or title within a group.* For example, a person may be responsible for taking certain types of information to group meetings, for keeping track of finances, or for recording agenda items for future meetings. Once a person is assigned one of these formal roles, other group members have expectations for that person. If the person does not follow through—by supplying the information or keeping the records—others will be disappointed, and the group's efforts may be undermined.

An **informal role** (sometimes called a **behavioral role**) is a *role that develops naturally or spontaneously within a group.* Informal roles emerge through interactions in the group, and they change to meet the group's emerging needs. Such roles reflect members' personality characteristics, habits, and typical ways of interacting in a group. If you are the type of person who likes to talk in front of others, you might take on the role of facilitator. On the other hand, if you are less talkative, you might take on behind-the-scene roles, such as conducting research or creating documents. Informal roles allow you to play to your strengths; of course, to develop informal roles, you may need to talk to other group members about your preferences and abilities.

Group member roles can be classified by their function as task, maintenance, or self-centered behaviors. **Task functions** are *behaviors that directly relate to the group's purpose, and they affect the group's productivity;* they are implemented to focus group members productively on their assignment. **Maintenance functions** are *behaviors that focus on the interpersonal relationships among group members; they are aimed at supporting cooperation and harmony.* Both task and maintenance functions are considered essential to effective group communication. On the other hand, **self-centered functions** are *behaviors that serve the needs of the individual at the expense of the group.* The person performing self-centered functions manipulates other members for selfish goals that compete with group goals. Task, maintenance, and self-centered functions can in turn be broken down into several categories, as you can see in Table 8.3.

## Group Climate and Cohesion

You have probably attended group meetings where people were so comfortable with one another that they found it hard to get beyond socializing and down to business. That relaxed atmosphere describes the **group climate,** which is *the emotional tone or atmosphere members create within the group.* Three factors that contribute heavily to group climate are trust, supportiveness, and cohesiveness.

| Table 8.3  Types of Task, Maintenance, and Self-Centered Functions | |
|---|---|
| **Type of Statement** | **Sample Statements** |
| **Task Functions** | |
| Initiating and orienting | "Let's make a list of what we still need to do." <br> "What has each member done since we last met?" |
| Information giving | "I was asked to find suitable venues for our event. Three possible locations exist." |
| Information seeking | "Who in the group has contacts in student government to check on that?" |
| Opinion giving | "I'm not sure that is the most effective way for us to raise funds." |

| | |
|---|---|
| Clarifying | "Paul, I'm not sure I understand the point you're trying to make. Can you clarify what you mean?" |
| Extending | "An additional benefit of pursing that idea is . . ." |
| Evaluating | "One problem I see with following this recommendation is . . ." |
| Summarizing | "So before we meet again next week, Mindy will talk to vendors and Mark will look at our expenses so far." |
| Coordinating | "If each member can get me their parts of the paper by Tuesday, I can compile them for further discussion at our next meeting." |
| Consensus testing | "Let's see if there is group agreement about this course of action." |
| Recording | "Let's make sure to get that in the minutes, so that we don't forget to follow up on that task." |

### Maintenance Functions

| | |
|---|---|
| Reinforcing norms | "Let's consider Mark's objections further. We decided to aim for consensus about all decisions." |
| Gatekeeping | "Pat, you look like you want to say something about the proposal." |
| Supporting | "I think Tara's point is well made, and we should look at it more closely." |
| Harmonizing | "Jared and Sally, I think there are areas where you agree, and I would like to suggest a compromise that might work for you both." |
| Tension relieving | "We're getting tired and cranky. Let's take a 10-minute break." |
| Dramatizing | "That reminds me of a story about what happened last year when . . ." |
| Showing solidarity | "We've really done good work here!" or "I'm so pleased with the decision we made tonight as a group." |

### Self-Centered Functions

| | |
|---|---|
| Withdrawing | "Do whatever you want; I don't care." |
| Blocking | "I don't care if we've already voted; I want to discuss it again!" |
| Status and recognition seeking | "I have a lot more expertise than the rest of you, and I think we should do it the way I know works." |

- **Trust** refers to *a belief that members can rely on each other.* Two types of trust relevant to group work are task trust and interpersonal trust. Task trust develops when members have confidence that others will get their jobs done in support of the group's goals. Interpersonal trust emerges when members perceive that others are working in support of the group, rather than trying to achieve personal gain or accomplish hidden agendas.

- Supportiveness refers to an atmosphere of openness in which members care about each other.

Working against trust and supportiveness in groups is the quality of defensiveness. To help you consider the impact supportiveness and defensiveness can have on group climate, Table 8.4 presents types of defensive and supportive behavior, illustrating each type with an example.

- **Cohesiveness** is the *attachment members feel toward each other and the group.* Highly cohesive groups are more open, handle disagreement more effectively,[17] and typically perform better[18] than groups with low levels of cohesiveness. More supportiveness and less defensiveness contribute to greater cohesion.

Although cohesiveness is generally desirable, dangers arise from too much cohesion. **Groupthink** is *a phenomenon that occurs when the desire for cohesion and agreement takes precedence over critical analysis and discussion.* According to sociologist Irving Janis, groupthink can destroy effective decision making. Several historical decision-making blunders have been attributed to groupthink, including the escalation of the Vietnam conflict, the space shuttle *Challenger* disaster, and possibly the *Columbia* shuttle disaster over Texas.[19] Although groupthink may be difficult for members to detect, researchers have identified the following observable signs:

- An illusion of invulnerability
- An unquestioned belief in the morality of the group
- Collective efforts to rationalize faulty decisions
- Stereotypical views of enemy leaders as evil, weak, or ineffective
- Censorship of alternative viewpoints
- A shared illusion that all members think the same thing
- Direct pressure on members expressing divergent opinions

Although Janis originally asserted that these were the characteristics that led to groupthink, and consequently resulted in a bad decision, recent studies suggest that these characteristics actually occur after the group has already made the poor decision.[20] Once groups make decisions, members try to create and reinforce a consensus in support of the decision, even in the face of evidence that the decision was poor, which leads to the groupthink characteristics.

**Table 8.4** Defensive and Supportive Behaviors and Statements

| Behavior | Description | Sample Statement |
|---|---|---|
| **Defensive Behaviors and Statements** | | |
| Evaluation | Insulting another person's idea | "That's a completely ridiculous idea." |
| Control | Dominating or insisting on your own way | "I've decided what we need to do." |
| Manipulating | Pushing compliance | "Don't you think you should try it my way?" |
| Neutrality | Claiming that you don't care how others feel | "It doesn't matter to me what you decide." |
| Superiority | Pulling rank, maximizing status differences | "As group leader, I think we should . . ." |
| Certainty | Being a "know-it-all" | "You guys are completely off base. I know exactly how to handle this." |
| **Supportive Behaviors and Statements** | | |
| Description | Describing your own feelings without making those of others wrong | "I prefer the first option because . . ." |
| Problem orientation | Searching for the best solution without predetermining what that should be | "We want to produce the best results, and that may mean some extra time from all of us." |
| Spontaneity | Reacting honestly and openly | "Wow, that sounds like a great idea!" |
| Empathy | Showing you care about the other members | "Jan, originally you were skeptical. How comfortable will you be if the group favors that option?" |
| Equality | Minimizing status differences by treating members as equals | "I don't have all the answers. What do the rest of you think?" |
| Provisionalism | Expressing opinions tentatively and being open to others' suggestions | "Maybe we should try a different approach . . ." |

Groupthink is possible in nearly every group. To prevent it, members should seek all pertinent information, carefully assess the credibility of information relevant to the decision at hand, assign members to present counterarguments, and maintain a commitment to finding the best possible outcome as supported by the available evidence.

## Decision Making and Problem Solving

Generally, effective problem solving involves five steps: (1) discussing criteria for an acceptable solution, (2) brainstorming and identifying alternatives, (3) evaluating each alternative, (4) implementing the plan, and (5) evaluating the outcomes based on the original criteria. Each step is a potential antidote for groupthink.

**Discussing Critical Criteria Criteria** are *the standards by which a group must judge potential solutions to a problem.* For example, a solution's potential effectiveness ("Will it work?"), acceptability ("Will people vote for our proposal?"), and cost ("Does this option keep us within the budget?") are common criteria. Discussing these criteria allows a team or group to reflect on its values and reasons for doing something in a new or different way. Group members will not always agree on what the critical criteria are, but agreeing is very important to the decision-making process. The more similar the group members are in age, gender, ethnicity, background, attitudes, values, and beliefs, the easier they can agree on criteria.

Two kinds of criteria are common. Absolute criteria are those that must be met; the group has no leeway. Important criteria are those that should be met but the group has some flexibility. Group members should give the highest priority to absolute criteria. Ideas that do not meet the standard of absolute criteria should be ranked on how well they meet the standard for important criteria. Consider an organization that wants a new location for business. Its absolute criteria might be the maximum cost of the building and the accessibility of the parking and entrances. Important criteria might be having other industry close by and being near public transportation.

**Identifying Alternatives** One technique that can promote innovation and creative thought in groups is brainstorming.[21] While brainstorming, group members are free to identify multiple, succinct ideas and are asked to defer any judgment (positive or negative) until all ideas have been identified. Critical evaluation kills creativity, which is why the evaluation stage takes place *after* the group has run out of ideas.

A facilitator can guide brainstorming by first giving group members a few minutes to consider the question. This can help generate a range of possibilities. As ideas are presented, the facilitator records and displays them. Once ideas become repetitive, the facilitator wraps up the process, and the analysis and evaluation begin.

**Evaluating Each Alternative** At this stage, the group uses the criteria they identified earlier to judge the efficacy of the ideas generated through brainstorming. To do so, it is useful to analyze the listed ideas and determine whether

# GLOBALLY

## WORKING COHESIVELY IN DIVERSE GROUPS

Most work groups, and even classroom groups, have at least one member for whom English is a second language. You might assume that having group members with differing levels of English proficiency will diminish the cohesiveness of the group, but that assumption is incorrect.

Research shows that having various primary languages represented in a group does not impede cohesiveness as long as members have frequent interactions.[22] However, other group members should make sure that English-as-a-second-language (ESL) members are fully included. Strategies for helping non-native speakers feel included are (1) providing written information in advance, (2) asking someone in the group to take notes that can be copied and distributed to all, (3) viewing difference as a group strength, and (4) matching tasks to members' abilities.

Finding out the strengths of all group members is important. Second-language speakers may not speak as often, but this does not mean they do not have highly developed skills in other areas, like computers, artwork, record keeping, and so on. Finding each member's strengths and using them to the group's advantage demonstrate effective and ethical leadership. If you are a non-native speaker, practice being assertive. Ask questions when something is not clear to you. Let others know about skills you have that could be useful to the group.

some can be combined into meaningful categories—for example, ideas related to location, to cost, or to accessibility. Solutions failing to meet absolute or important criteria are quickly eliminated, with the primary focus on those that meet absolute criteria. Later in the chapter, you will read about managing conflict in groups, as conflict can easily arise during group problem solving and decision making.

**Implementing the Plan** After your group has spent a significant amount of time considering group goals, project criteria, and each possible idea or recommendation, it is time to test or fully implement ideas. If you have enough time, you might test some of your ideas with a smaller group of people who can provide feedback. Organizations do this all the time in what are called focus groups. Focus groups help companies refine product development, testing, and implementation. For example, if you are hoping to get other college students interested in attending a charity event you are planning, you might form a small group of students who meet your ideal target market and ask them to give you feedback. They can tell you if they would come to your event or what they think of your promotional materials. You might explore how you could adapt your plan to make it more appealing to them. Once the group feels comfortable with the plan that has been developed, members should consider the best way to implement it and decide who will take on the various responsibilities for carrying it out.

**Evaluating the Outcomes Based on the Original Criteria** After you have carried out your plan, you will need to reconvene as a group to evaluate it. The group should discuss and analyze how the outcome compared with its expectations. Did the group meet its goals? What can be learned from project implementation that can be carried into future projects? Engaging in this type of cyclical learning and evaluation at the end of a project helps ensure that groups continue to grow and learn in their work together.

## ORGANIZATIONAL LEADERSHIP

As you work in groups, whether in the workplace or elsewhere, you will have opportunities to be a leader and even more opportunities to be led. What makes a good leader? Is leadership a skill people are born with? Can anyone learn to be a leader? As you will see, leadership by and large depends on effective communication skills.

### Communication Skills for Leaders

People sometimes use the terms *leadership* and *management* interchangeably. Although some leaders perform management functions and vice versa, the roles and functions of leaders versus managers differ in significant ways. As Figure 8.2 demonstrates, **leadership** is *the process of using communication to influence the behaviors and attitudes of others*, whereas **management** is *the process of using communication to maintain structure, order, harmony, and the efficacy of procedures and practices.*

Think about the role of the president of the United States. This leader is expected to establish a vision and use language in a way that excites others to be a part of that vision. A manager, on the other hand, monitors the organization and removes obstacles that prevent the execution of a leader's vision. Managers ensure that employees come to work on time, follow proper protocol and procedures for getting things done, and execute the organizational priorities as outlined.

Research highlights the following as some of the most important communication competencies associated with leadership:

**Figure 8.2** Leadership vs. Management

| Leaders and Leadership | Managers and Management |
|---|---|
| ■ **Leadership** is *the process of using communication to influence the behaviors and attitudes of others.*[23] | ■ **Management** is *the process of using communication to maintain structure, order, harmony, and the efficacy of procedures and practices.* |
| ■ Leaders challenge the status quo and establish a strong vision for the future. Leaders motivate and inspire people toward the established change initiatives. | ■ Managers maintain the status quo. They monitor the organization and remove obstacles that prevent the execution of established priorities. |

- The ability to communicate ideas to the group clearly and appropriately without dominating the conversation
- The ability to communicate a clear grasp of the task facing the group
- The ability to facilitate discussion
- The ability to encourage dialogue rather than forcing their own ideas on the group
- The ability to place group needs over personal concerns
- The ability to display respect for others during interaction
- The ability to share in the successes and failures of the group [24]

## Types of Power and Leadership

In general, people become leaders in one of two ways: they are designated as such or they emerge. A **designated leader** is *someone who has been appointed or elected to a leadership position* (such as a chair, team leader, coordinator, or facilitator). An **emergent leader** is *someone who exerts influence toward the achievement of a group's goal but who does not hold the formal position or role of leader.*

Having a designated leader can add stability to a group, but emergent leaders have their value as well. For example, a designated leader can focus resources and energy on central priorities, so that others in the group can focus on other functions. An emergent leader can be helpful for groups that confront a range of issues; moreover, it is nice for different people to step up to the front and lead the team from time to time, depending on the new challenge or issue. For example, a group of faculty members might be asked to develop a new recruiting strategy, and the person in the group with the most knowledge in this area might emerge as the leader. Then, when the group is asked to revise graduate student practices, someone more versed in that area can lead the group. As is the case with roles and types of groups, emergent leaders may also turn into designated leaders.

How do leaders, designated or emergent, gain their ability to influence others? They do this through the use of **power,** which is *the ability to influence others.*[25] In general, leaders use five kinds of power:

- *Reward power* is based on the ability to give followers what they want and need—for example, a leader who often uses pay bonuses to show appreciation for a job well done.
- *Punishment power* is based on the ability to withhold from followers what they want and need. An extreme form of punishment power is **coercion,** in which *compliance is forced through hostile acts.* A prime example is a parent who tries to get a child to comply by threatening to take away privileges, such as use of the Internet. Employers can threaten demotions or termination.

- *Referent power* is based on others' admiration and respect. Charisma is an extreme form of referent power that inspires strong loyalty and devotion from others. Your professors have referent power due to their ability to influence potential employers on your behalf through recommendations.

- *Expert power* is based on knowledge or expertise. A person who is sought out for a company because he or she has an established record for knowing how to implement new ideas has expert power. As students studying a specialized area or field, you are increasing your expert power.

- *Legitimate power* is given to a person because of a title, position, or role. Although legitimate power is important in influencing people, it is most effective when used in tandem with other bases of power. Consider a child who asks a parent why she has to go to bed at 8 PM. If the parent responds, "Because I say so," the child is more likely to rebel than if the parent also uses expert power to explain the reasons behind family rules.[26]

Depending on the kinds of power they use and the way they use it, leaders can be classified as one of three basic types: democratic, laissez-faire, or autocratic.

- *Democratic leaders* encourage members to participate in group decisions, even major ones. For example, a democratic leader asks, "What suggestions do you have for solving our problem?"

- *Laissez-faire leaders* take almost no initiative in structuring group discussions or actions. A laissez-faire leader is more like a nonleader, who is likely to say something along the lines of "I don't care; whatever you want to do is fine with me."

- *Autocratic leaders* maintain strict control over their group, including making assignments and giving orders. A typical autocratic leader says, "Here's how we'll solve the problem. First, you will . . ." Autocratic leaders ask fewer questions than do democratic leaders but they answer more; compared with democratic leaders, they make more attempts to coerce and fewer attempts to get others to participate.[27]

Groups vary in the amount of structure and control their members want and need, but research findings about style have been consistent. Most people in the United States prefer democratic groups and are more satisfied in democratically rather than autocratically led groups.[28] However, most scholars believe that the style should match the needs of the situation. For example, if you are in a group working on a class project and the deadline is tomorrow, a democratic leadership style might not be effective, because it takes longer to generate decisions.

## CULTIVATING POSITIVE RELATIONSHIPS IN SMALL GROUPS

Many issues that arise in the work environment, and in all small groups, can bring about conflict. You can learn to interact in ways that will minimize the occurrence of conflict, and you can cultivate strategies for dealing with conflict when it does arise. There is much you can do to interact in small groups in ways that will help move effective group processes forward. We begin by reviewing strategies that may help minimize conflict among group members through more effective small-group interactions.

## Interacting Effectively in Small Groups

Each member of a group must take responsibility to support the group's functions and to interact in ways that will advance group processes. How can you best do that? The ability to speak with polish is not essential, but the ability to speak clearly is. The following advice will help you interact effectively in small groups and teams, whether at work or elsewhere.

1. *Relate your statements to preceding remarks.* Clarify the relevance of your remarks to the topic by linking them to an idea raised by another group member:
   - Briefly mention the previous speaker's point—for example, "I want to piggyback on Bill's comment by noting that we can meet our goal by . . ."
   - Then state your own point clearly and concisely.
   - Summarize how your point adds to the comments made by others—for example, "I agree with Bill. We need to fund-raise, but we can't get so caught up in raising money that we forget about our goal of volunteering."

2. *Communicate your ideas with clear and simple language.* You don't need to impress others with your vocabulary or long, complex sentences. For example, you don't need to say, "I unequivocally recognize the meaningful contribution made by my colleague." Saying "I agree" works just as well. Here are some guidelines for communicating simply and clearly in group discussions:
   - After connecting your idea to that of the previous speaker, state your point and then provide one piece of supporting information or additional explanation.
   - Give group members a context for your remarks. Not all comments are critical; some are just ideas. Letting others know how you intend your remark to be taken—that is, as a recommendation for going forward, a critical piece of evidence, or an idea for brainstorming—may influence how they react and respond.
   - When done, ask if anyone needs you to clarify your point.

3. *Get to the point quickly.* Don't be long-winded. The main advantage of small groups is their ability to approach a problem interactively and hear multiple points of view on a topic. If you monopolize the discussion, or leave little time for others to contribute to the group dialogue, that advantage may be diminished or lost completely. To learn to speak concisely, try the following:

- Write down your idea before speaking. People tend to be wordier when they are trying to figure out what they want to say. If you've thought it out ahead of time, you'll be able to get right to the point.

- Try to talk for no more than one minute at a time. Of course, this time limit is arbitrary; however, one minute should be enough time to get an idea out for consideration, and you can always answer questions to clarify as needed.

4. *State one point at a time.* A group member making a presentation may certainly state several points. However, during give-and-take discussion, stating only one idea promotes efficiency and allows others to respond:

- As a group, appoint a process observer to keep the discussion moving and to prevent any member from bringing up more than one idea at a time. After the process observer intervenes a few times, these behaviors become second nature.

- If you have several ideas, provide the less important points to group members in written form for later reflection. Save discussion time for the most important ideas.

By following these simple strategies, you establish norms that allow your small group to function effectively, and you take advantage of all members' expertise.

### Achieving Communication Competence

Every workplace, as well as every small group, includes a variety of people, each with a unique personality. Maintaining positive relationships with all these individuals can be a challenge requiring effective verbal and nonverbal communication skills. Three key communication qualities can enhance workplace relationships: immediacy, supportiveness, and interaction management.

**Immediacy** When people engage in *communication behaviors intended to create perceptions of psychological closeness with others,* they are enacting **immediacy.** Immediacy can be created both verbally and nonverbally. Calling people by their first names, using "we" language, and telling stories are verbal behaviors that promote immediacy. Smiling, reducing the physical distance between those in the interaction, and using animated gestures and facial expressions are nonverbal behaviors that promote immediacy.

Using immediacy has been shown to have positive effects in the workplace. For instance, it can improve the relationship between supervisors and subordinates[29] and encourage people to engage in higher levels of self-disclosure.[30] Immediacy reflects the popular notion that it is not necessarily what you say but how you say it that matters.

**Supportiveness** People engage in **supportive communication** when they *listen with empathy, acknowledge the feelings of others, and* *engage in dialogue to help others maintain a sense of personal control.* Of course, supportive communication is an important skill in all contexts. To enhance your supportive communication skills, consider the following strategies.

1. *Listen without judging.* Being judgmental while listening to a co-worker's explanation of a problem can cause you to lose your focus on what he is really saying.

2. *Validate feelings.* Even if you disagree with something your co-workers say, validating their perceptions and feelings—for example, "What you're saying makes a lot of sense, Maria"—is an important step in building a trusting relationship.

3. *Provide both informational and relational messages.* Supportive communication includes both helping and healing messages. Simply listening to someone vent is as important as providing advice.

4. *Be confidential.* When co-workers share feelings and personal reflections, maintaining their trust is essential. Telling others or gossiping will destroy your credibility as a trustworthy co-worker. [31]

**Interaction Management** Workplace communication is somewhat different from other types of communication situations, because conversations tend to flow between the technical jargon associated with the workplace and other topics brought up to relieve stress and pass time. Thus, computer technicians might talk about megabytes and megapixels one minute and speculate about who will be voted off *Dancing with the Stars* the next. But this kind of topic switching can occur in any group setting—for example, when people switch topics from their personal lives to tasks that need attention.

Competent communicators engage in interaction management, which is an approach to communication that allows a clear flow between topics and ideas and in which people are aware of the communication styles and preferences of those around them and adapt appropriately. Pausing, changing pitch, listening carefully, and responding appropriately are skills related to interaction management. Being an effective communicator with co-workers and clients, or in any group, requires carefully observing the communication preferences of others. Recognizing that one person is consistently task-focused, whereas another always likes to chit-chat about family is important; adapting your interactions will help you fit in and achieve individual and group objectives.

## Managing Conflict

Communicating in organizations is not easy. In fact, a pervasive part of organizational life is conflict, both destructive and productive. Destructive conflict can harm relationships, whereas productive conflict can create a needed impetus for organizational change and development. People often view conflict negatively because they associate it with anger. However, **conflict** *occurs anytime two or more people have goals they perceive to be incompatible.* When one employee wants to work late to finish a joint project but another wants to go home to be with his family, conflict can occur. In short, conflict is a fact of life, the rule rather than the exception. You can use a variety of techniques to manage conflict productively,[32] including any of those listed and described in Table 8.5.

In addition to the general techniques in Table 8.5 for managing conflict, consider the tips in Table 8.6 related to conflict and communication throughout your career in groups and teams where people will have differences of opinion.

### Preparing for Ethical Dilemmas

You are likely to encounter several types of ethical dilemmas in organizations. Three common ones are aggressive communication, dishonesty, and sexual harassment.

When working in organizations, particularly those with a customer service focus, it is not uncommon to encounter situations in which anger turns to aggression. **Verbal aggressiveness** is *communication that attacks the self-concepts of other people in order to inflict psychological pain.*[33] This kind of aggression is common in organizational settings, although it is sometimes unrecognized by management. A recent summary of literature on workplace aggression identified the following types, some of which overlap:

- *Abusive supervision.* This occurs when a supervisor engages in sustained hostile behavior, both verbal and nonverbal. This does not, however, rise to the level of physical aggression.

| Table 8.5 | A Variety of Techniques for Managing Conflict |
|---|---|
| Avoidance | ■ In using the avoidance style, you deny the existence of conflict or work around it. Although avoidance can provide time to think through a situation, continued avoidance allows conflict to simmer and flare up with more intensity. |
| Competition | ■ In using the competition style, you view conflict as a battle and advance your own interests over those of others. Although competition may work for some situations, if your co-workers perceive that you view conflict as a win–lose situation every time, and that you must always win, they may come to question whether you really listen to and value their perspectives. |
| Compromise | ■ In using the compromising style, you are willing to negotiate away some of your position as long as the other party is willing to do the same. Compromise can be an effective strategy, because both parties get at least some of what they want. |
| Accommodation | ■ In using the accommodation style, you set aside your views and accept those of others. Accommodation can maintain harmony in relationships, but sometimes at the expense of airing your own perspectives and opinions. |
| Collaboration | ■ In using the collaborative style, you rely on thoughtful negotiation and reasoned compromise whereby both parties agree that the negotiated outcome is the best possible alternative under the circumstances. Although collaboration takes more time and effort to enact, it typically results in the best possible outcome for all parties. |

**Table 8.6** Conflict Management and Communication Tips

**Not all conflict is effectively managed through more communication.** You will invariably encounter people with experiences and perspectives different from your own. Sometimes the best thing to do is agree to disagree without trying to change someone else's perspective.

- - - - - - - - - - - - - - - - - - - - - - - - - - - - - - - - - - - - - - - - - - - -

**When you do communicate about disagreements with others, listen just as much, if not more, than you speak.** Communication is interactive, dynamic, and interdependent. This means that your responses to others should be based on what they say to you. When people spend too much time thinking about what their next point will be, rather than listening to what others are contributing to the dialogue, conflicts persist.

- - - - - - - - - - - - - - - - - - - - - - - - - - - - - - - - - - - - - - - - - - - -

**Paraphrase your understanding of other people's positions as you engage in managing conflict with them.** Listen and try to understand new ideas. Sometimes simply by paraphrasing those ideas you can illuminate the source of a conflict. Also, by demonstrating that you are working to understand other people's positions, you may help them feel less guarded and defensive.

- - - - - - - - - - - - - - - - - - - - - - - - - - - - - - - - - - - - - - - - - - - -

**Not every conflict is resolvable.** This is why the term *conflict* management is preferred over conflict *resolution*. Sometimes a resolution is not needed. People might simply need you to listen to what they have to say. By listening, you validate others' feelings.

- - - - - - - - - - - - - - - - - - - - - - - - - - - - - - - - - - - - - - - - - - - -

**Do not engage in conflict management when you are overly emotional.** You never want to say something in a conflict that you will come to regret. Avoid saying such things by telling people when you need more time and space to think before you engage in more open discussion with them.

- - - - - - - - - - - - - - - - - - - - - - - - - - - - - - - - - - - - - - - - - - - -

**When you engage in conflict management with people, use "I" language instead of "you" language.** It is easier to be open to someone else's opinions when they are phrased as individual perceptions. Refrain from speaking on behalf of large groups or making overly general claims like "everyone in this group thinks you're a slacker." Statements like this cause defensiveness and are unproductive. You might instead say something like "I feel you can make stronger contributions to this project."

- - - - - - - - - - - - - - - - - - - - - - - - - - - - - - - - - - - - - - - - - - - -

**Learn to separate conflict disagreements from the person airing the conflict.** It is possible to dislike an idea and still highly value the person who contributed it. Be mindful of your nonverbal messages as you engage in conflict management, and remember that messages contain a content dimension as well as a relational one. When interacting with people who are unable to separate conflict disagreements from the person airing the conflict, be more cautious in what you say. You may even decide that more discussion is counterproductive.

- *Bullying.* Bullying occurs when *one or more individuals ridicule, make offensive statements to or about, tease, socially isolate, or otherwise abuse one or more other individuals over an extended period of time.*

- *Incivility.* This occurs when a person demonstrates frequent rude behavior that may or may not have the intent of being harmful. Uncivil people may or may not know they are being rude.

- *Social undermining.* Whereas incivility can occur unwittingly, **social undermining** is intentional and often planned. It is an *action meant to socially isolate another person from a larger group.* [34]

Verbal aggressiveness can cause embarrassment, feelings of inadequacy, humiliation, hopelessness, despair, and depression. If you feel you are the victim of workplace aggression, consult a human resources manager, a union representative, or a trusted manager for advice.

Several high-profile events during the recent economic crisis underscored the impact of dishonesty in organizational communication. Specifically, financial institutions were blamed for not being honest when extending risky mortgages to individuals who went on to purchase homes they could not afford. The widespread lack of honesty and ethics played a large role in eroding consumer confidence during the crisis. All organizational members share the responsibility for behaving and communicating with honesty. When you suspect someone is being dishonest, it is important to say something to the individual and not allow people to practice unethical behavior. This type of assertive communication skill can be difficult, but it is critical in preventing a culture in which dishonest behaviors and interactions are commonplace. The fears that drive people to dishonest behaviors at work (e.g., the fear of offending a colleague or the fear of embarrassment for admitting when they're wrong) can often be countered by establishing open communication with co-workers.

**Sexual harassment** is a form of workplace aggression, defined by the Equal Employment Opportunity Commission (EEOC) as

> unwelcome sexual advances, requests for sexual favors, and other verbal or physical conduct of a sexual nature if (1) submission to the conduct is made a condition of employment, (2) submission to or rejection of the conduct is made the basis for an employment decision, or (3) the conduct seriously affects an employee's work performance or creates an intimidating, hostile, or offensive working environment.[35]

Simply put, *sexual harassment is unwelcome, unsolicited, repeated behavior of a sexual nature.* The EEOC definition outlines two, sometimes overlapping types of sexual harassment. The first type, quid pro quo, occurs when an employee is offered a reward or is threatened with punishment based on his or her participation in a sexual activity. For example, a supervisor might say, "I'll give you Friday off if you meet me at my place tonight." The second type of sexual harassment creates a hostile work environment, meaning that conditions in the workplace are sexually offensive, intimidating, or hostile and affect job performance. For example, if two males talk explicitly about the physical features of a female colleague in her presence, and she is offended by this exchange, sexual harassment has occurred.

A major obstacle to ending sexual harassment is the tendency of victims to avoid confronting the harasser. Most instances of sexual harassment are neither exposed nor reported. Instead, the victim usually avoids the situation by taking time off, transferring to another area, or changing jobs. The perpetrator is usually someone with authority and status—with power over the victim—

and the victim feels that exposure or confrontation will backfire. Organizations take sexual harassment very seriously, and most have confidential channels for reporting problems. Although unpleasant to confront, sexual harassment must be reported through the appropriate organizational channels.

Although not all ethical issues can be eliminated with effective communication practices, some of the strategies recommended throughout this chapter can create a more positive and enjoyable work environment. Why do we end this chapter by discussing some of these negative aspects of organizational workplace culture? Such discussions may empower you to take a confident stance if you observe someone isolating another person in an organization or engaging in unproductive and aggressive communication practices.

 **CHAPTER REVIEW**

This chapter provided you with a foundation for communicating in organizations and small groups of various types and sizes. You learned how to assess an organization's culture to determine the roles and norms that move its processes forward. You also learned how to approach and resolve conflict, a skill that is as important to the small group situation as it is to your one-on-one interpersonal relationships. Finally, you now have a better understanding of what is meant by leadership and how to enact the role of a leader effectively and ethically. With all these skills, you will be well prepared to work in groups in the classroom and workplace. As you move forward with your career, use all of these skills to determine your own role within your organization and to cultivate positive relationships with those around you.

## KEY TERMS

coercion, 148
cohesiveness, 143
conflict, 152
criteria, 145
designated leader, 148
differentiation and specialization, 134
emergent leader, 148
formal communication, 135
formalization, 135
formal (positional) role, 140

group climate, 141
groupthink, 143
hierarchy, 133
immediacy, 151
informal (behavioral) role, 141
informal communication, 137
interdependent, 138
leadership, 147
maintenance functions, 141
management, 147

norms, 139
organizational culture, 131
power, 148
role, 140
self-centered functions, 141
sexual harassment, 155
small-group communication, 138

social undermining, 154
strategic ambiguity, 135
supportive communication, 151
task functions, 141
trust, 143
verbal aggressiveness, 153

## STUDY QUESTIONS

1. Discuss the three main ways you can analyze an organization to learn about its culture. Use one of these methods to analyze the organization of your school.

2. Identify a few concrete strategies for interacting in small groups, and explain why these strategies would improve group functioning overall.

3. What is the difference between management and leadership? What role does communication play in enacting this difference?

4. What are three strategies for cultivating positive relationships in organizations?

# part 3

# Public Speaking Basics

In this section you will learn skills that will help you be a more competent communicator in public settings. You will learn how to select a topic and how to analyze an audience, as well as how to organize your presentation and gather information and supporting materials. Finally, you will learn about how you can apply delivery skills to overcome the very natural fear of public speaking.

# Topic Selection and Audience Analysis

Imagine that you have been asked to provide a talk for a class at your local high school. You are given a great deal of freedom on the topic. How do you decide on the subject matter? How will you narrow the scope of the topic you choose? Often deciding on an appropriate topic will depend on the audience you are going to address. In this chapter, we will consider the best steps to take when choosing a topic that is right for you and your audience.

LEARNING OBJECTIVES

*After reading this chapter, you should be able to:*

- Know how to select an appropriate topic.
- Explain strategies for narrowing your topic.
- Use observation, inference, questionnaires, and the Internet to analyze your audience.
- Apply three levels of analysis to discover specifics about your audience.
- Demonstrate how to adapt yourself, your language, your topic, your purpose, and your thesis statement to your audience.

## HOW TO SELECT AN APPROPRIATE TOPIC

Finding a topic that is right for you and your audience can be a challenge for a beginning speaker. Some speakers spend far too little time finding a suitable topic and end up speaking on something that audience members cannot connect with; others spend too long searching for topics, get forced into making a last-minute decision, and sacrifice valuable preparation time. Although you should devote adequate attention to thoughtful topic selection, this step should require only a small amount of your speech preparation time. In this section you will learn some strategies for making an efficient, effective choice, beginning with two ways to quickly generate a list of ideas.

### Survey Your Interests

Public speaking starts with the self—with what you know, have experienced, or are willing to learn. To survey your interests, consider

- What do you like best and least at work, about family life, about your community, and about our government, politics, and policies?

- How do you spend your leisure time—what do you like to read, what kinds of movies do you enjoy, and what television programs do you watch regularly?

- Do you enjoy sports and exercise? Do you regularly attend, or watch, certain sports but ignore others? Do you enjoy working out?

- What causes take up your time and energy? Do you work for environmental groups, do you care about the disparity between the rich and the poor, or do you buy only organic food?

- What particular issues bother you personally that you want to bring to the attention of others: discrimination, environmental concerns, or access to healthcare, for example?

If you choose a topic that is important to you, you will already know more about it than you will know about a topic you simply choose at random. In addition, you will be more motivated to do research on the topic and learn even more about it. Because of your interest, you will probably speak with more gusto when you deliver your talk. You will, in turn, create more audience attention and enthusiasm.

### Use Brainstorming

After you have surveyed your interests, you might consider brainstorming to generate multiple topics on which to speak. **Brainstorming** consists of *thinking of as many topics as you can in a limited time, so that you can select one that will be appropriate for you and your audience.* Selecting a topic from a list of many you've generated through brainstorming can be much easier than trying to think of just one perfect idea. In Chapter 8 you learned about how brainstorming in a group is useful in problem solving and small-group decision making. Similarly, individual brainstorming can help you find topics for your public speeches, reports, and term papers.

Basic brainstorming is fairly straightforward, as demonstrated in the steps outlined in Figure 9.1. First, give yourself a limited amount of time, such as five minutes, and without trying to think of titles or even complete thoughts write down as many potential topics as you can. Second, select the *three* items from your list that appeal to you the most as topics for your speech. Third, from those three topics choose the *one* you think would most appeal to both you and your audience.

### Assess Your Knowledge of and Commitment to the Topic

Once you have chosen a topic that interests you, you need to determine how much more or less information about the topic you have than your audience has. Ideally, you should know more about the topic than does your audience. Next, you can add to what you know by talking to others, reading, and visiting relevant websites, resources for supporting material that are discussed in greater detail in Chapter 11.

But even a topic about which you're well informed is not a good choice for a presentation unless you feel some commitment to it. **Commitment** is *a measure of how much time and effort you put into a cause.* Do you volunteer in a childcare center, at a hospital, at the library, or at a food pantry? Have you had friends or relatives die of careless habits, diseases, or addictions? Do you work for a political party when it is time to vote?

Although important, commitment to a topic may not be enough to overcome poor preparation and speech performance. Research has found that it is not; the strongest predictor of speech performance is the work put into preparation.[1]

After all these considerations of your interest, knowledge, and commitment to the topic, you need to think about one other factor: the timeliness of the topic. Have you ever watched an old movie and observed how differently people used the telephone in the past? You no doubt observed how stylized the clothing was. You may have even noticed how much smoking occurred in the past compared with today. Technology, clothing, and behavior change over time. Similarly, topics also change over time.

**Figure 9.1** Brainstorming, a Simple but Useful Process

| List as many ideas as you can. | → | Select the three most appealing ideas. | → | Narrow to one idea most appealing to you and your audience. |

## Determine Your Topic's Age

Topics, like people, live, change, and die. You will want to consider the age and development of your subject matter, as well as the age and development of your audience. Some topics have endured for decades, if not centuries:

- How much should government be allowed to intervene in our lives?
- Should the United States use military force to promote democracy?
- What can we do for the poor and marginalized in our society?
- What can we do about the privileged and overrewarded in our society?
- Should concern for the environment limit our exploration for oil?

Although these are appropriate speech topics, the speaker might need to be diligent in determining something fresh and new about the topic.

On the other hand, some topics become dated rather quickly. You may know about the temperance movement only from a history course, and these days you don't hear many speeches on the evils of drinking alcohol. However, if you had been alive before and after the Civil War, this topic would have been relevant. Today people are more likely to speak on the ill effects of smoking or taking illegal drugs.

Think about the speeches you hear in other classes, and more particularly in your communication class. Are you likely to hear some of the same topics over and over again? You might hear a number of speeches on abortion, euthanasia, capital punishment, drunk driving, drug legalization, eating disorders, and term limits for elected officials. Familiar topics may not be the best choice. Audience members may stop listening early when they hear yet another presentation on a common topic.

At the same time, you should not believe that a topic that has recurred is always prohibited. Current events can quickly recast an overly familiar topic into one that is relevant for the present. For example, the topic of gun control may have been considered outdated a few years ago, but more recent tragedies involving guns, including the mass shootings at the Aurora, Colorado, movie theater and at Sandy Hook Elementary School in Newtown, Connecticut, render this topic highly relevant again.

## NARROW YOUR TOPIC

Many beginning speakers choose a topic that is too broad for their time limit. Animal cruelty, buying a car, and overcoming an addiction may meet the requirements of importance, knowledge, and commitment, but they are too broad. If you carefully narrow a topic *before* you begin your search for

| Table 9.1 | Possible Presentation Topics | |
|---|---|
| Privacy on social media sites | Keeping drugs out of sports |
| Protecting yourself from foodborne illnesses | Personality tests |
| Reducing the national debt | Computer viruses |
| Food preservatives | Violence in videogames |
| Humans' effects on the environment | Biosystems engineering |
| Benefits for vets | Who are the libertarians? |
| Genetic cloning | Changing nature of families |
| Conflict-resolution strategies | Healthy eating |
| Why tuition keeps rising | What are orphan trains? |
| Successful job hunting | Stop moving jobs overseas |

additional information, you can save much time and even more frustration. Chapter 11 describes one way to narrow your topic—*concept mapping*, a technique for visually diagramming your primary topic and subtopics and the relationships among them.

Another way is to choose a broad and even abstract category, such as love, and list as many smaller topics as you can that are loosely related to it:

- The development of love over time
- Platonic love
- Obsessive love
- Crushes and "falling in love"
- How parents can demonstrate their love for a child
- Same-sex love
- Unconditional love
- Is it possible for a person to really love another person?

How will you know when your topic is narrow enough? Consider (1) the amount of information available about it, (2) the amount of time you have for your speech, and (3) whether you can discuss the topic in enough depth to keep audience members interested.

Still another approach is to look at the examples of topics provided on the Internet. (You could look, for example, at the site "Speech Topics Help: 10,000+ Speech Topics" at www.speech-topics-help.com/.) Table 9.1 also lists some possible topics.

## AUDIENCE ANALYSIS

Next, you will need to determine your topic's importance to the audience. For example, you may be a committed environmentalist who knows a great deal about sustainable agriculture, you may have lived on a small farm, and you may have good ideas about how to practice organic farming. However, if most of your audience members have never set foot outside a large metropolitan area, you may have a challenge discussing sustainable agriculture with them. This topic probably has less relevance and importance for your audience than it does for you. **Audience analysis** is *the collection*

and interpretation of audience characteristics through observation, inference, question-naires, and the Internet. In this section we will discuss three levels of audience analysis and then four methods for gaining this information.

## Three Levels of Audience Analysis

**Captive and Voluntary Audiences** The simplest level of audience analysis is to make a distinction between captive and voluntary audiences. A **captive audience** *did not choose to hear you or your speech*; therefore, they will take more convincing than voluntary audiences. Your classmates are a largely captive audience. A **voluntary audience** *choose to hear you speak about a particular topic*. A voluntary audience is easier to manage, because they actually seek information or ideas. A captive audience may recognize that they have no choice but to listen to your talk. They might be less critical and more agreeable than a voluntary audience. A voluntary audience, on the other hand, may have higher expecta-tions for a speaker, since they took time or paid money to hear the speech. At the same time, they may already agree with the topic and the speaker's point of view, since they volunteered to be part of the audience.

**Demographics** The second level of audience analysis involves discovering the audience's demographics. The term *demographics* means "the characteristics of the people." **Demographic analysis** is *the collection and interpretation of data such as name, age, sex, hometown, year in school, race, major subject, religion, and organiza-tional affiliations.* Seasoned public speakers usually rely heavily on demographic information. You can collect demographic analysis through observation, infer-ence, questionnaires, and the Internet.

A skilled speaker may guess that people who are Unitarian are open to mul-tiple ideas. Students majoring in engineering may be highly logical and seek scientific explanations, whereas those in the humanities value narrative as proof and appreciate artistic strokes in language. Older people may be more likely to be widely traveled but also more set in their beliefs. Younger people may be less experienced but more adaptive to new technology. These judgments, of course, are not universal; we all need to be careful not to stereotype, a topic covered in Chapter 6, on intercultural communication. A knowledgeable speaker wisely goes on to learn more about the audience's attitudes, beliefs, and values than simply relying on demographic information.

**Attitudes, Beliefs, and Values** The third level of audience analysis is to discern the audience's attitudes, beliefs, and values on an issue before giving the speech. How can you learn about these matters? Questionnaires and the Internet might be most useful as methods of discovery.

An **attitude** is *a predisposition to respond favorably or unfavorably to a person, an object, an idea, or an event*. Attitudes are quite stable and often difficult to change. You can assess the attitudes of audience members through questionnaires, as mentioned earlier; careful observation; or even informal conversations in which you ask the right questions. The following are some examples of attitudes:

| | | |
|---|---|---|
| Anti-government | Pro-business | Pro-conservation |
| Anti-gun control | Pro-green | Pro-technology |
| Anti-pollution | Pro-choice | Pro-diversity |
| Anti-immigration | Pro-life | Anti-refugee |
| Pro-animal rights | Anti-tax | Pro-free trade |

For example, if you know that many of your classmates are pro-immigration and a few are originally from Mexico, you would be wise to steer clear of that discussion if your attitudes conflict with theirs. And if some of the women in your class enjoy telling stories about their grandmothers' and mothers' feminist activity in the 1960s, you probably do not want to share your conservative views about women's rights. You might also conclude that these women are probably liberal on the rights of other groups and avoid speaking against abortion and gay rights.

A **belief** is *a conviction*. Beliefs are usually more enduring than attitudes, but our attitudes often spring from our beliefs. Some examples of beliefs follow:

Hard work pays off.

Good people will go to heaven.

Taxes are too high.

Work comes before play.

Anyone can get rich.

Government should be small.

Education pays.

Wickedness will be punished.

Knowing your audience's beliefs about your topic can be a valuable aid in informing and persuading them.

The strength of beliefs suggests that they are important to know about the people with whom you interact. Have you

## GLOBALLY

### SEEK HUMAN VALUES

Some colleges have such diverse audiences that audience analysis seems impossible. Even different parts of the United States exhibit differences. The South, for example, has a reputation for being more polite, less aggressive, and less direct in trying to influence others.[2] Although challenging, an audience with a rich mix of races, religions, and languages invites the speaker to find topics that we relate to as human beings. Most people of the world seek safety, security, food, shelter, and loving relationships.

Many other values are highly variable. Where does a person go when he is in trouble? To whom do you go as a last resort? Does anyone provide for others over a lifetime, or can we expect support and nurturance for only a period of time? Should we expect that some people will sacrifice for us? Should we sacrifice for others? Who has the final say in your social network? Should it be the oldest person, the youngest person, the loudest person, or the most credible person? Even our most intimate relationships are viewed differently across social groups and cultures.

COMMUNICATING

ever had a conversation with someone who bashed your beliefs? She may have ridiculed the president of the United States or a senator or representative for whom you campaigned. She may have stated that the current healthcare system will not work, it is too expensive, and most people do not understand how to receive quality care. She may have added that people should pay for their health-care and that, if they cannot afford it, they do not deserve it. Unknowingly, she is disagreeing with your beliefs. This is even more pronounced in a public speech.

A **value** is *a deeply rooted belief that governs our attitude about something.* Both beliefs and attitudes can be traced to a value we hold. A questionnaire for ranking values is provided in the section on methods of analyzing the audience.

The values your audience members hold and the order in which they rank them can provide important clues about their attitudes and beliefs. The relationships among attitudes, beliefs, and values are illustrated in Figure 9.2. If you know that many of your classmates are majoring in business, you might infer that they hold the attitudes, beliefs, and values in Figure 9.2. On the other hand, what if most of the students in your class are philosophy majors who want to become more educated simply because they love ideas and new knowledge?

**Figure 9.2** The Relationship Among Attitudes, Beliefs, and Values

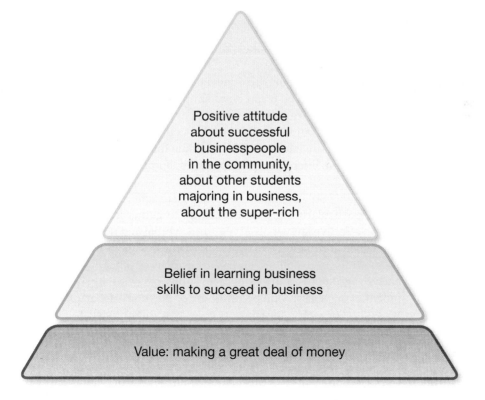

Positive attitude about successful businesspeople in the community, about other students majoring in business, about the super-rich

Belief in learning business skills to succeed in business

Value: making a great deal of money

# BUILDER

## "SIZE UP" YOUR AUDIENCE

Some of us are better than others at sizing up an audience. Whatever your skill level, you should practice analyzing audience characteristics. You might learn about the audience by looking at them, listening to their informal conversations, or observing their changes in behavior in response to other speakers. For example, ask yourself the following questions:

- What is the approximate age range of the audience?
- What cultures and ethnicities are represented?
- How many audience members commute to school versus living on campus?
- How many have traveled to other parts of the world?
- How many are active in campus or community organizations?

If they are music majors and are not planning on teaching music, what might you infer? Simply knowing the majors of your classmates may provide you with helpful information and a start on understanding what they value. This knowledge, in turn, helps you avoid some topics and consider others.

### Four Methods of Audience Analysis

Why should you analyze your audience? Suppose you are giving a speech arguing that a state should not take away an individual's right to belong to a union. To give an effective presentation, you should know not only state law (some states prohibit unions by denying workers the right to strike) but also how most of the individuals in your audience feel about unionization. If they agree with your view, you will probably take a different persuasive approach than if they disagree.

Audience analysis for public speaking is similar to target marketing in advertising and public relations. It can be as simple as "eyeballing" a group to estimate their age, sex, and race or as complicated as polling a group of people to discover their feelings on your topic. The insights you gain about them will help you make your speech more effective. Let's examine four methods of analyzing an audience: observation, inference, questionnaires, and the Internet.

**Observation** Effective public speakers must engage in active observation, using their five senses—particularly sight and hearing—to gather information about their audience. An effective lawyer observes jurors' verbal and nonverbal behavior and decides which arguments, evidence, and witnesses are influencing them. Activists and fundraisers usually spend years watching others and learning which approaches, arguments, and evidence an audience is most likely to accept.

As a student, your classroom presents an opportunity to acquire these observational skills. For every speech you give, you might listen to 20 or 25 given by others, each of which gives you a unique opportunity to discover your classmates' responses. Do they prefer speakers who come on strong or speakers who talk to them as equals? Do they like speeches about work, leisure, or ambition? Do they respond well to numbers and statistics, stories and examples, graphs and posters, or PowerPoint and Prezi? Observing and recording your classmates' responses to a variety of speakers, topics, and visual resources will give you a rich base of information about this audience.

**Inference** To draw an **inference** is to make *a tentative generalization based on some evidence.* The more evidence on which an inference is based, the more likely it is to be accurate. We infer from a man's wedding band that he is married, and from a fellow student's military uniform that she has served in the army. We are basing these inferences on thin data, but they are probably correct.

An *indirect* inference is one we draw by observation. You might, for example, have noticed that most of the students at your college hold part-time jobs (an observation). You might infer that most students, like you, find the school expensive, the financial aid to be limited, and the cost of area housing high. If students need to work, you might avoid persuasive topics that encourage your classmates to engage in expensive hobbies and recreational activities. Instead, you might consider topics such as "good food on a budget," "ways to have fun without spending any money," and "how budgeting can work for you."

A *direct* inference is based on deliberately gathered data. You could ask either orally or in writing how many students in the class have part- or full-time jobs; how many are married, have families, and/or have grown children; how many hope to become wealthy; whether they were raised in an urban or a rural setting; and how many have strong religious ties. The answers to these questions provide valuable information about your audience.

**Questionnaires** A more formal way to collect data on which you can base inferences is to ask your audience to fill out a **questionnaire** in which you present *questions developed to obtain demographic and attitudinal information.*

You can gather and summarize demographic information from questions similar to the following:

_____ 1. I am a
     a. first-year student.
     b. sophomore.
     c. junior.
     d. senior.

_____ 2. I am
     a. 17–21 years old.
     b. 22–35 years old.
     c. 36–45 years old.
     d. over 45.

_____ 3. I am
     a. single.
     b. married.
     c. divorced or separated.
     d. widowed.

_____ 4. I have
     a. no children.
     b. one child.
     c. two children.
     d. more than two children.

The audience members do not have to identify themselves by name to provide this information. In fact, keeping the questionnaires anonymous encourages honest answers and does not reduce the value of the information. You do not need advanced math skills to find helpful information in such a questionnaire. Simply note the categories that are most common—for example, most students are married and have children. Note the categories into which no one falls. If most of the students are single and have no children, a speech on daycare, nutrition for babies and young children, or how to balance school, career, and your personal life is probably not appropriate.

You can collect attitudinal information in at least three ways. One way is to ask questions that place audience members in identifiable groups, as these questions do:

_____5. I am

    a.  active in campus organizations.

    b.  not active in campus organizations.

_____6. I see myself as politically

    a.  conservative.

    b.  liberal.

    c.  independent.

_____7. I see myself as

    a.  strongly religious.

    b.  moderately religious.

    c.  not religious.

 **MEDIA**

CONSIDERING

## PRACTICE INFORMATION LITERACY THROUGH USER-GENERATED CONTENT

Social media can be a helpful tool when it comes to framing a speech topic and deciding what information to explore further. Consider the two most popular social media platforms, Facebook and Twitter. As you research and prepare your speech, how might you make use of their unique functionalities? Here are two ideas:

- *Survey your Facebook network.* Ask friends what information they think your audience is likely to know and/or not know about your topic. Their answers will help guide your library research.
- *Check out Twitter.* Twitter is especially helpful for learning about trends in people's thinking about a particular topic. Use the Twitter search function to see what people are currently saying about your topic.

However you decide to explore your topic, keep an open mind. The information you find on social media can also guide you to other sources. Don't stop your search after you land at a relevant organization's Facebook page. Explore that page for links to other resources related to your topic.

The second way to gain attitudinal information is to ask people to rank their values, using a scale like that in Table 9.2. These rankings can provide additional information about the audience's attitudes and beliefs. If you can persuade some of your classmates, or the entire class, to do this, you will have information to help you prepare your speech. How does your ranking compare with those of your classmates? What other values might help you with your speech?[3]

The third way to collect data about people's attitudes is to list concepts and then ask the respondents their attitudes toward them, such as by using an attitudinal scale like the one in Table 9.3. The respondents' reactions to these and similar words or phrases can provide information that will help you adapt your speech to your audience.

Compile data that indicate the attitudes within your class on one of the topics listed in Table 9.3. What does this information tell you about how to approach your audience on this topic? Clearly, if the audience is sympathetic to your position, you will need to do less to inform them about the idea. You can also go further in persuading them to be even more proactive on the issue than they have been. If they are opposed to your ideas, you will need to offer both sides of the information, if informing, and/or a two-sided appeal, if persuading. Even though you might feel strongly about legalizing a lower drinking age, a majority of your classmates may disagree. You do not have to reject your topic, but you will need to tailor it for an audience with attitudes that are different from yours. The information you can gain through questionnaires is invaluable and may outweigh the effort you make to gather it.

**Table 9.2   Ranking Values**

Rank-order five of the following values in their order of importance to you, with 1 being the most important and 5 being the least.

| ____ Wisdom | ____ Wealth | ____ Fame |
|---|---|---|
| ____ A world at peace | ____ Security | ____ Health |
| ____ Freedom | ____ Fulfillment | ____ Love |
| ____ Equality | ____ Education | ____ Faith |

**Table 9.3   Attitudinal Scale**

Next to each word or phrase, indicate your attitude toward it by writing in the appropriate number:
(1) strongly favor, (2) mildly favor, (3) neutral, (4) mildly disfavor, or (5) strongly disfavor.

____    a. Internet censorship

____    b. Government bailouts of business

____    c. Gun control

____    d. Stricter immigration policies

____    e. Healthcare reform

____    f. Lowered drinking age

____    g. Military spending

____    h. Medical marijuana

**The Internet**  The Internet offers considerable information about the characteristics of first-year college students, including their attitudes, beliefs, and

values, as well as how they spend their time. For example, www.city-data
.com provides demographic data for the town or city you are researching.
Information is provided about the area's levels of income, levels of education,
and amount of crime committed. You can also learn about the marital status
and sexual orientation of the people in the city or town. Finally, you can find
out what kinds of automobiles people drive and the lengths of the commute
they have.

Another website, which is both useful and entertaining, is www.claritas
.com/MyBestSegments. On this site you can enter a zip code to learn about the
largest segments of people, cleverly titled "Simple Pleasures," "Young and Rus-
tic," and "Golden Ponds." You will learn that "young and rustics" tend to be
renters with lower to middle incomes, households without children, and some
college education. These demographic groups can be further probed for detailed
information.

In addition, the websites of many universities provide a detailed study of
their students, going beyond surface demographics—for example, the ratio of
males to females and the number of international students. Each college and
university displays this information in different places on its website, but you
will not have difficulty locating it. In short, the Internet can be a source of information on your classroom audience.

### Tips for Analyzing Your Audience

In addition to the methods of audience analysis described in this section, take
some time before you speak to consider some basic questions regarding what
you know about the audience. You can use the following questions as a kind of
checklist, referring back to it at different points in the speech preparation process.

1. Who invited you to speak? What is the relationship between this person (or
   these people) and the audience? Is the audience likely to be eager to hear
   you, or are they required to attend?
2. What can the person who invited you to speak tell you about the audience?
   Will this person be biased, or can you trust her information?
3. Where will you be speaking? Does the environment offer a warm, hospita-
   ble atmosphere? Is the room arranged so audience members will be actively
   listening to you, or are they likely to be distracted by others, by their phones,
   or by other noise in the environment?
4. How are the audience members similar to or different from you? Establish
   your commonalities and consider how you can build on them.
5. What do you know about their backgrounds, hometowns, experiences, and
   attitudes? Can you link these to your topic and main points?
6. Do their beliefs and values line up with yours? How can you emphasize
   these areas of agreement? If they do not, how can you show that your differences are not important?

## ADAPT TO THE AUDIENCE

Audience analysis yields information about your listeners that enables you to adapt yourself and your message. A speech is not imposed on a collection of listeners; a message is negotiated between a speaker and an audience. Actually, communicators often adapt to their audience's characteristics, even when they are unaware that they are doing so.[4] You cannot be successful at public speaking unless you are willing to learn about your potential audience and adapt to them.

### Adapting Yourself

A number of studies have demonstrated the positive effects of adapting to the audience's attitudes: the audience has better recollection of the message, better feelings about the speaker, and attitudes consistent with those of the speaker.[5] A public speaker prepares for an audience by adapting to their expectations. How you look, how you behave, and what you say should be carefully tailored to your audience. You might speak informally and in casual clothes if you are talking to a group of friends. If the audience is a religious group gathered in a church, synagogue, or mosque, you should probably wear more formal clothes and avoid colloquial language.

### Adapting Your Language

The language you use in your speech, as well as your gestures, movements, and even facial expressions, should be adapted to your audience. You can use slang with your classmates, but you would not use words like *self-call* and *all-nighter* with a professional group. Similarly, you would not make humorous faces, wink, or stick your tongue out in a formal setting.

An example of questionable adaptation to an audience was discussed by Colin Powell on *Meet the Press* on January 13, 2012. Specifically, Powell was referencing racist attacks by Republicans on President Obama and called the party on its use of racial code words like *shuckin' and jivin'*, a racial era slave term, and *lazy*. Regarding the latter, Powell explained, "It may not mean anything to most Americans, but to those of us who are African Americans, the second word is shiftless and then there's a third word that goes along with that."[6] Powell may have identified one of the reasons these Republicans did not carry the day in the 2012 presidential election. You can learn from their errors.

### Adapting Your Topic

Public speakers should be permitted to speak on nearly any topic; after all, the First Amendment provides some protection for free speech. But practical considerations may lead you to avoid certain subjects, which will typically be unique to specific situations and contexts. You might exercise caution in speaking boldly about politics and religion in many public speaking situations. You can talk frankly about these topics when you know you are with like-minded people. Controversial topics, such as gay marriage, the role of the government in bailing big businesses out of debt, banning the ownership of pit bulls, and increased public surveillance may be fine for the classroom, but you should find out from your teacher if he has a list of topics that are taboo. For a number of reasons, some instructors restrict the topics on which students may speak.

When we consider topics outside the classroom, it is important to recall the origin of public speaking in ancient Greece. The ancients were well aware of the importance of public debate and oratory. They felt that democracy was possible only through the open discussion of ideas. The founders of the United States similarly valued public speaking, as the First Amendment to the Constitution was devoted to the freedom of speech. Public speaking fosters critical thinking and engagement as citizens.

You should not assume that freedom of speech suggests that you can say anything at any time to any person. Instead, you need to pay special attention to your language choices, your audience analysis and adaptation, and even your delivery choices. For example, it is easy to sound cynical or sarcastic if you do not respect your opponents' points of view. As you speak on controversial topics, you are exercising your constitutional rights. The care you take in your treatment of the topic demonstrates your sensitivity to the rights of others.

### Adapting Your Purpose and Thesis Statement

After you have selected your topic, you need to determine your specific purpose in speaking. The **specific purpose** is *the purpose stated precisely as an outcome or behavioral objective and in terms of the audience.* In other words, your specific purpose includes your topic, your audience, and your precise goal in speaking to them. Here are some examples of specific purposes:

> *My audience will be able to explain the difference between Windows 2000 and Mac OS X platforms.*

> *My audience will be able to identify three benefits of cross-racial adoptions.*

> *My audience will be able to explain the increase in violence against women in particular countries.*

> *My audience will be able to distinguish among military guns, machine guns, handguns, and hunting guns.*

Next, you will determine your **thesis statement,** *a complete statement that reveals the content of your presentation.* The thesis statement is similar to the central idea of a written composition; it forecasts the speech and is often stated early on, generally in the introduction. Here are some examples of thesis statements:

*The fat-soluble vitamins—A, D, E, and K—are essential to good health and can be found in foods such as eggs, fish, nuts, seeds, cabbage, and cauliflower.*

*You might help a friend or classmate if you know three of the signs of drug abuse, including abrupt changes in school attendance and school work, unusual anger or outbreaks of temper, and deterioration of physical appearance and grooming.*

*The U.S. government needs to balance safety and privacy concerns as a result of terror attacks.*

Just as a speech topic should be adapted to the audience, so should the purpose and thesis statement. For example, would a speech on computer platforms be appropriate in your classroom setting? You might talk about specific essential vitamins and minerals to your speech class, but would that thesis be appropriate for a group of nutritionists? Would you need to adapt to the audience of nutritionists with a more sophisticated treatment of the topic and a slightly different thesis statement? The topic, purpose, and thesis statement are related to each other and should be appropriate for your audience. Figure 9.3 shows the relationship among the topic, purpose, and thesis statement.

**Figure 9.3** From Topic to Thesis Statement

# YOURSELF

## How Do I Know What to Talk About When I Have to Make Presentations in School, in the Community, and at Work? I Don't Think I Know Enough About Anything to Be Confident About Choosing a Topic.

Many speakers are baffled about an appropriate topic for a speech. At first, the possibilities seem without limit. You are bombarded with information on social media, on television, and in classes. What topic is best for you? Or you might have a very different experience and feel that you have nothing to speak about.

To help you find a topic, you can use brainstorming, surveying your interests, determining what is important to the audience and to you, and assessing your knowledge and commitment to the topic. Ask yourself these questions: How do I spend the bulk of my time each day? What do I feel passionate about? What activities absorb all of my attention and interest? This kind of self-appraisal may open doors to the discovery of topics important to you.

Most likely you will need to narrow your topic for the prescribed length of the speech. Do not forget to analyze your audience by observing them, drawing inferences, and even conducting questionnaires and surveys. Consider whether the audience is captive or voluntary; what the demographic features of your audience might be; whether the topic and audience are young or old; and the likely attitudes, beliefs, and values of the audience. All of these considerations will lead you to a topic that is appropriate for you, your audience, and the occasion.

 **CHAPTER REVIEW**

You now know that, when you have a public speaking assignment, you will begin to prepare by selecting a topic that is appropriate for you. The topic should be fresh and relevant to your contemporary audience. Moreover, you should feel confident that the topic is one you already know something about—and ideally you will know more about it than does your audience. You may also need to narrow the topic to be appropriate for the assignment. Next, you need to consider the audience in more depth: Is the topic you have chosen important to the audience? Is it appropriate for them, given who they are and what their attitudes, beliefs, and values are likely to be? Now that you know how to gain information about your audience, these questions can be answered in several ways. You can use observation, inference, question-naires, and even the Internet. Finally, you can adapt yourself, your language, your topic, and your purpose and thesis statement to your audience.

## KEY TERMS

attitude, 165
audience analysis, 164
belief, 166
brainstorming, 161
captive audience, 165
commitment, 162
demographic analysis, 165

inference, 169
questionnaire, 169
specific purpose, 174
thesis statement, 174
value, 167
voluntary audience, 165

## STUDY QUESTIONS

1. What are some of the methods you can use to select a topic for a speech? Choose one of those methods, and spend 10 minutes selecting a topic for a speech you might give to your classroom audience. Was the method you chose effective? Were the topics you listed reflective of your interests and knowledge?

2. What advice would you give a classmate who is having difficulty narrowing her topic?

3. How can knowing something about your audience's beliefs help you get your message across?

4. What are the four methods you can use to analyze an audience? Can you think of a time, outside the classroom, when you've put one of these methods to use? What were the results?

5. Experienced speakers know how to adapt to their audience. What are some of the ways you can adapt to your audience?

# 10

# Organizing Your Presentation

Your speech will be more likely to accomplish its goals if you can gain and hold your audience's attention, make smooth transitions between major sections, and end with a clear statement of what you want your audience to take away. This chapter will teach you about organization by discussing the key elements of a speech—the introduction, the body, and the conclusion—as well as how to outline your speech effectively.

## LEARNING OBJECTIVES

*After reading this chapter, you should be able to:*

- Explain the five functions an effective introduction fulfills.
- Describe the six principles for outlining the body of a presentation.
- Explain the four functions an effective conclusion fulfills.
- Demonstrate an understanding of the purpose of a reference list.

## THE INTRODUCTION

The **introduction** is *the first part of your presentation,* where you fulfill the five functions listed in Figure 10.1. Within the first few minutes of a speech, audience members decide whether they will listen to you. In part, they are deciding whether your topic is important enough to gain their attention. For these reasons you will want to put sufficient time and effort into developing an engaging introduction.

You do not need to fulfill these five functions in the order they are presented in Figure 10.1. However, your instructor may prefer this order for all speeches. For other instructors, the functions may occur in any particular order. Gaining audience attention often comes at the beginning, but maintaining attention is an important function throughout the speech. Forecasting the speech's organization often comes toward the end of an introduction, but even that function does not have to be saved for last.

One student, who spoke on the value of eating organic food, began with forecasting the development and organization of the speech. He said, "Due to the expanding global population and rapidly depleting natural resources, processed food is becoming ever more prominent in our society. I will talk to you first about some gross facts about processed foods and then I will discuss the nutritious value of organic foods." He followed this forecast with a statement to

**Figure 10.1** The Five Functions of Introductions

Gain and maintain audience attention.

Arouse interest.

State the purpose or thesis.

Establish qualifications.

Forecast development and organization.

gain and maintain the attention of his audience, as well as to arouse interest in the topic:

*Considering the college student lifestyle, ramen noodles sound like a quick and appetizing dish. The cost-effective and easily fixed meal provides us with temporary satisfaction. However, very few ever ponder what components go into producing such processed foods and how effectively these large corporations monitor the quality of their products. The FDA allows companies to sell food with four rodent hairs in it per 100 grams.*

He then stated his purpose, or thesis, and finished the introduction with his qualification to speak on the topic.

## Gaining and Maintaining Audience Attention

Gaining and maintaining attention means involving your audience in your topic. Here are some suggestions for doing so successfully:

| | Suggestion | Example |
|---|---|---|
| 1. | Bring to the presentation the object or person about which or whom you are going to speak. | Bring organic food to sample in a speech on organic food. |
| 2. | Invite your audience to participate. | Have everyone stand up and perform the exercise you are teaching. |
| 3. | Let your clothing relate to your presentation. | A nurse talking about the dangers of not getting a flu shot wears her scrubs. |
| 4. | Exercise your audience's imagination. | Have the audience members close their eyes and imagine they are slipping into a cool Minnesota lake when Miami is humid and steamy. |
| 5. | Start with sight or sound. | Play "Smoke on the Water" before your speech on the Montreux Jazz Festival. |
| 6. | Arouse audience curiosity. | Speak in another language for a few seconds with no explanation until afterward. |
| 7. | Role-play. | In a speech on saving a heart attack victim, have someone demonstrate the signs of a heart attack; the speaker then takes appropriate steps. |

| | | |
|---|---|---|
| 8. | Show a very short video. | Show a video of a German in lederhosen playing an instrument in a Munich field. |
| 9. | Present a brief quotation. | Read a short excerpt about Theodore Roosevelt's reaction to the untimely death of his wife. |
| 10. | State striking facts or statistics. | Contrast the 3,000 people who died on September 11, 2001, with the 23,000 Americans who died in a single battle, the Battle of Antietam, on April 17, 1862, in the Civil War. |
| 11. | Self-disclose. | Tell audience members something about yourself—related to the topic—that they would not otherwise know: "I lost a job opportunity because of entries on my Facebook page." |
| 12. | Tell a story, a narration. | Tell a story about one of your famous (or infamous) ancestors. |

These suggestions for gaining and maintaining audience attention certainly are not the only possibilities; they are suggested to help you think creatively about your own process. Be careful of gaining the audience's attention by doing something unrelated to your topic or something that is overly dramatic. Do not begin with mundane statements such as "Today I am going to . . ." or "My speech topic is . . ." Also, do not tell jokes unless you are especially adept at humor. In addition, you might want to try your humor on a subset of your audience or with a group of friends. Finally, resist bringing a pet or a very young or very old relative as your attention-getter. You may not be able to control their actions.

### Arousing Audience Interest

The second function of an introduction is to arouse audience interest in the subject matter. The best way is to show clearly how the topic is related to the audience. In a speech on Asperger syndrome, you could share how many people have been diagnosed with this disease and the percentage of increase each year. Translate those numbers into the likelihood that members of the audience will parent a child with Asperger or will have a friend or neighbor who will experience it in their family. By making the topic relevant to those in your audience, you are sure to arouse their interest.

### Stating the Purpose or Thesis

The third function of an introduction is to state the purpose or thesis of your speech. People learn more, and are more likely to be persuaded, if they know the speaker's goal. Occasionally, you will want to wait a little longer to share the goal of a persuasive speech, particularly if you think your audience will initially be opposed to your message.

You will recall from Chapter 9 that a thesis statement is a complete sentence that reveals the content of your presentation. An example of a thesis statement is "People should be allowed to marry each other whether they are of the opposite sex or of the same sex for at least three reasons." The purpose explains your specific goal in terms of the audience—for instance, "My audience should be able to identify at least three reasons people should be allowed to marry each other whether they are of the opposite sex or of the same sex."

The following are two additional examples of statements of purpose or thesis:

*Thesis statement for an informative speech*: "Identity theft can be avoided, and I will explain five methods you can easily implement."

*Purpose for the same speech*: "My audience should recall at least three of the five methods by which they can avoid identity theft."

*Thesis statement for a persuasive speech*: "After listening to me, you will be eager to join our movement to change the grading system at this college."

*Purpose for the same speech*: "My audience will understand why the grading system at this college should be changed and will be willing to help make that change."

Notice that the thesis statement is written to the audience and can be used in the speech. The purpose is written before the thesis statement and is written for the speaker as she is planning the speech and the introduction. The purpose is not delivered orally.

## Establishing Your Qualifications

The fourth function of an introduction is to describe any special qualifications you have to enhance your credibility. You can talk about your experience, your research, the experts you interviewed, and your own education and training in the subject. Simply stating that you read about the topic or that you studied a topic in high school is insufficient to establish credibility. Be wary about self-praise, but explain why you can speak about the topic with authority. The following is an example of establishing credibility through self-disclosure: "You probably have noticed that I wear a military uniform on one Friday each month. This is because I fought in the Middle East and now serve in the National Guard—yes, I am a weekend warrior."

## Forecasting Development and Organization

The fifth function of an introduction is to forecast the organization and development of the presentation. The forecast previews the main points you plan to cover. Audience members feel more comfortable when they know what to expect.

You might want to forecast the development and organization of your speech just after you have stated the thesis statement, since it is an expansion on the thesis statement. In a speech in favor of same-sex marriages, a speaker might add the following after the thesis statement:

> *Five strong reasons exist for why same-sex people should be allowed to marry; I am hopeful that you will agree with, and recall, at least three of the five reasons at the end of the presentation. First, it is unconstitutional to discriminate against a specific group of people. Second, homosexuality is not a choice and should not be punished. Third, gay marriage does not hurt anyone, and it does not hurt society. Fourth, gay marriage will increase child adoptions. Finally, gay marriage will bring financial gains for state and local governments.*

Before we move on to a discussion of the body of your presentation, we will look at some tips for strengthening your introduction by avoiding common mistakes:

1. Do not start talking until you are up in front and settled. Starting your speech on the way up to the lectern is bad form.

2. Do not simply announce your topic; offer an interesting statement to gain the audience's attention.

3. Avoid saying negative things about you or your abilities: "I'm not used to public speaking," "I've never done this before," or "I couldn't be more nervous than I am right now." You are supposed to build your credibility in the introduction, not give an audience more doubts about your ability.

4. Do not let your nonverbal unease overcome your message. Crossing your legs, refusing to look at the audience, jingling the change in your pocket, repeatedly pushing your hair off your face—all of these signal to the audience your lack of confidence. Act confident even if you are not.

5. Do not say negative things about your message: "I didn't have much time to prepare this speech," "I couldn't find much information on my topic," or "I really don't know much about this issue." Do the best you can to convey your message, but do not tell the audience to disregard your message.

## THE BODY

The **body** of a presentation is *the largest part of the presentation, in which you place your arguments and ideas, your evidence and examples, your proofs and illustrations, and your stories and testimonials.* You need to decide what information to include and what to exclude. You also need to decide what you will talk about first, last, and in the middle. Your entire message should be included in the body. The introduction introduces this message, and the conclusion reinforces or reminds your audience of the message. New material should not appear in the conclusion; material introduced in the introduction should be expanded upon in the body.

As mentioned early in this chapter, most speakers begin composing their presentations with the body rather than the introduction, because they need to know the content of the presentation to write an effective introduction. However you decide to draft and organize your speech, you should not underestimate the importance of outlining.

### The Principles of Outlining

An **outline** is *a written plan that uses symbols, margins, and content to reveal the order, importance, and substance of your speech.* An outline is used to prepare your speech; it is not to be used in the delivery of the presentation. The outline is a simplified, abstract version of your speech. You will find that learning how to outline can provide you with a useful tool in your classes and at work.

Outlining is easy to learn if you keep six principles of outlining in mind:

*Principle 1: Link the outline to the purpose.* All the items of information in your outline should be directly related to your specific purpose and thesis statement. You will recall that we defined and discussed these terms in Chapter 9. Imagine that you are providing an informative speech about a constitutional amendment in your state. Your purpose might be to have the audience describe the scenario if the amendment is defeated and to describe the situation if the amendment passes. Your thesis statement might be "My audience will understand the proposed ethical standards for public officials, including a revised code of ethics and more effective ways of enforcing this code." You may want to encourage others to stop texting and driving: "Texting and driving results in accidents, deaths, and other long-term consequences."

*Principle 2: Your outline is an abstract of the message you will deliver.* As a simplification, the outline should be less than every word you speak but should include all important points and supporting materials.

*Principle 3: Each sentence in the outline is a single idea.* That is, the outline should consist of single units of information, usually in the form of complete sentences, each of which expresses a single idea.

*Principle 4: Your outline symbols signal importance.* The **main points,** or *most important points,* are indicated with Roman numerals, such as I, II, III, IV, and V. A 5- to 10-minute message should probably have from one to three main points. **Subpoints** *support the main points,* are of less importance, and are indicated with capital letters, such as A, B, C, D, and E. Ordinarily, two subpoints under a main point are regarded as the minimum. Nothing is magic about the number two; rather, the rule of division states that one item cannot be divided into fewer than two parts.

*Principle 5: Your outline margins signal importance.* The larger the margin on the left, the less important the item is to your purpose. However, the margins are coordinated with the symbols explained previously; thus, the main points have the same left margin, the subpoints have a slightly larger left margin, the sub-subpoints have a still larger left margin, and so on. The following outline demonstrates how margins illustrate importance.

---

**I. Many American families have adopted Russian children in the past.**

    A. People who were unable to adopt American babies for a variety of reasons turned to other countries, including Russia.

    B. The babies who were adopted were sometimes ill, had life-threatening diseases, or became criminals as adults.

       1. These problems were due in part to the lack of touching and care for the infants.

       2. These problems also occurred because of fetal alcohol syndrome.

**II. In 2012, Russia passed an adoption ban.**

    A. The ban was retaliation for the United States' enactment of the Magnitsky Act, which was a human rights bill that targeted some Russian officials.

    B. The ban punished Americans, but it also punished Russian children who were left in institutions without parents.

**III. The future of adopting Russian children is unclear: what is clear is that both Russian children and potential American parents have been abused.**

---

*Principle 6: Use parallel form.* If you are writing a sentence outline, all of your statements should be full sentences. If you are doing a rough draft, all of your statements should be fragments, or phrases. You should not mix sentences, fragments, clauses, single words, and other disjointed thoughts.

## The Rough Draft

Before you begin composing your outline, you can save time and energy by (1) selecting a topic that is appropriate for you, your audience, your purpose, and the situation; (2) finding arguments, examples, illustrations, quotations, stories, and other supporting materials from your experience, from written and visual resources, and from other people; and (3) narrowing your topic, so that you can select the best materials from a large supply of available items.

Once you have gathered materials consistent with your purpose, you can begin by developing a **rough draft** of your outline—*a preliminary organization of the outline*. The most efficient way to develop a rough draft is to choose a limited number of main points important for your purpose and your audience.

Next, you should see what materials you have from your experience, from written and visual resources, and from other people to support these main ideas. You need to find out if you have any materials that support your subpoints— facts, statistics, testimony, and examples. In short, you assemble your main points, your subpoints, and your sub-subpoints for your speech, always with your audience and purpose in mind.

The following is an outline exemplifying what a rough draft of a speech looks like.[1]

*Your rough draft can have sentences, phrases, or just a word or two to indicate your overall plan for presentation.*

*Your rough draft should be easy to change; it will evolve as you decide what to keep and what to discard based on your research of your topic.*

*Your rough draft is an early plan containing cues about what you want to say.*

---

**Blogging**

**Introduction**

My immediate purpose is to help my audience understand the origins, current uses, and future of blogging.

I. **What is blogging and what is its importance now and in the future?**

   A. What is blogging?

   B. Why important?

II. **History**

   A. Origin

      1. When?

      2. Who?

   B. Original uses

III. **Present**

   A. Reasons for popularity

   B. Complications

IV. **Future**

   A. Trends

   B. Genres

V. **Conclusion: Blogging is growing exponentially because of its many possibilities.**

---

A rough draft of a speech does not necessarily follow parallel form, nor is it as complete as the sentence outline, which often develops out of the rough draft. When you are ready to finalize your outline, you have several options. Key-word and sentence outlines are two possibilities.

## The Sentence Outline

A **sentence outline** *consists entirely of complete sentences.* Although it does not contain all the words that will be in the delivered speech, it does provide a complete guide to the content.

The sentence outline that follows is based on a student's speech. The immediate purpose of the presentation was to explain the reasons students should eat breakfast. The action goal of the speech was to persuade classmates to get in the habit of eating breakfast every day. Notice that every entry in the outline is a sentence.[2]

---

**Why All College Students Should Eat Breakfast**
**Michael Burns**

**Introduction**

I.  **Many people choose to sleep 30 minutes longer every day rather than take the time to eat breakfast.**

    A.  How many of you ate breakfast this morning? Your cup of coffee does not count. (*show of hands*)

    B.  College students who eat breakfast perform better in classes and are healthier.

    C.  Eating breakfast should be a part of all college students' daily schedules.

**Body**

II.  **There are many reasons eating breakfast is beneficial.**

    A.  Breakfast is a great way to jumpstart your metabolism and your day.

    B.  Students who eat breakfast are healthier than students who don't.
        1.  The Centers for Disease Control and Prevention reports that people who eat breakfast are less overweight than people who don't.
        2.  The *American Journal of Clinical Nutrition* claims that people who eat a breakfast that includes a glass of orange juice have a stronger immune system.

    C.  Students who eat breakfast also perform better in school.
        1.  Mayo Clinic doctors have reported that people who eat breakfast regularly have more energy and are able to focus longer on tasks.

---

2. The American Dietetic Association claims that students who eat breakfast are more likely to have better concentration and problem-solving skills than students who don't eat breakfast.

**Conclusion**

**III. As college students, we need to eat breakfast daily.**

    A. Eating breakfast every day will make us healthier.

    B. Eating breakfast every day will improve our performance in classes.

    C. Eating breakfast should be just as important to our daily schedules as taking a shower.

## The Key-Word Outline

A **key-word outline** is *an outline consisting of important words or phrases to remind you of the content of the speech.* This outline shrinks the ideas in a speech considerably more than does a sentence outline. The following key-word outline came from a student's speech. Notice how the key-word format reduces the content to the bare essentials.[3]

**The Youth Vote**
**Amanda Peterson**

**Introduction**

**I. Politicians ignore youth vote**

    A. Mostly 18- to 24-year-olds don't vote

    B. Statistics on voting

    C. Forecast of the reasons

**Body**

**II. Youth apathetic to politics**

    A. Sports & beer more interesting

    B. Don't know who represents them

### III. Politics unappealing

    A. Partisanship

    B. Political scandals

**Conclusion**

### IV. What solution?

    A. More focus on youth

    B. More attention on campus

## Organizational Patterns

The body of a presentation can be outlined using a number of organizational patterns. Four of them are summarized in Table 10.1.

The **time-sequence pattern** is *a method of organization in which the presenter explains a sequence of events in chronological order.* This pattern can be used in both informative and persuasive speeches. The following brief outline is organized in a time-sequence pattern.[4]

| **Table 10.1** Four Common Organizational Patterns for the Body of a Speech | | |
| --- | --- | --- |
| **Organizational Pattern** | **What It Is** | **Exemplary Topics** |
| Time-sequence | Chronological order | The future of social media<br>Development of the land grant colleges |
| Cause/effect | Discusses cause(s) and results | The causes and effects of inflation<br>The causes and effects of binge drinking |
| Problem/solution | Describes a problem and proposes a solution | Eliminating nuclear waste<br>Helping battered women |
| Topical-sequence | Identifies 3 to 5 qualities or types of a person, place, or thing | Four reasons to buy a used car<br>Three benefits of trade school |

> **How Ford Drove the Auto Industry**
> **Jared Fougner**
>
> **Purpose:** I plan to highlight the history of the Ford Motor Company in the United States from its beginnings to today so my audience will be informed about this important foundation of a truly American industry.
>
> I. Ford started the auto industry.
>
> II. In the early years, Ford experimented, developed mass production, and created cars that no other company was creating.
>
> III. In the middle years, Ford released the F-series pickup trucks.
>
> IV. In modern times, Ford innovated and competed in an ever-tightening market.

In using a **cause/effect pattern,** *the presenter first explains the causes of an event, a problem, or an issue and then discusses its consequences, results, or effects.* Generally, this pattern is used in persuasive speeches. The presentation may be cause/effect, effect/cause, or even effect/effect. The following outline shows an example of the cause/effect pattern.[5]

> **Confessions of a Smoker**
> **Linzey Crockett**
>
> **Purpose:** This speech by a confessed smoker notes the potential effects of smoking on smokers' health, including early death.
>
> I. Smoking has physiological effects on heart and blood.
>
> II. Carbon monoxide increases while oxygen depletes when you smoke.
>
> III. As the cigarette burns close to your mouth the dangerous toxins concentrate in the cigarette butt.
>
> IV. Smoking cigarettes can and will lead to pulmonary problems like lung cancer and emphysema, diseases that lead to an early death.

The third pattern of organization, used most often in persuasive presentations, is the **problem/solution pattern,** in which *the presenter describes a problem* *and proposes a solution.* A message based on this pattern can be divided into two distinct parts, with an optional third part in which the presenter meets any anticipated objections to the proposed solution.

Here you can see what a problem/solution speech in outline form looks like:[6]

---

**Routine Body Shrinking**

I. From the time that I was in elementary school, I was overweight.

II. Over the last decade many high-quality studies have proven the benefits of exercise.

III. In five years a well-planned workout regimen helped me lose 130 pounds.

IV. Launching and sustaining a well-structured exercise routine yields benefits uncovered in studies and demonstrated in my own life.

---

The **topical-sequence pattern,** used in both informative and persuasive presentations, *emphasizes the major reasons the audience should accept a point of view by addressing the advantages, disadvantages, qualities, and types of a person, place, or thing.* The following topical-sequence outline informs the audience about global warming.[7]

---

**Global Warming: What Can You Do?**

**Purpose:** This speech attempts to persuade the audience about implementing steps to avoid even greater global warming and damage to the earth.

I. One smart choice is to buy at a farmer's market to avoid shipping costs and to obtain fresher food.

II. Another smart choice is to buy a fuel-efficient car because such vehicles leave a smaller carbon footprint.

III. Unplug unused electronics because anything turned on means your energy supplier has to burn something that can emit carbon dioxide.

---

### Transitions and Signposts

Transitions and signposts connect the parts of the speech. A **transition** *typically includes a brief flashback and a brief forecast that tells your audience when you are moving from one main point to another.* Examples of transitions are provided in Table 10.2.

**Signposts** are *ways in which a presenter signals to an audience where the presentation is going.* Whereas transitions are often a sentence or two, signposts can be as brief as a few words. Transitions review, state a relationship, and forecast; signposts merely point. Some examples of signposts are listed in Table 10.3.

### Tips for Using Note Cards

A key-word outline fits easily on 3-by-5-inch or 4-by-6-inch note cards or on 8½-by-11-inch paper. If you choose note cards, the following suggestions may be useful:

| Table 10.2 Examples of Transitions |
| --- |
| *Transition from one main point to another:* "Now that we have seen why computers are coming down in cost, let us look next at why software is so expensive." |
| *Transition from a main point to a visual aid:* "I have explained that higher education is becoming more and more expensive. This bar graph will show exactly how expensive it has become over the past 5 years." |
| *Transition that includes a review, an internal summary, and a preview:* "You have heard that suntanning ages the skin, and I have shown you the pictures of a Buddhist monk and a nighttime bartender who hardly ever exposed themselves to direct sunlight. Now I want to show you a picture of a 35-year-old woman who spent most of her life working in direct sunlight." |

| Table 10.3 Examples of Signposts | |
| --- | --- |
| "First, I will illustrate . . ." | "A second idea is . . ." |
| "Look at this bar graph . . ." | "Another reason for . . ." |
| "See what you think of this evidence . . ." | "Finally, we will . . ." |

1. Write instructions to yourself on your note cards. For instance, if you are supposed to write the title of your speech and your name on the board before your presentation begins, write that instruction on the top of your first card.

2. Write on one side of the cards only; you may need to use more cards with your key-word outline on one side only, but writing on both front and back is more likely to result in confusion.

3. Number your note cards on the top, so that you are unlikely to confuse their order. If you drop them, you can quickly reassemble them.

4. Write out items that might be difficult to remember. Extended quotations, difficult names, unfamiliar terms, and statistics are items you may want to include on your note cards to reduce the chances of error.

5. Practice delivering your presentation at least two times using your note cards. Effective delivery may be difficult to achieve if you have to fumble with unfamiliar cards. You also need to remember that the note cards can interfere with your gestures.

6. Write clearly and legibly.

## THE CONCLUSION

The **conclusion,** *the end or final part of the speech,* fulfills four functions, which are listed in Figure 10.2. These functions need not be fulfilled in the order shown in the figure, but normally they are all fulfilled in the last minutes of a presentation.

**Figure 10.2** The Four Functions of a Conclusion

Forewarn the audience that you are about to finish.

Remind the audience of your central idea and the main points of your presentation.

Remind the audience what they should think or do in response to your speech.

End the speech in a way that makes the audience want to think or do what you recommend.

The first function of a conclusion is to warn the audience that the end of the presentation is near. One student signaled the end of her speech by saying, "Five minutes is hardly time to consider all the complications of this issue . . ." By stating that her time was up, she signaled her conclusion. Another said, "Thus men have the potential for much greater role flexibility than our society encourages . . ." The word *thus*, like *therefore*, signals the conclusion of a logical argument and indicates that the argument is drawing to a close.

The second function of a conclusion, reminding the audience of your central idea and the main points of your message, can be fulfilled by restating the main points, summarizing them briefly, or selecting the most important point for special treatment. This reminder of the central idea parallels the statement of the purpose and thesis statement in the introduction.

The third function of a conclusion is to specify what you expect audience members to think or do as a result of your presentation. You may want the audience to simply remember a few of your important points, to sign a petition, or to talk to their elected representatives.

The fourth function of a conclusion is to end the presentation in a manner that makes audience members want to think or do as you recommend. You can conclude with a rhetorical question: "Knowing what you know now, will you feel safe riding with a driver who has had a few drinks?" You can end with a quotation: "As John F. Kennedy said, 'Forgive your enemies, but never forget their names.'" You can use a literary passage: "We conclude with the words of Ralph Waldo Emerson, who said, 'It is one light which beams out a thousand

## MEDIA

### LEARN TO EASILY STORE AND ORGANIZE YOUR WEBSITE LINKS

If you find that you have a hard time locating websites after initial discovery, use online resources to help you stay organized and save time. Live Binders (www.livebinders.com) is an online storage and organization resource that lets you easily mark information that you find on the Internet and organize it into subcategories.

■ Let's say you are constructing a speech on driving regulations and safety standards. You might come across a story you like in the online version of the *New York Times.* With Live Binders you can mark and store the article under a category like "Introduction Material" to examine again later.

■ Perhaps you also locate some interesting state and national statistics on different governmental websites. You could mark and store these websites for later review and possible inclusion in your speech. You might call this category "Resources for Main Points."

As you explore and locate materials, create more refined online categories that reflect main point areas of your speech.

stars; it is one soul which animates all men.'" Or you can conclude with an action that demonstrates the point of your presentation—for example, quickly assembling an electric motor for the class and showing that it works.

The following is the conclusion of a speech by a first-year student about car phones and teen accidents. The side notes indicate how she fulfilled the functions of a conclusion.

## SAMPLE CONCLUSION THAT FULFILLS THE FOUR FUNCTIONS

As you can see, car accidents are the leading cause of death for adolescents 15–20 years of age; therefore, a cell phone in adolescents' hands can be a recipe for disaster. I hope you are now aware of the dangers of teens using cell phones while driving. If you want further evidence, please ask me later.

*Warns that ending is near*

I have covered the basics: 6,000 teens die each year because of car accidents, teenagers' judgments deteriorate greatly with distractions, and 50% of teenagers crash within the first six months of receiving their license.

*Reminds audience of main points: summary*

Cell phone distractions can be easily prevented and can save lives. A law against teen use of cell phones while driving has worked in the first state that adopted such a law. Our state should join them. Next time you hear talk about this proposed law, I hope you will think about the facts I have shared with you and tell others why teenagers should not be allowed to talk on cell phones while driving.

*Specifies what the audience should do*

If you want to keep the roads safer for you and all of your family and friends, you will help get this law in place in our state.

*Ends by recommending an action*

# BUILDER

## LEARN WHAT TO AVOID IN YOUR CONCLUSION

After you have organized your conclusion, review it with these suggestions in mind:

- Do not end abruptly with no forewarning.
- Remind the audience of your main points, but do not provide a detailed replay of everything in your speech.
- Do not say negative things about your own presentation: "Well, I guess that didn't go so well" or "I probably should have done more research."
- Do not let your own nonverbal communication signal a poor presentation by letting your voice trail off at the end or by dropping your arms and looking defeated.

## THE REFERENCES

When you have completed your outline, you may be asked to provide a list of **references,** or *the sources you used in your presentation.* The main idea behind a reference list is to inform others of what sources you used for your speech and to enable them to check those sources for themselves. Each entry in your references should be written according to a uniform style. Several accepted style manuals can answer your questions about the correct format: *The Publication Manual of the American Psychological Association* (APA), *The MLA Handbook*, and *The Chicago Manual of Style.* Since some teachers prefer MLA and others prefer APA, you should ask your instructor's preference.

## CHALLENGE YOURSELF

### Once I Find Out What I'm Going to Say or Write, How Do I Organize My Thoughts in a Reasonable Manner?

Perhaps you have listened to a speaker who seemed totally disorganized, or who did not have an introduction that gained and maintained your attention or stated the purpose of the talk. Maybe the speaker did not prepare you for ending the talk. He was talking energetically and then just stopped without forewarning. Maybe he did not conclude with a memorable statement that helped you recall his message. Or perhaps he did not tell you exactly what he wanted you to know or do at the end of the speech.

The way you organize your speech can make all the difference in how effectively you get your message across. Always keep in mind the strategies we've covered in this chapter:

- Carefully and creatively consider the functions of your introduction: gaining and maintaining audience attention, arousing audience interest, stating the purpose or thesis of the speech, establishing your own qualifications to speak on the topic, and forecasting the development and organization of the speech.

- Think about the various ways you can organize the body of the speech:
  Should you place the most important information first or last? Which organizational plan should you use? How can transitions and signposts help you help the audience follow your train of logic?

- Do not skip the steps of creating a rough draft, followed by a sentence outline, and then a key-word outline that you can actually use to deliver your speech.

- In the conclusion, don't forget to signal that you are almost done speaking, to state exactly what you want the audience to know or do, and to summarize your content in a way that provides a memorable ending.

After you believe you have organized your message as imaginatively and distinctly as you can, ask a friend or your instructor to examine your sentence or key-word outline. What advice can he or she offer? Do you tend to have a weak spot in your organization? Most of us do. Consider your weaknesses and pay special attention to them as you polish and prepare your speech.

- You can learn about APA style at www.apastyle.org/;
- You can learn about MLA at http://owl.english.purdue.edu/own/resource/747/01; and
- You can learn about the Chicago style at www.chicagomanualofstyle.org/.

The reference list is included in your written document; it is not read during the speech. Instead, you will use **oral citations** during the speech at the appropriate time when you are providing specific material you wish to quote or paraphrase. Generally, *you will provide the name of the source, how recent the information is, and the source's qualifications.* Here is an example of an oral citation: "*USA Today* on April 19, 2013, reported that the 'Boston Blast' shone the light on Massachusetts governor Deval Patrick." This source would be listed in the references following correct MLA or APA style.

 **CHAPTER REVIEW**

In this chapter you learned how to organize a speech into an introduction, a body, and a conclusion. Now that you are aware of the functions of introductions and conclusions, you can craft effective presentations that will capture your audience's attention and leave them with a memorable point or call to action. But how will you hold your audience's attention between the introduction and conclusion? Use the six principles for outlining the body of the speech and stay organized by subdividing your main points and subpoints. An organized speech is much more interesting and easier to follow than a disorganized one. You also now know your options for choosing from four organizational patterns: time-sequence, cause/effect, problem/solution, and topical-sequence. As you plan your speech, give thought to the organizational pattern that will best serve your purpose, whether it is to persuade or to inform.

**KEY TERMS**

body, 183
cause/effect pattern, 190
conclusion, 193
introduction, 179
key-word outline, 188
main points, 184

oral citation, 197
outline, 184
problem/solution pattern, 190
references, 196
rough draft, 186
sentence outline, 187

## STUDY QUESTIONS

1. What are the five functions of an introduction? Choose one of these functions and describe a time when you were responsible for putting it to use, whether it was in speaking or in writing.

2. How do a rough draft, a sentence outline, and a key-word outline differ from each other?

3. What are the four functions of a conclusion? Which of those functions might you consider most critical in a persuasive presentation, and why?

4. Turn on a radio or television news program or podcast. Listen carefully for oral citations throughout the piece, and keep an informal list of all the sources mentioned. Do any of the sources you listed peak your interest as a listener? How might a list of references help you, as a member of an audience, learn more about this topic?

# Gathering Information and Supporting Materials

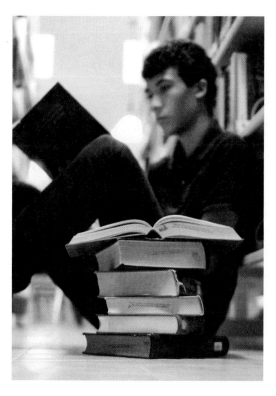

When it comes to researching and writing your speech, finding and evaluating supporting material is a critical step in the process. The information you present will need to suit your public speaking goal. It should also suit the needs of your listeners, whose thoughts, feelings, beliefs, and actions will be influenced by the information and evidence you put forward.

LEARNING OBJECTIVES

*After reading this chapter, you should be able to:*

- Explain the challenges of gathering information in the digital age.
- Demonstrate knowledge of the diverse resources available to you through your library.
- Demonstrate effective use of the Internet for finding sources of information.
- Explain the ways you can use practical experience in gathering information.
- Evaluate and properly cite your resources in an oral and a written format.

## GATHERING INFORMATION IN A DIGITAL WORLD

Let's say you are thinking of buying a car. After speaking to trusted friends and family members about their experiences with vehicles, you decide that a used car is the most practical choice. Next, you might turn to online consumer reports and reviews, recent newspaper articles, recall notices, and independent research studies; you might conduct instant polls among your social networks or an informal interview with a trusted friend who happens to work in the automotive industry.

In each case, your search for relevant information about used vehicles constitutes research. By using a variety of information sources and evaluating them for reliability and relevance, you bring greater insight to your goal of finding the right car, and you are better prepared to make an informed decision.

### Data, Information, and Knowledge

Just as you gather information about cars so you can make a high-quality decision about a purchase, you gather information for your speech topic so you can communicate a high-quality message to your audience. To achieve this goal, you need to understand how a researcher creates meaning from data and information, then shares it with others as knowledge. Figure 11.1 explains what is meant by the terms *data*, *information*, and *knowledge*.

**Figure 11.1** The Meaning of *Data*, *Information*, and *Knowledge*

**Data** are *facts collected from a particular source.*

**Example:** A runner might wear a special watch that conveys data about her heart rate, pacing, and patterns during a marathon.

**Information** is *a selective group of facts that you might reference to better understand a set of data.*

**Example:** A family might organize data about all of their purchases in a financial program, like QuickBooks, in order to see general trends related to their financial management.

**Knowledge** is *information with meaning attached to it.* Knowledge is a key component of problem solving.

**Example:** The marathon runner uses information about her running patterns to make decisions about conserving energy for the remainder of the race.

**Example:** The family tracking their yearly expenditures could use the information they gather to make a budget in order to save for a new purchase.

**Data** are *facts that have been collected from a particular source,* such as the data a runner collects when wearing a device that measures heart rate. **Information** is *the selective groups of facts that help us understand sets of data.* The runner who keeps a record of her body's physiological patterns when she runs a certain distance might use that information to determine whether to try running a marathon instead of a half-marathon. **Knowledge** is *information with meaning attached to it.*[1] The same runner would use the information she has collected about her physical abilities to focus her training or to pace herself during a long run.

In other words, when you collect data from a variety of sources, you can then organize it as information of a particular kind; when that information carries meaning that helps you make decisions or think critically about a problem, it takes the form of knowledge. Consider another example:

- A lot of complex *data* exist about alternative energy sources and use trends.

- If you focus on and collect facts about wind energy, you are forming an *information* base on that topic.

- When you are able to understand this information enough to articulate a position, perhaps reporting some of the benefits and drawbacks of investing in wind-generated energy, you are demonstrating your *knowledge* on that subject.

Once you understand the differences among data, information, and knowledge, you can use the results of your research to present a meaningful message to your audience.

### Information Literacy

As a presenter, you can successfully transfer knowledge to your audience by studying and practicing information literacy. **Information literacy** is *the ability to locate, evaluate, and incorporate important information into your own knowledge base.*[2] For example, an information-literate student developing a speech on renewable energy would carefully examine each potential source, keeping in mind the quality of the source in relation to the subtopics he is developing. On the other hand, a student who struggles with information literacy skills would simply select the first sources she comes across, regardless of their quality or relevance to the overall topic.

Your task is not simply to find information on a specific topic but, rather, to find information that helps your audience understand that topic better. With an increasing amount of information at your fingertips, you may find it difficult to convert data and information into useful, situated knowledge—that is, knowledge that you and your audience can use when discussing the topic with others. If you are struggling to recall information presented to you after a speech, chances are the speaker failed to produce useful knowledge from his research.

Consider the sheer amount of information on social networking sites like Facebook, YouTube, and Twitter, on which users generate loads of new content every minute. Some information science scholars argue that we are merely generating a lot of useless data[3] that does not necessarily contribute to our knowledge.

The ability to recognize and filter out irrelevant and inadequate information is an important skill.[4] By honing this skill, you will be better able to sort through information you have gleaned from a range of sources, from a survey on a social media site to your library's digital holdings, and share that information with your audience.

## Information Overload and Information Anxiety

The terms *information overload* and *information anxiety* refer to the overwhelming experience of sorting through and evaluating the information you encounter on a daily basis. **Information overload** is *the experience of having more data and information than you have the capacity to process in a given time period.*[5] **Information anxiety** is *the experience of stress you feel due to an inability to access, understand, or process information that is necessary to your goal or the task at hand.*[6]

To some extent, having access to plenty of information can help you make good decisions. But having too much information can lead to anxiety, making it difficult to process any new information you encounter.[7]

You have likely experienced anxiety and overload before, and chances are you will again. When this happens, make use of the research techniques discussed in this chapter. One of the best strategies for avoiding information overload and anxiety is to start your search for information early. Leave yourself plenty of time to find the best information, as well as to deal with the emotions that might accompany that search.

## The Information-Gathering Process

The information-gathering process can be broken down into five critical steps: defining the problem, using diverse strategies, scanning and evaluating, integrating, and organizing. Table 11.1 outlines these steps and offers examples and tips for applying them to your own information searches.[8]

The first step to any information search should be to define your problem clearly and adequately, which will help you avoid information overload. For example, if you begin by considering your own knowledge base and determining what useful information you can add to that base, you immediately limit the scope of your information search. Rather than having to sort through every

**Table 11.1** The Information-Gathering Process

| Define the Problem | Use Diverse Strategies | Scan and Evaluate the Information | Integrate the Information | Organize the Information |
|---|---|---|---|---|
| Before you begin, define your information problem(s) and consider your goals. | Use a range of search techniques and terms:<br>■ "College students and healthcare"<br>■ "College students and health information"<br>■ "College students and health problems" | As one of your main topics, you might choose to discuss where college students go to find health information and how these decisions impact their health. As you scan, you might ask yourself<br>■ What Internet resources do college students use for information on health?<br>■ How many students follow up by seeing a medical professional? | This is an opportunity to relate your journal article sources to anecdotes, interviews, and other sources of information. | Organize and present your information in order to stress particular points. |
| In a speech about healthcare for college students, you might define your problem this way: "I'm curious about the unique healthcare issues college students face." | *Tip:* Use your library's online catalog and search engines to explore your topic. For instance, pay attention to titles of books and journals that pop up often. | | You might integrate the information you found about college students using the Internet with information you gained from an interview with someone who works at your university health center. | Consider a way of grouping the information into subtopics—for example, "Costs of Healthcare," "Available Services," and "Care Concerns." |
| *Tip:* As you find more information and learn more about your topic, redefine your problem. | | Discard sources that do not focus specifically on the college student population. | *Tip:* Create an annotated bibliography in which you summarize your insights from each source. | Remember, your method of organization should enhance the audience's current understanding of the topic. |
| | | *Tip:* You don't have to use everything in a source. For example, use only the parts of a research study that relate to your specific topic. | | *Tip:* After completing an annotated bibliography, consider how your insights group together to form your whole topic. |

interesting fact you discover in relation to your topic, you will simply evaluate what is relevant to the problem as you have defined it.

For help in considering the diverse subdimensions of your topic before you search for information, construct a concept map, as discussed in Chapter 9. Doing so will help you identify areas in which you need to supplement your knowledge with additional facts or with greater depth of coverage or analysis.

## CONSIDERING

### CREATE A CONCEPT MAP ON YOUR COMPUTER, TABLET, OR SMARTPHONE

If you decide to create a concept map, take advantage of the free software available online.

- Edraw Mindmap (www.edrawsoft.com/freemind .php): This website offers freeware software that enables you to diagram and revise your own concept maps. There are a variety of templates you might find more or less useful, depending on the complexity of your topic.
- Total Recall—Mind Map (www.glamtropez.com /totalrecall/): This free application for iPhone, iPod, or iPad enables you to create concept maps of any size or color. These maps can also be shared through e-mail.

Using either of these programs, you can continue to think about and refine your topic from almost anywhere.

Figure 11.2 shows a concept map created to explore the topic of college students and healthcare. A student who creates a concept map like this one might discover she wants to pursue greater coverage of the resources available for students who abuse alcohol.

As you continue your research and find new information, you can revise your initial concept map to illustrate more clearly the relationships between aspects of your topic, such as student use of the Internet to research health questions. Remember to use only information that is most clearly related to your topic.

### GATHERING INFORMATION FROM LIBRARY RESOURCES

More and more libraries are replacing stacks of books and racks of magazines and journals with computers, providing increased access to digital subscriptions and holdings.[9] **Reference librarians,** *librarians who are specially trained in finding and evaluating information,* can assist navigating this wide range of resources by helping you think of unique search terms. Reference librarians can also guide you in using the computerized technologies, such as the **online library catalog system,** *a program that allows you to explore all the types of print and multimedia holdings and collections of the library.* Even as the digital functions supported by college and university libraries continue to evolve, the library is still the best place to go for assistance in gaining access to a wide range of useful resources.

### Use Books, Articles, and Periodicals

An effective information search makes use of a variety of sources. Your library's resources include books, magazines, newspaper articles, journal articles, encyclopedias, sourcebooks, government documents, almanacs, and multimedia sources, as well as its own special collections. But the most commonly used sources are books, newspapers and magazines, and scholarly journals, described in Table 11.2.

As you search for information to use in your presentation, focus on the most reliable information you can find. Scholarly articles summarize and build on the research of others and therefore reflect the most current scholarly investigations of your topic. Books and magazines likewise contain information that builds on

**Figure 11.2** A Concept Map Exploring the Topic "College Students and Healthcare"

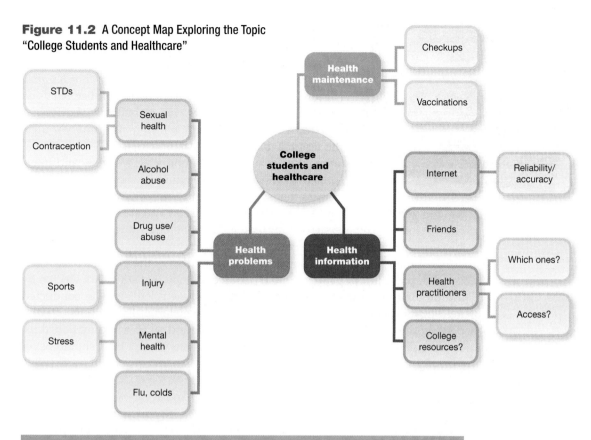

---

**Table 11.2** Books, Newspapers and Magazines, and Scholarly Journals

**Books**

- Contain in-depth information
- Are useful for understanding the general issues, themes, and fundamental principles related to your topic
- Often provide a sense of the history and development of your topic, as well as the interrelationships between your topic and other issues

**Newspaper and Magazine Articles (popular press sources)**

- Are a great place to start when gauging human interest and understanding current trends, issues, and debates
- Provide diverse perspectives with regard to the core issues related to a topic
- Offer ideas for the introduction or conclusion of a speech, when you might want to include examples of the experiences of others

**Scholarly Journal Articles**

- Provide an understanding of current and past investigations and research of a topic
- Often have the highest level of peer review before publication

the work of others. When citing from these sources, keep in mind the difference between primary sources and secondary sources, laid out in Figure 11.3.

A **primary source** is *original source material or research.* A **secondary source** is *a source of information that builds on or comments on another's material or research.* The further removed a piece of information is from its primary source, the less reliable it is. For example, if you read a journal article by an author who conducted a survey and interpreted its results, you are citing a primary source when you discuss that survey in your speech or paper. On the other hand, if you cite *Newsweek*'s summary of that survey, you are referring to a secondary source. The *Newsweek* summary is someone else's interpretation of the survey findings, which is fine to use as long as you are aware of the potential for errors or for a point of view that may differ from that of the primary researcher.

Wikipedia is a popular secondary source. Wikipedia listings are written by a community of users rather than, for instance, the scientists who conducted investigations and produced the primary source material. The authors of Wikipedia entries may or may not be relaying credible and reliable information; thus, you should refrain from citing Wikipedia as a source, much as you should never formally cite Facebook, Twitter, or other user-generated content as credible sources in a speech.

On the other hand, user-generated content (like Facebook and Twitter) can help you begin your search for new or noteworthy information. But you should always ground any social media insights in scholarly evidence and primary sources. For example, if your social media friends constantly talk about television shows, movies, and the Internet, you might decide to develop a speech about media addiction in the age of digital communication. Next, you might supplement your own insights by visiting the library and exploring online databases for relevant and credible information on this topic.

Use primary sources whenever possible. If you find a published summary of research and the summary is from a secondary source, use the information

**Figure 11.3** Primary Sources Versus Secondary Sources

| Primary Sources | Secondary Sources |
|---|---|
| ■ *Original material*<br>■ For instance, citing the results of a recently conducted survey | ■ *Material that builds on or comments on another's research*<br>■ For instance, a newspaper article's summary of a primary source, such as survey results |

in the summary to locate the actual study (the primary source), and then read and cite directly from that primary source. Newspaper journalists often provide one or two sentences about research studies published in scholarly journals. For example, you might read a summary reporting that many elementary school lunches are high in calories and contribute to our national obesity epidemic. To strengthen your research, find the study and examine it for yourself. Doing so will give you greater insight into the following:

- How many people were part of the study?
- What region of the country was sampled?
- What are some of the most pertinent demographic characteristics of the schools that participated in the study?

Understanding such factors will help you draw more accurate conclusions and present more reliable information to your audience.

The *way* you present your information is as important as the information you present. Remember that a study's conclusions are almost always preliminary. In a famous instance, researchers studying the impact of working conditions on productivity concluded that environmental factors, like the brightness of the lights in a factory, were responsible for increased levels of productivity. After further analysis, however, they discovered that it was not the lighting that positively affected productivity but, rather, the attention paid to the workers by the researchers who were present to conduct the study. This phenomenon, now known as the Hawthorne effect, is an important reminder that research is an ongoing process. Because we cannot study all variables at once, we must draw and state conclusions cautiously.

The best approach, then, is to make "soft" statements about research studies you cite. For example, you might say, "This study suggests," "This study implies," or "This study provides some indication that," instead of "This study proves" or "This study concludes." Remember also to focus your remarks on the new insights generated by a study, which can be found in the "Results" and "Discussion" sections of published articles. Finally, sometimes writers of journal articles use discipline-specific jargon and terminology. Simplify the language and conclusions of journal articles in a way that is appropriate for your audience.

### Use Electronic Databases

Many libraries invest in computer programs that give cardholders full remote access to electronic databases and subscriptions. Whether or not you choose to research remotely, visit the library and ask for help in using these tools.

Reference librarians can teach you how to use the unique features each database offers.

Many libraries subscribe to well over a hundred electronic databases that provide abstracts and full-text articles from a range of sources. Some of the most commonly used library databases are listed in Table 11.3. If your library does not subscribe to these databases, ask your reference librarian if you have access to similar databases that may include specialized information about your topic.

## Use Surveys and Statistics as Evidence

When collecting information from books, popular press sources, and scholarly journal articles, you will encounter surveys and statistics that may be useful in supporting your overall speech topic.

**Surveys** are *studies that ask a sample of the population a limited number of questions in order to discover public opinions on a particular set of issues.* Surveys, or polls,

| Table 11.3   Commonly Used Periodical Indexes |
|---|
| **Academic Search Complete** |
| ■ Academic Search Complete is updated daily with articles in a wide range of disciplines from over 4,000 scholarly publications. |
| **Communication and Mass Media Complete and Communication Abstracts** |
| ■ Databases index over 250 journals in communication and media use, updated bimonthly. |
| **LexisNexis and Factiva** |
| ■ These are often used to access full-text articles from newspapers and magazines, as well as transcripts of news broadcasts and legal cases. Factiva has over 10,000 sources from 159 countries. |
| **Education Full Text** |
| ■ Education Full Text incorporates publications from over 770 education journals, with more than half of the journals indexed as peer-reviewed publications. |
| **Medline** |
| ■ Medline is a medical database index from the National Library of Medicine incorporating over 4,000 journals related to healthcare and medicine. |
| **Readers' Guide to Periodical Literature** |
| ■ This includes over 300 magazine abstracts and 200 full-text magazines published in the United States. |
| **Humanities Abstracts and Social Sciences Index** |
| ■ These indexes reference both full-text articles and abstracts in art, literature, politics, social psychology, and crime. |

synthesize the experiences of hundreds or thousands of people. One person's experience with alcohol can have an impact on an audience, but a survey indicating that one-third of all U.S. adults abstain, one-third drink occasionally, and one-third drink regularly provides better support for an argument about the extent of alcohol use in this country. If you're considering citing survey results, first consider these important questions:

*How trustworthy is the survey source?* An important critical thinking question to ask is, Who sponsored the survey? A respected newspaper, an objective television or radio network, or a nonpartisan university can produce trustworthy surveys, but a political party, a company that sells a product related to the survey, or a group with a cause related to the survey topic will likely produce a survey that is biased.

*How broad was the sample?* Did the survey include the entire nation, the region, the state, the city, the campus, or the class? Larger samples represent a broader viewpoint. In the context of political and other polls, you probably have heard mention of a "margin of error." A survey conducted by sampling a small subset of individuals, and whose results are generalized to a much larger population, contains a significant margin of error. Larger sample sizes reduce the margin of error, which can boost confidence in the accuracy of a poll's results.

*Who was included in the survey?* Were people selected randomly, or did they volunteer to respond to the questions? From what population were they drawn? If survey responses come from people who called in to a radio talk show, the results will include only the views of people who listen to that show and have an interest in the topic. If people are randomly selected to be in a survey, the results are less likely to be biased by a particular viewpoint. As another example, if you conduct a poll only through Facebook, you are drawing from one kind of population; if you conduct a paper–pencil sur-vey at a shopping mall, you include a different kind of population. Scholarly articles always include information about sampling methods; other publications may be less careful about doing so.

*How representative was the survey sample?* For example, *GQ* readers or motorcycle enthusiasts (mostly young males, in both cases) are not typical of the population as a whole, yet many magazines targeted at a specific population survey their readers for opinions, which they then may generalize to the population as a whole, introducing a margin of error.

*Why was the survey done?* Was the survey performed for any self-serving purpose—for example, to attract more readers—or did the government conduct the study to help establish policy or legislation? If the survey

**CONSIDERING**

## MEDIA

### KNOW WHERE TO FIND RELIABLE AND TRUSTWORTHY STATISTICS

As you've learned, you must take caution in evaluating online sources of information. Source credibility should be a top priority for you as a researcher. The following three government websites are excellent resources for numbers and surveys you can trust.

- The Bureau of Labor Statistics (www .bls.gov/) reports on employment and economics.
- The Congressional Budget Office (www .cbo.gov/) reports on U.S. spending.
- The Census Bureau (www.census.gov/) provides demographic information about U.S. populations, including information on race, ethnicity, income, education, and so on.

All three of these government sources are nonpartisan, meaning they are not controlled by any one political party.

sponsor appears to have an agenda, such as selling tobacco products or cell phones, the possibility of bias in the findings or in the sampling is increased.

**Statistics** are *numbers used to summarize information or compare quantities.* They can be used as evidence, but they can be difficult to interpret. To make things easier for your audience, instead of saying, "Honda sales increased 47%," you could round off the figure to "nearly 50%." You could report the number of Honda car sales this year compared with last year. Finally, you could clarify the comparison—for example, by saying, "That is the biggest sales increase experienced by any domestic or imported car dealer in our city this year."

Because numbers are sometimes easier to understand when they appear in print, the public speaker often has to simplify, explain, and translate. For example, instead of saying, "North High had 323,462 high school graduates," say "North High had over 300,000 graduates." Other ways to simplify a number like 323,462 include writing the number on a board or poster and clarifying by using a comparison, such as "Three hundred thousand high school graduates are equivalent to the entire population of Lancaster."

You can greatly increase your effectiveness as a speaker if you illustrate your numbers by using visual resources, such as pie charts, line graphs, and bar graphs. When you have such aids, you can both say and show your figures. Also try using visual imagery—for example, "That amount of money is greater than all the money in all our local banks" or "That many discarded tires would cover our city 6 feet deep in a single year."

### GATHERING INFORMATION FROM THE INTERNET

Outside of the library, the most frequently used information source is the Internet. In this section we will review how to conduct effective Internet searches for relevant and accurate information on your topic.

## Use Search Engines and Virtual Libraries

The Pew Internet and American Life Project (www.pewinternet.org) is a non-profit organization that researches and studies the ways people incorporate digital technologies into their daily lives. Most recently, Pew reported that 85% of American adults use the Internet daily. For 91% of those participants, using a search engine to find information was their primary activity.[10]

A **search engine** is *a website that is used specifically to search for information.* We use search engines daily for everything from securing directions to exploring online product reviews and examining recent health trends and concerns. As useful as search engines can be, they also have some downsides. For example, they provide a lot of irrelevant information that you, the researcher, need to sift through. Also, they do not always clearly identify the credentials of the authors of the information they turn up. In other words, information found through search engines needs to be carefully evaluated.

Although search engines are the most common means of searching the Internet, another useful tool is a virtual library source. **Virtual libraries** *provide links to websites where some level of review for relevance and usability of the information has been conducted.* A source is not typically listed as part of a virtual library unless it has appeared in an academic journal, at a scholarly convention, or on a reputable website, such as a university or government agency website. Figure 11.4 presents a list of useful search engines and virtual libraries.

**Figure 11.4** Useful Search Engines and Virtual Libraries

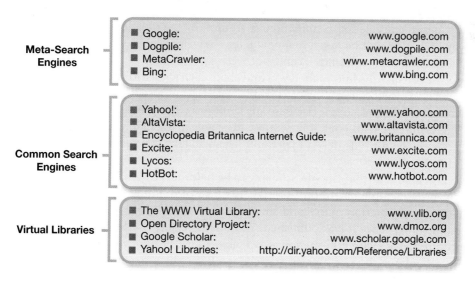

| Meta-Search Engines | |
|---|---|
| Google: | www.google.com |
| Dogpile: | www.dogpile.com |
| MetaCrawler: | www.metacrawler.com |
| Bing: | www.bing.com |

| Common Search Engines | |
|---|---|
| Yahoo!: | www.yahoo.com |
| AltaVista: | www.altavista.com |
| Encyclopedia Britannica Internet Guide: | www.britannica.com |
| Excite: | www.excite.com |
| Lycos: | www.lycos.com |
| HotBot: | www.hotbot.com |

| Virtual Libraries | |
|---|---|
| The WWW Virtual Library: | www.vlib.org |
| Open Directory Project: | www.dmoz.org |
| Google Scholar: | www.scholar.google.com |
| Yahoo! Libraries: | http://dir.yahoo.com/Reference/Libraries |

## Use Google Scholar

As a beginning researcher, you might struggle to determine which sources are the most critical to your topic. Google Scholar will help you identify what are known as **seminal sources,** *foundational studies or pieces of information that have been heavily cited and have helped advance a line of scholarly inquiry.*

Sometimes the hardest part of putting together a puzzle is seeing how each piece relates to the larger image being constructed. When you use Google Scholar to conduct a search, the results will include the seminal sources related to your topic of investigation. Returning to the puzzle analogy, this site will show you what articles serve as corner and edge pieces of the puzzle that is your overall research topic. For example, Figure 11.5 shows what you would see if you were to conduct a search on Google Scholar using the search term "cyberbullying."

- Examining the sources that have cited at least one of these three seminal articles would provide over 1,000 articles published since 2006. The published work related to any one of these three seminal sources could inform the entirety of a speech on cyberbullying, since you would not likely need to examine and analyze more than 300 sources.

- One of the benefits of Google Scholar is that it pulls information from a variety of disciplines. For the topic of cyberbullying, the top three sources are in different fields—child psychology, school psychology, and criminal justice.

- Google Scholar also pulls information from conference proceedings, which do not have as much peer review as other sources. With this in mind, it is your responsibility to evaluate the information in the green line.

Let's say you want to examine only the second source in the search shown in Figure 11.5. You could copy the source information, take it to your library, and request the article for examination. If you follow the blue link that says "Cited by 381," you will be taken to a new page that shows only the 381 sources that have cited this book since it came out.

If you take the information you find about each source to your library, you can get assistance locating each article. In fact, some campuses and universities have integrated their electronic database subscriptions with Google Scholar searches. If this is the case with your library, you will be able to log in to your library account and click on the blue title (a hyperlink). This will take you to a digital copy of the journal article.

A final way that Google Scholar can be helpful is by leading you to sources that are directly related to the scope of your topic. Simply type in the title of a source in quotation marks and then search through every item that has cited your source since it was published. You might be surprised to learn how much additional relevant information is available.

Applying these strategies to each largely cited source of information helps you find the most precise information in a large body of relevant sources.

**Figure 11.5** A Google Scholar Search for Articles on Cyberbullying

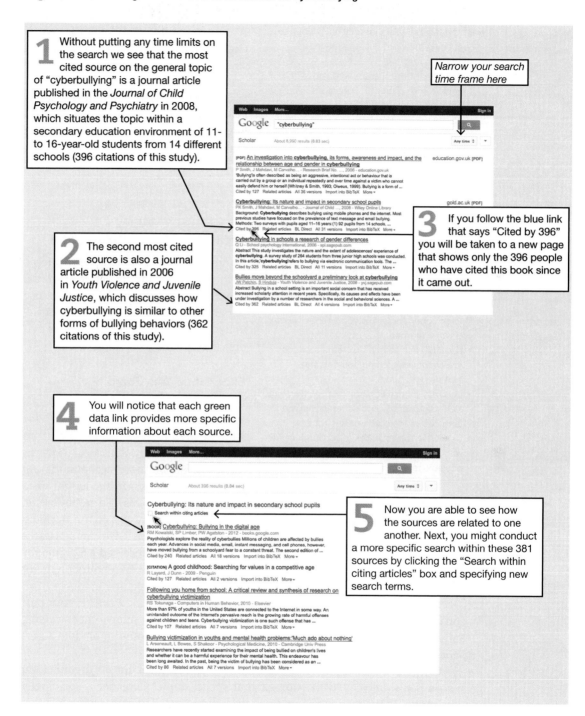

1 Without putting any time limits on the search we see that the most cited source on the general topic of "cyberbullying" is a journal article published in the *Journal of Child Psychology and Psychiatry* in 2008, which situates the topic within a secondary education environment of 11- to 16-year-old students from 14 different schools (396 citations of this study).

*Narrow your search time frame here*

2 The second most cited source is also a journal article published in 2006 in *Youth Violence and Juvenile Justice*, which discusses how cyberbullying is similar to other forms of bullying behaviors (362 citations of this study).

3 If you follow the blue link that says "Cited by 396" you will be taken to a new page that shows only the 396 people who have cited this book since it came out.

4 You will notice that each green data link provides more specific information about each source.

5 Now you are able to see how the sources are related to one another. Next, you might conduct a more specific search within these 381 sources by clicking the "Search within citing articles" box and specifying new search terms.

| Table 11.4 | Tips for Information Searching on the Internet |
|---|---|
| Word Stemming | ■ By default, browsers identify any webpage containing the word you entered in the search box.<br>• A search for the speech acronym *INFORM* would return sites with the words *informative, information, informal,* and *informing.*<br>• To prevent this result, type your search term with a single quote at the end: '*INFORM*' |
| Phrase Search | ■ If you are looking for a phrase, put the entire phrase in quotation marks.<br>• Typing in *campus safety* will return all sites that contain the two words *campus* and *safety* anywhere on the site. Placing the phrase in quotation marks will return only sites using the phrase in its entirety: "*campus safety.*" |
| Boolean Operators | ■ Boolean operators allow you to specify *what* you want returned.<br>• Use *AND* in a search box (e.g., *tobacco AND addiction*) to find sources that include both terms.<br>• Use *NOT* in a search box (e.g., *PowerPoint NOT Microsoft*) to find sources with the term before the operator but not after it.<br>• Use *OR* in a search box (e.g., *Gauguin OR van Gogh*) to find sites with one of two possible terms. |
| Parentheses | ■ Using parentheses allows you to combine Boolean search operators.<br>• Typing the search (*media AND violence*) *NOT television* will result in websites containing the terms *media* and *violence* but not *television.* |

## Use Internet Search Tools and Resources

A general understanding of search engine logic and functions, such as the strategic use of parentheses, quotation marks, and Boolean operators, will help you limit your searches to the most relevant sources. Table 11.4 offers tips on how to make the most of your Internet searches.

## GATHERING INFORMATION THROUGH PERSONAL EXPERIENCE AND INDEPENDENT RESEARCH

Another way to gain insight into a topic is through personal experience or the experiences of others. When you use **personal experience,** *you relate something that actually happened to you* as evidence for your speech topic.

### Experience Your Topic

Let's say you are working on a speech about excessive parking fines for student-commuters. You plan to advance the claim that local government should be more accommodating to students who park in residential areas around campus. This is a policy issue. Your personal story as a commuter who can't afford the expensive campus parking lots and who received a $25 fine for parking more than two hours on a city street can be compelling evidence. You have to be careful, however, if your personal experience is unusual. You would have to show that many other students suffered the same treatment, or your "evidence" would sound more like a personal gripe.

One way to gain personal experience is to volunteer for an organization whose goals are related to your general speech topic. Consider a sociologist who moves to the neighborhood he is studying in order to gain deeper insights into the way that community functions, or an investigative reporter who takes a job at the restaurant chain whose unfair employment practices she will later reveal in an article. Think of all the material you could gather in just a few hours of working on a local political campaign, in an animal shelter that takes in abused animals, or in your community, cleaning up a nearby park after a storm.

Your experiences volunteering, including the conversations you have and the activities you observe, can find their way into your speech. For example, say you are asked to develop an informative speech about providing healthcare for older adults. To research this topic, you could volunteer for a few hours at a senior center or an assisted living home and interact with both the staff and the residents. Experiencing some aspect of your topic firsthand offers many benefits. You might make contact with people who would make good interview sources. Moreover, volunteering demonstrates that you care about your speech topic, boosting your credibility as a speaker.

## Conduct Independent Research

Another way to become more directly involved with your topic is to conduct independent research. For example, most classes gather in the minutes before class begins, a brief time when you could ask your classmates their opinion about an issue you plan to discuss. You do not need to construct an entire survey; however, if you decide to, you can refer to Chapter 9, where this topic is discussed in detail. Maybe you just want to know how many of your classmates have a particular position on the topic you wish to discuss—for example, what they think of campus parking fines. In your presentation, you can reveal the results.

If you do not have strong, direct experience with your topic, you can engage in independent research by interviewing an expert. Your goal in the interview should be to get the expert talking about his or her experiences and to gather stories you might use as supporting material in your speech. You can do this by constructing open-ended questions—for example, "Can you describe for me an unusual case you have experienced while working as a campus security officer?" or "What do you think the current needs are in relation to campus security?" Either of these questions would generate **expert testimony,** or *information from a source who has enough credibility to speak about a specific topic.* Attorneys often use expert testimony in court—for example, evaluations of psychologists and physicians, to support the innocence or guilt of an individual. Expert testimony can be powerful and persuasive. However, although personal experience and independent research can enhance the overall quality of a speech, they should never be the sole basis for your argument. Make sure you also ground your speech in evidence from scholarly journal articles and books.

## EVALUATING, CITING, AND DOCUMENTING YOUR SOURCES

As you gather and evaluate a diversity of sources, and incorporate those sources into your knowledge base, always keep in mind the importance of source credibility. We have already discussed source credibility to some extent in the context of library and Internet research. But in this section we look at another means of evaluating sources and, especially, avoiding plagiarism by citing sources accurately and often.

## CHALLENGE YOURSELF

### I Am Familiar With Good Habits for Finding and Evaluating Sources, but How Do I Know If I've Chosen the Best Sources? How Do I Know When I Can Stop Seeking New Information?

Recent research published in the *Journal of Information Science* supports that, by and large, students are familiar with the practices associated with evaluating sources, like those listed in Table 11.5. However, the same study suggests that students are more likely to use the sources that are most accessible to them, rather than those that are most pertinent to their research goals.[11]

Your struggle begins with selecting the best and highest-quality sources to suit the needs of your topic and your audience. In this chapter you've learned some of the steps you can take to improve your information-searching practices. But how will you know when you are done seeking new information? Consider the following tips for managing your research process:

1. *Begin the process early.* The processes laid out in this chapter take time. Rushing is likely to lead to increased anxiety and a lower-quality product.
2. *Don't try to do all the research in one sitting.* Doing anything for too long diminishes your ability to focus on important details. Break up your research into at least three sessions, each focused exclusively on the development of each main point.
3. *Before initiating your second research session, evaluate, synthesize, and integrate the information from your first session.* The information you found in your first session may guide your subsequent research.
4. *Trust yourself.* Your goal is not to find out everything there is to know about your topic. Rather, you should aim to bring out an interesting and unique perspective. Your audience will know if you are genuinely interested in your topic; your enthusiasm is likely to advance their understanding.

Your credibility is at stake every time you address an audience. You want to use information that will enhance your credibility and show people that you care enough about their time to bring them the very best information you can find on your topic.

## Evaluate Sources of Information

As you begin evaluating, citing, and documenting sources, familiarize yourself with a technique known as data triangulation. **Data triangulation** is *the process of verifying and confirming the results or insights from one source of information with other types of information on the same topic.* For example, if you are working on a speech about global warming, you might want to incorporate some of what you read in Al Gore's 2006 book *An Inconvenient Truth.* However, because the book came out more than seven years ago, you might decide to verify that the claims advanced in the book are consistent with more current research on global warming. By checking your sources against each other using data triangulation, you ensure the credibility of the information you are presenting, as well as that of yourself as a speaker.

Whatever sources you evaluate, you can apply a consistent set of criteria to test their credibility. Specifically, ask yourself the questions outlined in Table 11.5. Throughout your research process, continue to ask these questions about every one of your sources. If you can answer yes to all these questions with

| **Table 11.5** Criteria for Testing Source Credibility | |
|---|---|
| Are there clear markers of credibility for the source? | ■ Be cautious of sources without a clear author who has identified credentials.<br>• *Examine the credentials of the author.* Ask yourself, Does the author have a degree or obvious expertise regarding the subject?<br>• *Examine the credentials of the publishing source.* Many journals require double-blind reviews of submissions before publication. Is this true of your source? |
| Is the source objective? | ■ Look for biases in the organization hosting or sponsoring the information or funding the research.<br>• Researching a speech on gun control, you might be especially critical in evaluating information found on the National Rifle Association (NRA) website.<br>• If you are researching Internet addiction, you might be expecially wary of any information sponsored by Microsoft. |
| Does the source draw appropriate conclusions? | ■ Credible sources draw conclusions that are appropriate for the study. For example, much survey research is conducted in such a way that the results cannot be applied beyond the study sample.<br>• Examine the Results and Discussion sections of a research study to verify that the conclusions it draws are grounded in the study's results.<br>• Use data triangulation.<br>• Ask yourself, Do the authors draw conclusions that go beyond the data? |
| Is the information in the source current? | ■ Scientific research is self-correcting over time. This means that additional research may detect flaws in earlier thinking and conclusions. Thus, refrain from using sources of information that are out of date.<br>• If you are putting together a speech about smoking and health, do not use antiquated sources that might downplay the dangers of smoking. |

## CONSIDERING

### MEDIA

### LEARN TO USE OWLS TO CITE YOUR SOURCES PROPERLY

The Purdue Online Writing Lab (OWL) is an excellent resource for learning how to cite information properly in the text of your speech outline, as well as on your reference list. APA style is typically used to cite sources in the social sciences, whereas MLA is most often used in the humanities.

- For APA style guidelines, visit http://owl.english.purdue.edu/owl/section/2/10/.
- For MLA style guidelines, see http://owl.english.purdue.edu/owl/section/2/11/.

Using these resources will ensure that you are giving your sources proper written credit and doing so in the format designated by your instructor.

certainty, you increase the chances that your sources are valid and trustworthy.

### Avoid Plagiarism

Being clear about where you found the evidence you use in your outline and your speech is very important. In doing so, a process called documenting your sources, you rightfully credit the work of other writers and researchers, avoid the very serious consequences of plagiarizing, and demonstrate that you are a credible speaker who has put a lot of good work into gathering and interpreting information. Therefore, once you identify a source you want to use, cite it properly in three places: the reference list for your speech (or paper), the body of your written work, and the oral delivery of your speech.

An effective **bibliographic reference** is *the complete citation information about a source that you include in the references or works cited at the end of your speech outline.* Your outline should also include **internal references,** *citation information about specific evidence as you present it in the body of your speech.* Table 11.6 gives examples of the two most common formats for written citations in a "references" or "works cited" list—the American Psychological Association (APA) style and the Modern Language Association (MLA) style. Your instructor generally specifies which style you should use. Although the rules may seem picky, using proper citation form is extremely important to good scholarship, as well as to your instructor in assessing your work.

You will also want to make sure you properly cite your sources during your speech. Such **oral citations** *make specific reference, where appropriate, as you present them, to each source you used.* An effective oral citation provides the following three pieces of information:

1. The author(s) of the piece
2. The date of publication (for a web source, the date it was last updated or was accessed)
3. The name of the publication

**Table 11.6** Proper APA and MLA References

| | APA References | MLA References |
|---|---|---|
| **Newspaper Article— General Style** | Last Name, First Initial. (year, month day). Title of article. *Title of Newspaper,* pp. first page, last page. | Author(s). "Title of Article." *Title of Newspaper* day month year: first page, last page. Medium of publication. |
| **Newspaper Article— Example** | Manjoo, F. (2012, October 22). Keeping loved ones on the grid. *The New York Times*, pp. D1, D7. | Manjoo, Farhad. "Keeping Loved Ones on the Grid." *The New York Times* 22 October 2012: D1, D7. Print. |
| **Journal Article— General Style** | Last Name, First Initial, Author, B. B., & Author, C. C. (year). Title of article. *Title of Journal, volume* (issue), first page–last page. doi: reference number | Author(s). "Title of Article." *Title of Journal* Volume. Issue (year): first page–last page. Medium of publication. |
| **Journal Article— Example** | Kanter, M., Afifi, T., & Robbins, S. (2012). The impact of parents "friending" their young adult child on Facebook on perceptions of parental privacy invasions and parent–child relationship quality. *Journal of Communication*, *62*(5), 900–917. doi: 10.1111/j.1460-2466.2012.01669.x | Kanter, Maggie, Tamara Afifi, and Stephanie Robbins. "The Impact of Parents "Friending" Their Young Adult Child on Facebook on Perceptions of Parental Privacy Invasions and Parent–Child Relationship Quality." *Journal of Communication* 62.5 (2012): 900–917. Print. |
| **Website— General Style** | Last Name, First Initial. (date of last update). *Site title*. Retrieved from URL | *Name of the Individual Webpage*. Name of the Publisher, year. Medium of Publication. Day month year accessed. |
| **Website— Example** | Pennsylvania State University. (October 12, 2012). *Penn State takes actions on many Freeh report recommendations*. Retrieved from http://live.psu.edu | *Penn State Takes Action on Many Freeh Report Recommendations*. Penn State University, 2012. Web. 12 October 2012. |
| **Interview— General Style** | Last Name, First Initial. (year, month day) *Personal Communication*. | Last Name, First Name. Personal Interview. Day month year. |
| **Interview— Example** | Hanson, M. (2012, September 10). *Personal Communication*. | Hanson, Mary. Personal Interview. 10 September 2012. |

*Note:* Journal articles that use continuous pagination from issue to issue of the same volume do not need to include the issue number in proper APA style. If an article does not have a doi (digital object identifier) number, you do not have to provide it. Interview references are not typically included in an APA reference list. However, you may want to include some information about interviews you conducted, so that you can count them among your sources.

You do not need to state the exact title of each source. Simply provide enough information that your audience members can locate your sources if they want to examine your evidence in greater depth. Figure 11.6 provides an example of how you can create an oral citation for a newspaper article, a journal article, a website, and an interview.

In general, during your presentation, do not go too long without referring to a source. Although your instructor will likely tell you the requirements for using sources in your speech, a good rule of thumb is to incorporate one oral reference for each minute of your speech. Using this rule, if you are preparing a five- to six-minute speech, you should orally cite five or six unique sources of information.

**Figure 11.6** Oral Citations for Newspaper Articles, Journal Articles, Websites, and Interviews

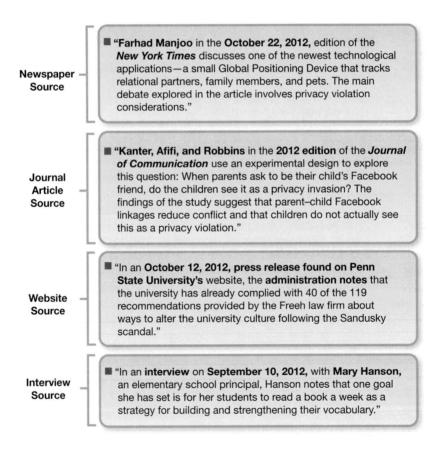

Newspaper Source

- "**Farhad Manjoo** in the **October 22, 2012,** edition of the **New York Times** discusses one of the newest technological applications—a small Global Positioning Device that tracks relational partners, family members, and pets. The main debate explored in the article involves privacy violation considerations."

Journal Article Source

- "**Kanter, Afifi, and Robbins** in the **2012 edition** of the **Journal of Communication** use an experimental design to explore this question: When parents ask to be their child's Facebook friend, do the children see it as a privacy invasion? The findings of the study suggest that parent–child Facebook linkages reduce conflict and that children do not actually see this as a privacy violation."

Website Source

- "In an **October 12, 2012, press release found on Penn State University's** website, the **administration notes** that the university has already complied with 40 of the 119 recommendations provided by the Freeh law firm about ways to alter the university culture following the Sandusky scandal."

Interview Source

- "In an **interview** on **September 10, 2012,** with **Mary Hanson,** an elementary school principal, Hanson notes that one goal she has set is for her students to read a book a week as a strategy for building and strengthening their vocabulary."

# CHAPTER REVIEW

This chapter has explored some of the ways you can ground your speeches and written work in the most current, credible, and valuable sources of information. With so much information at hand, you have the very important job of applying these strategies and thus turning data and information into useful knowledge for your audience. By using a diverse range of resources, including your library's holdings, the Internet, and your personal experiences, and methodically triangulating your sources and data, you help ensure that the information you pass on to your audience is both relevant and accurate. Finally, you now know how to evaluate and cite your sources in oral and written formats.

## KEY TERMS

bibliographic reference, 218
data, 201
data triangulation, 217
expert testimony, 215
information, 201
information anxiety, 202
information literacy, 201
information overload, 202
internal references, 218
knowledge, 201
online library catalog system, 204

oral citations, 218
personal experience, 214
primary source, 206
reference librarians, 204
search engine, 211
secondary source, 206
seminal sources, 212
statistics, 210
surveys, 208
virtual libraries, 211

## STUDY QUESTIONS

1. Name and explain the stages of an effective information-gathering process. How, if at all, does access to digital resources affect these stages?
2. Consider each of the following types of sources, and describe the kind of information you might find in each: books, newspaper articles, and scholarly journal articles.

3. How is Google Scholar different from your typical search engine?

4. Name a topic you could research that would allow you to draw from your personal experience. Name a topic you could research that would be enriched by surveying people in your community. Explain why you chose those topics.

5. What steps would you take to evaluate a source for credibility and document it to avoid being accused of plagiarism?

# Communication Apprehension and Delivery

In this chapter we will take a close look at the causes and symptoms of the fear of public speaking, as well as some tips for managing them. Even as you learn to manage the fear of public speaking, you need to practice your presentation for effective delivery.

LEARNING OBJECTIVES

*After reading this chapter, you should be able to:*

- Explain the relationship between delivery and communication anxiety.

- Describe the causes and symptoms of communication apprehension, as well as ways to manage them.

- Describe the four modes of delivery and explain the advantages and disadvantages of each.

- Understand how to apply the vocal aspects of delivery when giving a speech.

- Demonstrate the proper use of your body when delivering a speech.

- List some delivery tips for non-native speakers of English.

## WHY CARE ABOUT DELIVERY SKILLS?

Some people believe that it's not what you say, but how you say it, that really counts. According to others, the reverse is true. Actually, both what you say *and* how you say it are important. To better understand this, let's first discuss what *delivery* means.

### What Is Delivery?

**Delivery** is *how your voice and body affect the meaning of your presentation.* Effective speakers use their words, voice, and body to communicate a message in a compelling manner. Consider the points in Figure 12.1 about the importance of delivery skills.[1]

How you look and sound while delivering a presentation affects whether audiences will decide to listen to you. If you look confident and poised, if you speak smoothly and without unintended hesitation, and if your voice sounds strong and authoritative, your audience will perceive you as someone they should listen to.[2]

Perhaps the most striking fact about delivery is how quickly its impact is felt: audiences decide in seconds or, at the most, minutes whether they find you credible as a speaker. Observe fellow students, and watch your instructors, supervisors, managers, and executives at work. Do you judge their competence by how they look and sound? You will likely find that many judg-

**Figure 12.1** Unpacking Delivery

Effective delivery contributes to the credibility of the speaker.

Student audiences characterize the poorest speakers by the vocal and physical aspects of their delivery.

Speakers who are fidgety and nervous; whose voices are monotonous; who maintain little eye contact; and who show little animation or facial expression are perceived as having poor delivery skills.

ments about speakers' credibility come from their poised appearance and confident voice.

A common cause of poor delivery is public speaking anxiety. A fidgety speaker who makes little eye contact is displaying symptoms of nervousness, which negatively affect her delivery.[3] A presenter who speaks too quickly or softly will lose the attention of the audience. In the next section we aim to demystify public speaking anxiety by examining, first, the reasons speakers get nervous and, second, some strategies for managing those feelings, before and during the speech.

## What Is Communication Apprehension?

Given the role of mediated forms of communication in our lives—and the diminishing role of face-to-face interactions—it's no wonder that many of us struggle with nervousness when asked to speak in front of others.

**Communication apprehension (CA)** is *the fear of communicating with other people, whether that interaction is real or anticipated.*[4] CA can be triggered not only by the act of speaking in front of others but also simply by the thought or anticipation of that interaction. You may not experience any anxiety about your speech until the moment you enter the classroom the day of your presentation. In fact, seeing others present before you do can be just as nerve-racking as presenting yourself.

Nervousness often leads us to make mistakes or to present ourselves in a way that does not look or feel natural. You might even be wondering what you can gain from discussing these fears. Talking about your fears can help, as can reminding yourself that you are not alone. In a recent study, college students were asked to list their biggest fears, and speaking to a group of people was the most commonly identified fear.[5] Over 800 college students listed speaking in front of a group more frequently than any other fear, including the fear of experiencing financial problems, death, or loneliness, as illustrated in Figure 12.2.

## Experiencing Communication Apprehension

Before examining modes of delivery and the vocal and bodily aspects of presenting, you first need to understand the reasons for communication apprehension and what you can do to overcome it.

CA happens across a range of contexts. Some people experience anxiety only when thinking about speaking in front of groups, whereas others get nervous about interacting one-on-one; some of us experience anxiety in both cases.[6]

**Figure 12.2** The Top Fears of College Students

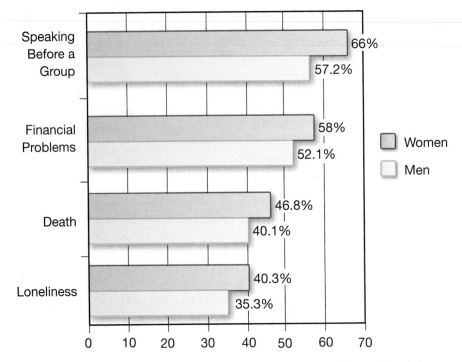

**Source:** Dwyer, K. K., & Davidson, M. M. (2012). Is public speaking really more feared than death? *Communication Research Report, 29*, 99–107.

Generally speaking, **trait apprehension** is *communication anxiety in a variety of settings and under diverse circumstances.*[7] **State apprehension,** on the other hand, is *communication anxiety in a limited number of settings or circumstances,* such as only when speaking to a large group of people, or only while being evaluated. Most people experience some degree of state apprehension, commonly referred to as stage fright or public speaking anxiety.

We often are our own worst critics and incorrectly believe that our audience is judging our presentation skills as harshly as we do. Most often the reverse is true. Because your peers will also be expected to get up and speak, they are more likely to sympathize with your anxiety than to disapprove of it.

The goal of this chapter is not to help you get rid of your anxiety altogether. Experiencing too little or too much anxiety can reduce the overall effectiveness of your communication with your audience. For example, if your anxiety levels are too low, you might overestimate your abilities, underprepare, or establish too casual and relaxed a tone. When your anxiety levels are too high, your delivery can suffer, as when your speech speeds up, your breathing changes, or your body temperature rises and causes your face to turn red.

Everyone has felt anxiety, and moderate amounts can actually improve your delivery. Use the time you give to preparation and practice to reduce any fears to manageable levels, so that they help rather than hinder your delivery. Athletes, musicians, and speakers all feel anxiety when performing, but they practice over and over until they are comfortable in front of an audience.

When we talk about CA, it is important to keep the goals of public speaking in mind. For example, your goal in speaking is to communicate information or to persuade your audience, so your focus falls on creating a message that will work on a particular audience; a speaker who focuses on the audience and message tends to forget about the dry mouth and shaky knees he may experience. Factors such as the structural elements and content of your speech can likewise affect anxiety levels. For example, when you forget to prepare sufficient notes, or to develop your topic and organize it using an outline, you are more likely to experience higher levels of CA.

But what if you do all you can to prepare and still experience anxiety before presenting? Even when you don't achieve perfect delivery, you can still meet the goal of communicating to your audience. Just think of all the famous speakers throughout history who have communicated important messages to large groups of people despite imperfect delivery and high anxiety levels. For instance, the popular movie *The King's Speech* depicts King George VI of England overcoming his stammer and fear of public speaking to rouse his people during World War II. Abraham Lincoln reportedly suffered extreme shyness, despite having delivered his memorable and stirring Gettysburg Address.

## REDUCE YOUR FEAR OF PUBLIC SPEAKING

In the same way that athletes train and practice to improve their skills, getting over speech anxiety requires commitment and practice. Three techniques that can help you reduce and manage your anxiety levels are systematic desensitization, cognitive restructuring, and skills training. One or more of these techniques may be right for you.

### Systematic Desensitization

The first technique we will discuss, **systematic desensitization,** *focuses on progressive relaxation, visualization, and active engagement exercises to help you overcome public speaking anxiety.* To practice systematic desensitization, begin by performing a relaxation exercise in your mind. You will continue to perform the same exercise in progressively more uncomfortable or anxiety-producing scenarios.

For instance, you might begin by doing the exercise while in a completely calm and relaxed state, such as when you get home in the evening or just before going to bed. Eventually, you will work up to using the same technique while preparing to speak in front of a group, perhaps on your way to class. The following steps describe one way to use this technique in preparing for a speech:

1. Turn off the lights; lie down and think of a situation in which you are totally relaxed and free of stress.
2. Take a deep breath, hold it for a few seconds, and then exhale, repeating with each new breath.
3. Feel the tension leave your body as you exhale each breath.
4. When you reach a relaxed state, visualize yourself doing a small speaking task successfully, such as telling a personal story you know well.
5. Next, practice doing the small activity you visualized in the previous stage. For example, if you are using that personal story to introduce your speech, practice a larger portion of your introduction out loud and by yourself.

 **YOURSELF**

**CHALLENGE**

## I Am Really Afraid to Give a Presentation to a Large Group. I Have Not Done Much Speaking and I Am Worried About How I Will Appear. Can I Do Anything to Relax and Enjoy Speaking?

Many times we avoid thinking about or working on a speech until the last possible minute.[8] This is a bit like ripping off an adhesive bandage—trying to do everything in one quick motion. This approach actually increases public speaking anxiety.

Research supports that devoting more time to practice before giving your speech will actually lower your anxiety and improve your delivery.[9] Following some simple preparation steps will help you reduce your anxiety and increase your enjoyment of public speaking.

- Practice your speech the first few times using your formal outline, which will have much of your speech content written out.
- Practice the content out loud. You can pronounce anything more effectively in your head than when you say it out loud. Identify words that are hard for you to say, as well as places where you get tripped up; then correct your delivery before the day of the presentation.
- As you practice, mark up your outline, noting the places where you seem to know the content pretty well, as well as the places where you struggle to recall what to say next. You might decide to add transitions or signposts in the places where your memory fails you.
- Since you won't be reading directly from your outline when you present, create note cards to take with you to the podium. Do not read them word-for-word, however; instead, they should be designed to assist you where you need it most.
- Finally, rehearse using the note cards, so that you are familiar with their contents on the day of the speech. Again, note the places where you continue to have difficulty thinking about what comes next. Either underline or highlight these places to provide yourself with delivery cues.

You do not need to rehearse your speech with a real audience until you are comfortable on your own. If you are feeling particularly nervous, try combining these steps with the systematic desensitization technique described in this chapter.

6. Finally, start over again with relaxation. This time visualize doing something slightly more difficult than you did before, such as delivering the first main point in the body of your speech. Follow the same sequence of steps.

Once you have practiced these elements successfully in your mind, you must practice them out loud in order to experience the full effects of this anxiety-reduction technique. For example, you might first begin by practicing delivering a smaller portion of your speech to a wall, then in front of a mirror, and finally to progressively larger groups of people whom you trust.

Although this approach takes time to employ successfully, research shows that many speakers find it to be highly effective.[10] One reason is that you begin by imagining successes, such as visualizing telling a story you know well, and then build on those positive experiences in the safety of your own imagination.

## Cognitive Restructuring

The second method for reducing anxiety in a communication situation is to use the power of positive thinking, also known as **cognitive restructuring.** This method works by *analyzing negative perceptions and developing coping statements for dealing with a variety of situations.* For example, one common negative thought is "If I forget a part of my speech, I will not do well." But the truth is, one small mistake will not make or break the speech. No one expects a perfect performance.

Our thoughts have a powerful impact on how we experience events, in both positive and negative ways. Sometimes we analyze situations too quickly and attach negative perceptions to them without being mindful of our assumptions. Taking a step back from our assumptions, analyzing our thought processes, and developing coping statements can help break down negative thinking.[11] A coping statement that focuses on what to do if such a thing occurs helps rebuild negative thoughts into positive ones—for example, "I will practice with my note cards, so that I know where I might have issues with memory, and if I forget a part of my speech, I will look at my cards and go to the next piece of information."

To use cognitive restructuring more broadly, you can take the following steps:

1. Create a list of all the irrational and negative self-talk dialogue you experience when thinking about public speaking.

2. Analyze each negative statement and identify a few of the unrealistic or overly negative assumptions you are making in the statement.

3. Develop a coping statement for each negative thought on your list. Be specific and spend as much time thinking about how to overcome those negative thoughts as you did considering them in the first place.

4. Practice the coping statements often until they automatically come to mind when you find yourself contemplating the negative dialogues.

Cognitive restructuring can also help you perceive the public speaking situation differently.[12] Instead of seeing your classroom speech as just another assignment in a required course, you can reframe the situation more positively. For example, speaking to your class is your personal opportunity to sway the thinking of 20 to 30 people who ordinarily would not have come together to listen to your ideas. In other words, you can cope with your negative feelings by redefining the situation as a valuable opportunity to demonstrate what you know, and to help others in the process.

### Skills Training

The third technique for getting over public speaking fears is practice. **Skills training** is *the systematic work you do, through instruction and practice, to develop your public speaking skills.* Rehearsal may sound like common sense, but research supports that consistent practice is one of the most successfully applied techniques for improving public speaking and reducing anxiety.[13]

The first step in using this technique is to recognize that public speaking is a skill that requires work. A student who really wants to become an effective communicator should

- Read and listen for basic instruction.
- Plan a presentation following the instructor's assignment.
- Analyze the audience.
- Practice and deliver the speech.

Furthermore, coaching from the instructor and classmates can help you develop better skills. You are already undertaking this recommendation by reading this book and taking a class in which you will develop greater competence in public speaking.

One example of the skills approach in action is the practiced use of eye contact. Many beginning speakers spend way too much time looking at their notes or PowerPoint slides and too little time maintaining eye contact with their audience. As discussed in Chapter 10, beginning speakers should use a key-word outline for note cards instead of a script, in order to deliver an extemporaneous speech instead of a memorized one. The extemporaneous mode of delivery will encourage eye contact. Over a series of speech-giving opportunities, you will learn to rely much less on your notes and much more on your message and audience.

### Choosing the Right Anxiety-Reducing Technique for You

Now that you are aware of three useful approaches for overcoming CA, you might be wondering which technique you should use. Actually, you can benefit from all these strategies, because each targets different aspects of public speaking anxiety.[14] You might also confer with your instructor to develop a plan that considers your particular anxieties and skills and emphasizes the strategies that will be most helpful to you.[15]

As you can see, working on your delivery skills and managing public speaking anxiety go hand in hand. An important message delivered poorly will fail to engage listeners; however, the same message delivered with confidence and skill can succeed in influencing and informing your audience.

## THE FOUR MODES OF DELIVERY

The four modes of delivery are extemporaneous, impromptu, manuscript, and memorized. In your public speaking class, you may be asked to try the impromptu mode for certain assignments. However, most classroom presentations require the extemporaneous mode.

The four modes of delivery vary in the amount of preparation they require. Although all are possible choices for your presentation, speakers are least likely to use the manuscript and memorized modes. The manuscript and memorized modes encourage accuracy but discourage eye contact, audience adaptation, and conversational style. Also, the memorized mode requires much more preparation time than a class with a number of assigned speeches can afford. That is why most public speaking classrooms encourage students to use the extemporaneous mode.

### The Extemporaneous Mode

A presentation delivered in the **extemporaneous mode** is *carefully prepared and practiced, but the presenter delivers the message conversationally without heavy dependence on notes.* This mode is message- and audience-centered, with the presenter focused not on the notes but on the ideas being expressed. This mode is characterized by considerable eye contact, freedom of movement and gesture, the language and voice of conversation, and the use of an outline or key words to keep the presenter from reading or paying undue attention to a written script.

Although this mode lends a speech the appearance of spontaneity, don't be fooled; extemporaneous delivery only appears to be spontaneous. Like a talented musician who makes a complicated composition look easy after hours of practice, you need to work hard to make your presentation seem smooth and easy. Extemporaneous delivery allows you to be very flexible and adaptable, to focus on conveying your message to that particular audience. You do not need to use the same words you used when practicing the speech, and you can repeat or explain if you see that the audience is puzzled.

You have seen this mode of delivery in the classroom, in some professors' lectures, sometimes in the pulpit, often in political and legal addresses, and usually in presentations by experienced speakers. This is the mode you will find most useful outside the classroom.

As a student in the communication classroom, you need to avoid overrehearsing your presentation to the point that you memorize it. Most communication instructors and audiences respond negatively to presentations that sound memorized. Any presentation that sounds memorized—and most memorized presentations do—never lets the audience get beyond the impression that the speaker's words are not really his or her own, even if they are.

### The Impromptu Mode

With the **impromptu mode,** *you deliver a presentation without notes, plans, or formal preparation and with spontaneity and conversational language.* You use the impromptu mode when you answer a question in class, when you say who you are, and when you give people directions on the street. You cannot say much in these situations unless you know the answers. Ordinarily, this mode of delivery requires no practice and no careful choice of language, but it does require that you know something about the topic.

The impromptu mode encourages you to "think on your feet" without research, preparation, or practice, so the advantage of the impromptu mode is that you learn how to handle questions about your speech, inquiries about you in a job interview, or questions in class or on the job. The disadvantage of the impromptu mode is that you really do have to know something to provide an adequate response.

### The Manuscript Mode

As its name implies, in the **manuscript mode** you *deliver a presentation from a script of the entire speech.* The advantage of this mode is that the presenter knows exactly what to say and reads the words to the audience while giving as much attention to the audience as possible. The disadvantages are that the written message invites a speaker to pay more attention to the script than to the audience and it discourages eye contact and audience feedback.

Politicians, especially those who are likely to be quoted, as well as clergy and professors sometimes use this mode of delivery. Students are rarely asked to use this mode, except when reading a quotation from part of a presentation to the class.

### The Memorized Mode

A presentation delivered in the **memorized mode** is *committed to memory.* This mode requires considerable practice and allows plenty of eye contact, movement, and gestures. However, this mode discourages the speaker from responding to feedback, from adapting to the audience during the speech, and from choosing words that might be appropriate at the moment. In other words, memorization removes spontaneity and increases the danger of forgetting.

Politicians, athletes, and businesspeople—those who speak to the same kinds of audiences about the same subjects—often memorize their speeches. Even professors, when they teach a class for the third time in a week, may memorize the lesson for the day.

## Choosing the Right Mode of Delivery for Your Presentation

The mode you choose should be appropriate for the message, audience, and occasion. Students use the extemporaneous mode most often in learning public speaking, because that mode teaches good preparation, adaptation to the audience, and a focus on the message. Nonetheless, your mode of delivery does not determine your effectiveness.

Comparing extemporaneous and memorized modes, two researchers concluded that the mode is not what makes a speaker effective. Instead, the speaker's ability is more important. Some speakers are more effective with extemporaneous speeches than with manuscripts, but others use both modes with equal effectiveness.[16]

Frequently, the situation, or context, invites a particular mode of delivery. In a spontaneous toast of a bride and groom, the audience expects a brief, impromptu expression of congratulations; at a political rally, a politician gives some variation of a speech she has delivered many times and in many places (extemporaneous mode); an attorney reads a will to the expectant family (manuscript mode); and an experienced public speaker includes some passage that he has memorized. In the classroom context, the instructor determines the expected mode of delivery.

## THE VOCAL ASPECTS OF PRESENTATION

Studying the vocal aspects of presentation is like studying music. The words of a presentation are like musical notes. As people speak, they create a melody. Think of a song that has been covered by two different musicians. Just as musicians can make the same notes sound quite different, affecting their audiences according to the rhythm and mood, for instance, presenters can alter the way they say words in order to get the audience to respond in various ways.

Some of these vocal aspects were covered in Chapter 4, where you learned briefly about nonword sounds. The nine **vocal aspects** of presentation are *projection and volume, rate, pauses, fluency, pitch, pronunciation, articulation, enunciation,* and *vocal variety.*

### Projection and Volume

**Projection** is *speaking loudly enough for all to hear,* whereas **volume** is *the relative loudness of your voice.* Audiences (and instructors) get distracted or annoyed when they cannot hear the presenter. You need to be conversational but with a slightly higher volume than you are used to using.

Volume is more than just loudness. Variations in volume can convey emotion, importance, suspense, and changes in meaning. You can use a stage whisper in front of an audience, just as you would whisper a secret to a friend. You can speak loudly and strongly on important points, letting your voice carry your conviction.

Volume can change with the situation. For example, a political rally may be filled with loud, shouted cheers bursting with enthusiasm, whereas a eulogy may be delivered at a lower, respectful volume. An orchestra never plays so quietly that patrons cannot hear, but the musicians vary their volume. Similarly, a presenter who considers the voice an instrument learns how to project softly, loudly, and somewhere in between to convey meaning.

### Rate

**Rate** is *the speed of delivery, or how fast you say your words.* The normal rate for Americans is between 125 and 190 words per minute, but this rate varies widely. You need to remember that your rate of delivery depends on you—how fast you normally speak—and on the situation, audience, and subject matter. People tend to speak more slowly and quietly at a funeral, children listening to a story understand better at slower rates, and complex materials may require more patient timing and more repetition.

Most speech instructors like a presentation to sound conversational yet more formal and careful than street talk. The best advice is to adopt the rate of speaking you use when you talk with others in a conversation. Of course, in front of an audience, you speak as you would in conversation but with a louder voice (increased volume). Try to have a comfortable rate that is slower than a bullet train but not as slow as to induce sleep in your audience.

### Pauses

The third vocal characteristic of speech delivery is the **pause,** *an absence of vocal sound used for dramatic effect, transition, or emphasis.* Presentations are often a steady stream of words without silences, yet pauses can be used for dramatic effect and to get an audience to consider content. The speaker may begin a speech with rhetorical questions:

> *Have you had a cigarette today? Have you had 2 or 3? 10 or 11? Do you know what your habit is costing you in a year? A decade? A lifetime?*

After each rhetorical question, a pause allows audience members to answer the question mentally. These are pauses correctly used for effect.

On the other hand, **vocalized pauses** are *breaks in fluency that negatively affect an audience's perception of the speaker's competence and dynamism.* These "ahhhs" and "mmhhs" are disturbing and distracting. Unfortunately, even some experienced speakers have the habit of filling silences with vocalized pauses.

One technique that can help increase awareness of the use of vocalized pauses is to have someone who is listening to the speaker drop a marble into a can every time a vocalized pause is used. The resulting punishment, the clanging of the cans, can help break the speaker's habit. You might also ask a friend to simply count every time you vocalize a pause and note problematic areas of the speech, so that you know where to practice less use of vocalized pauses as you prepare to present to an audience. Many audiences would prefer a little silence to a series of vocalized pauses.

### Fluency

The fourth vocal characteristic of delivery is **fluency,** *the smoothness of the delivery, the flow of the words, and the absence of vocalized pauses.* Fluency cannot be achieved by looking up words in a dictionary or by any other simple solution. Fluency is not even very noticeable, but lack of fluency is obvious. Listeners are more likely to notice errors than the seemingly effortless flow of words in a well-delivered speech. Also, you can be too smooth. A speaker who seems too slick or smooth-talking is sometimes perceived as dishonest. One study showed the importance of fluency: audiences tended to perceive the speaker's fluency and smoothness of presentation as a main determinant of his or her effectiveness.[17]

To achieve fluency, presenters must be confident about the content of their speeches. By knowing what they are going to say and practicing the words over and over, speakers can reduce their use of disruptive repetition and vocalized pauses. If presenters focus on the overall rhythm of the speech, their fluency improves. Speakers must pace, build, and time the various parts of the speech to unite them into a coherent whole.

### Pitch

The fifth vocal characteristic of delivery is **pitch,** *the highness or lowness of a speaker's voice—the voice's upward and downward movement and the melody produced by the voice.* Pitch is what makes the difference between the "ohhh" you utter when you earn a poor grade in a class and the "ohhh" you make when you see someone really attractive. The "ohhh" looks the same in print, but when the notes turn to music, the difference between the two expressions is vast.

The pitch of your voice can make you sound either lively or listless. As a speaker you learn to avoid the two extremes: the lack of change in pitch that results in a monotone and the repeated changes in pitch that result in a singsong delivery. The best public speakers use the full range of their normal pitch (Figure 12.3).[18]

Presenters make many subtle changes in meaning by producing changes in pitch. The speaker's pitch tells an audience whether the words are a statement or a question, whether the words mean what they say, and whether the presenter is expressing doubt, determination, irony, or surprise.

Presenters learn pitch control only through regular practice. An actor who is learning to deliver a line has to practice that line many times and in many ways before being sure that most people in the audience will understand the words as intended. An effective presenter rehearses a presentation before friends to discover whether this will be the case. You may sound angry when you do not intend to, doubtful when you mean to sound certain, or frightened when you are only surprised. You may not be the best judge of how you sound to others, so practice with someone who can tell you honestly how you sound.

### Pronunciation

The sixth delivery characteristic is **pronunciation,** *the act of correctly articulating words.* The best way to avoid pronunciation errors is to go to an Internet source like Dictionary.com, which provides an audio symbol "◀))" that reveals how to pronounce words. Following is an example of what Dictionary.com says about the word *Urdu,* an Asian language. Notice the symbol of a speaker; click on the symbol and the website will provide an audio pronunciation of the word.

Of course, any standard hardcover or online dictionary provides a pronunciation table to help you with new and unusual words. Listening to broadcasters, teachers, and even presenters in your class can increase your vocabulary. But if you still have some misgivings about how to pronounce a word, you should ask your instructor for assistance before the day of your presentation.

### Articulation

The seventh delivery characteristic is **articulation,** *the production of sounds,* which is another important part of enunciation. An example of articulation problems

> From Dictionary.com:
>
> ■ **Urdu** ◀)) [*oor*-doo, **ur**-; *oor*-**doo**, ur-] one of the official languages of Pakistan, a language derived from Hindustani, used by Muslims, and written with Persian-Arabic letters.

**Figure 12.3** The Control of Pitch

Controlling pitch does more than make a presentation sound pleasing.

> Changes in pitch can help an audience remember information.

> Voices perceived as "good" are characterized by a greater range of pitch, more upward and downward inflections, and more pitch shifts.

> Certainly, one of the important features of pitch control is that pitch can alter the way an audience responds to the words spoken.

are when you order "dry toast" (without butter) and get "rye toast" or when you asked for a "missing statement" and get a "mission statement." Other times articulation is a problem because you are unfamiliar with a word. For example, a student giving a speech on euthanasia (assisted suicide) had a fine topic, but he called his topic "ee-then-as-ee-ah" instead of articulating it the correct way, which sounds like "youth-in-Asia."

Among the common articulation problems are the dropping of final consonants and "-ing" sounds ("goin'," "comin'," and "leavin'"), the substitution of "fer" for "for," and the substitution of "ta" for "to." An important objective in public presentations, as in all communication, is to articulate accurately.

### Enunciation (Pronunciation Plus Articulation)

**Enunciation,** the eighth vocal aspect of speech delivery, is *the pronunciation and articulation of sounds and words.* Lack of enunciation often occurs because we don't say whole words or we slur over them. A person who says "I'm gunna be leavin' in the mornin' if I'm feelin' bedder," is trying to say, "I am going to be leaving in the morning if I am feeling better." Another example of enunciation is someone who says "sumpinz up" when she means "something is up."

Rehearsing in front of friends, roommates, or family is a relatively safe way to try out your vocabulary and pronunciation on an audience. Your objective should be to practice unfamiliar words until you are comfortable with them. Also, be alert to the names of people you quote, introduce, or cite in your speech;

audiences are impressed when a student speaker correctly pronounces such names as Goethe, Monet, and de Chardin. And your instructor will be impressed if you ask during speech preparation how to pronounce a certain word. That approach is better than just mispronouncing it in a presentation in front of class or at work.

## Vocal Variety

The ninth vocal aspect of speech delivery—one that summarizes many of the others—is **vocal variety.** This term refers to *voice quality, intonation patterns, inflections of pitch, and the duration of syllables.* Studies show that vocal variety improves the effectiveness of public presentations:

- A very early study of reading out loud found that audiences retain more information with large variations in rate, force, pitch, and voice quality.[19]
- More recently, researchers studied an audience's comprehension of prose and poetry and found that comprehension decreased 10% when the presenter delivered material in a monotone voice.[20]
- Audience members understand more when listening to skilled speakers than when listening to unskilled speakers.[21] They also recall more information both immediately after the speech and at a later date.
- Skilled speakers are more effective, whether the material is organized or disorganized, easy or difficult.[22]
- Good vocalization was found to include fewer but longer pauses, greater ranges of pitch, and more upward and downward inflections.[23]

If you learn how to manage the vocal aspects of delivery, you will be well on your way to impressing listeners with how you look and sound as a speaker. You will also find yourself more comfortable and confident in your role as a public speaker.

## THE BODILY ASPECTS OF PRESENTATION

The importance of delivery has been recognized for thousands of years. In the *Rhetoric ad Herennium,* Cicero observed that "delivery is the graceful regulation of voice, countenance, and gesture." This section focuses on the **bodily aspects** of delivery, or *how to use your body to convey meaning.*

### Gestures

**Gestures** are *movements of the head, arms, and hands used to illustrate, emphasize, or signal ideas in a speech.* People rarely worry about gestures in conversation, but when they give a speech in front of an audience, arms and hands seem to be bothersome. Perhaps people feel unnatural because public speaking is an unfamiliar situation.

Do you remember the first time you drove a car, the first time you tried to swim, or the first time you kissed? The first time you give a speech, you might not feel any more natural than you did then. Nonetheless, physically or artistically skilled people make their actions look easy. A skilled golfer, a talented painter, and a graceful dancer all perform with seeming ease. Beginners make a performance look difficult. Apparently, we have to work diligently to make physical or artistic feats look easy.

What can you do to help yourself gesture naturally when you deliver your presentation? The answer lies in connecting your feelings to your behavior. When speakers really care about a topic, you can see their passion in the way they deliver their message: they are more animated, their face shows a range of emotion, their voice is strong, and their eyes connect with yours. Students speaking on a variety of topics from environmental awareness to business ethics have demonstrated that passion and conviction translate into effective delivery.

In addition to focusing on finding a topic you are passionate about, you should also concentrate on your message. Being self-conscious about your delivery or trying to focus too much on a "perfect" delivery can backfire and cause your delivery to seem unnatural. Some students trained in competitive debate exhibit unnatural delivery behaviors that actually cause audience members to

**CONSIDERING MEDIA**

## RESPOND TO SPEAKERS ON YOUTUBE

New technology invites you to create videos that can be viewed and shared on platforms like YouTube or Vimeo. How can you use these new technologies to improve your delivery?

- Record a video of your speech and upload it to YouTube or Facebook.
- Ask your network of friends to watch and critique your presentation.
- If you find you are having particular problems, such as vocalizations or a lack of eye contact, your friends will be helpful in pointing them out.
- You may even decide to generate discussion about the focus of your speech and obtain quotes or ideas that you can integrate into it.

Social media resources give us ways to get feedback from more people than ever before. Who knows—your speech may even go viral!

become focused so much on delivery that they lose the message of the speech. You should concentrate on your message and do your best to present natural delivery behaviors in your speech.

Another way of learning to make appropriate gestures is to practice a speech in front of friends who are willing to make helpful suggestions. In time, and after many practice sessions, public speakers learn which arm, head, and hand movements seem to help and which seem to hinder their message. For instance, actors spend hours rehearsing lines and gestures, so that they will look spontaneous and unrehearsed on stage. Through practice you, too, can learn to gesture naturally, in a way that reinforces rather than detracts from your message.

### Facial Expressions

Your face is the most expressive part of your body. **Facial expressions** consist of *the nonverbal cues expressed by a speaker's face.* Eyebrows rise and fall; eyes twinkle, glare, and cry; lips pout or smile; cheeks can dimple or harden; and a chin can jut out in anger or recede in yielding. Some people's faces are a barometer of their feelings; others' faces seem to maintain the same appearance whether they are happy, sad, or pained.

Because you do not ordinarily see your own face while speaking, you may not be fully aware of how you appear to an audience. In general, speakers are trying to maintain a warm, positive relationship with the audience, and they signal that intent by smiling as they would in conversation with someone they like. However, the topic, the speaker's intent, the situation, and the audience all help determine the appropriate facial expressions in a public speech. You can discover the appropriateness of your facial expressions by having friends, relatives, or classmates tell you how you look when practicing your speech. You can also observe how your instructors use facial expressions to communicate.

### COMMUNICATING GLOBALLY

#### EYE CONTACT COMMUNICATES DIFFERENT MESSAGES FROM CULTURE TO CULTURE

Strong eye contact during a presentation does not communicate the same thing in all cultures. For instance, speakers from nondominant cultures may not use eye contact as expected by the dominant culture. Most Americans think direct eye contact signals respect and attention to the listener, but some cultures inside and outside the United States believe that direct eye contact signals disrespect or defiance of authority. Some Native American[24] and Latino cultures, for example, regard direct eye contact as disrespectful, and some African cultures perceive it as a threat. What does eye contact signal to you? What might it mean to your classroom audience?

### Eye Contact

Another physical aspect of delivery important to a public speaker is **eye contact,** or *the extent to which a speaker looks directly at the audience.* In conversation we use eye contact to signal turn taking: we can look away while conversing but resume eye contact to signal the other person's turn to speak. Eye contact can also evoke other meanings in presentations:

- Too much eye contact—"staring down the audience"—is too much of a good thing, but too much gazing at notes—lack of eye contact—is poor delivery.

- Audiences prefer the maintenance of good eye contact,[25] and good eye contact improves source credibility.[26]

- Eye contact in a presentation signals your relationship with the audience. If you look at your audience in a friendly way, you signal a warm relationship with them.

- The belief that a person who cannot look you in the eye during conversation may not be telling the truth can be applied to public speaking situations; a speaker's averted eyes may invite the audience to think that he is not telling the truth, even if he is.

- A public speaker who rarely or never looks at audience members may appear disinterested in them, and the audience may resent being ignored.

- A public speaker who looks over the heads of audience members or scans them so quickly that eye contact is not established may appear to be afraid of the audience.

The proper relationship between audience and speaker is one of purposeful communication. You signal that sense of purpose by treating audience members as individuals with whom you wish to communicate, by looking at them for responses to your message.

How can you learn to maintain eye contact with your audience? One way is to know your speech so well that you have to glance only occasionally at your notes. A speaker who does not know the speech well is manuscript-bound. Delivering an extemporaneous speech from key words or an outline is a way of encouraging yourself to keep an eye on the audience. One of the purposes of extemporaneous delivery is to enable you to adapt to your audience, which is not possible unless you are continually observing their behavior to see if they appear to understand your message.

Another way of learning to use eye contact is to scan your entire audience and address various sections as you progress through your speech. Concentrating on the head nodders may also improve your eye contact: in almost every audience, some individuals overtly indicate whether your message is coming across; these individuals usually nod yes or no with their heads. Some speakers find that friendly faces and positive head nodders improve their delivery.

## Movement

The fourth physical aspect of delivery is **bodily movement,** *what a speaker does with his or her entire body during a* *presentation.* Sometimes the situation limits a speaker's movement, as might the presence of a fixed microphone, a lectern, a pulpit, or any other physical feature of the environment. The length of the speech can also make a difference; a short speech without movement is less difficult for both speaker and audience than is a very long speech without movement.

Good movement is appropriate and purposeful. A "caged lion" who paces back and forth to work off anxiety is moving inappropriately and purposelessly in relation to the content of the presentation. You should move for a reason, such as walking a few steps when delivering a transition, thereby literally helping your audience "follow you" to the next idea. Some speakers move forward on the points they regard as most important.

Because of the importance of eye contact, speakers should always strive to face the audience, even when moving. Some other suggestions on movement relate to the use of visual aids. Speakers who write on the board during a speech have to turn their backs on the audience. Avoid turning your back by using PowerPoint or Prezi, writing information on the board between classes, preparing a poster ahead of time, or projecting your images on a screen.

You can learn through practice and observation. Watch your professors, teaching assistants, and fellow students when they deliver their speeches to determine what works for them. They may provide positive or negative examples. Similarly, you need to determine what works best for you when you practice your speech. Use a form like that in Figure 12.4 to evaluate your nonverbal delivery.

## DELIVERY TIPS FOR NON-NATIVE SPEAKERS

If you are a student who speaks English as a second language, you may be particularly concerned about your delivery. After all, you must try to remember what you want to say, select the appropriate words, and pronounce them correctly. These concerns differ greatly from one person to another, depending on how comfortable you are with your topic and spoken English. Here are some suggestions for how to work on delivery issues that may be of unique concern to you:

1. *Recognize that you are not alone.* For most speakers, the actual delivery of the speech is what causes the most anxiety. Even native speakers worry that they will forget what they intend to say or that they will say something incorrectly. If you have anxiety about delivery, your classmates will certainly empathize with you.

2. *Give yourself time.* Most of the other suggestions on this list require that you have some extra time to devote to improving your delivery. Perhaps you may need to begin working on your speeches much earlier in comparison with many of your classmates.

3. *Check pronunciation.* With several online pronunciation dictionaries, you can look up words and hear them pronounced. For new and unfamiliar words or words with many syllables, such resources can help you practice correct pronunciation.

**Figure 12.4** An Evaluation Form for Nonverbal Aspects of Delivery

## Evaluation Form for Nonverbal Aspects of Delivery

To summarize the material on vocal and bodily aspects of delivery, you should examine the sample evaluation form below. Use this scale to evaluate yourself and others on each of the following items: 1 = excellent, 2 = good, 3 = average, 4 = fair, 5 = weak.

### Vocal Aspects of Delivery

_____ Pitch: upward and downward inflections
_____ Rate: speed of delivery
_____ Pause: appropriate use of silence
_____ Volume: loudness of the voice
_____ Enunciation: articulation and pronunciation
_____ Fluency: smoothness of delivery
_____ Vocal variety: overall effect of all of the above

### Bodily Aspects of Delivery

_____ Gestures: use of the arms and hands
_____ Facial expression: use of the face
_____ Eye contact: use of the eyes
_____ Movement: use of the legs and feet

4. *Talk with your instructor about reasonable goals.* If you are still working on several pronunciation or grammar issues, you can use your public speaking class as an opportunity to improve. With your instructor's help, identify a short list of items that you can work on over the course of the term. Your practice efforts will be more focused, and your instructor will have a clearer idea of what to concentrate on when giving feedback. If you do not set such objectives beforehand, both you and your instructor may have difficulty concentrating on specific and attainable areas for improvement.

5. *Understand that eye contact is important.* Especially if you come from a culture that does not emphasize eye contact, you should recognize that American audiences value this nonverbal delivery characteristic. To improve your eye contact, you should first get more comfortable maintaining eye contact during conversation. As your eye contact improves during one-on-one interactions, you can work on improving eye contact during speeches.

6. *Practice using audio or video recordings.* By listening to and/or watching yourself, you will be better able to isolate specific ways to improve your delivery. While observing a recording, make a list of two to four things you could do to improve your delivery; then practice the speech, focusing on those items.

## CHAPTER REVIEW

In this chapter we examined several factors related to improving your delivery. We began by learning what *delivery* means and the many reasons to care about delivery skills. Perhaps the most important reason is the likelihood that you will experience nervousness, or CA, before or during a speech. CA can interfere with your ability to present a stronger message. However, by working on your delivery skills, you can combat CA and get your message across effectively. You also learned several strategies that have helped people manage and reduce CA, as well as the four modes of delivery and their appropriate applications. We explored some of the delivery skills that are critical to creating a lasting impression on an audience. Finally, you now know how non-native speakers can engage in additional skills training if language issues are a concern.

## KEY TERMS

articulation, 236
bodily aspects, 238
bodily movement, 241
cognitive restructuring, 229
communication apprehension
    (CA), 225
delivery, 224
enunciation, 237
extemporaneous mode, 231
eye contact, 240
facial expressions, 240
fluency, 235
gestures, 238
impromptu mode, 232
manuscript mode, 232

memorized mode, 232
pause, 234
pitch, 235
projection, 233
pronunciation, 236
rate, 234
skills training, 230
state apprehension, 226
systematic desensitization, 227
trait apprehension, 226
vocal aspects, 233
vocalized pauses, 235
vocal variety, 238
volume, 233

## STUDY QUESTIONS

1. How might someone who suffers from state apprehension differ from a person who suffers from trait apprehension?

2. What are the steps of cognitive restructuring, and what are the goals of practicing this technique?

3. When might a manuscript mode of delivery be more appropriate for delivering a speech than an extemporaneous mode?

4. Explain three of the seven vocal aspects of a presentation, and create a goal that you might focus on each area you identify for your next speech.

5. What are the four bodily aspects of presentation? As a listener, which do you find most effective, and why?

6. What advice would you give to non-native speakers to help them feel more comfortable in preparing to deliver a speech?

# Speaking to Inform and Persuade

Here you will refine your informative and persuasive speaking skills, which you can then apply in any number of speaking contexts. For example, in the final chapter you will see how your refined speaking skills will continue to benefit you, even after you complete your degree. As you enter the workforce, your résumé, cover letter, and interview style will reflect your ability to inform a potential employer of your skills, as well as to persuade that employer to consider you seriously as a candidate.

# Public Presentations to Inform

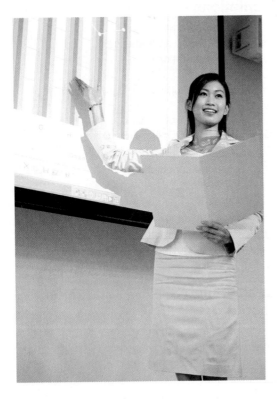

This chapter will help you prepare and deliver an informative presentation. The goal of informative speaking is to enhance your audience's knowledge and understanding of a topic. First, you will learn how to determine your goal and purpose. Next, you will become familiar with the skills and techniques for presenting information effectively. Finally, you will see some helpful examples of an outline and note cards for an informative presentation.

LEARNING OBJECTIVES

*After reading this chapter, you should be able to:*

- Understand the various goals and purposes of informative presentations.
- Effectively present information to an audience.
- Apply the following basic informative skills to your presentations: defining, describing, explaining, illustrating, using analogies, narrating, and demonstrating.
- Effectively use visual resources to inform.
- Explain the appropriate use of note cards when delivering an informative speech.

## PREPARE AN INFORMATIVE PRESENTATION

When you set out to prepare an informative presentation, you must first consider your goals in speaking. To begin, answer the following questions:

1. Why are you delivering the speech? What are your intent, purpose, and goal for informing your audience?
2. What topics lend themselves to informative speaking?
3. What immediate and long-term actions do you expect from your audience as a result of your informative presentation?

Long-range goals were discussed in Chapter 9, on topic selection and audience analysis. You may want to review that information as it applies to informative speeches.

### What Is Your Goal?

Before you can attempt to speak informatively on a topic, you need to identify your specific goal, or the information you wish to convey. You may want to increase what the audience knows about a topic, teach them something useful, clear up complicated matters, demonstrate something they would find helpful, show how objects or items are related to each other, or share information they might initially think of as boring but that you enliven with your speech. Table 13.1 lists these general goals and provides specific examples for each.

| Table 13.1 Common Goals of Informative Presentations and Examples of Topics | |
|---|---|
| **Goals of Informative Presentations** | **Topic Examples** |
| **To increase what your listeners know about a topic** | ■ The newest trends in green design for houses<br>■ New clothing designers emerging with spring fashions<br>■ What is nanotechnology? |
| **To help your audience learn useful information** | ■ Early steps for avoiding the flu<br>■ Chinese customs for greeting and leaving<br>■ Travel tips for visitors to Mexico |
| **To clarify complex issues** | ■ How does identity theft work?<br>■ How might the United States address its economic problems?<br>■ Who was Ponzi? |
| **To demonstrate something useful** | ■ How to save a life with the Heimlich maneuver<br>■ The correct way to lift weights<br>■ Do-it-yourself wiring |
| **To show how things relate in space** | ■ How to make a man's sport coat<br>■ Using electronics in a green residence<br>■ Where the major islands of the Caribbean are |

## What Is Your Purpose?

The **immediate behavioral purposes** of your presentation—*the actions you expect from an audience during and immediately after a presentation*—can be fairly straightforward for an informative presentation:

1. *Define words, objects, or concepts.*

   "After hearing my presentation, I want my audience members to be able to provide a meaningful definition for the concept of *eminent domain*."

   **Sample statement of purpose for a presentation to define:**

   "My purpose is to have my listeners be able to explain to me what powers the government has because of the laws surrounding eminent domain and what the impact can be on private citizens."

2. *Describe objects, people, or issues.*

   "After hearing my presentation, my listeners can describe in a way we can all understand the controversy caused by plans to build a new athletic stadium."

   **Sample statement of purpose for a presentation to describe:**

   "My purpose is to have my listeners correctly explain back to me the main parts of the controversy surrounding the new athletic stadium."

3. *Distinguish between things.*

   "After hearing my presentation, the audience should be able to distinguish between socialist and democratic positions on state ownership."

   **Sample statement of purpose for a presentation to distinguish between things:**

   "My purpose is to have my audience show me that they can tell the difference between a socialist position and a democratic position on state ownership."

4. *Compare and/or contrast items.*

   "After hearing my speech, my audience should be able to contrast a real diamond with a cubic zirconia."

   **Sample statement of purpose for a presentation to compare and/or contrast:**

   "Upon completion of my presentation, members of the audience will be able to accurately identify a cubic zirconia in a collection of authentic diamonds."

## EFFECTIVELY PRESENT INFORMATION TO AN AUDIENCE

Audience analysis can help you determine how much the audience members already know and how much you will have to tell them. For example, imagine that you want to talk about the erratic nature of the stock market. If audience members regularly invest in the stock market, they probably know a great deal about market fluctuation and strategies to maximize their investments. However, if your audience is a typical group of undergraduate students, they may need to learn about basic terminology, some history of the stock market, and some examples of good and poor times to invest.

Audience analysis can also help you take advantage of the following tips for presenting information:

- Create information hunger.
- Demonstrate information relevance.
- Use extrinsic motivation.
- Select and design your content.
- Avoid information overload.
- Organize your content.

Each of these tips are discussed in detail in this section. If you have already read Chapter 10, you know a great deal about audience analysis. If you have not yet read that chapter, you may want to read it now to fully understand the material here.

### Create Information Hunger

An informative presentation is more effective if the presenter can create **information hunger,** *a need for information in the audience.* This is because, when you arouse the audience's interest, they are likely to learn more.

## MEDIA

### CONSIDERING

### LEARN HOW PREZI CAN ENHANCE YOUR INFORMATIVE PRESENTATION

Many people use PowerPoint to complement their informative presentations. But PowerPoint is limited in its functionality. More impressive and up-to-date is Prezi (www.prezi.com), a free presentation software option available online. Here are some of its benefits:

- It is not constrained by the static slide approach; it allows you to pan and zoom, giving your ideas a visual flair.
- It allows you to incorporate sounds, images, and videos into your presentation.
- It facilitates real-time collaboration with peers.
- It offers fun and informative tutorials for learning its many applications.

The next time your presentation calls for an engaging visual aid, sign on to Prezi and begin designing.

## WHAT INFORMATION IS ALLOWED?

Our country has freedom of speech written into the Constitution and Bill of Rights, but even in the United States most universities have restrictions on what you can do for an informative presentation.

Probably you cannot give a demonstration speech on how to operate an assault weapon; some religious colleges would not welcome speeches that oppose positions firmly held by the sponsoring church; and strong talk against another culture might end up as prohibited "hate speech."

Similarly, you need to exercise care in informing co-cultures and cultures about their own beliefs and practices. For example, a person from a dominant culture who chooses to explain and describe female Muslim attire may be perceived by Muslims as insulting. When talking to people from another culture or co-culture, you need to be sensitive about what information they may perceive to be insulting or disrespectful.

One method of creating information hunger is to use **rhetorical questions,** which are *questions asked for effect, with no answer expected,* to introduce an informative speech: "Are you aware of the number of abused children in your hometown?" or "Do you know how to get the best college education for your money?" Depending on the audience, these rhetorical questions could arouse interest.

Another method is to tap into the audience's curiosity. For example, you might state, "I have discovered a way to add 10 years to my life," or "The adoption of the following plan will ensure lower taxes." In addition, a brief quiz on your topic early in the speech arouses your audience's interest in finding the answers. Unusual clothing related to the topic of your speech (for example, an EMT uniform) is likely to arouse interest in why you are so attired, and an object you have created (for example, a homemade windmill that is as tall as you) will probably inspire the audience to wonder how you made it. Rhetorical questions and audience curiosity are just two of the many ways to create information hunger.

### Demonstrate Information Relevance

Another factor that can connect an audience with an informative presentation is **information relevance,** *the importance, novelty, and usefulness of the information to the audience.* Thus, when selecting a topic for an informative presentation, you should carefully consider how relevant it will be to that particular audience. Skin cancer might be a better topic in the summer, when students are sunbathing, than in the winter, when they are studying for finals. A presentation on taxes could be awfully dull; a speech on how present tax laws cost audience members more than they cost the rich might be more relevant, and a speech on three ways to reduce personal taxes might be even more so. However, if your audience happens to be composed of young people who have never paid taxes, none of the three topics might be relevant. Similarly, a speech on raising racehorses, writing a textbook, or living on a pension might be informative but not relevant because of the financial status, occupation, or age of the listeners. Thus, you should exercise some care in selecting a topic that interests the audience, as covered in Chapter 9.

### Reveal Extrinsic Motivation

The third factor in relating an informative presentation to an audience is **extrinsic motivation,** *the reasons outside the presentation that audience members will benefit from listening to the presentation.* An audience is more likely to listen to and comprehend a presentation if they have good reasons for doing so, especially if they see some potential benefit or reward for themselves.[1] A teacher who tells students to listen carefully because they will be tested at the end of the hour is using extrinsic motivation. A speaker uses extrinsic motivation by telling audience members that, in this speech, they will learn ways to increase their own energy and creativity.

Extrinsic motivation is related to the concept of information relevance. An audience member who would ordinarily lack interest in the economy might find that topic relevant when it is linked to learning about employment trends for college graduates. The audience member's interest in being employable is an extrinsic motivation for listening carefully to the presentation.

Extrinsic motivations need to be mentioned early in a presentation. For example, a statement like "You will need this background material for the report due at the end of this week" provides extrinsic motivation for managers who hear this message from their employer. Similarly, in an informative presentation, you may be able to command more attention, comprehension, and action from audience members if you provide them with some good reasons outside the presentation for attending to your message.

### Design Informative Content

The fourth factor that can help your audience relate to an informative presentation is your selection of **informative content,** *the main points and subpoints, illustrations, and examples used to clarify and inform.* The following principles can help you select your speech content:

- *Audiences tend to remember and comprehend generalizations and main ideas better than details and specific facts.* You should limit your presentations to two to five main points.

- *Relatively simple words and concrete ideas are significantly easier to retain than are more complex materials.* Long or unusual words may dazzle an audience, but they may also reduce their understanding. Keep the ideas and words at an appropriate level.

- *Humor can make a dull presentation more interesting, but humor does not seem to increase information retention.*

Humor also improves the audience's perception of the speaker's character and can increase her authoritativeness when a presentation is dull.

- *Early remarks about how the presentation will meet the audience's needs can create anticipation and increase the chances that the audience will listen and understand.* Whatever topic you select, you should tell audience members early in your presentation how the topic is related to them. This will increase the chances that they will listen.

- *Calling for overt audience response or behavior increases comprehension more than does repetition.* Having an audience do something—such as raise their hands or stand up if they've had a particular kind of experience—provides feedback to the speaker and can be rewarding and reinforcing for both the presenter and the listeners.

### Avoid Information Overload

The dangers of information overload while gathering and evaluating sources are discussed in Chapter 11. However, as an informative speaker, you must also be wary of the amount of information you present to others. Recall that information overload occurs when you provide more information than the audience can absorb, whether in quantity, complexity, or both. The danger of information overload is that the audience may quit listening to your talk, dismiss your topic, or view you as having less credibility. Information overload is illustrated in Figure 13.1.

The solution to information overload is to focus on a limited number of main points, include only the best supporting materials, and keep the message at a level the audience can understand. For example, one man wanted to discuss

**Figure 13.1** Information Overload in Quantity and Complexity

## Information Overload of Quantity

- The speaker tells more than audience members ever wanted to know about a subject, even when they are interested.

- The speaker tries to cram as much information as possible into the time allowed. Unfortunately, this cramming of information decreases understanding.

## Information Overload of Complexity

- The speaker uses language or ideas that are beyond the capacity of the audience to understand.

- An engineer who unloads detailed formulas on the audience, or a philosopher who soars into the ethereal heights of abstract ideas, may leave the audience feeling frustrated and more confused than before the speech.

# BUILDER

## LEARN TO INVOLVE YOUR AUDIENCE

You have probably attended a presentation in which the speaker asks for audience participation. In fact, in any class that isn't a lecture, you are part of an audience whose participation isn't merely requested but is required. An informative speaker might involve an audience in the following ways:

- Ask audience members to perform the task being demonstrated—for example, two people dance after you explain the technique of a waltz.
- Have them stand, raise hands, or move chairs to indicate their understanding of the speaker's statements: "Raise your hand if you are familiar with local building codes."
- Have them write answers that will indicate understanding (e.g., "List three ways to lower your blood pressure").

When it's your turn to present, involving your audience is a great way to hold their attention.

stem cell research. Although this topic is complex and the scientific knowledge about it can be overwhelming, he made the speech highly understandable. He talked about what stem cells are; then he described adult stem cells, embryonic stem cells, umbilical cord stem cells, and pluripotent stem cells. Because he explained the simpler stem cells first, the class could easily grasp the more complex pluripotent stem cells.

### Organize Content

In an informative presentation, you can help the audience learn the content by following these organizational recommendations:

1. Tell audience members what you are going to tell them (in the introduction), tell them (in the body), and then tell them what you told them (in the conclusion).
2. Use transitions and signposts to increase their understanding.
3. Tell your audience which points are most important.
4. Repeat important points for better understanding.

Audiences can more easily grasp information when they are invited to anticipate and to review the organization and content of your speech. That is why the body of your presentation is bracketed by a preview of what you are going to say and a summary or review of what you've said.

## SKILLS FOR AN INFORMATIVE PRESENTATION

When giving an informative presentation, you can rely on certain skills to help you convey your information most effectively. In particular, informative presentations call for the skills of defining, describing, explaining, illustrating, using analogies, narrating, and demonstrating.

## Defining

Many people think that definitions are merely explanations found in a dictionary. However, they are much more than that, and there are multiple ways of defining things:

- A **comparison** *shows the similarity between something well known and something less known.* A student explained that tying a bow tie (unfamiliar to most) is the same as tying a shoelace (familiar to all), but since we are unaccustomed to tying a shoelace around our neck, a bow tie is challenging.
- A **contrast** *clarifies by showing differences*—for example, "He was taller than you, he was more heavy set than you, and his hair was darker."
- A **synonym** *defines by using a word or words that are close or similar in meaning to the one you are trying to define*: "A depressed person feels demoralized, purposeless, isolated, and distanced from others."
- An **antonym** *defines an idea by opposition*: "A good used car is not full of dents, does not have high mileage, is not worn on the seats, does not leak lots of oil, and has not been involved in a serious accident."
- An **operational definition** *defines by explaining a process.* An operational definition of a cake is the sequence of actions depicted in a recipe.

Definitions are anything but dull; in fact, they are often the cause of great controversy. Consider the following questions pertaining to definitions: When does a collection of cells become a *fetus*? When does a fetus become a *premature child*? Is a *soul* produced with the meeting of sperm and egg? Can *marriage* be between same-sex partners?

## Describing

Describing requires presenters to be concrete rather than abstract, specific instead of general, and accurate instead of ambiguous. It also includes using **imagery,** *figures of speech that hit at the senses and stimulate listeners' synapses to see, hear, and feel what the words are saying.*

Look at the following description of Reggie Watts, who started his career as a singer with bands but became a stand-up comedian and performance artist.

> He arrives on stage with enormous amber rings dripping like tree sap from his fingers, his Afro a Miracle-Gro spider plant. Sometimes he's painted a pinkie nail pink. He might be wearing a ridiculous sweater.[2]

The writer's use of imagery is highlighted. In only two sentences, the words bring this person to life. What this writer demonstrates is that words can paint pictures in the mind that appeal to the senses.

Strong, descriptive imagery is also in the following portrayal of Watts's voice. The highlighted words are especially effective in describing his voice as if it were an entire band.

> Then he lays down a track. He starts with the sound of a kick drum, from deep in his throat, recorded into a loop sampler—a small machine often used by guitarists to layer melodies. He adds a snare with a few controlled exhales. A couple of high notes with his tongue against his teeth. And then he starts to sing, in French or gibberish German. Morphing imperceptibly into a cockney slang, he seems to be talking about something from a human-resources manual or a dating disaster.[3]

Do these words help you picture what Reggie Watts looks and sounds like? You can perform similar magic with your own words if you recognize the potential of speaking with imagery.

## Explaining

An **explanation** is *a means of developing an idea that simplifies or clarifies it while arousing audience interest.* An important step in explaining is analyzing, deconstructing, or dissecting something to help the audience understand it. Unless you become skilled at dissecting a concept, your explanation may leave audience members more confused than they were before your presentation. You have to determine what you can do to make a difficult concept more palatable for and accessible to the audience. For example, a biology professor in an article about global warming[4] expressed the problem by explaining how animals and plants are migrating north or climbing higher, if they can, to survive:

> Wild species don't care who is in the White House. It is very obvious they are desperately trying to move to respond to the changing climate. Some are succeeding. But for the ones that are already at the mountain top or the poles, there is no place for them to go. They are the ones that are going extinct.[5]

In this instance the biology professor knew that global warming is a fairly vague concept. He chose one sign of global warming to reference the idea. Everyone can understand the migration of animals and plants in need of water, food, and tolerable temperatures.

### Illustrating

An **illustration** *clarifies by showing what something is.* For instance, if you are talking about lung cancer, you might show photos of affected and unaffected lungs. In discussing the difference between all-wheel and 4-wheel drive, you could show an illustration of the two systems with a diagram. Illustrations can consist of photos, drawings, the objects themselves, or "word pictures."

Stories, or narratives, can also provide illustrations. For example, Aesop tells the fable of the lion and the mouse. The mouse awakens the lion by jumping on his head. The lion awakens and is angry. He is about to eat the mouse when he observes that the mouse has made him laugh, and he spares his life. Not too much later, the lion is ensnared and the mouse comes to his rescue. This children's story illustrates that even the small and the weak can sometimes be of help to the large and the strong. Poetry, too, can touch the senses and illustrate ideas that are otherwise difficult to explain.

### Using Analogies

An **analogy** is *a comparison of things that are otherwise dissimilar.* "Analogies prove nothing that is true," wrote Sigmund Freud, "but they can make one feel more at home." In other words, linking the known with the unknown can help someone grasp an idea.

The introduction of the iPad, iPod touch, and iPhone was confusing to many potential consumers. Which one or ones should they buy? One advertisement used an analogy; it said that the iPad was like a commuter, the iPhone was like a social networker, and the iPod touch was like a budget-conscious partner in this trio. The analogy worked well in explaining their differences and in suggesting who might want to purchase each one.

Here is another example of an analogy: the U.S. Congress's decision making is like a tug-of-war between two fairly equal teams, neither of which will yield to the other. As a result, nobody wins or loses, but neither does much movement occur. If you are trying to inform an audience on a new or unfamiliar idea, consider linking it to something the audience already knows, and use that to form an analogy.

### Narrating

**Narration** is *the oral presentation and interpretation of a story, a description, or an event.* Narration occurs throughout a range of presentation styles and scenarios, such as the following:

- The dramatic reading of lines from a play, a poem, or another piece of literature

- The voice-over on a series of slides or a silent film to illustrate a point in a speech

- The reading of a letter, a quotation, or a selection from a newspaper or magazine

- The telling of a story or an anecdote from one's life

A person who does the play-by-play account of a ballgame is narrating, and so is a presenter who explains what a weaver is doing in an informative presentation on home crafts.

To use narration is to move a little closer to oral interpretation of literature, or even acting, because the narration can be more dramatic than the rest of the presentation. The sections of your presentation that require this kind of special reading also require special practice. If you want to include a few lines of poetry in your presentation, you need to rehearse them, so that they have the desired impact.

## Demonstrating

**Demonstrating** is *showing the audience what you are explaining.* Some topics are communicated best through words, others through demonstration. You can talk about CPR, the Heimlich maneuver, fashion trends, and weight lifting, and you can read about these subjects. But nothing aids in the understanding of these topics better than seeing and doing CPR, practicing the Heimlich maneuver, seeing the latest fashion trends, and lifting some weights while learning about them.

Demonstrations are commonly used in everyday life. For example, chefs prepare food on television. Physicians demonstrate a variety of procedures and techniques for medical students. People who want to buy new cars and computers familiarize themselves with products via demonstrations. Clearly, demonstrating is a useful skill in informing others, and one you might try in your informative presentation.

## USE VISUAL RESOURCES TO INFORM

Visual aids reinforce your verbal message, as well as help you gain and maintain audience attention. Table 13.2 provides some examples of topics and the visual resources you could use to supplement them.

Once you decide which visual resources you will use in your presentation, and how you will use them, you should prepare for any scenario in which the resource might fail, such as the following:

- A speaker has prepared a PowerPoint presentation but encounters compatibility issues when using it with another computer system.

**Table 13.2** Examples of Topics and Visual Resources

| Topic | Visual Resource |
| --- | --- |
| How to change your own oil | ▪ Use PowerPoint or Prezi photos. |
| How to succeed in marathons | ▪ Come in running clothes; show the audience how to prepare for, start, and continue the race. |
| How to make a simple dessert | ▪ Bring and mix the ingredients for a pie and have the audience salivating as they anticipate dessert. |
| How to play croquet | ▪ Use croquet mallets and balls. |
| How to tie knots for rock climbing | ▪ Tie the knots as you describe them. |

# CHALLENGE YOURSELF

## How Can I Use Visual Resources Effectively in My Informative Presentation?

As you have already learned, visual resources are not always effective. All of us have watched the hapless speaker who could not exhibit her Prezi because of differences in computer systems, could not show her photos because they were too small, or could not get her dog to perform the tricks it had been taught.

What advice will help you use visual resources effectively?

- *Be audience-centered.* Do not use foul-smelling, offensive, or disturbing resources.
- *Be ethical.* Do not use dangerous or inappropriate items.
- *Keep the content clear and relevant.* Do not overwhelm the audience with too many facts or figures.
- *Explain the visual resource.* Do not assume that the audience understands its relevance.
- *Understand that using resources takes time.* Explaining a visual resource will take at least two minutes.
- *Do not be too simple or too complex.* Consider the audience's level of knowledge on the topic.
- *Strive for professionalism.* Sloppy drawings, print that is too small to be read, and audio that is too soft to be heard will undermine your presentation.
- *Hide the resource when it is not in use.* They are distracting before and after they are used.

In addition to following this advice, consider a few additional tips that your audience is likely to appreciate: Make sure everyone in the room can see your visuals. Check the visibility of your visual resources before your speech, during practice; if the classroom is 25 feet deep, have a friend or family member determine if the visual can be read from 25 feet away. Finally, do not stand in front of the visual you wish the audience to see; step aside and speak to your audience, not your visual.

- A presenter plans on singing a particularly poignant aria but has laryngitis on the day of the presentation.

- Someone brings photos to be projected on the screen, but the photos are so tiny that no one can see them.

- A friend agrees to role-play during a speech but has a conflict and must cancel at the last minute.

Being prepared with a backup plan is essential. Regardless of the types of visual resources you use, you need to practice extensively with them so that they will enhance your presentation rather than distract from it.

## A SAMPLE INFORMATIVE SPEECH OUTLINE AND NOTE CARDS

The following is an informative speech outline that was written by Christa Galbraith, a first-year student. The outline is not perfect, but it is a good example of an informative speech. You will note that this is a complete-sentence outline. Following the outline are the student's note cards, which she used to deliver the speech.

A complete-sentence outline and note cards are helpful in the planning and preparation of your speech. However, keep in mind that you would never read either one word-for-word during your delivery. The best practice is to put away the outline and take only your note cards with you to the podium.

### Informative Speech Outline
### Christa Galbraith

I. **Introduction**

A. **Attention Getter:** For the past nine years, Darfur, Sudan, has been a war-torn region where hundreds of thousands of innocent people have died. The death toll has caused this war to be classified as a Sudanese genocide.

B. **Listener Relevance:** We all must be educated about the injustices happening around the world, as it is our responsibility to speak up and help those in need.

C. **Speaker Credibility:** I first heard about the genocide in Darfur in my eighth-grade English class. My teacher was very concerned with human rights and wanted us to be passionate about helping those who were struggling. We spent the semester writing letters to U.S. Congress, starting petitions, and making educational videos for the morning news in the hopes of creating awareness and intervention.

D. **Thesis Statement:** The genocide in Darfur is a complex regional conflict that has affected the lives of millions of people.

E. **Preview:** Today, I want to discuss four main points relating to the genocide in Darfur: the basic composition of Sudan and Darfur, the conflict itself, peace agreements, and the current climate.

## II. Body

A. **Main Point #1:** Darfur is a region in western Sudan (show picture) that is composed of two main ethnic groups—those who identify as Arabs, and those who identify as Africans. The Arabs tend to live in Northern Darfur, while the Africans reside in Southern Darfur.

   1. **Supporting Point #1:** The Sudanese government, which is mainly composed of Arabs, is believed to favor the country's Arab citizens, who alienated the Africans living in the region.

   2. **Supporting Point #2:** According to Debra A. Miller, the editor of *Current Controversies,* there is also a pronounced difference in the location of Darfur's natural resources. The north has control of the majority of the farmland, while the south is rich in oil. Naturally, this caused tension, as each group wanted some of the other's resources, while keeping their own for themselves (*Current Controversies* p. 19).

   **Transition:** The clear division and competition of ethnic groups in Darfur caused unrest and civil war. As the conflict escalated, the government failed to adequately step in. Many Africans felt they weren't being protected.

B. **Main Point #2:** In April of 2003, two African rebel groups—the Sudan Liberation Army and the Justice of Equality Movement—attacked a military airfield at al-Fashir, killing 75, capturing 23, and destroying seven bombers and helicopter gunships (Miller, *Current Controversies* p. 19). This humiliated the government and proved that their soldiers were not trained well enough to stop the rebel forces.

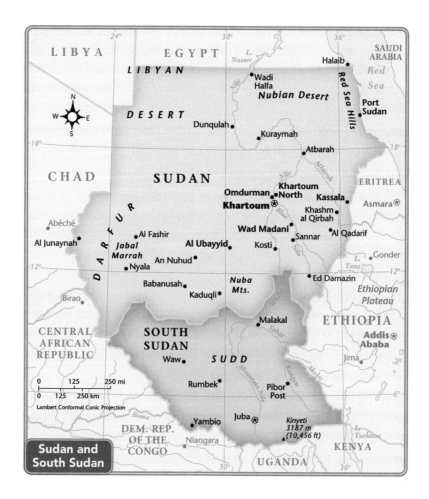

Sudan and
South Sudan

1. **Supporting Point #1:** As an act of punishment, the Sudanese
   government supplied a volunteer group of Arab militants—called
   the Janjaweed—with weapons and communication equipment. The
   Janjaweed then destroyed an entire Darfurian village, murdering and
   displacing its residents. Robert O. Collins, the author of *A History of
   Modern Sudan*, explains that they killed and mutilated the men, raped
   the women, and abducted or killed the children before burning down
   their homes, stealing their livestock, torching their fields, and destroying
   all their public buildings (*A History* . . . p. 289). About 300,000 people
   have been killed.

2. **Supporting Point #2:** Those who survive the attacks are forced to congregate in refugee camps, either near the border of Chad, or in Chad itself. Here they are exposed to disease, malnutrition, and separation from their families. Approximately 2 million people have been displaced.

**Transition:** As violence escalated, the Sudan Liberation Movement saw the need for peace talks with the Sudanese government.

C. **Main Point #3:** Peace talks have been largely unsuccessful.

1. **Supporting Point #1:** According to the U.S. Department of State Archives, the first peace agreement was signed in 2006 and required the government to disarm the Janjaweed, provide $30 million for displaced victims, and $300 million, plus $200 million each year after to rebuild the region (U.S. Department of State Archives).

2. **Supporting Point #2:** However, the violence continued and the need for a second peace agreement arose. The second peace agreement was signed in 2011 and required a compensation fund for victims.

**Transition:** Again, this peace agreement has failed to produce results, and the violence in Darfur continues to worsen.

D. **Main Point #4:** According to U.S. Ambassador Smith, in a Darfurian radio interview, "the security situation has deteriorated" since 2011 (Radio Dabanga Interview).

1. **Supporting Point #1:** The interviewer, Kamal Elsadig, pressured the Ambassador to address issues such as the bombing and murder in civilian areas, as well as the rape that continues in much of Darfur. There is also a lack of water, food, and medical supplies (Interview).

2. **Supporting Point #2:** Many have called 2012 the bloodiest year yet.

**Transition:** Though the genocide in Darfur started several years ago, it continues today, and the violence has only escalated.

V. **Conclusion**

A. **Thesis Restatement:** Millions of people have been affected by this nine-year-long genocide over natural resources, ethnic differences, and government revenge.

B. **Main Point Summary:** Hundreds of thousands of Africans are being murdered by the Janjaweed military as an act of revenge. Their villages are terrorized, destroyed, and scattered, causing families to be split up and citizens to take refuge in camps. Peace agreements have been ineffective, and the violence continues today.

C. **Clincher:** We must not turn a blind eye to the injustice and tragedy happening in Sudan. When the safety and rights of others are being undermined, all of our rights are at risk.

## References

Collins, Robert. *A History of Modern Sudan*. New York: Cambridge University Press, 2008. 289. Print.

Miller, Debra. *Current Controversies: Darfur*. Farmington Hills: Greenhaven Press, 2009. 18–19. Print.

"Q&A: Sudan's Darfur Conflict." *BBC News* 23 Feb 2010, n. pag. Web. 11 Oct. 2012. <http://news.bbc.co.uk/2/hi/africa/3496731.stm>.

Smith, Ambassador, dir. "Sudan: Ambassador Smith." Dir. Kamal Elsadig. Radio Dabanga: 19 Sep 2012. Web. 11 Oct 2012. <http://allafrica.com/stories/201209200049.html>.

United States Department of State. *Darfur Peace Agreement*. 2006. Web. <http://web.archive.org/web/20080220140754/http://www.state.gov/r/pa/prs/ps/2006/65972.htm>.

---

### Card #1

Past 9 years–Darfur, Sudan–war-torn–Sudanese genocide.

Educated about the injustices . . . speak up and help those in need.

Learned of genocide in Darfur–eighth grade.

Complex regional conflict–affected millions of people.

Four points: composition of Sudan and Darfur, conflict, peace agreements, and current climate.

**Card #2**

Darfur-western Sudan (show picture)-two main ethnic groups: Arabs in North and Africans in South.

Sudanese government favors Arabs and alienated the Africans.

Debra A. Miller-Current Controversies, a pronounced difference in location of natural resources. The north-farmland; the south-oil.

**Card #3**

Miller-April of 2003, two African rebel groups-the Sudan Liberation Army and the Justice of Equality Movement-attacked a military airfield at al-Fashir, killing 75, capturing 23, and destroying 7 bombers and helicopter gunships.

Humiliated government; showed soldiers were not trained well enough to stop rebel forces.

As punishment, government supplied Arab militants-Janjaweed-with weapons & communication equipment.

Destroyed villages, murdering and displacing its residents.

## Card #4

Robert O. Collins—*A History of Modern Sudan*—kill and mutilate the men, rape the women, and abduct or kill the children before burning down their homes, stealing their livestock, torching their fields, and destroying their public buildings.

About 300,000 people killed.

Those who survive—forced to congregate in refugee camps—exposed to disease, malnutrition, and separation from families.

Approximately 2 million people have been displaced.

Violence escalated, Sudan Liberation Movement sought peace talks with the government.

## Card #5

Peace talks—unsuccessful.

U.S. Department of State Archives—first peace agreement, 2006, required the government to disarm the Janjaweed, provide $30 million for displaced victims, and $300 million, plus $200 million each year after to rebuild the region.

Violence continued; need for a second peace agreement arose.

Second peace agreement—2011, required compensation fund.

This peace agreement, too, has failed.

**Card #6**

U.S. Ambassador Smith, in radio interview, "the security situation has deteriorated" since 2011.

Interviewer, Kamal Elsadig, pressured Ambassador to address bombing, murder in civilian areas, as well as rape.

Lack of water, food, and medical supplies.

2012, the bloodiest year yet.

Millions affected-9-year genocide: natural resources, ethnic differences, and government revenge.

Thousands of Africans are being murdered by the Janjaweed military.

When the safety and rights of others are being undermined, all our rights are at risk.

## CHAPTER REVIEW

In this chapter you learned how to prepare and deliver an informative presentation. When you are setting out to convey information to an audience, identifying your goal and purpose is always the first step. What immediate and long-term actions would you like your audience to take as a result of your speech? Asking this question can help you identify your goal and purpose, as well as to test whether the speech was a success. Just as important is using the skills you have learned for presenting information effectively. Make use of definition, description, explanation, illustration, analogies, narration, and demonstration and you will keep your audience interested and engaged. Finally, be prepared. The sample sentence outline and note cards in this chapter can help you prepare and deliver your next informative speech.

## KEY TERMS

analogy, 258
antonym, 256
comparison, 256
contrast, 256
demonstrating, 259
explanation, 257
extrinsic motivation, 253
illustration, 258
imagery, 256

immediate behavioral purpose, 250
information hunger, 251
information relevance, 252
informative content, 253
narration, 258
operational definition, 256
rhetorical questions, 252
synonym, 256

## STUDY QUESTIONS

1. What is informative speaking? Describe a time when you delivered an informative presentation, in or outside the classroom.

2. What is the difference between the overall goal and the specific purpose of an informative presentation?

3. What are the seven important skills of an informative speaker, and how does each contribute to a presentation?

4. Give an example of a particularly effective or ineffective use of visual resources in a presentation you've attended. Explain why the visuals worked well or did not.

5. What is the purpose of an outline and note cards when it comes to giving your presentation?

# 14

# Public Presentations to Persuade

**In persuasive speaking, your focus is on your imme-
diate purposes as well as on your long-range goals—
after all, your aim is to persuade your audience to
take some action. When you finish this chapter, you
will be able to use evidence to support and argue for
your position, describe and provide examples of the
three logical forms of proof, and demonstrate the
skills used for persuading.**

LEARNING OBJECTIVES

*After reading this chapter, you should be able to:*

- Understand the various goals and purposes of persuasive presentations.
- Know how to effectively introduce your purpose and argument.
- Demonstrate effective use of arguments and evidence.
- Describe and provide examples of the three logical forms of proof.
- Demonstrate effective use of the skills for persuading: providing examples, using comparison and contrast, and using testimonials.

# PREPARE A PERSUASIVE PRESENTATION

A **persuasive presentation** is *a message strategically designed to induce change in the audience in some way consistent with your purpose.* The following are some examples of persuasive topics:

*New rules are needed for drug use among athletes.*

*Teachers need to unionize.*

*Construction and building practices must become greener.*

*Alternative forms of energy must be found.*

*Our legislature must pass laws to control college tuition.*

Most people misunderstand how persuasion works. Some people think it is all about getting people to do something they would not otherwise do. Actually, *forcing people to unwillingly think or behave as you wish* is not persuasion but **coercion.** Likewise, *tricking people or using fraudulent means to gain compliance* is not persuasion but **manipulation.** Both coercion and manipulation override a person's ability to choose, to make a decision based on sound information and ideas, and are therefore not used by ethical speakers. Persuasion is strategic, but it is neither coercive nor manipulative.

## What Is Your Immediate Purpose?

Your presentation should have an **immediate purpose,** *a statement of what you intend to accomplish.* You may want to review that concept as presented in Chapter 13, on informative speeches. Given that a single presentation to a captive audience is unlikely to produce dramatic results, you need to be realistic. Thus, a realistic purpose might be something like this: "My immediate purpose is to have my listeners write down the e-mail addresses of legislators so they can communicate with them about lowering our tuition."

## What Is Your Long-Range Goal?

In the context of a persuasive speech, you also want to consider your **long-range goal,** *a statement of purposes that could be achieved with continuing efforts to persuade.* You know, for instance, that you are not going to produce a lot of action from a one-shot effort to persuade listeners that more regulation is needed regarding steroid and designer-drug use among athletes. But you also know that, the more your audience hears about this issue from many sources, the more likely something will be done about it. With these thoughts in mind, you could state your long-range goal like this: "My long-range goal is to encourage my listeners to learn more about this issue over time so eventually they may join the effort to push for rules against the use of performance-enhancing drugs in sports."

## INTRODUCE YOUR PERSUASIVE PRESENTATION

The introduction for your persuasive presentation has characteristics similar to those of other types of introductions: it seeks to gain and maintain attention, relates the topic to the speaker, and forecasts the organization and development of the presentation. However, a persuasive introduction differs from other kinds of introductions in the way it reveals the purpose of the presentation.

### Revealing the Purpose of the Presentation

In an informative presentation, you state clearly at the outset what you want to accomplish and tell the audience what you want them to learn. In a persuasive presentation, however, your listeners may reject your intention to change their thinking or behavior unless you prepare them to listen to you. To do so, you need to analyze the audience to determine when and how you should reveal your immediate purpose.

Have you heard of the "foot-in-the-door" technique? This technique is based on the idea that door-to-door salespeople try to put their foot in the door so home dwellers cannot shut the door without at least listening to the whole sales pitch. Similarly, when you warm your audience to your idea rather than blurting it out at the beginning, you are practicing a kind of foot-in-the-door strategy.

How much are you asking of your audience? Figure 14.1 explains two possible scenarios. If you aren't asking for much of a change from your audience, you should reveal your purpose and action steps in your introduction. If you think your audience will resist your call for action, reveal your purpose at the outset;

**Figure 14.1** Asking for a Change

## How much are you asking of your audience?

### Not asking for much of a change?

Reveal your purpose in the introduction of the speech— or your introducer may even reveal the purpose for you.

### Need to convince your audience to accept your immediate purpose?

Provide your reasons first and reveal your action step toward the end of the presentation.

then explain the actions you wish them to take at the end, after you have made a strong case.

If you ask your listeners for too much change, you are likely to get a **boomerang effect**—that is, *the audience will like you and your message less after the presentation than they did before.* To avoid the boomerang effect, analyze your audience and decide when you should reveal your purpose.

### What Purposes Are Persuasive?

Most persuasive presentations in the classroom have one of two immediate purposes, adoption or discontinuance, explained and illustrated in Figure 14.2. **Adoption** means that *listeners start a new behavior as a result of the persuasive presentation*—for example, they start exercising after you present the risks and

**Figure 14.2** Examples of Adoption and Discontinuance

The purpose of this poster is *adoption*, meaning that it aims to persuade viewers to do something new—to walk, bike, or take public transportation instead of driving.

This poster persuades viewers to *discontinue* a behavior—in this case, texting while driving.

prevalence of diabetes. The persuader has some proof of effectiveness if people in the audience state on a post-presentation questionnaire that they are going to take up some new behavior.

**Discontinuance** is *a persuasive purpose rooted in convincing listeners to stop some current behavior*—for example, to stop taking so much sick leave or to cut down on caffeine intake. Discontinuance and adoption are challenging persuasive purposes well worth your efforts in a presentation. They can change your listeners' lives in very positive ways.

### Why Should You Try to Persuade?

Despite decades of messages discouraging overeating, encouraging exercise, and discouraging smoking, U.S. adults are the fattest people on earth, exercise way too little, and continue to die in large numbers from obesity and smoking-related diseases. Given that a multitude of campaigns have failed to change these behaviors, you might start to wonder how anyone would expect you to succeed in a classroom presentation. But you should feel encouraged to know that, in the classroom, you will benefit from the opportunity to address your audience directly, face-to-face.

Face-to-face efforts are more persuasive than public service campaigns for at least three reasons. One is that face-to-face communication is among the most effective modes we have. Consider the difference between a public service announcement on television discouraging bulimia and a classroom presentation on the same subject by a classmate who confesses to bulimia and reveals the awful, life-threatening effects of the disease. Which mode—a TV spot or the person herself—would have the most influence on you? As you consider this question, remember that, although we can see almost any entertainer on video, thousands of us show up for concerts because we want to see an entertainer in the flesh.

Face-to-face communication is also compelling because it offers the possibility of spontaneous behavior. For example, Bruce Springsteen postponed the tour he had planned to promote his latest album so he could lend support to President Obama's campaign, and this unexpected move brought attention to both him and the presidential campaign. More recently, Springsteen has used the stage to speak out against greed in the banking industry—combining entertainment with persuasion in an extremely effective way. Although you might not have the star power of a Springsteen, you may find that people in your classroom audience respond well to your in-person message, delivered in real time, because of its potential to present them with something new, spontaneous, and relevant to them.

The third reason your face-to-face presentation can be especially effective is that your classmates are a captive audience. Thus, you have an opportunity in the classroom to speak about something that really matters to you and to persuade people who might never otherwise have gone to hear a speech about this topic. As members of the classroom audience, they learn about a topic from you, and your persuasive speech has the potential to change their thinking or behavior.

## HOW DO YOU PERSUADE?

To persuade others—whether in school, at home, or at work—you must choose strategies that will work best on your listeners. In other words, audience analysis is key to making the most of the strategies described in this section.

### Using Argument to Persuade: Fact, Policy, and Value

Many listeners respond positively to speakers who know how to present a logical argument. Lawyers and debaters are well versed in logical **argument,** *a form of discourse that attempts to persuade.* Arguments consist of propositions, which are the points to be discussed or considered in the argument, and they concern questions of fact, policy, or value.

An example of a **proposition of fact**—*an assertion that can be proved or disproved*—is "College student debt is the highest in history."[1] To demonstrate the accuracy of this fact, you can cite Mark Whitehouse's article in the *Wall Street Journal* that had the headline "Number of the week: Class of 2011 most indebted ever." Or you could cite any number of authoritative sources on this subject, because college student loan debt now exceeds credit card debt.[2]

An example of a **proposition of policy**—*a proposal of a new rule*—is President Obama's student loan forgiveness program:

> Under the terms of this program, anyone who makes his monthly payments for twenty years after leaving college is eligible to have his/her remaining balance forgiven. . . . Individuals who spend ten years in public service positions become eligible to have their loans forgiven at that point rather than having to wait the full twenty years. This means that their debt is forgiven in half the time and their debt reduced significantly sooner.[3]

An example of a **proposition of value**—*a statement of what we should embrace as good or bad, right or wrong*—is "We must put security above First Amendment freedoms." To demonstrate the merit of this proposition, you would provide evidence that airline searches, wiretapping, and profiling are more important than our right to protection against unreasonable searches, our expectation of privacy, and our right not to be singled out for negative treatment because of race or ethnicity. Why? Because those violations of rights keep us safe, and we want security more than we want freedoms.

### What Is the Difference Between Evidence and Proof?

The term **evidence** refers to *anything, physical or verbal, that helps in forming a conclusion or judgment,* such as DNA results or witness testimony. **Proof,** on the other hand, is *any evidence that the receiver believes.* You might present statistics as *evidence* to support your argument that this country needs a policy solution to the student-debt crisis. If, however, an audience member questioned the source of the statistics or the way the numbers were collected and analyzed, your evidence would not constitute *proof* for that listener. If a lawyer for the prosecution introduces DNA as *evidence* in a criminal trial, but the lawyer for the defense questions the way the DNA was collected or stored, the evidence may not be convincing *proof* for the judge or jury. The relationship between evidence and proof is illustrated in Figure 14.3.

## How Can You Test Evidence?

To make your argument as strong as possible, ensure that the evidence you present meets the **tests of evidence,** *standards for demonstrating validity.* To determine if your evidence is strong, ask these questions:

1. Is the evidence consistent with other known facts?
2. Would another observer draw the same conclusions you have, based on this evidence?
3. Does the evidence come from unbiased sources?
4. Is the person who is the source of the evidence qualified by education and/or experience to make a statement about the issue?
5. Is the person who is the source of the evidence credible based on background and reputation?

**Figure 14.3** The Relationship Between Evidence and Proof

6. If the evidence is based on personal experience, how typical is that personal experience?

7. If statistics are used as evidence, are they from a reliable source; comparable with other known information; and current, applicable, and interpreted so the audience can understand them?

8. If studies and surveys are used as evidence, are they authoritative, valid, reliable, objective, and generalizable?

9. Are your inferences appropriate to the evidence you are presenting?

10. Have you overlooked any important counterevidence?

An example may help you understand these questions and how to use them. A study was recently conducted at the University of Copenhagen, Denmark. Men between the ages of 20 and 30 who were obese and had a sedentary lifestyle were placed in three groups. The first group did not exercise; the second group exercised about 30 minutes per day or until they burned 300 calories; and the third group exercised about 60 minutes per day or until they burned 600 calories. Although we might guess that the third group lost the most weight, the group that exercised 30 minutes a day actually lost more.[4] If you were one of the researchers in this study, and you stopped there, concluding that you now had evidence against exercise as a tool for weight loss, you would have failed to fully test your evidence. You would especially have failed to consider questions number 1, 2, and 10.

Why? The researchers did not stop with that evidence. In looking at the participants' food journals, they discovered that, as participants in the third group increased their exercise, they also increased the amount of food they ate. In short, there was a more complex reason the members of the third group lost less weight than those in the second group. The researchers concluded, therefore, that shorter amounts of exercise may be more helpful for those trying to lose weight.[5] The point is that, for statistics to be considered *authoritative, valid, reliable, objective, and generalizable,* they must be viewed in context. And those who present and interpret them in an argument must not overlook any important counterevidence.

## THREE FORMS OF PROOF

To persuade an audience you need to know some methods of doing so. Aristotle in his *Rhetoric* wrote about three modes of proof: ethos, pathos, and logos.

**Logos** refers to *persuasion by using logical argument.*

**Ethos** refers to *the reputation, authority, and integrity of the speaker.*

**Pathos** refers to *the use of emotional means of persuasion.*

Over the centuries, these methods have been refined but are still visible everywhere, from advertisements and movie trailers to classroom and office presentations.

**Figure 14.4** The Structure of an Inductive Argument

## Logos, or Logical Proof

One logical structure you can use to formulate your arguments is known as inductive reasoning. An **inductive argument** *provides enough specific instances that the listener can make an inferential leap to a generalization or conclusion.* Consider the example in Figure 14.4, which illustrates the structure of an inductive argument for more government programs and support. A series of individual instances, such as unrepaired roads and highways, can lead to an inferential leap, which in turn might lead an audience to conclude that more government support is needed.

Another logical structure, illustrated in Figure 14.5, is deductive reasoning. A **deductive argument** *uses a general proposition applied to a specific instance, or minor premise, to draw a conclusion.* This logical structure is called a **syllogism,** meaning that it *contains a generalization (a major premise) applied to a particular instance (a minor premise) that leads to a conclusion.*

## Ethos, or Source Credibility

You can persuade some listeners simply because you have earned the right to speak, but your credentials and reputation are important as well. Competence, trustworthiness, and dynamism are all elements of a speaker's ethos. With your personal power, expertise, charisma, or personality, you can gain the compliance of your audience, so you will want to let them know what your credentials are.

**Figure 14.5** The Structure of a Deductive Argument

You will also want to establish your credibility by being well prepared and demonstrating that you have done your homework.

### Pathos, or Emotional Proof

The **fear appeal,** *a message designed to frighten or alarm an audience so they will be persuaded to act,* is one of the most common appeals to emotion:

- Political ads focus on impending economic collapse and suggest that only one political party can protect us from our enemies.
- Financial gurus make us feel that we are risking financial ruin if we don't heed their advice.

Fear appeals get us to brush our teeth, use deodorant, and buy certain clothing. As a speaker you can use fear appeals in an ethical manner if you do not exaggerate the threat, and if you offer reassurance as well.

| **Table 14.1**  The Monroe Motivated Sequence |
| --- |
| **Step 1: Attention** |
| ■ *Gain and maintain audience attention*, and determine a way to focus it on the content of your presentation. |
| **Step 2: Need** |
| ■ Once you have the audience's attention, demonstrate how the speech is relevant to them.<br>■ *Arouse a need* for the change you suggest in your persuasive presentation. |
| **Step 3: Satisfaction** |
| ■ Your speech either presents the information the audience needs or suggests a solution to their needs. You *satisfy the audience* by meeting their needs with your plan. |
| **Step 4: Visualization** |
| ■ Reinforce your idea in the audience's minds by getting them to *see* how your information or ideas will help them. |
| **Step 5: Action** |
| ■ Once the audience has visualized your idea, *plead for action*.<br>■ The audience might remember your main points in an informative presentation and state them to others, or the audience may go out and do what you ask in a persuasive presentation. |

**Source:** This organizational pattern was originally provided by Ehninger, D. & Monroe, A. H., in their multiple editions of *Principles and types of speech communication.* The most current version of the book is German, K. M., Gronbeck, B. E., Ehninger, D., & Monroe, A. H. (2012). *Principles of public speaking* (18th ed.). Old Tappan, NJ: Pearson.

In media campaigns regarding teen pregnancy, pathos and fear appeals have been used in a balanced way. Health promoters have found that the most successful antipregnancy campaigns include a variety of strategies—for example, they combat positive attitudes toward pregnancy as well as negative attitudes about birth control. They also emphasize negative consequences of sexual intercourse.[6] These messages address emotional issues, but without making exaggerated claims and while providing reassurance.

In contrast, messages that shock people with fear (such as the grim and gripping reenactments of alcohol-related car crashes) often are not effective and may be viewed as unethical. When the appeal to fear is too extreme, the response may be increased anxiety, aggression toward the source of the message, and in some cases unhealthy behaviors to reduce anxiety (for example, alcohol or drug use).[7] Consequently, an extreme fear appeal is also counterproductive.

## ORGANIZE YOUR PERSUASIVE MESSAGE

How do you organize your presentation to achieve your persuasive purpose? Recall the many organizational strategies provided in Chapter 10: the time-sequence pattern, cause/effect pattern, problem/solution pattern, and topical-sequence pattern. Another possibility is the Monroe Motivated Sequence, which is especially useful for persuasive presentations, especially when the audience is reluctant to change or to accept a proposed action.

### The Monroe Motivated Sequence

Developed by University of Iowa professor Alan Monroe, the **Monroe Motivated Sequence,** *an organizational pattern that includes the following steps: attention, need, satisfaction, visualization, and action,* has been used successfully for four decades and is popular for having five easy-to-follow steps, outlined in Table 14.1. Following is an example of a speech using the Monroe Motivated Sequence.

---

### We Need More Than Antibiotics to Treat Infections

**Purpose:** My audience will be able to state the advantages of using multiple drugs to kill dangerous bacteria in our bodies.

**Thesis Statement:** Serums and phages should be considered, in addition to antibiotics, to kill bacteria.

**Attention Stage:** What is the largest cause of death in the United States? If you have listened to the speeches in this class, you might conclude that it is automobile accidents. Although it is true that automobile accidents kill about 32,000 people a year, a close rival in frequency are infections caught in hospitals. Last year, 30,000 people died from fatal infections they contracted while staying in the hospital. The 30,000 people included newborns, children, middle-aged people, and elderly patients.

**Need Stage:** Why did all these people die when modern medicine boasts a range of antibiotics with proven effectiveness? Some bacteria are antibiotic-resistant. Last year, in Europe alone, 25,000 people died from bacteria that did not respond to antibiotics. Further, a chief medical officer labeled antibiotic resistance a "ticking time bomb."

**Satisfaction Stage:** Some pre-antibiotic medications—including serum therapy and bacteriophages (viruses that attack bacteria)—may provide a solution. In the past, medical doctors turned to antibiotics, instead of serums and phages, because antibiotics proved to be a successful treatment for infections. Today, largely because of overuse, we are learning that antibiotics are becoming much less effective. Moreover, serums and phages are more selective in the bacteria they will attack, making them an even more attractive alternative to antibiotics.

**Visualization Stage:** Imagine a world in which a child in Guatemala who has *Shigella* diarrhea and does not respond to antibiotics is still alive and has a chance to live a fulfilling life. Imagine the middle-aged man who was admitted to the Medical Center at the University of Virginia in 2010—arguably one of the finest medical centers in the world—did not die from an infection treated with antibiotics. Imagine a world where no one needs to worry about dying from an infection treated only with antibiotics.

**Action Stage:** What can we do to maximize the effectiveness of medicine to rid our bodies of bacteria? We must insist that scientists continue to do research on serums, phages, and other treatments, as well as explore new medical approaches. We also need to insist that our physicians do not take an easy way out by treating all bacteria by antibiotics. Ignoring alternatives to antibiotics may be a matter of life and death for you or someone you love.

## Ethical Considerations

**Ethics** are *a set of principles for right conduct.* Many of our standards for ethical behavior are codified into law. Others are not, but violating them still leads to consequences. The following are some generally accepted ethical standards that govern the preparation and delivery of a persuasive presentation.

1. *Accurately cite sources.* Give credit to the writers, researchers, and thinkers who have provided information you have used.
2. *Respect sources of information.* Demonstrate their credibility as completely as possible.
3. *Respect your audience.* Do not attempt to trick or manipulate them.
4. *Respect those who disagree with you or who offer rebuttals to your argument.* Attack your opponent's evidence, sources, or logic—but not your opponent.

## SKILLS FOR PERSUASIVE SPEAKING

Even when your aim is to persuade, you can draw on the skills for informative speaking that were presented in Chapter 13. The three skills that lend themselves particularly well to persuasive speaking are providing examples, using comparison and contrast, and using testimonials.

### Providing Examples

**Examples** are specific instances used to clarify your point. They are among the most common clarifying materials. A single, very strong example can help convince an entire audience. For instance, in an argument designed to motivate everyone to vote, you could present a case in which a few more votes would have meant a major change in election results.

Two types of examples are factual and hypothetical. A **factual example** is *based on real circumstances.* Here's one about the expanding role of social media: "Several online memorial sites on Facebook illustrate how social networking sites have started to serve a larger role than simply helping people connect." This is a factual example because it's about a feature of social media (memorial sites on Facebook).

In contrast, a **hypothetical example** is *a fictional but realistic example.* One of your instructors may state on the first day of class, "A good excuse for a student missing class is that he or she has a serious auto accident, ends up in the hospital, and has a signed medical statement from a physician to prove hospitalization for a week. A poor excuse is a student who overslept for a 4 P.M. class and has no explanation for his or her behavior." Either type of example can be brief or extended, but an ethical speaker will reveal whether an example is factual or hypothetical.

# CHALLENGE YOURSELF

## How Can I Get Others to Agree With Me, to Understand What I Know and Believe, and to Switch to My Side on Important Issues?

You probably already know that persuasion is one of the most difficult of all communication situations. Have you ever tried to persuade a teacher to accept a late paper, to change the grading of an exam, or to give you a higher grade in the class? Perhaps you have attempted to persuade your partner to accompany you on an expensive trip. Maybe you have even endeavored to convince a friend to vote for a different person or to stop using drugs. How successful were you in your endeavors?

In addition to what you've learned in this chapter, consider the advice of Robert Cialdini, a professor at Arizona State University. Professor Cialdini wrote the popular book *Yes—50 Scientifically Proven Ways to Be More Persuasive,* in which he offers the following six principles.

### Principle of Reciprocity

People are more likely to say yes to you if you have said yes to them first. If a classmate needs help with a project, show a willingness to step in. You will likely find that he will provide support to you when you ask for it.

### Principle of Commitment and Consistency

People have a deep desire to be consistent. Thus, you are more likely to persuade people if you can show them that your position is consistent with their positions on similar matters. For example, you might argue that your friend should support a candidate because environmental issues are a priority for that candidate and your friend has always been concerned with environmental issues.

### Principle of Authority

This idea is related to the concept of ethos, mentioned in the chapter. Audiences are persuaded by people in authority and people with expertise. The more you draw on your expertise, whatever it may be, the more likely you are to be persuasive.

### Principle of Social Validation

People are more willing to take a recommendation if they see that people similar to them have adopted the proposal. Testimonials from those who agree with you are invaluable as tools of persuasion.

### Principle of Scarcity

People find products more attractive to the degree that they are scarce or limited in availability. "Going out of business" sales work because people believe they have a limited time to make a purchase.

### Principle of Liking

People are more likely to respond to people they know and like. If you nurture relationships with those in your audience, you are more likely to be persuasive to them.

Now that you know some of the principles of persuasion, and have examples of how you can use them, take opportunities to apply them in your class presentations, as well as your day-to-day life.[8]

## Using Comparison and Contrast

As defined in Chapter 13, comparison clarifies by linking a familiar instance with an unfamiliar one. If your audience is familiar with one city but not another, you might acquaint them with the unfamiliar city by highlighting what it has in common with the one they know: "New York City and Los Angeles both have immense populations, locations on an ocean, and large international ports." Or you can use contrast, which *emphasizes differences*: "Contrasted with New York City, Los Angeles has far more square miles, a more extensive road system, and a less developed mass transit system." These key similarities and differences help characterize the two cities.

Imagine a friend is attempting to persuade you to buy an electric car, but you have only ever driven gasoline-fueled cars. To make her argument, your friend might point out differences in the impact on the environment and cost to run each type of vehicle (contrast) while explaining similarities in the comfort of the ride and handling (comparison). Comparison and contrast can be used in informative speeches, but they are particularly appropriate for persuasive messages.

## Using Testimonials

**Testimonial evidence** consists of *written or oral statements of others' experience used to substantiate or clarify a point*. We can identify three types of testimonial evidence. **Lay testimony** *consists of statements made by ordinary people that substantiate or support what you say*: a student explains why fellow students should vote for the candidate you have argued is the best. **Celebrity testimony** *consists of statements made by a public figure who is known to the audience*. When former-representative Gabrielle Giffords campaigns for gun-control legislation or Bruce Springsteen endorses Barack Obama, they are offering celebrity testimony, and this can be extremely persuasive. Such testimonies are also known as endorsements. Stronger than lay testimony and celebrity testimony is expert testimony. **Expert testimony** *includes statements made by someone who has special knowledge or expertise about an issue or idea*. You might quote a mechanic about problems with an automobile, an interior decorator about quality fabrics, or a political scientist about the possible outcomes of an election.

## A SAMPLE PERSUASIVE SPEECH OUTLINE AND NOTE CARDS

The following complete-sentence outline was written by a first-year college student, Calla Price. This outline helped the student plan and organize her talk. She did not use the outline when she delivered her speech; instead, she used the note cards that follow this outline.

## Persuasive Speech on Texting and Driving
## Calla Price

## Introduction

I. **Attention Getter:** Coffee Creamer, named after its color, was my Chevy S-10. That old pickup now sits out in one of our pastures reminiscing on the days before it was totaled. Miserable truck, it just sits there, alone, mangled, and useless after a texting-and-driving accident. The truck might not fear the consequences of texting and driving, but I do.

II. **Listener Relevance:** You have probably written or read a text on your phone while driving, at least once; you may have even had an accident.

III. **Speaker Credibility:** I rolled over my Coffee Creamer because of texting and driving. I could have been killed.

IV. **Thesis Statement:** Texting and driving needs to stop.

V. **Preview:** Sometimes accidents end in fatalities. Frequently they bring other consequences that can lead to life-altering physical or emotional impairments. Let's try to find a solution to this problem; let's imagine together what driving could be without a fear of a texting-and-driving accident.

## Body

I. **First Main Point:** Texting and driving is dangerous. It is a serious problem in the United States because of the frequency with which it occurs.
A. The dangers of texting and driving are appalling.

B. Texting while driving is a serious distraction that increases a driver's chances of getting into an accident.

C. According to Lisa A. Gardner in a journal article "Wat 2 Do Abt Txt'n & Drv'n," three safety risks are directly related to this behavior.

1. First, texting takes some of the mental focus away from the task of driving.

2. Second, texting requires drivers to take one hand off the wheel.

3. And third, in order to read or write a text, drivers have to look away from the road.

D. The effects of texting-and-driving accidents range from financial burdens to long-term health problems.

   1. Fixing car damage costs money, something most college students don't have.

   2. Mental health problems can arise after an accident.

      a. Anxiety, depression, and post-traumatic stress disorder (PTSD) are common side effects.

      b. Anne Cameron describes PTSD as having many symptoms including reliving the event, feeling shame or guilt, being irritable or angry, and experiencing problems with memory.

      c. PTSD symptoms can disappear for years and be triggered again by an unrelated event.

**Transition:** Clearly, texting while driving is problematic. But the solution is not so clear, because the motivations to text and drive vary from person to person.

II. **Second Main Point:** Texting and driving is a relatively new issue, which means that we are still on the lookout for effective solutions. We do know, however, that in order to solve this problem we need to influence people's decisions directly, and establish laws and regulations against texting and driving.

   A. Influencing people to stop texting and driving might be one of the most successful ways of stopping the problem.

      1. According to Gardner, peer pressure has been instrumental in changing people's perception—making drunk driving and driving without a seatbelt, for instance, not only illegal, but socially unacceptable. Asking friends not to text and drive while you are in the car may be the most effective way to make them understand you are not comfortable with it. But that is not an easy thing to do. To avoid hard feelings with a friend, Nancy Jackson writes, "Avoid calling or texting your friends if you know they are driving at the time." Ask them not to text you if you are driving as well. These requests should get your message across.

      2. Technology also can help influence people. For example, there are now easy-to-install apps that use GPS technology to sense when

you are driving, and they send automatic replies to people who text or call when you are on the road. In an article for *USA Today*, Julius Genachowski explains that "new apps block texting or web surfing when the phone is in motion."

B. Laws and regulations against texting and driving also influence people's decisions.

1. Currently thirty states and the District of Columbia have made texting and driving illegal. Thirty-one states have laws that restrict teens from using their phones while driving. Penalties range from state to state. The national government is regulating states with and without texting and driving laws. According to Jackson, if a state does not have certain laws in place, federal aid for highway maintenance is reduced by 25%.

2. The national government is also making mandatory the development of technology to aid in the prevention of texting and driving, and accidents generally, for cars produced in the U.S.

**Transition:** Can you imagine a world where the solutions worked, and texting and driving wasn't a problem?

**III. Third Main Point:** If texting and driving were considered socially unacceptable, lives would be saved. Moreover, medical bills and mental health problems would be prevented. Think of the benefits of making this problem unacceptable.

A. The accident rate would decrease.

1. Accidents would still happen, but the number of accidents that are really serious or hard to get over would decrease.

2. How many people do you know who have had a texting and driving accident? How many of them drove away with an unwrecked car, an unhurt body, or a healthy mental state?

B. The fear of accidents that were not your fault would decrease as well.

1. More drivers would be paying better attention.

2. Think of how much more attention you have to give others when you know they are texting and driving. Imagine not having to watch other drivers' every move. Imagine not having to worry about your own children texting and driving because our generation put an end to it.

**Transition:** I cannot stress enough the dangers of texting and driving. I hope I have convinced you to stop putting your life, money, and mental health on the line for the sake of sending a text.

## Conclusion

**I. Thesis Statement:** Think of the consequences before you pick up the phone and start texting and driving, or before you let a friend do it.

**II. Main Point Summary:** Put an end to texting and driving.

**III. Clincher:** Texting is not a live-or-die situation. Texting and driving is.

## References

Cameron, A. (2007). Exploring posttraumatic stress disorder. *Lesbian News, 33*(3), 24.

Gardner, L. A. (2010). Wat 2 Do Abt Txt'n & Drv'n (aka: What to Do About the Problem of Texting While Driving?). *CPCU Ejournal, 63*(11), 1–13.

Jackson, N. (2011). *DN'T TXT N DRV. Current Health Teens, 37*(7), 6–9.

Julius, G. (2012). Time to put the brakes on texting and driving. *USA Today*. Retrieved from www.usatoday.com/story/opinion/2012/09/24/column-put-the-brakes-on-texting-and-driving/1588157/10

Teens Aware of Texting Dangers, Yet Carry On. (2011). *Professional Safety, 56*(12), 18.

As explained in Chapter 13, on informative speaking, a complete-sentence outline and note cards with brief notes can be helpful in the preparation of your speech. However, the idea is not to read from either one while presenting. The complete-sentence outline is a planning tool; the note cards can accompany you to the podium for reference as you speak. The following note cards might be used to deliver the persuasive speech on texting and driving.

**Card #1**

Coffee Creamer-Chevy S-10.

You have probably written or read a text while driving.

I rolled my truck-I could have been killed.

Texting and driving needs to stop.

Some accidents end in fatalities or other life-altering consequences.

Try to find a solution: Imagine what driving could be without a fear of texting and driving.

**Card #2**

Texting and driving-dangerous.

Happens frequently in U.S.

Lisa A. Gardner in a journal article "Wat 2 Do Abt Txtn & Drvn,"-three safety risks:

- Takes away some of the mental focus.
- Requires drivers to take one hand off the wheel.
- Requires drivers to look away from the road.

The effects of texting and driving accidents:

- Fixing car damages costs money, which most of us do not have.
- Mental health problems: Anxiety, depression, and post-traumatic stress disorder. Anne Cameron describes PTSD-reliving the event, feeling shame or guilt, being irritable or angry, and experiencing problems with memory.

## Card #3

Texting and driving-new issue.

Need to look for effective solutions.

Need to influence people's decisions directly.

- Gardner-peer pressure has been instrumental in changing people's behaviors.
- Nancy Jackson writes, "Avoid calling or texting your friends if you know they are driving at the time."
- Technology-easy-to-install apps that use GPS technology to sense when you are driving and send automatic replies to people who text or call when you are on the road.
- USA Today, Julius Genachowski-"new apps block texting or web surfing when the phone is in motion."

## Card #4

Need to establish laws and regulations against texting and driving.

- 30 states + District of Columbia = texting and driving illegal.
- 31 states have laws that restrict teens from using their phones while driving.
- Penalties vary.
- National government-regulating states-Jackson-if a state does not have certain laws in place, federal aid for the highway maintenance is reduced by 25%.
- National government-mandatory to develop technology.

**Card #5**

Texting and driving-socially unacceptable-lives would be saved.

Benefits of making this problem unacceptable:

- Accident rate would decrease.
- Fear of accidents that were not your fault would decrease.

Think of the consequences before you pick up the phone and start texting and driving, or before you let a friend do it.

Put an end to texting and driving.

Texting is not a live-or-die situation. Texting and driving is.

## CHAPTER REVIEW

In this chapter you learned about persuasive speaking and how to prepare and present a persuasive speech. In persuasion, identifying your immediate purpose and long-term goals will help you determine when and how to present your argument, as well as help you to use effective evidence. Familiarity with the three logical forms of proof and the skills for persuasion will also help you become a more effective persuasive speaker.

### KEY TERMS

adoption, 273
argument, 275
boomerang effect, 273
celebrity testimony, 284
coercion, 271
deductive argument, 278

discontinuance, 274
ethics, 282
ethos, 277
evidence, 275
examples, 282
expert testimony, 284

## STUDY QUESTIONS

1. Draft a list of possible goals of a persuasive speech. How does the nature of the ultimate goal of persuasion differ from that of informative speaking?

2. When should persuasive speakers reveal their purpose? Why does the timing of this revelation matter?

3. How does proof differ from evidence? Describe one scenario from the news, or from your own life, in which evidence was presented that did not qualify as proof.

4. Name and define the three forms of proof. Can you think of a famous public speech that uses two of those three forms? Describe how the speaker used each form of proof to persuade the audience.

5. What are the steps in the Monroe Motivated Sequence? Do you consider the Monroe Motivated Sequence to be an effective means of persuasion? Why or why not?

6. Name the skills that lend themselves to persuasive speaking, and give an example of how you might use each in a persuasive presentation.

# 15

# Using Communication Skills As You Enter the Workplace

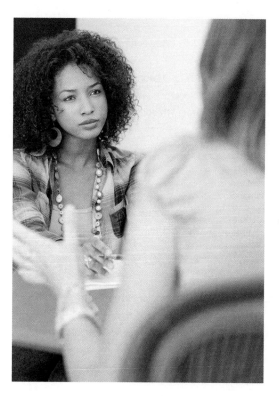

Throughout your career, your education will give you a competitive advantage. In particular, strong communication skills will be vital in every step of the process. This chapter shows how you can communicate your expertise, experience, and education in compelling ways to land one of the estimated 54.8 million job openings during this decade.

LEARNING OBJECTIVES

*After reading this chapter, you should be able to:*

- Discuss some of the contemporary jobs in the communication field.

- Describe your skills effectively in a résumé.

- Create a compelling cover letter for a job application packet that highlights why a company should hire you.

- Know how to present yourself effectively and appropriately during a job interview.

- Respond to behavioral-based job interview questions to create a lasting impression about you as a candidate.

- Identify at least three ways to network effectively throughout college.

## CONTEMPORARY JOBS IN COMMUNICATION

What can you do with a communication degree? The communication field covers many subdisciplines, including public relations, advertising, business communication, journalism, corporate training, and marketing. Some students combine their communication courses with other courses, such as health and wellness, and go on to work in health campaigns against tobacco, excessive alcohol use, or obesity. Others combine communication with political science to serve as a legislative assistant or political analyst. Still others take business courses to prepare themselves to be corporate recruiters, training specialists, or sales representatives. Table 15.1 lists some of the contemporary jobs recent communication graduates have found.

The National Association for Colleges and Employers conducts an annual survey to study trends in national industry demands, hiring, and employment-

**Table 15.1** Contemporary Jobs in Communication

| Title | Organization | Title | Organization |
| --- | --- | --- | --- |
| Speech writer | Political campaign | Tour guide | Travel firm |
| PR professional | Major hospital | Manager | Major hotel |
| Audio editor | Film production firm | Community affairs liaison | Medium-sized city |
| Writer/reporter/editor | Newspaper/magazine/television | Fundraiser | Small college |
| Social media manager | Retail company | Small-business owner | Privately employed |
| Teacher | High school | Teller | Bank |
| Business consultant | Independently employed | Event planner | Medium-sized city |
| Web designer | City government | Flight attendant | Major airline |
| Administrative assistant | Investment firm | Government lobbyist | Small midwestern state |
| Creative planner | Advertising firm | Salesperson | Insurance company |
| Motivational speaker | Consulting firm | Project manager | Publisher |

related practices. Its 2013 Job Outlook survey included representatives from 244 organizations and revealed that hiring new employees with communication skills training is a top priority. In fact, according to employers, a degree in communication is among the top five undergraduate degrees they seek.[1] Figure 15.1 lists the top five skills that employers look for in a potential employee (on a 1–5 scale ranking), regardless of the candidate's major area of study. Effective verbal communication skills rank at the top of the list.

When it comes to seeking employment, most likely the first opportunity you will have to demonstrate your competence as a communicator will be in writing. Most companies will not take the time to interview you unless your résumé and cover letter stand up to the highest level of scrutiny. Thus, you will need to know how to communicate your skills and training effectively to potential employers.

## PRODUCING A WINNING RÉSUMÉ

Human resource professionals use a variety of tools—from surveys to background checks—to screen job applicants. But when it comes to your candidacy, the professional résumé remains the most important source of information about you.[2]

A good résumé is your starting point in any job search, and it is likely to be critical for securing an interview and an eventual offer of employment. To create a successful résumé, you must consider its style, content, and format.

### Style

**Style** refers to *the way you use language and grammar to construct your written materials.* Although style can range from very formal to very informal, you will want to set a more formal tone in your résumé. Avoid using slang, casual language,

**Figure 15.1** The Skills Most Commonly Sought by Employers

## MEDIA

### EXPLORE ONLINE RESOURCES FOR IMPROVING YOUR RÉSUMÉ

Social media sites like LinkedIn, which provides a virtual forum for posting and updating your qualifications and skills, have quickly gained status among employers and recruiters. While it is important to keep your social media sites up-to-date when you are on the job market, a printable resume remains an important feature of your application package.

The following website resources can help you improve the overall quality of your résumé.

- Boston College Grouped Action Verbs List (www.bc.edu/offices/careers/skills/resumes/verbs .html): This general website provides useful resources for résumé writing, including a list of action verbs grouped by nine different skill set areas (management, communication, clerical, research, technical, teaching, financial, creative, and helping skills).
- Purdue University OWL Resume Resources (http://owl.english.purdue.edu/owl/section/6/23/): This website has 10 sections on how to prepare and critique a résumé. You can even complete an online résumé workshop.

Although it is always a good idea to visit your school's career center, and to run your résumé by friends and colleagues, you should also take advantage of the resources available online.

or emoticons; such attempts to be overly cute or friendly will almost certainly backfire. A sample résumé is shown in Figure 15.2.

Several stylistic conventions are unique to résumés. For example, to describe your skills on your résumé, you should use descriptive clauses that begin with action verbs, rather than using complete sentences beginning with the pronoun "I." Many experts recommend action verbs like *planned, supervised*, and *conducted*.[3] These words get employers' attention, because they are concrete and indicate what the applicant has done.

Notice in Figure 15.2 that descriptive clauses related to current employment begin with present-tense action verbs, whereas those related to previous experience begin with past-tense action verbs. Some commonly used action verbs are listed in Table 15.2.

### Content

Style considerations, of course, mean nothing without the right content. The key content includes your contact information, education, experience, skills, and honors and activities. Without contact information the rest of your résumé is useless. Every résumé you

**Figure 15.2** A Sample Chronological Résumé

**YOUR NAME**

email@emailaddress.com

Campus Address:
Street address
City, STATE zip code
(xxx) xxx-xxxx

Permanent Address:
Street address
City, STATE zip code
(xxx) xxx-xxxx

---

**OBJECTIVE**  To lead company efforts in employee training, mentoring, and relations

**EDUCATION**  **Bachelor of Science in Communication Studies**
Major Concentration: **Applied Communication**
Minors: **Human Resource Management** and **Public Relations**
Degree to be conferred: May 2014
Kent State University, Kent, OH
GPA: 3.92

**SIGNIFICANT**
**COURSEWORK**
- Comm. in Small Grps and Teams
- Organizational Communication
- Public Relations
- Leadership and Communication
- Communication & Conflict
- Org Training and Development
- Human Resource Management
- Layout, Editing, and Design

**INTERNSHIP**  *Personalized System of Instruction*        January 2013–May 2013
School of Communication Studies, Kent, OH
- Guided students in their preparation of four speeches for the Introduction to Human Communication course
- Mentored student development of effective study habits for the course
- Assisted the course instructor with lectures, assignments, and in-class developmental exercises
- Evaluated student progress with the instructor in weekly meetings

**RELATED**
**EMPLOYMENT**
*Assistant Manager*        June 2011–current
Local Restaurant, Kent, OH
- Train new associates on relevant policies and procedures
- Prepare sales reports and established weekly goals with associates
- Mentor associates in effective customer service strategies
- Conduct associate performance appraisals and quarterly reviews

**HONORS &**
**ACTIVITIES**
- Lambda Pi Eta National Communication Assoc. Honor Society, President
- School of Communication Studies Senior Scholar, Award Recipient
- Dean's list, 6 semesters in a row

**REFERENCES**
Name
Professional Title
Company
(xxx) xxx-xxxx
E-mail address

Name
Professional Title
Company
(xxx) xxx-xxxx
E-mail address

Name
Professional Title
Company
(xxx) xxx-xxxx
E-mail address

**Table 15.2** Action Verbs for Résumés

| | | | |
|---|---|---|---|
| Accomplished | Formulated | Ordered | Succeeded |
| Adapted | Generated | Participated | Supervised |
| Administered | Handled | Performed | Supplied |
| Analyzed | Headed | Persuaded | Supported |
| Balanced | Identified | Prepared | Tabulated |
| Disbursed | Managed | Revised | Uploaded |
| Examined | Modified | Searched | Verified |
| Executed | Notified | Selected | Volunteered |
| Explained | Obtained | Sponsored | Won |
| Filed | Offered | Streamlined | Wrote |

send out must include complete information about how to reach you, including your e-mail address.

Next, you should pay attention to the information you highlight. Try to think like an employer and keep in mind the prominent functions of the job you are applying for. Then tailor the content to speak to the most crucial aspects of that job. Provide specific information that quantifies your skills and experience; be consistent, concise, and neat.

*Quantify information.* As much as possible, provide concrete information to illustrate the scope of your accomplishments. For example, "Managed a $30,000 budget for Organization X" is much more precise than "Managed the yearly operating budget."

*Be consistent.* Whatever stylistic decisions you make about your résumé, adhere to them. If you use bullets to list your job duties, use bullets throughout your résumé. If you put periods at the ends of your bulleted descriptions, do so consistently. If you indent one job title five spaces and underline it, make sure all your job titles are indented five spaces and underlined. Being consistent shows potential employers that you pay attention to detail and are well organized, both of which are qualities that employers value.

*Be concise.* You do not have to put all your information in a résumé. In fact, view it as an appetizer; you can offer the main course in an interview. Most experts agree that, unless you have more than seven years of work experience, your résumé should not be longer than one page.[4]

*Be neat.* Given that employers have very limited time to spend reading your résumé, it must make an excellent overall impression. Employers judge you and your capabilities in part on the physical appearance of your résumé. Hiring managers will have a hard time ignoring poor proofreading and sloppiness, and your chances of securing an interview will significantly decrease.

Some résumés, as you can see in Figure 15.1, include an **objective statement,** *an articulation of your goal for the résumé.* This statement usually appears first, just below your contact information. Objective statements are important, because they allow you to tailor your credentials and goals to the needs of a particular organization and job description (or the formal duties and scope of a position).[5] The following are examples of objective statements:

- *To apply programming skills in an environment with short deadlines and demanding customers*

- *To achieve consistent improvement in sales profitability of units under my supervision*

Employers also want to see your educational credentials. In summarizing your education, you should include the degrees you have been awarded, your education completion dates (or anticipated completion dates), the schools you've attended, your majors and minors, and your honors or scholarships. The latest U.S. census information, illustrated in Figure 15.3, indicates that completing a bachelor's degree places you among the most highly educated people in the country.[6] Earning a college degree demonstrates to future employers that you are motivated, dedicated, and driven, and completing your degree while earning high grades, working part-time, or involving yourself in extracurricular activities improves your chances of landing a job. If your work history is limited, these educational experiences can help bolster your potential as a job candidate.

Whether you are a freshly minted college graduate or an experienced individual changing jobs or careers, employers will also look at the types of jobs you have held, as well as your job tenures, job duties, and professional accomplishments. When describing your work experience, include a job title, the name of the organization, the dates of your employment, and a description (using action verbs) of your major responsibilities and achievements.

**Figure 15.3** Educational Attainment in the United States

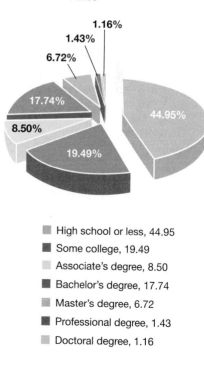

- ■ High school or less, 44.95
- ■ Some college, 19.49
- ■ Associate's degree, 8.50
- ■ Bachelor's degree, 17.74
- ■ Master's degree, 6.72
- ■ Professional degree, 1.43
- ■ Doctoral degree, 1.16

In the list of your previous job duties, list those that are most critical to the job you are applying for first, with the least relevant one last on the list. In adapting your résumé to a particular job, include key words and phrases from the posted job description. In large organizations, the staff uses electronic databases to search through hundreds of résumés to find perfect matches between jobs and people. If your résumé contains key words from the job advertisement, it is more likely to make the cut.

Some résumés also include a skills section highlighting the candidate's abilities, ranging from the ability to use specialized computer applications to fluency in multiple languages. The skills section of a résumé should be tailored to the job description of the position for which you are applying.

Many college students end their résumés with a list of their campus activities and honors. Involvement in campus and community organizations shows that you are a well-rounded person and are community-minded.

## Format

There are two main ways to organize your résumé: chronologically, as shown in Figure 15.2, and functionally, as in Figure 15.4. A **chronological résumé,** which *organizes your credentials over time,* is what most people envision when they think of a résumé. This has long been the standard and, despite technological advances allowing for electronic résumés, it continues to be the most widely accepted format. The purpose of a chronological résumé is to demonstrate your accomplishments over time. You begin with your present or most recent job and continue back to past jobs (see Figure 15.2).

A **functional résumé** *organizes your experience by the type of function performed.* If you have had a variety of career paths (such as retail, sales, and advertising), a functional résumé allows you to group these experiences according to the skills you developed and the duties you performed, rather than the places where you developed or performed them. Graduating college students can use a functional résumé to group "professional experience" separately from "other work experience," which may include jobs that do not directly relate to your career goal but nonetheless illustrate your work ethic.

Functional résumés give you an opportunity to focus on the skills and attributes you bring to the work you do. As a college student, perhaps you have held several short-term jobs and worry that your frequent changes in employment will scare off new employers. Your attributes might come from a range of places, such as community-engaged class projects, or groups to which you belong, such as sororities or fraternities. In such cases, a functional résumé will help you identify the unique experiences you've had, as well as the skills you've gained from them.

If you decide to put together a functional résumé, begin by studying the job for which you are applying. Next, before you begin drafting, make sure you

**Figure 15.4** A Sample Functional Résumé

**YOUR NAME**

email@emailaddress.com

Campus Address:
Street address
City, STATE zip code
(xxx) xxx-xxxx

Permanent Address:
Street address
City, STATE zip code
(xxx) xxx-xxxx

**OBJECTIVE**   To lead company efforts in employee training, mentoring, and relations

**SKILL SUMMARY**   Over ten years of experience in customer relations, employee relations, training, project development, and management. Skills across organizations:

- Customer Service & Relations
- Research Skills
- Teamwork/Collaboration
- Teaching & Training
- Microsoft Office Suite
- Staff Supervision
- Organizational Management
- Report Writing
- Professional Presentations

**RELEVANT SKILLS**

**LEADERSHIP AND MENTORING SKILLS**
- Instituted an anonymous online employee feedback and response mechanism
- Coordinated diverse service personnel for accurate and timely food delivery
- Trained new employees on the implementation of a shadow mentorship program
- Motivated employees to be more proactive and independent in their areas

**PROBLEM-SOLVING AND DECISION-MAKING SKILLS**
- Researched and reconciled cash and accounting discrepancies
- Interviewed and hired job candidates
- Responded to unexpected crises and problems from food shortages to missed shifts

**CUSTOMER RELATIONS SKILLS**
- Listened to and resolved customer concerns and complaints
- Implemented a new procedure for customer complaint responses
- Designed and maintained physical space with customer needs in mind
- Corresponded with the corporate office about staff training and development

**EMPLOYMENT HISTORY**

| | |
|---|---|
| **Assistant Manager**, Target | 2012–present |
| **Accounting Office**, Walmart | 2011–2012 |
| **Customer Service Specialist**, JCPenney | 2010–2011 |
| **Assistant Kitchen Manager**, Red Robin | 2009–2010 |

**EDUCATION**   **B.S., Communication Studies**, Kent State University        Expected: 2014
- Major Concentration: **Applied Communication**
- Minors: **Human Resource Management** and **Public Relations**

**HONORS**
- Lambda Pi Eta National Communication Assoc. Honor Society, President
- School of Communication Studies Senior Scholar, Award Recipient

**REFERENCES**

| | | |
|---|---|---|
| Name | Name | Name |
| Professional Title | Professional Title | Professional Title |
| Company | Company | Company |
| (xxx) xxx-xxxx | (xxx) xxx-xxxx | (xxx) xxx-xxxx |
| E-mail address | E-mail address | E-mail address |

know what attributes the employer is looking for; this is an important step no matter which résumé format you choose. Where can you find that information? Start with the job description, the company's website, and blogs or articles discussing your field. Employers were recently asked to rank a lengthy list of attributes from 0 to 100, based on how important they are to an individual's job candidacy. Figure 15.5 lists the top 10 attributes employers seek when evaluating résumés. The percentage aligned with each attribute reflects the average ranking each attribute received.[7]

You might consider using some of the attributes listed in Figure 15.5 as categories in your functional résumé. Some of these, like competent written communication skills, should be demonstrated in the way you present your résumé as well—avoid grammatical errors and use strong action verbs in describing your attributes.

Many colleges and universities have career centers whose staff will critique your résumé and cover letter for free. They also have resources to help you conduct a successful job search and produce a winning résumé. Stop in to your school's career center well before your senior year and become familiar with the services and resources available.

**Figure 15.5** The Top 10 Attributes Employers Look for on a Résumé

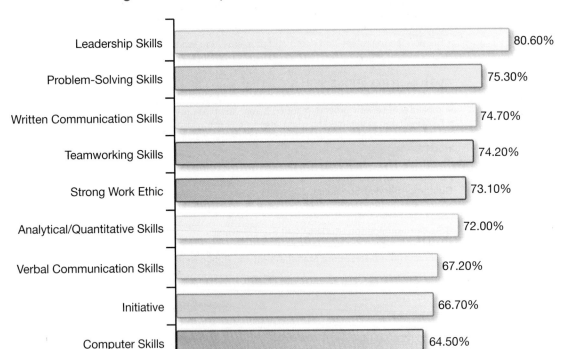

| Attribute | Percentage |
|---|---|
| Leadership Skills | 80.60% |
| Problem-Solving Skills | 75.30% |
| Written Communication Skills | 74.70% |
| Teamworking Skills | 74.20% |
| Strong Work Ethic | 73.10% |
| Analytical/Quantitative Skills | 72.00% |
| Verbal Communication Skills | 67.20% |
| Initiative | 66.70% |
| Computer Skills | 64.50% |
| Technical Skills | 64.00% |

## WRITING A CONVINCING COVER LETTER

A **cover letter** *persuasively illustrates the ways in which you and your credentials match the job description,* and it typically accompanies your résumé. The main objective of a cover letter is to show how your skills and qualifications can be of value to the organization. You can refer the reader to an enclosed résumé for more detail on your qualifications and experience. However, your cover letter should not simply repeat the information in the résumé.

Like any persuasive document, a cover letter has four main sections designed to achieve the reader's (1) attention, (2) interest, (3) desire, and (4) action (Figures 15.6 and 15.7).[8] Below the addresses (yours and that of the person you are writing to), your cover letter should gain the reader's *attention* by stating some basic facts: the position for which you are applying, how you heard about it, and your general qualifications. In the second paragraph, you need to arouse the reader's *interest* and demonstrate your *desire* for the job. This is where you describe your major experiences and strengths as they relate to the job. If possible, mention one or two accomplishments that illustrate your proficiency and effectiveness.

In the third paragraph, you need to suggest action. State that you would like to learn more about the organization and to have a face-to-face meeting, which is the *action* you are hoping for. Finally, express your appreciation for the reader's time and/or consideration.

As mentioned earlier, a cover letter is an opportunity to demonstrate your writing skills; take care with respect to grammar, spelling, and other mechanics, so that you avoid making mistakes that could turn off a potential employer. You would be surprised at how easily a credible applicant is dismissed simply because of correctable errors. If you opt to send e-mail queries to potential employers, remember that they are cover letters, too. Make them formal and persuasive, and include your résumé as an attachment.

## MASTERING THE JOB INTERVIEW

Before you have the opportunity to meet with a potential employer in a face-to-face interview, chances are you will be expected to participate in either a phone or a video-format interview. This is even more likely if the job for which you are interviewing is in another city, state, or country. Advances in interactive communication technology have made these forms of interviewing far less expensive and more reliable than they were even a few years ago.

In a phone interview, you can do several things to use the format to your advantage. If you are being interviewed by a group of people over the phone, keep a notepad handy. When people introduce themselves to you at the beginning, write down each person's name and some type of personal identifier, such as the sound of the person's voice, that will make it easier for you to remember who

**Figure 15.6** The Parts of a Cover Letter

**HEADING**
Your Name
Address
City, STATE, zip code
Phone
e-mail address

**INSIDE ADDRESS**                                                          **DATE**
Name, Title
Department, Organization
Address
City, STATE, zip code

**SALUTATION:**    Use title and last name if available (e.g., Dear Dr. Smith or Dear Ms. Jones). Do not use a first name unless you know the person well and are sure this is acceptable. If you do not have a name, use the title (e.g., Dear Employment Manager).

**PARAGRAPH I:**    Gain *attention* and state *purpose:* Indicate the position or type of work for which you are applying. Mention how you heard about the opening or the organization. You may also want to provide a general overview of your qualifications for the position as a preview statement for your letter.

**PARAGRAPH II:**    Arouse *interest* and demonstrate *desire.* Describe your major strengths as they relate to the position you are seeking. If possible, mention one or two recent accomplishments that illustrate your proficiency and effectiveness. Refer the reader to the enclosed résumé for more detail on your qualifications and experience.

**PARAGRAPH III:**    Suggest *action.* Restate your strong interest in the position or organization and your desire for a face-to-face meeting. Include a statement about how the reader may contact you. Finally, express your appreciation for the reader's time and/or consideration.

**COMPLIMENTARY CLOSE** (Sincerely yours,)
(Leave 3 blank lines)
**NAME**
**POSTSCRIPT** (Enclosure; Enc.)

**Figure 15.7** A Sample Cover Letter

---

**Excited Applicant's Name**
Street address
City, STATE zip code
(xxx) xxx-xxxx
email@emailaddress.com

March 20, 2013

Hiring Official's Name
Human Resources, Fab Designs
City, STATE zip code

Dear Hiring Official's Name,

I am writing with interest in a content development position at Fab Designs, a top public relations firm providing high-level professional services to its clients. I hope you will find that my education and experience have prepared me for a position with your firm.

As a content developer at Create, I took on a variety of leadership roles. I led the company's transition to a new design software program and trained all staff in its use, an initiative that helped to increase our sales and make procedures more efficient. I also trained interns in company procedures, as well as managed their day-to-day work flow. I am now interested in putting my content development and leadership skills to use at a larger public relations firm.

For all of these reasons, I am very excited to learn about positions at Fab Designs. I hope to have the opportunity to discuss my qualifications with you in person, and I will look forward to hearing from you soon.

Sincerely,

Excited Applicant
Enclosure

---

is speaking. Then, use the interviewers' names as much as possible during the interview to demonstrate that you are friendly and a good listener.

Before you go into any interview, you should know as much as you can about the organization and the functions of the job. Carry out a phone interview in a place where you can spread out all of your notes to use as a reference, if you need them. Choose a location that will be free of distractions, so that you can concentrate as much as possible on the interviewers and the questions being asked.

Another popular format for employment interviews is interactive video. Several Internet-based programs enable video interviews, including Skype, Facetime, ooVoo, and Google Video, each with advantages and drawbacks.[9] Testing any of these technologies beforehand with a friend can help you learn how to use the program, how your image comes across on video, and the optimal lighting and camera angle to achieve the image you desire during your interview.

During video interviews pay attention to nonverbal communication. Use a set of headphones, if possible, to cut down on distortion and feedback that might be picked up by your or the interviewer's microphone. Also, professional attire is just as important for a video interview as it is with face-to-face interviews; dress professionally.

Carefully consider the environment where you are planning to conduct your video interview. Select a professional location that will positively reinforce your overall credibility with the interviewer—not your home, unless you have a professional office or another location that is free of personal possessions and other potentially distracting objects. Arrange to be interviewed where you can be hard-wired to the Internet for your connection (e.g., Ethernet or cable connection); don't take chances by relying on the signal strength and quality of a wireless connection. Do whatever you can to remove any possible distortions or distractions that may occur during a video interview; if someone's voice cuts in and out or your interview has to be disconnected and reconnected, you will lose valuable time that could have been spent interacting with the employer and asking relevant questions.

Do not be surprised if you undergo several rounds of interviews for a position with different people (and in different formats) or experience a group interview, in which multiple people evaluate your responses at the same time. During the interview you must present yourself as a potential asset to the organization, which requires using both verbal and nonverbal communication. Specifically, you want to create a good first impression, speak with clarity, and demonstrate interest.

### Create a Good First Impression

First impressions are critical in a job interview. You have about 30 seconds to create a positive first impression. One of the most obvious ways is to dress appropriately. The general rule is to match the style of dress of the interviewer. You can learn about the company's dress code by asking someone who works there, by visiting the organization to observe people, or simply by asking a receptionist at the company. However, if you cannot acquire information about the dress code, you are better off to dress more professionally than casually when you show up for an interview.

Taking the time to look professional will demonstrate that you care about the job and your first impressions. For professional positions, conservative dress is typically appropriate—that means dark suits, white shirts or blouses, standard ties for men, dark socks or neutral hose, dark shoes. Be modest in your use of jewelry and cologne. Of course, arrive on time and take cues from the interviewer on how to act while also trying to present yourself in an honest, positive way. For example, use a firm handshake when you meet the interviewer, and if the interviewer stands, you should remain standing.

### Speak With Clarity

The way you use grammar can deeply influence the impressions others form about you in professional settings, such as job interviews.[10] Even if you have to pause before responding to questions, organize your answers and avoid slurring your words. Never use potentially offensive language; always use proper grammar. Avoid vocalized pauses ("uh," "um"), verbal fillers ("you know"), and repetitive phrases ("things like that"). If you practice beforehand and you feel confident about your qualifications, you should be able to speak with clarity and precision.

### Demonstrate Interest

To be effective in interviews, you must demonstrate interest in the interviewer and the company. One of the most important and meaningful ways to do so is by maintaining strong eye contact with the interviewer.[11] Although you may believe that responding to questions is the central interviewing skill, good listening is also crucial, and it can improve your responses. Use body language to show interest. Smile, nod, and give nonverbal feedback to the interviewer, and thank the interviewer for his or her time and consideration of you as a candidate.

## MORE TIPS FOR THE INTERVIEW

Beyond the general interviewing tips discussed in the previous section, there are things you can do to increase your chances of having a successful interview: understand the job and the company and prepare for behavioral-based interview questions.

### Understand the Job

A **job description** *defines the content and scope of a position.* Although the format can vary, all job descriptions include at least some of the following information: job duties and responsibilities; the knowledge, skills, and abilities necessary to accomplish the duties; the working conditions; responsibilities in relation to co-workers, supervisors, and external stakeholders; and the extent of the supervision required.

You will have studied the job description in order to craft your résumé and cover letter, but it doesn't hurt to return to it before an interview. Doing so will signal to you the types of questions you may be asked and will help you think about your answers and how you will describe your qualifications.

## Understand the Company

Job applicants and interviewees lose all credibility when they cannot demonstrate even superficial knowledge of the organization to which they are applying. Taking time to carefully research the company will showcase your initiative, help you be conversant, and prepare you to ask better questions. When appropriate during an interview, signal that you know about the company. For example, if you are asked why you would like to work for the company, say something specific about the company that you admire or have found out from your research.

Besides using obvious sources of information in your research, like the company's website, check your library for specialized resources, such as the Lexis-Nexis Company Insight database or the Bloomberg Businessweek Company Insight Center. These sources can lead you to information about the company's finances, its executive officers, and other pertinent facts. Small businesses may not be indexed in such databases, however; a local library or chamber of commerce may have information about these.

## Prepare for Behavioral-Based Interview Questions

Some companies have transitioned to the use of **behavioral-based interview questions,** *which ask the interviewee to describe a situation or an experience that demonstrates skills that are relevant to the position at the company.* Behavioral-based interview questions force the applicant to respond with concrete answers.

The best way to prepare for behavioral-based interview questions is to think about your own work and life history and create what you might refer to as an **experience inventory,** *a story or two from your work history or life that relate to the position you seek and show what kind of person and worker you are.* The prompts in the following nine areas[12] should help you with your inventory:

- *Job skill and overall work experience.* Describe your most significant work accomplishments.
- *Intelligence.* Give an example of a time when you used your fact-finding skills to solve a problem.
- *Maturity and judgment.* Describe an important work decision you have had to make in the recent past. Whom did you consult, and how did you go about making that decision?
- *Responsibility.* Give an example of when you showed initiative and took the lead on a project. Or give an example of a time when you set a goal and achieved it.
- *Relationships.* Describe a project in which others you were working with disagreed with your ideas. What did you do? Or give an example of a time when you motivated others.

- *Resourcefulness.* How do you determine what gets priority in scheduling your time? Or describe a situation when you had several things to do in a limited time, such as study for multiple exams. What led up to the situation? How did you handle it? What was the outcome?

- *Work attitude.* Tell about a time you had to learn something new in a short period of time. Or have you ever had to discipline or counsel an employee or a group member? Explain.

- *Motivation.* Give an example of a time when you motivated others. Tell the most difficult customer service experience you have ever had to handle. What did you do, and what was the outcome?

- *Leadership.* Give an example of a time when you went beyond the call of duty in order to get the job done. Or tell about a time when you were in charge of something and had to let others help you.

When answering behavioral-based interview questions, keep the following guidelines in mind:

- *Be concise.* When preparing, think about the pieces of information that are critical to the point you want to make with a story. Expand or omit according to that central point or theme. Get to the point of your story quickly, so that you can also explain what it means.

- *Select examples that highlight important information about you.* An interviewer asks behavioral-based questions to determine what skills have emerged from your previous experiences. If an interviewer asked you to discuss a time that you used fact-finding skills to solve a problem, you could tell a story that showcased your skill in using the Internet to locate sound research-based sources. For example, you could say, "I know that when I think about problems I like to rely on proven expertise and that I'm good at locating a variety of pieces of evidence on the Internet quickly," and then tell a story that highlights the development of this skill.

- *Explain the moral, conclusion, or lesson learned from your experience.* One way to end a behavioral-based response is to identify explicitly what the story shows about you. If when telling your story you wish to highlight the value of persistence and a sound education, you might say, "When I started looking for sources for a paper, I first consulted my textbook and then I went to the library. Neither of these approaches worked. I then remembered a lesson a professor had taught about using Google Scholar to locate a range of sources on a topic. I applied what I had learned from this professor to the exploration of my paper topic and found exactly the type of information I was looking for. Therefore, not giving up on the task and relying on my education made the difference."

# BUILDER

## PRACTICE BEHAVIORAL-BASED INTERVIEWING

Ask a classmate or close friend to practice behavioral-based interviewing with you. Choose a real company or organization on which to base your questions. Take turns selecting one of the nine experience inventory areas (job skills and overall work experience, intelligence, maturity and judgment, responsibilities, relationships, resourcefulness, work attitude, motivation, and leadership), and ask each other a behavioral-based question tied to the company you are pretending to interview for.

- Was the experience concisely described?
- Did the example highlight important information about the interviewee?
- Was the moral or lesson learned from the experience clear to the interviewer?
- Did the answer clearly tie back to the organization?

Finish the exercise by offering each other tips on other experiences you might mention with regard to each subject area. What might you do to improve your experience inventory?

- *Connect this lesson to the organization, if possible.* The person asking you behavioral-based questions wants to see how your skills and values merge with the company's work practices. If you can see a way to make that connection for the interviewer, do so. Returning to the example about Internet research, you might say, "I imagine these Internet-based research skills and the need for persistence will also be extremely relevant to the job we're discussing."

### BUILDING CONNECTIONS

As you have seen, being able to present yourself effectively in writing and during interviews is crucial to your professional development. Another skill that will play a vital role in opening doors in your profession is building connections, also known as networking.

From your very first college class, you should begin to think about the professional contacts you are making and how you will make the most of those connections. For example, you should think of each of your instructors as a professional resource with connections that may benefit you. Your instructors might eventually write letters of recommendation for you, so going above and beyond what is expected of you in class will help you stand out in their eyes, resulting in stronger letters of recommendation.

#### Use Social Media to Expand Your Professional Network

One way to strengthen your professional network during college is to make effective use of job-related social media sites, like LinkedIn. They can help you build a strong professional network and learn about what other people in your field are doing with their careers. Don't wait to take steps to strengthen your digital presence—develop your résumé as your studies progress, update it frequently, and post it on a professional social media site.

LinkedIn is the largest professional network on the Internet, operating in over 200 countries with an estimated 187 million members worldwide.[13] Although you should certainly make use of your career center to locate possible job prospects, also post your credentials on LinkedIn, where job opportunities around the globe, and beyond your academic network, could present themselves. Furthermore, you can always use job-related social media to explore ideas with a larger network and get feedback from other professionals. LinkedIn allows professionals to display their credentials and network with people who have similar interests, regardless of where they live.[14]

Using social media can help with professional advancement opportunities as well. But keep in mind that you are not the only one using social media to network and learn about possible job prospects. Many human resource professionals use LinkedIn, Facebook, and other social networking sites to find out about the personal lives of job applicants.[15] Moreover, if you already have a job, but are looking for a better opportunity, protect your privacy and limit who has access to your profile.

One way to prevent possible breakdowns in your private information on social media is to carefully consider the information you make available.[16] Periodically review any posts, photos, comments, and tagged information available through any of your social media networks. Ask yourself if you're comfortable with future employers evaluating you based on that information.[17] If you find information that you or others have posted that could hurt your job search, delete it. Everything connected to you through social media impacts your reputation and networking potential. Use social media cautiously to help ensure that career and networking opportunities remain open to you.[18]

## Use Internships as a Networking Opportunity

With so many job openings, you might wonder, "Why should I take the time to complete an internship before applying for a job?" Much like your education, an internship is an investment in yourself and your future. It is true that many degree programs will not require you to complete an internship; however, required or not, an internship could be the best way to start your career.

If you find that putting together a résumé is difficult because you do not have enough work experience in your field, an internship can help you expand your résumé and improve your job prospects.[19] When organizations make hiring decisions, they look for people with strong practical experience. An internship is one way to extend and enrich your education beyond classroom learning.

Internships also give you a short-term, low-risk way to explore various career options.[20] If you are pursuing a degree in the healthcare industry, you might learn through internship experience that you prefer to work with children rather than adults. This knowledge will help you limit the types of positions you apply for and ensure that you will feel satisfied in the career you choose. Or you might like to go into business management but you don't know if you'd prefer to work for a large firm or small company. You could intern with companies of various sizes to learn more about being a leader in both small and large organizational systems. This will also prepare you to speak to prospective employers about your direct experiences in leading a variety of organizational teams.

Finally, internships are a great way to expand your professional network. When you begin your career search at the end of your degree program, weak ties will play a vital role in your job searches. **Weak ties** are *people whom you do not know very well and who do not have a strong relationship with you*, like co-workers, previous internship partners, neighbors, and general acquaintances. On the other hand, **strong ties** are *people with whom you have a well-developed relationship and to whom you turn for advice frequently.* Your strong ties may include close friends, family, and others you know well and trust. All of these connections—but your weak ties, in particular—can help you find job opportunities you may not find on your own.[21]

You should not downplay the value of completing an internship or taking temporary work for a company. In an internship role, you are being assessed as a potential employee in the industry while gaining practical skills that will bolster your résumé. Even though only some internships are paid, even those for which there is no financial compensation offer valuable opportunities to build your skills. In fact, you should think of internships as on-the-job interviews and opportunities to expand your professional network.

### Use the Informational Interview to Learn

One final thing that you can do to network, even as you complete your college degree, is to seek out information about the careers that interest you. You can do this by conducting informational interviews with professionals who hold positions to which you aspire. Ask a professional in your field how she got her start in the industry, what it takes to make it, and what advice she might give to someone trying to break into the field in a positive way. Everyone has something to teach you, and an informational interview will only strengthen your prospects. To ensure that you get the most out of informational interviews, there are a few simple steps you can follow before, during, and after the interview.

**Before the Interview.** Before informational interviews there are a few things you can do to be adequately prepared. First, do your homework. You should be knowledgeable about the company, the person you are interviewing, and any information that is readily available through Internet research. If you are not prepared, the person you are interviewing may feel that you do not value his time.

Second, prepare appropriate questions. The types of questions you ask reveal how much passion and preparation you have put forward. Therefore, you might ask a professional you admire what is unique about his job. Ask questions that can't be answered through information that is readily available.

Next, go into an informational interview with 5 to 10 questions to guide your time with the interviewee. You want to be prepared, but you do not want to be so rigidly connected to your questions that you miss opportunities to follow up on information that emerges out of the conversation.

Make connections to information you have uncovered in your research, and ask questions that take it further whenever possible. You might ask, "I read in your online profile that early in your career you didn't do much consulting work. How did you make the transition from one type of work to the other?"

Finally, before interviews, ask those you interview if they are comfortable with your using an audio recorder, so that you can focus on their responses and review them later. In addition to asking permission, make sure you have access to the technology. With the advances in smartphone devices and technology, there is a range of tools and applications you can use. If you do not have a way to record an interview, you can borrow a recorder from a friend or check one out from your local library.

## CHALLENGE YOURSELF

### How in the World Am I Going to Get a Job When I Graduate? I Have Limited Professional Experience and Am Not All That Great at Networking. What Should I Do?

When it comes to networking for your chosen career, informational interviews are an often overlooked method. It can be difficult to make contact with someone who has a wealth of experience in an area in which you hope to work. But keep in mind that people are often happy to talk about the work they do. Asking for professional advice from someone you see as successful is one of the highest forms of flattery. If you do your homework and demonstrate some knowledge of the person and his career, he will more than likely give you advice and perhaps be willing to help you in your job search down the road.

Everyone's professional journey is a little bit different. Don't feel that one person's pathway to success is the only one. After conducting an informational interview with someone you respect, be mindful of what is unique to that person's experience, as well as what you can apply to your own job-search process.

Don't give up. Anything that is worthwhile takes dedication and perseverance. If you consistently learn from others and apply what you learn, you will find that others will seek your advice, too.

**During the Interview.** When conducting an informational interview, there are several things you should keep in mind that will make the interview more enjoyable. First impressions are critical. Arriving early will help you manage a positive and professional first impression. Throughout the interview act courteously; when it's over express your appreciation for the person's willingness to talk with you.

Second, be flexible. Your interviewee may answer two or three of your planned questions at once. If this happens, adapt, jump ahead, and go with the flow of the interview. Read the nonverbal cues you learned in Chapter 3. If it becomes clear that your subject is talking about something she enjoys, ask an unplanned follow-up question. If she appears to be uncomfortable with the direction of the conversation, move on to another question.

Third, practice active listening techniques during the informational interview. Show that you care about the person's answers. To be sure that you understand the insights your subject is sharing, paraphrase his main points from time to time to demonstrate the care with which you are listening.

Finally, before you end an informational interview, allow the interviewee to ask you questions. Your subject may have questions or additional insights for you, so allow time for them, as well as time to share general reflections.

**After the Interview.** After an informational interview, take some time to think about and process what you heard during the interview. You may want to jot down some quick reflections or insights you do not want to forget. Make sure the person you interviewed feels appreciated for his time and insights; send a thank-you card in the mail. It's a novelty today to get a card rather than a quick thank-you e-mail. Be specific as you draft your thank you, and write one thing that you gained from the interview experience.

Finally, if appropriate, ask the people you interview if you can add them to your professional network. Ask if they use LinkedIn, and send a request. They then will be in your network when you finish your education and are looking for a job. You may have additional opportunities to network down the road.

 **CHAPTER REVIEW**

In this chapter you learned the communication skills that will help you secure employment. Presenting yourself effectively in writing (in your résumé and cover letter) and orally (in face-to-face interviews) will open up professional opportunities that would not otherwise be available to you. Think about networking well before you need professional connections; if you wait until the need is critical to your job search, you will find it more difficult to build those relationships. Critically thinking about the information you communicate in these contexts can be the difference between continuing your job search and landing your dream job.

## KEY TERMS

behavioral-based
   interview questions, 308
chronological résumé, 300
cover letter, 303
experience inventory, 308
functional résumé, 300

job description, 307
objective statement, 299
strong ties, 312
style, 295
weak ties, 312

## STUDY QUESTIONS

1. What are some of the career options related to studying communication? How might communication skills prepare you for a job in your field of choice?

2. Why should you use strong action verbs when creating job function descriptions? Choose three of the action verbs listed in Table 15.2, and draft one clause for each that describes your own present or past employment experience.

3. Consider the four main sections that make up a cover letter. How does each of these sections help you persuade a company to hire you?

4. How might you create a strong first impression at a job interview?

5. What are the nine behavioral-based interview question areas? Think of a question for each area that an interviewer might ask you. Next, answer those questions using the advice given in this chapter.

6. What would you do before, during, and after an informational interview to help you build more connections and network more effectively?

# GLOSSARY

**A**

**adoption** Listeners start a new behavior as a result of a persuasive presentation.

**ageist language** Language that denigrates people based on their age, whether young or old.

**agenda-setting** The process of shaping what topics are considered critical for discussion by society.

**aggressiveness** Occurs when people stand up for their rights at the expense of others' and care about their own needs but no one else's.

**alliteration** The repetition of the initial sound of a word.

**ambiguous words** Words that can be interpreted in multiple ways.

**analogy** A comparison of things that are otherwise dissimilar.

**analytical function** The use of critical thinking skills to evaluate and critique an issue or idea.

**androgynous** Referring to a person who possesses both stereotypically male and stereotypically female traits.

**antonym** Defines an idea by opposition.

**argument** A form of discourse that attempts to persuade.

**argumentativeness** A predisposition to recognize controversial issues, advocate positions, and refute opposing positions.

**articulation** The production of sounds.

**artifacts** Ornaments or adornments we display that hold communicative potential.

**asynchronous communication** Communication that occurs when the people involved experience a delay in interacting with one another and take turns being senders and receivers of information.

**attitude** A predisposition to respond favorably or unfavorably to a person, an object, an idea, or an event.

**attractiveness** Includes physical attractiveness, how desirable a person is to work with, and how much "social value" the person has for others.

**audience analysis** The collection and interpretation of audience characteristics through observation, inferences, questionnaires, and the Internet.

**automatic attention** We listen in spite of ourselves, without effort.

**autonomy and connectedness** Having an interest in being close to others, but also needing to maintain a separate identity.

**avoidance stage** When two partners avoid each other, desiring separation.

**B**

**bargaining** The process that occurs when two or more parties attempt to reach an agreement on what each should give and receive in a relationship.

**behavioral-based interview questions** Interview questions that ask the interviewee to describe a situation or an experience that demonstrates skills that are relevant to the position at the company.

**behavioral flexibility** The ability to adapt to new situations and relate in new ways when necessary.

**belief** A conviction, often thought to be more enduring than an attitude and less enduring than a value.

**bibliographic reference** The complete citation information about a source, which is included in the "references" or "works cited" section at the end of a speech outline.

**bodily aspects** How to use one's body to convey meaning.

**bodily movement** What a speaker does with his or her entire body during a presentation.

**body** The largest part of a presentation, in which the speaker places his or her arguments and ideas, evidence and examples, proofs and illustrations, and stories and testimonials.

**bonding stage** When a couple communicate their relationship to others.

**boomerang effect** When an audience likes a speaker and his or her message less after the presentation than they did before.

**boundary-crossing media** A communication channel whose personal and professional uses span communication contexts.

**brainstorming** Thinking of as many topics as possible in a limited time to select one that will be appropriate for the audience.

**C**

**captive audience** An audience that does not choose to hear a speaker or his or her speech.

**cause/effect pattern** An organizational pattern in which the presenter first explains the causes of an event, a problem, or an issue and then discusses its consequences, results, or effects.

**celebrity testimony** Statements made by a public figure who is known to the audience.

**channel** The means by which a message moves from the source to the receiver of the message.

**chronemics** The way people organize, relate to, and use time and the messages that result.

**chronological résumé** A document that organizes a job seeker's credentials over time.

**circumscribing stage** When the primary focus is on setting limits and boundaries on communication between two people.

**cliché** An expression that has lost originality and force through overuse.

**co-cultural groups** Groups that include but are not limited to women, ethnic minorities, gay and lesbian individuals, immigrants and refugees, physically or mentally challenged persons, and even neighborhood gangs and political groups that have formed to promote a cause.

**code** A systematic arrangement of symbols used to create meanings in the mind of another person or persons.

**codependency** The tendency to depend on the needs of, or control by, another.

**code sensitivity** The ability to adapt to the verbal and nonverbal language of the individual with whom we are communicating, regardless of cultural or co-cultural differences.

**code switching** Shifting from one treatment of language to another based on the audience and place.

**coercion** When compliance is forced through hostile acts.

**cognitive restructuring** A technique for reducing public speaking anxiety that focuses on analyzing negative perceptions and developing coping statements for dealing with a variety of situations.

**cohesiveness** The attachment members feel toward each other and the group.

**collectivist cultures** Cultures that value the group over the individual.

**commitment** A measure of how much time and effort people put into a cause.

**communication** The process of using messages to generate meaning.

**communication apprehension (CA)** The fear of communicating with other people, whether that interaction is real or anticipated.

**communication privacy management (CPM) theory** A theory that focuses on the processes people use to decide whether to reveal or conceal private information and how to manage the private information they share with others.

**comparison** Shows the similarity between something well known and something less known.

**complementarity** The idea that we sometimes bond with people who provide something we do not have; in turn we may have qualities or characteristics they lack.

**complementing** Goes beyond duplication of the message in two channels; the verbal and nonverbal codes add meaning to each other and expand the meaning of either message alone.

**compliance-gaining** Attempts to persuade another person to do something he or she might not ordinarily do.

**compliance-resisting** Occurs when targets of influence messages refuse to conform to requests.

**computer-mediated communication (CMC)** Human-to-human interaction using networked computer environments.

**conclusion** The end or final part of a speech.

**concrete language** Words and statements that are specific rather than abstract or vague.

**conflict** Occurs anytime two or more people have goals they perceive to be incompatible.

**conflict management** The use of language to resolve issues between or among individuals or groups.

**connotative meanings** The meanings people come to assign because of personal or individual experience.

**content** The literal meaning of a message.

**context** A set of circumstances including a physical setting, an occasion, or a situation.

**contradiction** When verbal and nonverbal messages conflict.

**contrast** Clarifies by showing differences.

**co-ownership rules** Privacy rules that clarify our expectations for how others will treat our disclosures.

**cover letter** A document that persuasively illustrates the ways in which a job seeker and his or her credentials match a particular job description.

**creative function** When imagination meets writing or speaking ability.

**criteria** The standards by which a group must judge potential solutions to a problem.

**cultivation effect** The effect of heavy television and media use, which leads people to perceive reality as consistent with media portrayals.

**cultural relativism** Viewing other cultures as objectively as possible, without judgment.

**culture** A unique combination of traditions and customs that is transmitted through learning and that shapes the beliefs and behavior of the people who live within them.

**D**

**data** Facts that have been collected from a particular source.

**data triangulation** The process of verifying and confirming the results or insights from one source of information with other types of information on the same topic.

**deceptive communication** The practice of deliberately making somebody believe things that are untrue.

**decoding** The process of assigning meaning to an encoded message.

**deductive argument** Uses a general proposition applied to a specific instance, or minor premise, to draw a conclusion.

**defensiveness** Occurs when a person feels attacked.

**delivery** How a person's voice and body affect the meaning of a presentation.

**demographic analysis** The collection and interpretation of data such as name, age, sex, hometown, year in school, race, major subject, religion, and organizational affiliations.

**demonstrating** Showing the audience what the speaker is explaining.

**denotative meaning** The agreed-upon meaning of a word, or the meaning found in a dictionary.

**description** Giving an account of observed behavior or phenomena.

**designated leader** Someone who has been appointed or elected to a leadership position.

**dialectic theory** A theory that suggests that relationships include contrary tendencies or opposing values.

**dialogue** A conversation, discussion, or negotiation.

**differentiating stage** When differences are emphasized, as opposed to commonalities.

**differentiation and specialization** The division of labor in an organization and the degree to which each individual has a unique role and responsibility.

**discontinuance** A persuasive purpose rooted in convincing listeners to stop some current behavior.

**dominant culture** The group that has the most power, influence, and rights.

E

**emergent leader** Someone who exerts influence toward achievement of a group's goal but who does not hold the formal position or role of leader.

**empathic listening** The attempt to understand another person.

**emphasis** Using nonverbal cues to strengthen a message.

**encoding** The process of translating an idea or a thought into words.

**enunciation** The eighth vocal aspect of speech delivery; the pronunciation and articulation of sounds and words.

**ethics** A set of principles for right conduct.

**ethos** The reputation, authority, and integrity of a speaker.

**ethnic group** Consists of people who share common cultural elements—for example, language or religion—as well as a common history.

**ethnocentrism** The belief that one's own group or culture is superior to all other groups or cultures.

**euphemism** A generally harmless word, name, or phrase that replaces an offensive or suggestive one.

**evidence** Anything, physical or verbal, that helps in forming a conclusion or judgment.

**examples** Specific instances used to clarify a point.

**experience inventory** A story or two from an individual's work history or life that relate to the position and show what kind of person and worker he or she is.

**experimentation stage** The stage in which people make an effort to find some common ground, including background, interests, attitudes, or values.

**expert testimony** Information from a source who has enough credibility to speak about a specific topic.

**explanation** A means of developing an idea that simplifies or clarifies it while arousing audience interest.

**explicit-rule culture** A culture in which policies, procedures, and expectations are more likely to be discussed or negotiated.

**extemporaneous mode** A carefully prepared and practiced presentation in which the presenter delivers the message conversationally, without heavy dependence on notes.

**extrinsic motivation** The reasons outside the presentation that audience members will benefit from listening to it.

**eye contact** The extent to which a speaker looks directly at the audience.

F

**facial expressions** The nonverbal cues expressed by a speaker's face.

**factual example** An example based on real circumstances.

**fear appeal** A message designed to frighten or alarm an audience so they will be persuaded to act.

**feedback** The receiver's verbal and nonverbal response to the source's message.

**figures of speech** Expressions that draw relationships that help listeners remember.

**fluency** The smoothness of the delivery, the flow of the words, and the absence of vocalized pauses.

**formal communication** Messages that follow prescribed channels of communication throughout an organization.

**formal (positional) role** An assigned role based on an individual's position or title within a group.

**formalization** The rules, procedures, and norms that may exist for carrying out work practices.

**functional résumé** A document that organizes a job applicant's experience by the type of function performed.

G

**gatekeeping** The process of determining what news, information, or entertainment will reach a mass audience.

**gestures** Movements of the head, arms, and hands used to illustrate, emphasize, or signal ideas in a speech.

**global communication** Exchanges between people whose communication practices, patterns, and understandings differ because they come from distinct cultures.

**grammatical errors** Violations of the formal rules of written and spoken language.

**group climate** The emotional tone or atmosphere members create within a group.

**groupthink** A phenomenon that occurs in a group when the desire for cohesion and agreement takes precedence over critical analysis and discussion.

**H**

**hearing** The act of receiving sound.

**hierarchy** The levels of responsibility and relationships within an organization.

**hostile work environment harassment** It "occurs when unwelcome comments or conduct based on sex, race, or other legally protected characteristics unreasonably interferes with an employee's work performance or creates an intimidating, hostile, or offensive work environment" (FCC).

**hurtful messages** Messages that create emotional pain or upset; they can encourage the end of a relationship.

**hyperbole** The use of exaggeration to make a point.

**hyperpersonal perspective** The understanding that, in certain circumstances, CMC can be beneficial and rewarding, and perhaps even preferable to face-to-face interactions.

**hypothetical example** A fictional but realistic example.

**I**

**identity management** The control (or lack of control) of what we communicate and what it conveys about us.

**illustration** Clarifies by showing what something is.

**imagery** Figures of speech that hit at the senses and stimulate listeners' synapses to see, hear, and feel what words are saying.

**immediacy** When people engage in communication behaviors intended to create perceptions of psychological closeness with others.

**immediate behavioral purposes** The actions a speaker expects from an audience during and immediately after a presentation.

**immediate purpose** A statement of what a speaker intends to accomplish in a speech.

**implicit-rule culture** A culture in which cultural rules are embedded in tradition and followed faithfully.

**impromptu mode** When a presentation is delivered without notes, plans, or formal preparation, with spontaneity and conversational language.

**individualistic cultures** Cultures that value individual freedom, choice, uniqueness, and independence.

**inductive argument** An argument that provides enough specific instances that the listener can make an inferential leap to a generalization or conclusion.

**inference** A tentative generalization based on some evidence.

**influence** The power a person has to affect other people's thinking or actions.

**informal communication** Any interaction that emerges out of social interactions among organization members rather than following the rules of the formal chain of command.

**informal (behavioral) role** A role that develops naturally or spontaneously within a group.

**information** The selective groups of facts that help people understand sets of data.

**information anxiety** The experience of stress due to an inability to access, understand, or process information that is necessary to a goal or task at hand.

**information hunger** An audience's need for information, as created by the presenter.

**information literacy** The ability to locate, evaluate, and incorporate important information into our own knowledge base.

**information overload** The experience of having more data and information than we have the capacity to process in a given time period.

**information relevance** The importance, novelty, and usefulness of information to an audience.

**informative content** The main points and subpoints, illustrations, and examples used to clarify and inform.

**initiating stage** The relational stage that begins with the first impressions someone has of a potential partner.

**instrumental function** Using language as a directive—a means of getting others to think or do something.

**integration stage** When two people begin to merge their lives.

**intensifying stage** When the communication between two people changes and deepens.

**intent** What a speaker wants to communicate.

**intercultural communication** Interactions between people from different cultural backgrounds.

**interdependence** A situation in which people are mutually dependent and have an impact on each other.

**internal references** Citation information about specific evidence presented in the body of a speech.

**interpersonal communication** The process of exchanging meaning in interpersonal relationships.

**interpersonal relationships** Associations between at least two people who are interdependent, who use consistent patterns of interaction, and who have interacted for an extended period of time.

**interpretation** The assignment of meaning to stimuli.

**intimate distance** Extends from the body outward to 18 inches; it is the distance used by people who are relationally close.

**intrapersonal communication** The kind of discussion and decision making that occurs within one's own mind.

**introduction** The first part of a presentation.

**J**

**jargon** The language particular to a specific profession, work group, or culture.

**job description** Defines the content and scope of a position.

**K**

**key-word outline** An outline consisting of important words or phrases to remind a speaker of the content of the speech.

**kinesics** The way we interpret nonverbal behavior related to movement, such as body language and facial expression.

**knowledge** Information with meaning attached to it.

**L**

**language** The code we use to communicate with each other.

**lay testimony** Statements made by ordinary people that substantiate or support what a presenter says.

**leadership** The process of using communication to influence the behaviors and attitudes of others.

**linkage rules** Privacy rules that clarify someone's need to have others exercise caution about sharing information with certain individuals.

**listening** The act of interpreting the sounds someone hears, to determine their meaning.

**listening for pleasure** We listen to relaxing, fun, or emotionally stimulating information.

**logos** Persuasion by using logical argument.

**long-range goal** A statement of purposes that could be achieved with continuing efforts to persuade.

**long-term memory** Memory reserved for facts, figures, and concepts that we know we have to remember.

**M**

**main points** The most important points in a speech.

**maintenance functions** Behaviors that focus on the interpersonal relationships among group members; they are aimed at supporting cooperation and harmony.

**management** The process of using communication to maintain structure, order, harmony, and the efficiency of procedures and practices.

**manipulation** Tricking people or using fraudulent means to gain compliance.

**manuscript mode** Delivering a presentation from a script of an entire speech.

**mass communication** Involves the use of print and electronic technology by professional communicators to share messages over great distances for large audiences.

**mass media** The specific means by which we use print and electronic technology to communicate.

**meaning** Whatever message someone is trying to convey to others, as well as how that message is interpreted.

**media convergence** The ways in which different technologies have evolved to perform similar outcomes or tasks.

**media literacy** The ability to think critically about mediated messages and how they influence us.

**mediated communication** Messages that are transmitted not directly from person to person but through some other communication tool, such as print, electronic, or digital communication devices.

**memorized mode** When a presentation is committed to memory.

**message** The verbal and nonverbal expression of the idea, thought, or feeling that one person (the source) wishes to communicate to another person or group of people (the receivers).

**metaphor** Creatively compares two things that do not at first seem alike.

**Monroe Motivated Sequence** A problem-solving organizational format (including the steps of attention, need, satisfaction, visualization, and action) that encourages an audience.

**M-time** A monochromatic time schedule that compartmentalizes time to meet personal needs and to separate tasks from social activities.

**multitasking** Trying to do two or more tasks at once.

**N**

**narration** The oral presentation and interpretation of a story, a description, or an event.

**neologisms** New words or new meanings for old words that are in the process of entering common use.

**noise** Any interference in the encoding and decoding processes that reduces the clarity of a message.

**nonverbal codes** Nonword symbols, gestures, or vocalizations that communicate meaning.

**nonverbal communication** The process of using wordless messages to generate meaning.

**norms** The beliefs about how individual members should interact and behave in a particular context.

**novelty and predictability** The wish to be able to predict events in a relationship; to yearn for the original and new.

**O**

**objectics** The study of the human use of clothing and other artifacts as nonverbal codes.

**objective statement** An articulation of the goal for a résumé.

**observations** Descriptions of what someone has directly seen, touched, tasted, smelled, or heard.

**online library catalog system** A program that allows users to explore all types of print and multimedia holdings and collections of the library.

**operational definition** Defines by explaining a process.

**opinion leader** A range of people consistently turn to that person for advice and informed perspectives on issues.

**oral citations** Spoken citations that make specific reference, where appropriate, to each source used in a presentation.

**organization** Grouping stimuli into meaningful units.

**organizational culture** The attitudes, values, and beliefs that are common and that characterize the interactions of organization members and the way they work and behave.

**outline** A written plan that uses symbols, margins, and content to reveal the order, importance, and substance of a speech.

**P**

**paralinguistic features** The nonword sounds and nonword characteristics of language, such as pitch, volume, rate, and quality.

**paraphrasing** Restating another person's message by rephrasing in one's own words.

**pathos** The use of emotional means of persuasion.

**pause** An absence of vocal sound used for dramatic effect, transition, or emphasis.

**permeability rules** Privacy rules that clarify how much private information someone is comfortable with others sharing about specific topics.

**perception** The process of using the senses to acquire information about the surrounding environment or situation.

**perception checking** Involves checking in with one's conversational partner to ensure one has a common understanding of an event that has occurred or a common definition of a particular phenomenon.

**perceptual constancy** Past experiences lead a person to see the world in a way that is difficult to change.

**personal bias** Letting our own prejudices interfere with our ability to interpret information accurately.

**personal distance** Ranges from 18 inches to 4 feet, and it is the distance most Americans use for conversation and other nonintimate exchanges.

**personal experience** Something that actually happened to a speaker.

**personal space** The distance we maintain between ourselves and others; the amount of space we claim as our own.

**persuasive presentation** A message strategically designed to induce change in the audience in some way consistent with the speaker's purpose.

**phatic communication** The most casual and often briefest exchanges that are intended to recognize the existence of another person and demonstrate sociability rather than provide information.

**pitch** The highness or lowness of a speaker's voice; the voice's upward and downward movement; and the melody produced by the voice.

**power** The ability to influence others.

**prejudice** A negative attitude toward a group of people just because they belong to that group.

**primary source** Original source of material or research.

**privacy turbulence** When those allowed to access someone's private information have not upheld the stipulated obligations.

**problem/solution pattern** The organizational pattern in which a

presenter describes a problem and proposes a solution.

**profanity** Language that is vulgar, abusive, or disrespectful of things sacred.

**projection** Speaking loudly enough for all to hear.

**pronunciation** The act of correctly articulating words.

**proof** Any evidence that a receiver believes.

**proposition of fact** An assertion that can be proved or disproved.

**proposition of policy** A proposal of a new rule.

**proposition of value** A statement of what should be embraced as good or bad, right or wrong.

**proxemics** The study of the human use of space and distance.

**proximity** The location, distance, or range between persons and things.

**pseudolistening** Pretending to listen but letting the mind or attention wander to something else.

**P-time** A polychronic time schedule that views time as "contextually based and relationally oriented."

**public distance** Exceeds 12 feet and is the distance used most often in public speaking in such settings as lecture halls, churches, mosques, and synagogues.

**Q**

**questionnaire** A list of questions developed to obtain demographic and attitudinal information.

**R**

**race** A category of people distinguished by inherited features, such as skin color, facial features, or quality of hair.

**racist language** Language that is insulting because it associates skin color or ethnicity with stereotypical and usually negative characteristics.

**rate** The speed of delivery, or how fast we say our words.

**receiver** The intended target of the message.

**reference librarians** Librarians who are specially trained in finding and evaluating information.

**references** The sources used in a presentation.

**reflexivity** Being self-aware and learning from interactions with the intent of improving future interactions.

**regionalisms** Words and phrases specific to a particular region or part of the country.

**regulation** The use of nonverbal codes to monitor and control interactions with others.

**relational maintenance** When a couple begin establishing strategies for keeping the relationship together.

**repetition** Occurs when the same message is sent verbally and nonverbally, or when someone uses the same word choices over and over again to stress a central point.

**responsiveness** The idea that we tend to develop relationships with people who demonstrate positive interest in us.

**rhetorical questions** Questions asked for effect, with no answer expected.

**role** A part a person plays in a social context.

**rough draft** A preliminary organization of an outline.

**rules of engagement** Rules about initiating, conducting, and ending a verbal exchange.

**S**

**scanning and choosing** A process of taking in stimuli and choosing what to listen to and how.

**search engine** A website that is used specifically to search for information.

**secondary source** A source of information that builds on or comments on another's material or research.

**selection** The decisions we make to focus on some stimuli—sights, sounds, smells, and other sensations—and neglect others.

**selective attention** The sustained focus we choose to give to things that are important to us.

**self-centered functions** Behaviors that serve the needs of the individual at the expense of the group.

**self-disclosure** The process of making intentional revelations about ourselves that others would be unlikely to know and that generally constitute private, sensitive, or confidential information.

**seminal sources** Foundational studies or pieces of information that have been heavily cited and have helped advance a line of scholarly inquiry.

**sentence outline** An outline consisting entirely of complete sentences.

**sexist language** Language that excludes individuals on the basis of gender.

**sexual harassment** Unwelcome, unsolicited, repeated behavior of a sexual nature.

**short-term memory** Where we temporarily store information.

**signposts** Ways in which a presenter signals to an audience where the presentation is going.

**similarity** The idea that our relational partners usually like or dislike the same things we do.

**simile** Creatively compares two unlike things, using the word *like* or *as*.

**skills training** The systematic work done, through instruction and practice, to develop public speaking skills.

**slang** Informal, casual language used among equals.

**small-group communication** The interaction among three to nine people who are working together to achieve an interdependent goal.

**social distance** Ranges from 4 to 12 feet, and it is the distance used most often to carry out business in the workplace.

**social function** The use of language to build and maintain relationships.

**social media** A variety of websites that allow users to connect and interact with acquaintances, friends, family members, organizations, colleagues, and customers all over the world through the exchange of user-generated content.

**social undermining** An intentional and often planned action meant to socially isolate another person from a larger group.

**source** Initiates a message.

**specific purpose** The purpose stated precisely as an outcome or behavioral objective and in terms of the audience.

**stagnation stage** When relationships are sluggish and do not grow or progress.

**state apprehension** When someone experiences communication anxiety in a limited number of settings or circumstances.

**statistics** Numbers used to summarize information or compare quantities.

**status** Expressed by devoting attention to someone we think is particularly important.

**stereotype** To treat individuals as if they are the same as others in a given category.

**strategic ambiguity** Intentional uncertainty and vagueness.

**strong ties** Relationships that we are highly committed to and that we devote substantial energy to maintaining, regardless of individual circumstances that may occur.

**style** The way we use language and grammar to construct written materials.

**subpoints** Points that support the main points of a speech.

**substitution** Occurs when nonverbal codes are used in place of verbal codes.

**supportive communication** When communicators listen with empathy, acknowledge the feelings of others, and engage in dialogue to help others maintain a sense of personal control.

**surveys** Studies that ask a sample of the population a limited number of questions in order to discover public opinions on a particular set of issues.

**syllogism** A structure that contains a generalization (a major premise) applied to a particular instance (a minor premise) that leads to a conclusion.

**symbol** Represents an idea, a process, or a physical entity.

**synchronous communication** Communication that occurs when the people involved interact with one another at the same time as both senders and receivers of information.

**synonym** Defines by using a word or words that are close or similar in meaning to the one we are trying to define.

**systematic desensitization** A technique that focuses on progressive relaxation, visualization, and active engagement exercises to help presenters overcome public speaking anxiety.

**T**

**tactile communication (haptics)** The use of touch in communication.

**task functions** Behaviors that directly relate to a group's purpose; they affect the group's productivity.

**termination** When a relationship stops completely.

**territoriality** The need to establish and maintain certain spaces as our own.

**testimonial evidence** Written or oral statements of others' experience used to substantiate or clarify a point.

**tests of evidence** The standards for demonstrating validity.

**thesis statement** A complete statement that reveals the content of a presentation.

**time-sequence pattern** A method of organization in which the presenter explains a sequence of events in chronological order.

**topical-sequence pattern** An organizational pattern that emphasizes the major reasons the audience should accept a point of view by addressing the advantages, disadvantages, qualities, and types of a person, place, or thing.

**trait apprehension** When someone experiences communication anxiety in a variety of settings and under diverse circumstances.

**transition** Typically includes a brief flashback and a brief forecast that tell an audience when a speaker is moving from one main point to another.

**trouble talk** Exchanges in which people complain about something without expecting a solution.

**trust** A belief that members of a group can rely on each other.

**turning point** A transformative event that alters a relationship in some way.

**turn taking** When one person speaks and the other responds with a certain amount of give and take.

**U**

**uncertainty-accepting cultures** Cultures that tend to be tolerant of ambiguity and diversity; they are more often democracies than dictatorships or countries led by powerful royalties.

**uncertainty-rejecting cultures** Cultures that have difficulty with ambiguity and diversity.

**uses and gratifications (U&G) theory** A theory that suggests that people use social media to satisfy their own needs and desires.

**V**

**value** A deeply rooted belief that governs our attitude about something.

**verbal aggressiveness** Communication that attacks the self-concepts of other people in order to inflict psychological pain.

**verbal communication** The use of language to convey meaning.

**viral social media campaigns** Video messages created with the intentions that people will forward and discuss them through social media and that the messages will be widely seen.

**virtual libraries** Resources that provide links to websites where some level of review for relevance and usability of the information has been conducted.

**vocal aspects** The aspects of a presentation that involve the voice: projection and volume, rate, pauses, fluency, pitch, pronunciation, articulation, enunciation, and vocal variety.

**vocal cues** All of the oral aspects of sound except words themselves.

**vocalized pauses** Breaks in fluency that negatively affect an audience's perception of the speaker's competence and dynamism.

**vocal variety** Voice quality, intonation patterns, inflections of pitch, and the duration of syllables.

**volume** The relative loudness of a speaker's voice.

**voluntary audience** An audience that chooses to hear someone speak about a particular topic.

**W**

**weak ties** Personal relationships to which we are not as committed overall and in which we would not invest as much time and energy to maintain.

**word** A symbol that has been assigned meaning.

# ENDNOTES

## CHAPTER 1

1. *Why men don't listen?* BBC News. Retrieved from http://news.bbc.co.uk/2/hi/health/1044805.stm

2. Allen, M., Berkowitz, S., Hunt, S., & Louden, A. (1999). A meta-analysis of the impact of forensics and communication education on critical thinking. *Communication Education, 48,* 18–30.

3. Scott, E. (2011). *Conflict resolution skills for healthy relationships: The key to less relationship stress? Effective conflict resolution skills!* Retrieved from http://stress.about.com/od/relationships/a/conflict_res.htmAbout.com Guide

4. Ford, W. S. Z., & Wolvin, A. D. (1993). The differential impact of a basic communication course on perceived communication competencies in class, work, and social contexts. *Communication Education, 42,* 215–233.

5. Jolly, C. (2010, May 27). *Number of non-English-speaking households in the US rises.* Retrieved from www.k-international.com/blog/non-english-speakers-in-us/

6. Nichols, M. (2006, September 15). Listen up for better sales. *BusinessWeek Online,* 12.

7. Bates, J. (2004, December 15). Unaccustomed as I am . . . *Nursing Standard, 19*(14–16), 25.

8. Johnson, L. M., & Johnson, V. E. (1995, January/February). Help wanted—accountant: What the classifieds say about employer expectations. *Journal of Education for Business, 70*(3), 130–134.

9. Cano, C. P., & Cano, P. Q. (2006). Human resources management and its impact on innovation performance in companies. *International Journal of Technology Management, 35,* 11–27.

10. Hanzevack, E. L., & McKean, R. A. (1991). Teaching effective oral presentations as part of the senior design course. *Chemical Engineering Education, 25,* 28–32; Horton, G. E., & Brown, D. (1990). The importance of interpersonal skills in consultee-centered consultation: A review. *Journal of Counseling and Development, 68,* 423–426; LaBar, G. (1994). Putting together the complete hygienist. *Occupational Hazards, 56,* 63–66; Messmer, M. (1997, August). Career strategies for accounting graduates. *Management Accounting,* 4–10; Nisberg, J. N. (1996). Communication: What we hear, what we say vs. what they hear, what they say. *The National Public Accountant, 41,* 34–38; Ridley, A. J. (1996). A profession for the twenty-first century. *Internal Auditor, 53,* 20–25; Simkin, M. G. (1996). The importance of good communication skills on "IS" career paths. *Journal of Technical Writing & Communication, 26,* 69–78.

11. Perception. *Encarta Dictionary.* (2011).

12. Role. *Encarta Dictionary.* (2011).

13. Yahaya, A. (2009). The relationship of self-concept and communication skills towards academic achievement among secondary school students in Johor Bahru. *International Journal of Psychological Studies.* Retrieved from www.ccsenet.org/journal/index.php/ijps/article/view/3931

14. Mead, G. H. (1967). *Mind, self, and society from the standpoint of a social behaviorist* (Charles W. Morris, Ed.). Chicago: University of Chicago Press.

15. Hamilton, K. (1998, November 2). A very ugly gym suit. *Newsweek,* 52.

16. For further reading see Czubaroff, J. (2000). Dialogical rhetoric: An application of Martin Buber's philosophy of dialogue. *Quarterly Journal of Speech, 86,* 168–189.

17. Wiggins, J. A., Wiggins, B. B., & Zanden, J. (1993). *Social psychology* (4th ed.). New York: McGraw-Hill.

## CHAPTER 2

1. Leaper, C., & Gleason, J. B. (1996). The relationship of play activity and gender to parent and child sex-typed communication. *International Journal of Behavioral Development, 19,* 689–703.

2. Lindset, E. W., & Mize, J. (2001). Contextual differences in parent-child play: Implications for children's gender role development. *Sex Roles, 44,* 155–176.

3. McKay, B., & McKay, K. (2011, January 28). *Classical rhetoric 101—Invention.* Retrieved from www.artofmanliness.com/2011/01/26/classical-rhetoric-101-the-five-canons-of-rhetoric-invention/

4. Walther, J. (2012). Interaction through technological lenses: Computer-mediated communication and language. *Journal of Language and Social Psychology, 31,* 397–414.

5. Allen, M., Berkowitz, S., Hunt, S., & Louden, A. (1999). A meta-analysis of the impact of forensics and communication education on critical thinking. *Communication Education, 48,* 18–30.

6. Chung, J. (2013). Social networking in online support groups for health: How online social networking benefits patients. *Journal of Health Communication.* doi: 10.1080/10810730.2012.757396

7. Whorf, B. L. (1956). Science and linguistics. In J. B. Carroll (Ed.), *Language, thought and reality* (pp. 207–219). Cambridge, MA: MIT Press.

8. *Ordinary words with new meanings*. Retrieved from www.openforum.com/idea-hub/topics/technology/article/11-ordinary-words-that-have-new-meaning-in-social-media-1/

9. Ibid.

10. Genesee, F., & Bourhis, R. Y. (1982). The social psychological significance of code switching in cross-cultural communication. *Journal of Language and Social Psychology, 1,* 1–27.

11. Available at www.youtube.com/watch?v=hQM9lVejdqk

12. Federal Communications Commission. Retrieved from www.fcc.gov/encyclopedia/understanding-workplace-harassment-fcc-staff

13. *Ageist language.* (2012, February 12). Retrieved from virtuallinguist.typepad.com/the_virtual_linguist/.../ageist-language.html

14. *Slang. Commonly used American slang.* Retrieved from www.manythings.org

15. Ibid.

16. *What did he say??? Computer jargon explained.* Retrieved from www.jonstorm.com/glossary/

17. *Euphemism list.* Retrieved from www.euphemismlist.com/

18. http://muse.dillfrog.com/ambiguous_words.php

19. Wells, G. L., & Olson, E. A. (2003). Eyewitness testimony. *Annual Review of Psychology, 54,* 277–295.

## CHAPTER 3

1. Lapakko, D. (1997). Three cheers for language: A closer examination of a widely cited study of nonverbal communication. *Communication Education, 46,* 63–67.

2. Grahe, J. E., & Bernieri, F. J. (1999). The importance of nonverbal cues in judging rapport. *Journal of Nonverbal Behavior, 23,* 253–269; Vedantam, S. (2006, October 2–8). A mirror on reality: Research shows that neurons in the brain help us understand social cues. *Washington Post National Weekly Edition, 23*(50), 35.

3. Nikolaus, J., Roessing, T., & Petersen, T. (2011). The effects of verbal and nonverbal elements in persuasive communication: Findings from two multi-method experiments. *Communications: The European Journal of Communication Research, 36,* 245–271.

4. Mehrabian, A. (1971). *Silent messages.* Belmont, CA: Wadsworth.

5. Ekman, P. (1997). Should we call it expression or communication? *Innovations in Social Science Research, 10,* 333–344; Ekman, P. (1999). Basic emotions. In T. Dalgleish & T. Power (Eds.), *The handbook of cognition and emotion* (pp. 45–60). Sussex, UK: John Wiley; Ekman, P. (1999). Facial expressions. In T. Dalgleish & T. Power (Eds.), *The handbook of cognition and emotion* (pp. 301–320). Sussex, UK: John Wiley; Ekman, P., & Friesen, W. V. (1967). Head and body cues in the judgment of emotion: A reformulation. *Perceptual and Motor Skills, 24,* 711–724.

6. Paarvean, N. (2013, March 19). Why you really can tell what's your dog thinking: Scientists reveal we're evolved to identify animal emotions (which is hardly news to anyone who owns a pet). *Mail Online* reporting research published by Tina Bloom and Harris Friedman in *Behavioural Processes.*

7. Cash, T. F. (1980, July 7). If you think beautiful people hold all the cards, you're right, says a researcher. *People Weekly, 14,* 74–79; Kowner, R. (1996, June). Facial asymmetry and attractiveness judgment in developmental perspective. *Journal of Experimental Psychology, 22,* 662–675.

8. Brody, J. E. (1994, March 21). Notions of beauty transcend culture, new study suggests. *New York Times,* A14.

9. Williams, R. B. (2011, August 6). *Wired for Success* provides the findings of a study conducted by Biesanz, J., Human, L., & Lorenzo, G,. which was published in *Psychological Science.*

10. Rhode, D. L. (2010). *The beauty bias: The injustice of appearance in life and law.* Oxford, UK: Oxford University Press.

11. Cash, 164–182.

12. Knapp, M. L., Hall, J. A., & Horgan, T. G. (2014). *Nonverbal communication in human interaction* (8th ed.). Boston: Wadsworth, Cengage Learning.

13. Widgery, R. N. (1974). Sex of receiver and physical attractiveness of source as determinants of initial credibility perception. *Western Speech, 38,* 13–17.

14. Davies, A. P. C., Goetz, A. T., & Shackelford, T. K. (2008). Exploiting the beauty in the eye of the beholder: The use of physical attractiveness as a persuasive tactic. *Personality and Individual Differences, 45,* 302–306.

15. Hall, E. T. (1966). *The hidden dimension.* New York: Doubleday.

16. Ibid.

17. Burgoon, J. K. (1978). A communication model of personal space violations: Explication and an initial test. *Human Communication Research, 4,* 129–142.

18. Bruneau, T. J. (2007). Time, change, and sociocultural communication: A chronemic perspective. *Sign Systems Studies, 35*, 89–117.

19. Cecchini, M., Baroni, E., Di Vito, C., & Lai, C. (2011). Smiling in newborns during communicative wake and active sleep. *Infant Behavior & Development, 34*, 417–423.

20. Hertenstein, M. J. (2002). Touch: Its communicative functions in infancy. *Human Development, 45*, 70–94; Loots, G., & Devise, I. (2003). The use of visual-tactile communication strategies by deaf and hearing fathers and mothers of deaf infants. *Journal of Deaf Studies and Deaf Education, 8*, 31–43.

21. Aguinis, H., Simonsen, M. M., & Pierce, C. A. (1998). Effects of nonverbal behavior on perceptions of power bases. *Journal of Social Psychology, 138*(4), 455–475.

22. McCroskey, J. C., Heisel, A., & Richmond, V. (2001). Eysenck's Big Three and communication traits: Three correlational studies. *Communication Monographs, 68*, 360–366.

23. Lee, J. W., & Guerrero, L. K. (2001). Types of touch in cross-sex relationships between coworkers: Perceptions of relational and emotional messages, inappropriateness, and sexual harassment. *Journal of Applied Communication Research, 29*, 197–220.

24. Fisher, J. D., Rytting, M., & Heslin, R. (1976). Hands touching hands: Affective and evaluative effects of interpersonal touch. *Sociometry, 3*, 416–421.

25. Goldberg, S., & Lewis, M. (1969). Play behavior in the year-old infant: Early sex differences. *Child Development, 40*, 21–31.

26. Ibid., 241–248.

27. Jourard, S., & Rubin, J. E. (1968). Self-disclosure and touching: A study of two modes of interpersonal encounter and their inter-relation. *Journal of Humanistic Psychology, 8*, 39–48.

28. Kane, M. N. (2006). Research note: Sexual misconduct, non-sexual touch, and dual relationships: Risks for priests in light of the code of pastoral conduct. *Review of Religious Research, 48*, 105–110; Lee & Guerrero; Strozier, A. L., Krizek, C., & Sale, K. (2003). Touch: Its use in psychotherapy. *Journal of Social Work Practice, 17*, 49–62.

29. Kramer, E. (1963). The judgment of personal characteristics and emotions from nonverbal properties of speech. *Psychological Bulletin, 60*, 408–420.

30. Taylor, L. C., & Compton, N. H. (1968). Personality correlates of dress conformity. *Journal of Home Economics, 60*, 653–656.

31. Laurie, A. (2000). *The language of clothes.* New York: Holt.

32. Wohlrab, S., Fink, B., Kappeler, P. M., & Brewer, G. (2009, January). *Personality and Individual Differences, 46*(2), 202–206.

33. Horgan, T., & Smith, J. (2006). Interpersonal reasons for interpersonal perceptions: Gender-incongruent purpose goals and nonverbal judgment accuracy. *Journal of Nonverbal Behavior, 30*, 127–140.

34. Motley, M. T., & Camden, C. T. (1988). Facial expression of emotion: A comparison of posed expressions versus spontaneous expressions in an interpersonal communication setting. *Western Journal of Speech Communication, 52*, 1–22.

## CHAPTER 4

1. Janusic, L. A., & Wolvin, A. D. (2009). 24 hours in a day: A listening update to the time studies. *The International Journal of Listening, 23*, 104–120.

2. Salopek, J. (1999, September). Is anyone listening? Listening skills in the corporate setting. *Training & Development, 53*, 58–59.

3. Nett, W. (2011, September 23). Best Buy chairman says listening skills crucial to thriving business. *Lubbock Avalanche Journal.* Retrieved from http://lubbock online.com

4. LeBeau, P. (2009, June 25).Texting and driving worse than drinking and driving. Retrieved from www.cnbc.com/id/31545004/site/14081545

5. Thompson, W. F., Schellenberg, E. G., & Letnic, A. K. (2011, May 20). Fast and loud background music disrupts reading comprehension. *Psychology of Music.* doi:10.1177/0305735611400173

6. Skenazy, L. (2009, February 9). Smartphone apps great for marketing, bad for social skills. *Advertising Age*, np.

7. Junco, R., & Cotton, S. (2012, September). No A 4 U: The relationship between multitasking and academic performance. *Computers & Education, 59*(2), 505–514.

8. Martin, J., & Nakayama, T. (2011). *Experiencing intercultural communication* (p. 184). New York: McGraw-Hill.

9. Davidson, K. (2011). *Now you see it: How the brain science of attention will transform the way we live, work, and learn.* New York: Viking.

10. Miller, G. A. (1994). The magical number seven, plus or minus two: Some limits on our capacity for processing information. *Psychology Review, 101*, 343–352.

11. Gilbert, M. B. (1988). Listening in school: I know you can hear me—but are you listening? *Journal of the International Listening Association, 2*, 121–132.

12. Stansfield, S. (2008, December 16). Noise as a public health problem. *ASHA Leader*, 5–6.

## CHAPTER 5

1. Hughes, M., Morrison, K., & Asada, K. J. K. (2005). What's love got to do with it? Exploring the impact of maintenance rules, love attitudes, and network support on friends with benefits relationships. *Western Journal of Communication, 69*, 49–66.

2. Nice, M. L., & Katzev, R. (2009). *Internet romances: The frequency and nature of romantic online relationships.* Retrieved from www.scribd.com/doc/10983206/Internet_Romances_The_Frequency_and_Nature_of_Romantic_Online_Relationships

3. Retrieved from www.urban.org/publications/1000491.html

4. Centers for Disease Control and Prevention. *National marriage and divorce rate trends.* Retrieved from www.cdc.gov/nchs/nvss/marriage_divorce_tables.htm

5. Missouri Families.org. *Relationships: Quick answers.* Retrieved from http://missourifamilies.org/quick/divorceqa/

6. Wilcox, W. B. (2010). *The state of our unions: Marriage in America 2010.* Charlottesville, VA, & New York: National Marriage Project and Institute for American Values.

7. Armario, C. (2011, April 28). Single parents raise 25% of US children. *Boston Globe.* Retrieved from www.boston.com/news/nation/articles/2011/04/28/single_parents_raise_25_of_us_children; Mather, M. (2010, May). *Population Reference Bureau: U.S. children in single-mother families.* Retrieved from www.prb.org/Publications/PolicyBriefs/singlemotherfamilies.aspx.

8. Miller, G. R. (1976). *Explorations in interpersonal communication.* Beverly Hills, CA: Sage.

9. Knapp, M. L. (1978). *Social intercourse: From greeting to goodbye.* Needham Heights, MA: Allyn & Bacon.

10. McCroskey, J. C., & McCain, T. A. (1974). The measurement of interpersonal attraction. *Speech Monographs, 41*, 267–276.

11. Montgomery, B. M., & Baxter, L. A. (1998). *Dialectic approaches to studying personal relationships.* Mahwah, NJ: Erlbaum.

12. See, for example, Bullis, C., Clark, C., & Sline, R. (1993). From passion to commitment: Turning points in romantic relationships. In P. Kalbfleisch (Ed.), *Interpersonal communication: Evolving interpersonal relationships* (pp. 213–236). Hillsdale, NJ: Erlbaum; Surra, C. A. (1985). Courtship types. Variations in interdependence between partners and social networks. *Journal of Personality and Social Psychology, 49*, 357–375; Surra, C. A. (1987). Reasons for changes in commitment. Variations by courtship style. *Journal of Social and Personal Relationships, 4*, 17–33; Surra, C. A., Arizzi, P., & Asmussen, L. A. (1988). The association between reasons for commitment and the development and outcome of marital relationships. *Journal of Social and Personal Relationships, 5*, 47–63; Surra, C. A., & Hughes, D. K. (1997). Commitment processes in accounts of the development of premarital relationships. *Journal of Marriage and the Family, 59*, 5–21.

13. Baxter, L. A., & Pittman, G. (2001). Communicatively remembering turning points of relational development in heterosexual romantic relationships. *Communication Reports, 14*, 4.

14. Duck, S. (1994). Meaningful relationships: Talking, sense, and relating. Thousand Oaks, CA: Sage; Duck, S., & Sants, H. (1983). On the origin of the specious: Are personal relationships really interpersonal states? *Journal of Social and Clinical Psychology, 1*, 27–41.

15. Perse, E. M., & Rubin, R. B. (1989). Attribution in social and parasocial relationships. *Communication Research, 16*, 59–77.

16. Davis, M. H., & Oathout, H. A. (1987). Maintenance of satisfaction in romantic relationships: Empathy and relational competence. *Journal of Personality and Social Psychology, 53*, 397–498.

17. Pearson, J. C. (1992). *Lasting love: What keeps couples together.* Dubuque, IA: William C. Brown.

18. Sillars, A., Shellen, W., McIntosh, A., and Pomegranate, M. (1997). Relational characteristics of language: Elaboration and differentiation in marital conversations. *Western Journal of Communication, 61*, 403–422.

19. Infante, D. A., & Rancer, A. S. (1982). A conceptualization and measure of argumentativeness. *Journal of Personality Assessment, 45*, 72–80.

20. Gibb, J. R. (1991). *Trust: A new vision of human relationships for business, education, family, and personal living* (2nd ed.). North Hollywood, CA: Newcastle.

21. Ibid.

22. White, G. L. (2008). Romantic jealousy: Therapists' perceptions of causes, consequences, and treatments. *Journal of Couple and Relationship Therapy, 7*, 210–229.

23. Spitzberg, B. H., & Cupach, W. R. (2007). *The dark side of interpersonal communication* (2nd ed.). Mahwah, NJ: Erlbaum.

24. Floyd, K. (1997). Affectionate communication in non-romantic relationships: Influences of communicator, relational, and contextual factors. *Western Journal of Communication, 61*, 279–298; Floyd, K. (1997). Communicating affection in dyadic relationships: An assessment of behavior and expectancies. *Communication Quarterly, 45*, 68–80; Floyd, K., & Morman, M. T. (1998). The measurement of affectionate communication. *Communication Quarterly, 46*, 144–162; Floyd, K., & Morman, M. T. (2000). Reacting to the verbal expression of affection in same-sex interaction. *Southern Communication Journal, 65*, 287–299.

25. Floyd, K., & Burgoon, J. K. (1999). Reacting to nonverbal expressions of liking: A test of interaction adaptation theory. *Communication Monographs, 66*, 219–239.

26. LePoire, B. A., & Yoshimura, S. M. (1999). The effects of expectancies and actual communication on nonverbal adaptation and communication outcomes: A test of interaction adaptation theory. *Communication Monographs, 66*, 1–30.

27. Caplan, S. E., & Samter, W. (1999). The role of facework in younger and older adults' evaluations of social support messages. *Communication Quarterly, 47*, 245–264.

28. MacGeorge, E. L. (2001). Support providers' interaction goals: The influence of attributions and emotions. *Communication Monographs, 68*, 72–97.

29. Clark, R. A., Pierce, K. F., Hsu, K., Toosley, A., & Williams, L. (1998). The impact of alternative approaches to comforting, closeness of relationship, and gender on multiple measures of effectiveness. *Communication Studies, 49*, 224–239.

30. Wilson, S. R. (1998). Introduction to the special issue on seeking and resisting compliance: The vitality of compliance-gaining research. *Communication Studies, 49*, 273–275.

31. Marshall, L. J., & Levy, V. M., Jr. (1998). The development of children's perceptions of obstacles in compliance-gaining interactions. *Communication Studies, 49*, 342–357.

32. Saeki, M., & O'Keefe, B. (1994). Refusals and rejections: Designing messages to serve multiple goals. *Human Communication Research, 21*, 67–102.

33. Ifert, D. E., & Roloff, M. E. (1997). Overcoming expressed obstacles to compliance: The role of sensitivity to the expressions of others and ability to modify self-presentation. *Communication Quarterly, 45*, 55–67.

34. Deusch, M., & Kraus, R. M. (1962). Studies of interpersonal bargaining. *Journal of Conflict Resolution, 6*, 52.

35. Pearson, J. C. (1983). *Interpersonal communication: Clarity, confidence, concern.* Glenview, IL: Scott, Foresman.

36. Haggerty, G., Blake, M., & Siefert, C. J. (2010). Convergent and divergent validity of the relationship profile test: Investigating the relationship with attachment, interpersonal distress, and psychological health. *Journal of Clinical Psychology, 66*, 339–354.

37. Anderson, M., Kunkel, A., & Dennis, M. R. (2011). "Let's (not) talk about that": Bridging the past sexual experiences taboo to build healthy relationships. *Journal of Sex Research, 48*, 381–391.

38. Schneider, I. K., Konijn, E. A., Righetti, F., & Rusbult, C. E. (2011). A healthy dose of trust: The relationship between interpersonal trust and health. *Personal Relationships, 18*, 668–676.

39. Cleary Bradley, R. P., & Gottman, J. M. (2012). Reducing situational violence in low-income couples by fostering healthy relationships. *Journal of Marital and Family Therapy, 38*, 187–198.

40. Hawkins, A. J., & Ooms, T. (2012). Can marriage and relationship education be an effective policy tool to help low-income couples form and sustain healthy marriages and relationships? A review of lessons learned. *Marriage and Family Review, 48*, 524–554.

41. Williams, A. (2013, January 13). The end of courtship? *New York Times.* Retrieved from www.nytimes.com/2013/01/13/fashion/the-end-of-courtship.html

## CHAPTER 6

1. Kramarae, C. (1981). *Women and men speaking.* Rowley, MA: Newbury House.

2. Nasson, T. (2013). Gay celebrities, gay movie stars, gay actors. Retrieved from www.wildaboutmovies.com/features/GAY_CELEBRITIES.php

3. Austin, G., & Johnson, D. (2012, August 13). Hispanic or Latino: Which is correct? *Profiles in Diversity Journal.* Retrieved from www.diversityjournal.com/9724-hispanic-or-latino-which-is-correct/

4. Dodd, C. H. (1998). *Dynamics of intercultural communication* (5th ed.). New York: McGraw-Hill.

5. The future of the global muslim population: Projections for 2010–2030 (2011, January 27). *The Pew Forum on Religion and Public Life.* Retrieved from www.pewforum.org/The-Future-of-the-Global-Muslim-Population.aspx

6. Garcia, A. L., Miller, D. A., Smith, E. R., & Mackie, D. M. (2006). Thanks for the compliment? Emotional reactions to group-level versus individual-level compliments and insults. *Group Processes and Intergroup Relations, 9*, 307–324.

7. Czopp, A. M., Monteith, M. J., & Mark, A. Y. (2006). Standing up for change: Reducing bias through interpersonal confrontation. *Journal of Personality and Social Psychology, 90,* 784–803.

8. Swim, J. K., Hykers, L. L., Cohen, L. L., & Ferguson, M. J. (2001). Everyday sexism: Evidence for its incidence, nature, and psychological impact from three daily diary studies. *Journal of Social Issues, 57,* 31–53.

9. Hofstede, G. (1980). *Culture's consequences: International differences in work-related values.* Beverly Hills, CA: Sage.

10. Ibid.

11. Coleman, D. (1998, December 22). The group and self: New focus on a cultural rift. *New York Times,* 40.

12. Hofstede.

13. Know Britain: Commonwealth countries from A–J. Retrieved from http://www.know-britain.com/general/commonwealth_countries1.html

14. Ibid.

15. Samovar, L. A., Porter, R. E., & Stefani, L. A. (1998). *Communication between cultures* (3rd ed.). Belmont, CA: Wadsworth.

16. Dodd.

17. Ibid.

18. Ting-Toomey, S. (1997). Managing intercultural conflicts effectively. In L. A. Samovar & R. E. Porter (Eds.), *Intercultural communication: A reader* (8th ed., pp. 392–404). Belmont, CA: Wadsworth.

19. Ibid., 395.

## CHAPTER 7

1. BBC News. (2012, August 31). *Social media in China: What you need to know.* Retrieved from www.bbc.co.uk/news/world-asia-china-19399773

2. Chakroff, J. L., & Nathanson, A. I. (2008). Parent and school interventions: Mediation and media literacy. In S. L. Calvert & B. J. Wilson (Eds.), *The handbook of children, media, and development* (pp. 552–576). Oxford, UK: Blackwell.

3. Harrison, J., & Cantor, J. (1997). The relationship between media consumption and eating disorders. *Journal of Communication, 47,* 40–67.

4. Dominick, J. R. (2005). *Dynamics of mass communication: Media in the digital age.* New York: McGraw-Hill.

5. Thurlow, C., Lengel, L., & Tomic, A. (2004). *Computer mediated communication: Social interaction and the Internet.* Thousand Oaks, CA: Sage.

6. Rubin, A. M. (1984). Ritualized and instrumental television viewing. *Journal of Communication, 34,* 67–77.

7. Kim, J., & Haridakis, P. (2009). The role of Internet user characteristics and motives in explaining three dimensions of Internet addiction. *Journal of Computer-Mediated Communication, 14,* 988–1015.

8. Haridakis, P., & Hanson, G. (2009). Social interaction and co-viewing with YouTube: Blending mass communication reception and social connection. *Journal of Broadcasting and Electronic Media, 53,* 317–335.

9. Hinckley, D. (2012, September 19). Americans watch TV 34 hours a week, says Nielsen. *New York Daily News.* Retrieved from http://articles.nydailynews.com/2012-09-19/news/33957315_1_nielsen-dvrs-older-viewers

10. Huston, A., Donnerstein, E., Fairchild, H., et al. (1992). *Big world, small screen: The role of television in American society.* Lincoln: University of Nebraska Press.

11. Husemann, L. R., Dubow, E. F., & Yang, G. (2013). Why it is hard to believe that media violence causes aggression. In K. E. Dill (Ed.), *The Oxford handbook of media psychology* (pp. 159–171). New York: Oxford University Press.

12. *Youth violence: A report of the surgeon general.* (2001). Retrieved from www.surgeongeneral.gov

13. Linz, D., Donnerstein, E., & Adams, S. (1989). Physiological desensitization and judgment about female victims of violence. *Human Communication Research, 15,* 509–523.

14. Harrison & Cantor.

15. Chakroff & Nathanson.

16. Wilson, J., & Wilson, S. L. (1998). *Mass media/mass culture* (4th ed.). New York: McGraw-Hill.

17. Lim, J. (2006). A cross-lagged analysis of agenda setting among online news media. *Journalism and Mass Communication Quarterly, 83,* 298–312.

18. Bilandzic, H. (2006). The perception of distance in the cultivation process: A theoretical consideration of the relationship between television content, processing experience, and perceived distance. *Communication Theory, 16,* 333–355.

19. Gerbner, G. (1998). Cultivation analysis: An overview. *Mass Communication and Society, 1,* 75–77.

20. Reamer, N. D. (2012). *Mediated sexuality and teen pregnancy: Exploring the secret life of the American teenager.* Unpublished master's thesis, Kent State University.

21. Gennaro, C. D., & Dutton, W. H. (2007). Reconfiguring friendships: Social relationship and the Internet. *Information, Communication and Society, 10,* 591–618.

22. Jeong, S., Cho, H., & Hwang, Y. (2012). Media literacy interventions: A meta-analytic review. *Journal of Communication, 62,* 454–472.

23. Christ, W. G., & Potter, J. (1998). Media, literacy, media education, and the academy. *Journal of Communication, 48,* 5–15.

24. Child, J. T., & Petronio, S. (2011). Unpacking the paradoxes of privacy in CMC relationships: The challenges of blogging and relational communication on the Internet. In K. B. Wright & L. M. Webb (Eds.), *Computer-mediated communication in personal relationships* (pp. 21–40). New York: Peter Lang.

25. Rubin, A. M., & Haridakis, P. M. (2001). Mass communication research at the dawn of the 21st century. *Communication Yearbook, 24,* 73–97.

26. Correa, T., Hinsley, A. W., & Zuniga, H. G. (2010). Who interacts on the Web? The intersection of users' personality and social media use. *Computers in Human Behavior, 26,* 247–253.

27. Ibid.

28. Child, J. T., & Agyeman-Budu, E. A. (2010). Blogging privacy management rule development: The impact of self-monitoring skills, concern for appropriateness, and blogging frequency. *Computers in Human Behavior, 26,* 957–963.

29. Hunt, D., Atkin, D., & Krishnan, A. (2012). The influence of computer-mediated communication apprehension on motives for Facebook use. *Journal of Broadcasting and Electronic Media, 56,* 187–202.

30. Haridakis & Hanson.

31. Child, J. T., Haridakis, P. M., & Petronio, S. (2012). Blogging privacy rule orientations, privacy management, and content deletion practices: The variability of online privacy management activity at different stages of social media use. *Computers in Human Behavior, 28,* 1859–1872.

32. Walther, J. B. (1996). Computer-mediated communication: Impersonal, interpersonal, and hyperpersonal interaction. *Communication Research, 23,* 3–43.

33. Ibid.

34. Ellison, N. B., Hancock, J. T., & Toma, C. L. (2012). Profile as promise: A framework for conceptualizing veracity in online dating self-presentations. *New Media and Society, 14,* 45–62.

35. Walther.

36. Byron, K. (2008). Carrying too heavy a load? The communication and miscommunication of emotion by email. *Academy of Management Review, 33,* 309–327.

37. Gennaro, C. D., & Dutton, W. H. (2007). Reconfiguring friendships: Social relationship and the Internet. *Information, Communication and Society, 10,* 591–618.

38. Pempek, T. A., Yermolayeva, Y. A., & Calvert, S. L. (2009). College students' social networking experiences on Facebook. *Journal of Applied Developmental Psychology, 30,* 227–238.

39. Child, J. T., & Westermann, D. A. (2013). Let's be Facebook friends: Exploring parental Facebook friend requests from a communication privacy management (CPM) perspective. *Journal of Family Communication, 13,* 46–59.

40. Ibid.

41. Bartholomew, M. K., Schoppe-Sullivan, S. J., Glassman, M., & Dush, C. M. (2012). New parents' Facebook use at the transition to parenthood. *Family Relations, 61,* 455–469.

42. Child & Westermann.

43. Frankel, A. (2011, September 12). NLRB judge: Employees can bitch about their jobs on Facebook. *Thomas Reuters.* Retrieved from http://blogs.reuters.com/alison-frankel/2011/09/12/nlrb-judge-employees-can-bitch-about-their-jobs-on-facebook/

44. Frampton, B. D., & Child, J. T. (2013). Friend or not to friend: Coworker Facebook friend requests as an application of communication privacy management theory. *Computers in Human Behavior, 29,* 2257–2264.

45. Shea, V. (1995). *Netiquette.* San Francisco: Albion.

46. Himelboim, I., Lariscy, R. W., Tinkham, S. F., & Sweetser, K. D. (2012). Social media and online political communication: The role of interpersonal informational trust and openness. *Journal of Broadcasting and Electronic Media, 56,* 92–115.

47. Lazarsfeld, P., Berelson, B., & Gaudet, H. (1944). *The people's choice: How the voter makes up his mind in a presidential campaign.* New York: Columbia University Press.

48. Bosslet, G. T., Torke, A. M., Hickman, S. E., Terry, C. L., & Helfy, P. R. (2011). The patient–doctor relationship and online social networks: Results of a national survey. *Journal of General Internal Medicine, 26,* 1168–1174.

49. Ibid.

50. Petronio, S. (2002). *Boundaries of privacy: Dialectics of disclosure.* Albany: State University of New York Press.

51. Child, J. T., Pearson, J. C., & Petronio, S. (2009). Blogging communication, and privacy management: Development of the blogging privacy management measure. *Journal of the American Society for Information Science and Technology, 60,* 2079–2094.

52. Child, J. T., Petronio, S., Agyeman-Budu, E. A., & Westermann, D. A. (2011). Blog scrubbing: Exploring triggers that change privacy rules. *Computers in Human Behavior, 27,* 2017–2027.

53. Boyd, D. (2012, August 27). Tarrant County sheriff's deputy fired for posting rants on Facebook. *Star-Telegram.* Retrieved from www.star-telegram.com/2012/08/27/4209974/tarrant-county-sheriffs-deputy.html

54. Bracetti, A. (2012, May 10). 25 Facebook posts that have gotten people fired. *ComplexTech.* Retrieved from www.complex.com/tech/2012/05/25-facebook-posts-that-have-gotten-people-fired/

55. Poeter, D. (2012, March 16). Webcam peeper convicted in Rutgers cyberbullying case. *PCMag.* Retrieved from www.pcmag.com/article2/0,2817,2401701,00.asp

56. Goffman, E. (1959). *The presentation of self in everyday life.* New York: Anchor Books.

## CHAPTER 8

1. Cheney, G. (1983). The rhetoric of identification and the study of organizational communication. *Quarterly Journal of Speech, 69,* 143–158.

2. Sun, S. (2008). Organizational culture and its themes. *International Journal of Business and Management, 12,* 137–141.

3. Pacanowsky, M. E., & O'Donnell-Trujillo, N. (1983). Organizational communication as cultural performance, *Communication Monographs, 50,* 126–147.

4. Jones, E., Watson, B., Gardner, J., & Gallois, C. (2004). Organization communication: Challenges for the new century. *Journal of Communication, 54,* 722–750.

5. Cheney, G., Christensen, L. T., Zorn, T. E., & Ganesh, G. (2010). *Organizational communication in an age of globalization* (2nd ed.). Long Grove, IL: Waveland Press.

6. Putnam, L. L. (1982). Paradigms for organizational communication research: An overview and synthesis. *Western Journal of Speech Communication, 46,* 192–206.

7. Eisenberg, E. (1984). Ambiguity as strategy in organizational communication. *Communication Monographs, 51,* 227–242.

8. Milliken, F. J., Morrison, E. W., & Hewlin, P. F. (2003). An exploratory study of employee silence: Issues that employees don't communicate upward and why. *Journal of Management Studies, 40,* 1453–1476.

9. Sablich, J., Fessenden, F., & McLean, A. (2012). Timeline: The Penn State scandal. *New York Times.* Retrieved from www.nytimes.com/interactive/2011/11/11/sports/ncaafootball/sandusky.html

10. Milliken et al.

11. Susskind, A. M., Schwartz, D. F., Richards, W. D., & Johnson, J. D. (2005). Evolution and diffusion of the Michigan State University tradition of organizational communication network research. *Communication Studies, 56,* 397–418.

12. Fay, M. J., & Kline, S. L. (2011). Coworker relationships and informal communication in high-intensity telecommuting. *Journal of Applied Communication Research, 39,* 144–163.

13. Caudron, S. (1998). They hear it through the grapevine. *Workforce, 77,* 25–27.

14. Galanes, G. J., & Adams, K. H. (2009). *Effective group discussion.* New York: McGraw-Hill.

15. Wheelan, S. A. (2009). Group size, group development, and group productivity. *Small Group Research, 40,* 247–262.

16. Jana, R. (2009, March 23). Real life imitates real world. *BusinessWeek,* 42.

17. Kelly, L., & Duran, R. L. (1985). Interaction and performance in small groups: A descriptive report. *International Journal of Small Group Research, 1,* 182–192.

18. Barker, D. B. (1991, February). The behavioral analysis of interpersonal intimacy in group development. *Small Group Research, 22,* 76–91.

19. Ferraris, C. (2004, May). *Investigating NASA's intergroup decision-making: Groupthink and intergroup social dynamics.* Paper presented at the annual meeting of the International Communication Association Convention, New Orleans, LA.

20. Henningsen, D. D., Henningsen, M. L., Eden, J., & Cruz, M. G. (2006). Examining the symptoms of groupthink and retrospective sense making. *Small Group Research, 37,* 36–64.

21. Blomstrom, S., Boster, F. J., Levine, K. J., Butler, E. M., & Levine, S. L. (2008).The effect of training on brainstorming. *Journal of the Communication, Speech, & Theatre Association of North Dakota, 21,* 41–50.

22. Lauring, J., & Selmer, J. (2010). Multicultural organizations: Common language and group cohesiveness. *International Journal of Cross Cultural Management, 10,* 267–284.

23. Hackman, M. Z., & Johnson, C. E. (2003). *Leadership: A communication perspective* (4th ed.). Prospect Heights, IL: Waveland Press.

24. Barge, J. K., & Hirokawa, R. Y. (1989). Toward a communication competency model of group leadership. *Small Group Behavior, 20,* 167–189.

25. Wilmot, W. W., & Hocker, J. L. (2007). *Interpersonal conflict* (7th ed.). New York: McGraw-Hill.

26. French, J. R. P., & Raven, B. (1981). The bases of social power. In D. Cartwright & A. Zander (Eds.), *Group dynamics: Research and theory* (3rd ed.). New York: McGraw-Hill.

27. Foels, R., Driskell, J. E., Mullen, B., & Salas, E. (2000). The effects of democratic leadership on group member satisfaction. *Small Group Research, 31,* 676–702.

28. Brown, M. E., & Trevino, L. K. (2006). Socialized charismatic leadership, values congruence, and deviance in work groups. *Journal of Applied Psychology, 91,* 954–962.

29. Teven, J. J., McCroskey, J. C., & Richmond, V. P. (2006). Communication correlates of perceived Machiavellianism of supervisors: Communication orientations and outcomes. *Communication Quarterly, 54,* 127–142.

30. Lee, D., & LaRose, R. (2011). The impact of personalized social cues of immediacy on consumers' information disclosure: A social cognitive approach. *CyberPsychology, Behavior, and Social Networking, 14,* 337–343.

31. Albrecht, T. L., & Bach, B. W. (1997). *Communication in complex organizations: A relational approach.* New York: Harcourt Brace.

32. Wilmot & Hocker.

33. Infante, D., Riddle, B., Horvath, G., & Tumlin, S. (1992). Verbal aggressiveness: Messages and reasons. *Communication Quarterly, 40,* 116–126.

34. Herschovis, M. S. (2011). "Incivility, social undermining, bullying . . . oh my!": A call to reconcile constructs within workplace aggression research. *Journal of Organizational Behavior, 32,* 499–519.

35. *U.S. Equal Employment Opportunity Commission.* (n.d.). Retrieved from www.eeoc.gov/laws/types/sexual _harassment.cfm

## CHAPTER 9

1. Mazer, J., & Titsworth, S. (2008). *Testing a common public speaking claim: An examination of students' ego-involvement with speech topics in the basic communication course.* National Communication Association Convention, San Diego, CA.

2. Severson, K. (2011, November 2). Seeing social graces as waning in the South. *New York Times,* A16.

3. Sklare, G. B., Markman, B. S., & Sklare, A. Values clarification: It's just a matter of timing. *Personnel & Guidance Journal, 55,* 245–248.

4. Clark, H. H., & Murphy, G. L. (1982). Audience design in meaning and reference. In J. F. Le Ny & W. Kintsch (Eds.), *Language and comprehension* (pp. 287–296). New York: Elsevier; Higgins, E. T. (1981). The "communication game": Implications for social cognition and persuasion. In E. T. Higgins, C. P. Herman, & M. P. Zanna (Eds.), *Social cognition: The Ontario symposium* (Vol. 1, pp. 343–392). Hillsdale, NJ: Erlbaum.

5. Cappella, J. N. (2006). Integrating message effects and behavior change theories: Organizing comments and unanswered questions. *Journal of Communication, 56,* S265–S279; Dillard, J., Weber, K. M., & Vail, R. G. (2007). The relationship between perceived and actual effectiveness of persuasive messages: A meta-analysis with implications for formative campaign research. *Journal of Communication, 25,* 613–631; Dillard, J. P., and Ye, S. (2008). The perceived effectiveness of persuasive messages: Questions of structure, referent, and bias. *Journal of Health Communication, 13,* 149–168.

6. ProudProgressive. (2013, January 13). *Colin Powell slams Sarah Palin and the Republican Party's Obama racism.* Retrieved June 23, 2013.

## CHAPTER 10

1. Daniel Kalis, a teaching associate, gave this presentation.

2. Michael Burns, Basic Course Director at North Dakota State University, provided this outline for this chapter.

3. Amanda Peterson, an undergraduate at North Dakota State University, composed this outline for a communication course.

4. Jared Fougner, who became a graduate student and was from North Dakota, provided this talk.

5. Linzey Crockett, a student from Chicago, Illinois, wrote and delivered this speech.

6. Greg Heller, an ROTC student majoring in communication, wrote this talk.

7. Emily Holt, a first-year college student, composed this speech.

## CHAPTER 11

1. Child, J. T., & Shumate, M. (2007). The impact of communal knowledge repositories and people-based knowledge management on perceptions of team effectiveness. *Management Communication Quarterly, 21,* 29–54.

2. Gross, M., & Latham, D. (2007). Attaining information literacy: An investigation of the relationship between skill level, self-estimates of skill, and library anxiety. *Library & Information Science Research, 29,* 332–353.

3. King, B. (2011, January 18). Too much content: A world of exponential information growth. *The Huffington Post.* Retrieved from www.huffingtonpost.com/brett -king/too-much-content-a-world-_b_809677.html

4. Eisenberg, M. B. (2008). Information literacy: Essential skills for the information age. *Journal of Library and Information Technology, 28,* 39–47.

5. Eppler, M. J., & Mengis, J. (2004). The concept of information overload: A review of literature from organizational science, accounting, marketing, MIS, and related disciplines. *The Information Society: An International Journal, 20,* 325–344.

6. Bawden, D., & Robinson, L. (2009). The dark side of information: Overload, anxiety and other paradoxes and pathologies. *Journal of Information Science, 35,* 180–191.

7. Eppler & Mengis.

8. Brand-Gruwel, S., Wopereis, I., & Walraven, A. (2009). A descriptive model of information problem solving while using the internet. *Computers & Education, 53,* 1207–1217.

9. Child, J. T., Pearson, J. C., & Amundson, N. G. (2007). Technology talk: Public speaking textbooks' coverage of information retrieval technology systems. *Communication Quarterly, 55,* 267–281.

10. Pew Internet and American Life Project. (2012, February 1). Retrieved from www.pewinternet.org/Static-Pages/Trend-Data-(Adults)/Online-Activites-Total.aspx

11. Kim, K., & Sin, S. J. (2011). Selecting quality sources: Bridging the gap between the perception and use of information sources. *Journal of Information Science, 37,* 178–188.

## CHAPTER 12

1. Bettinghaus, E. (1961). The operation of congruity in an oral communication situation. *Speech Monographs, 28,* 131–142.

2. Henrikson, E. H. (1944). An analysis of the characteristics of some "good" and "poor" speakers. *Speech Monographs, 11,* 120–124.

3. Gilkinson, H., & Knower, F. H. (1941). Individual differences among students of speech as revealed by psychological test—I. *Journal of Educational Psychology, 32,* 161–175.

4. McCrosky, J. C. (1977). Oral communication apprehension: A summary of recent theory and research. *Human Communication Research, 4,* 78–96.

5. Dwyer, K. K., & Davidson, M. M. (2012). Is public speaking really more feared than death? *Communication Research Report, 29,* 99–107.

6. McCrosky.

7. Allen, M., & Bourhis, J. (1996). The relationship of communication apprehension to communication behavior: A meta-analysis. *Communication Quarterly, 44,* 214–226.

8. Pearson, J. C., Child, J. T., & Kahl, D. H. (2006). Preparation meeting opportunity: How do college students prepare for public speeches? *Communication Quarterly, 54,* 351–366.

9. Pearson, J. C., & Child, J. T. (2008). The gentle art of persuasion: The influence of biological sex, previous experience, and preparation time on classroom public speaking grades. *Basic Communication Course Annual, 20,* 101–137.

10. Ayres, J., & Hopf, T. S. (1985). Visualization: A means of reducing speech anxiety. *Communication Education, 34,* 318–323.

11. Ayres, J. (1988). Coping with speech anxiety: The power of positive thinking. *Communication Education, 37,* 289–296.

12. Bodie, G. D. (2010). A racing heart, rattling knees, and ruminative thoughts: Defining, explaining, and treating public speaking anxiety. *Communication Education, 59,* 70–105.

13. Pearson, Child, & Kahl.

14. Allen, M., Hunter, J. E., & Donohue, W. A. (1989). Meta-analysis of self-report data on the effectiveness of public speaking anxiety treatment techniques. *Communication Education, 38,* 54–76.

15. Dwyer, K. K. (2000). The multidimensional model: Teaching students to self-manage high communication apprehension by self-selecting treatments. *Communication Education, 49,* 72–81.

16. Hildebrandt, H. W., & Stephens, W. (1963). Manuscript and extemporaneous delivery in communicating information. *Speech Monographs, 30,* 369–372.

17. Hayworth, D. (1942). A search for facts on the teaching of public speaking. *Quarterly Journal of Speech, 28,* 247–254.

18. Black, J. W. (1942). A study of voice merit. *Quarterly Journal of Speech, 28,* 67–74; Woolbert, C. (1920). The effects of various modes of public reading. *Journal of Applied Psychology, 4,* 162–185.

19. Woolbert.

20. Glasgow, G. M. (1952). A semantic index of vocal pitch. *Speech Monographs, 19,* 64–68.

21. Black.

22. Beighley, K. C. (1952). An experimental study of the effect of four speech variables on listener comprehension. *Speech Monographs, 19,* 249–258.

23. Ibid.

24. Martin, J., & Nakayama, T. (2011). *Experiencing Intercultural Communication*. New York: McGraw-Hill, 178–179.

25. Cobin, M. (1962). Response to eye contact. *Quarterly Journal of Speech, 48*, 415–418.

26. Beebe, S. A. (1974). Eye contact: A nonverbal determinant of speaker credibility. *Speech Teacher, 23*, 21–25.

## CHAPTER 13

1. Petrie, C. R., Jr., & Carrel, S. D. (1976). The relationship of motivation, listening, capability, initial information, and verbal organizational ability to lecture comprehension and retention. *Speech Monographs, 43*, 187–194.

2. Tourtelot, N. (2008, December). Lunatic. *Esquire*, 167.

3. Ibid.

4. Harden, B., & Eilperin, J. (2006, December 4–10). Wild species and ski resorts are on the move. *Washington Post Weekly Edition*, 19.

5. Ibid.

## CHAPTER 14

1. Whitehouse, Mark. (2011, May 7). Number of the week: Class of 2011 most indebted ever. *Wall Street Journal*.

2. Collins, A. (2009). *The student loan scam: The most oppressive debt in U.S. history—and how we can fight back*. New York: Beacon Press.

3. Understanding Obama's student loan forgiveness program. (2011). Retrieved from obomastudentloanforgiveness.com

4. Rosenkilde, M., Auerbach, P., Reichkendler, M., Ploug, T., Stallknecht, B., & Sjodin, A. (2012, August). Body fat loss and compensatory mechanisms in response to different doses of aerobic exercise—a randomized controlled trial in overweight sedentary males. *American Journal of Physiology—Regulatory, Integrative and Comparative Physiology, 303*, R571–R579. doi: 10.1152/ajpregu.00141.2012

5. Ibid.

6. Witte, K. (1997, April). Preventing teen pregnancy through persuasive communications: Realities, myths, and the hard-fact truths. *Community Health. 22*(2), 137–154.

7. Prevention First. (2008). *Ineffectiveness of fear appeals in youth alcohol, tobacco and other drug (ATOD) prevention*. Springfield, IL: Author.

8. Goldstein, N. J., Martin, S. J., & Cialdini, R. B. (2009). *Yes—50 scientifically proven ways to be more persuasive*. New York: Free Press.

## CHAPTER 15

1. National Association of Colleges and Employers. (2013). *Job outlook 2013*. Retrieved from www.naceweb.org

2. Wright, E. W., Domagalski, T. A., & Collins, R. (2011). Improving employee selection with a revised resume format. *Business Communication Quarterly, 74*, 272–286.

3. Henricks, M. (2000). *Kinko's guide to the winning résumé*. United States of America: Kinko's.

4. Ibid.

5. Bennett, S. (2005). *The elements of resume style: Essential rules and eye-opening advice for writing resumes and cover letters that work*. New York: Amazon Books.

6. United States Census Bureau. (2013). *Educational attainment in the United States: 2009*. Retrieved from www.census.gov/hhes/socdemo/education/data/cps/2009/tables.html

7. National Association of Colleges and Employers.

8. Krizan, A., Merrier, P., & Jones, C. (2002). *Business communication* (5th ed.). Cincinnati: South-Western.

9. Smith, M. W. (2011, May 21). The best option for video calling. *USA Today*. Retrieved from http://usatoday30.usatoday.com/tech/products/2011-05-21-video-calls_n.htm

10. Lipovsky, C. (2006). Candidates' negotiation of their expertise in job interviews. *Journal of Pragmatics, 38*, 1147–1174.

11. Young, M. J., Behnke, R. R., & Mann, Y. M. (2004). Anxiety patterns in employment interviews. *Communication Reports, 17*, 49–57.

12. U.S. Department of Commerce National Oceanic & Atmospheric Administration. (2013). *Sample interview questions based on nine basic competency areas* [report]. Retrieved from www.esrl.noaa.gov/outreach/student_programs/HelpfulInterviewTips.pdf

13. LinkedIn. (2013, January 7). *About us*. Retrieved from www.press.linkedin.com/about

14. Roberts, S. J., & Roach, T. (2009). Social networking websites and human resource personnel: Suggestions for job searches. *Business Communication Quarterly, 72*, 110–114.

15. Ibid.

16. Child, J. T., Petronio, S., Agyeman-Budu, E. A., & Westermann, D. A. (2011). Blog scrubbing: Exploring triggers that change privacy rules. *Computers in Human Behavior, 27*, 2017–2027.

17. Frampton, B. D., & Child, J. T. (2013). Friend or not to friend: Coworker Facebook friend requests as an application of communication privacy management theory. *Computers in Human Behavior, 29*, 2257–2264.

18. Child, J. T., Haridakis, P. M., & Petronio, S. (2012). Blogging privacy rule orientations, privacy management, and content deletion practices: The variability of online privacy management activity at different stages of social media use. *Computers in Human Behavior, 28*, 1859–1872.

19. National Association of Colleges and Employers.

20. Branham, L. (2001). *Keeping the people who keep you in business: 24 ways to hang on to your most valuable talent.* New York: American Management Association.

21. Granovetter, M. S. (1973). The strength of weak ties. *American Journal of Sociology, 81*, 1287–1303.

# CREDITS

Skill Builder Box Cube design:
© Dragan Grkic/Getty Images RF

**PART OPENERS**
1-2: © Radius Images/Getty Images
RF; 1-3: © Goodshoot/Fotosearch
RF; 1-4: © Jacqueline Veissid/Getty
Images RF; 2-5: © Lars Niki RF; 2-6:
© Joseph Turs/Getty Images RF;
2-7: © Jupiterimages Images RF; 2-8:
© DLILLC/Corbis Images RF; 3-9:
© Spencer Grant/Science Source;
3-10: © Hill Street Studios/Getty
Images RF; 3-11: © Aldo Murillo/
Getty Images RF; 3-12: © Steve Hix/
Somos Images/Corbis RF; 4-13:
© Datacraft Co. Ltd./Getty Images
RF; 4-14: Library of Congress Prints
and Photographs Division, Depart-
ment of the Interior, National Park
Service [3b48901u]; 4-15: © Eric
Audras/Getty Images RF

**CHAPTER 1**
Page 3: © Jack Hollingsworth/
Getty Images RF; p. 4 (top): © Tetra
Images/Getty Images RF; p. 4
(bottom): © Getty Images RF; p. 7:
© Rolf Bruderer/Blend Images/
Getty Images RF; p. 8: © Image
Source, all rights reserved RF; p. 9:
© JGI/James Grill/Getty Images
RF; p. 12: © Spencer Grant/Science
Source; p. 13: © James DeVaney/Wire
Images/Getty Images; p. 15: © Doug
Pensinger/Allsport/Getty Images;
p. 16: © John Lund/Marc Romane/
age footstock RF

**CHAPTER 2**
Opener: © Radius Images/Getty
Images RF; p. 20 (top): © J. Hardy/
PaloAlto RF; p. 20 (bottom): © pho-
tosindia/Getty Images RF; p. 21:
© LWA/Dann tardif/Getty Images
RF; p. 22: © Fancy Photography/Veer
RF; p. 25: © SW Productions/Brand
X/Corbis RF; p. 26: © Paul Burns/
Photodisc/Getty Images RF; p. 28:
© Jose Luis Pelaez Inc./Blend Images
LLC RF; p. 31: © Radius Images/

Getty Images RF; p. 33: © PhotoAlto/
Alix Minde/Getty Images RF; p. 34:
NASA, ESA, and the Hubble Heri-
tage Team (STScl/AURA)

**CHAPTER 3**
Opener: © Goodshoot/Fotosearch
RF; p. 39: © L. Mouton/PhotoAlto
RF; p. 40: © Steve Debenport/
Getty Images RF; p. 42 (top): © JGI/
Jamie Grill/Getty Images RF; p. 42
(bottom): © Marnie Burkhart/
Corbis RF; p. 44: © Ariel Skelley/
Getty Images RF; p. 46 (top): © Clark
Brennan/Alamy RF; p. 46 (bot-
tom): © McGraw-Hill Education/
photographer, John Flourney; p. 47:
© Goodshoot/Fotosearch; p. 48:
© Realistic Reflections RF

**CHAPTER 4**
Opener: © Jacqueline Veissid/Getty
Images RF; p. 52: © Purestock/Getty
Images RF; p. 53: © Ingram Publish-
ing RF; p. 55: © Jacqueline Veissid/
Getty Images RF; p. 56 (top): CDC/
Cade Martin; p. 56 (bottom): © Rob-
ert Kohlhuber/Getty Images RF;
p. 57 (top): © Peathegee Inc./Getty
Images RF; p. 57 (bottom): © Platt-
form/Getty Images RF; p. 58: © Tom
Grill/Corbis Images RF

**CHAPTER 5**
Opener: © Lars Niki RF; p. 65:
© Steve Hix/Somos Images/Corbis
RF; p. 66: © Jakob Helbig/Cultura/
Corbis RF; p. 67: © Fuse/Getty
Images RF; p. 69: © Beau Lark/Cor-
bis; p. 70: © JGI/Jamie Grill/Getty
Images RF; p. 71: © JGI/Jamie Grill/
Blend Images LLC RF; p. 72: © Deb-
orah Jaffe/Corbis RF; p. 76: © Save-
break Media LTD/Corbis RF; p. 77:
© Andersen Ross/Blend Images
LLC RF; p. 79: © Lane Oatey/Blue
Jean Images/Getty Images RF; p. 80:
© Paul Berns/Tetra Images/Photoli-
brary RF; p. 81: © Don Mason/Blend
Images LLC RF

**CHAPTER 6**
Opener: © Joseph Turs/Getty Images
RF; p. 86 (middle): © Corbis RF; p. 86
(bottom): © McGraw-Hill Education;
p. 88: © Joe Raedle/Getty Images;
p. 89: © Fuse/Getty Images RF; p. 92:
© McGraw-Hill Education/Andrew
Resek, photographer; p. 93: © Joseph
Turs/Getty Images RF; p. 94: © Photo
by Spencer Platt/Getty Images; p. 95:
© Blend Images/Pete Saloutos/Getty
Images RF; p. 96: © Dave Moyer RF;
p. 98: © Stockbyte/Getty Images RF;
p. 100: © Eric Audras/Getty Images RF

**CHAPTER 7**
Opener: © Jupiterimages RF; p. 104:
© Uppercut RF/Getty Images RF;
p. 105 (top): © Csondy/Getty Images
RF; p. 105 (bottom): © Lars Niki RF;
p. 108: © Thanasis Zovoilis/Getty
Images RF; p. 110: © Mike Theiss/
National Geographic/Getty Images;
p. 111: © Lars Niki RF; p. 115 (top):
© Jim Arbogast/Getty Images RF;
p. 115 (bottom): © Sam Edwards/
Getty Images RF; p. 118: © Design
Pics/Kristy-Anne Glubish; p. 121:
© KidStock/Getty Images RF;
p. 122: © moorboard/Getty Images
RF; p. 123: © Digital Vision/Getty
Images RF; p. 125: Daniel Berehulak/
Getty Images

**CHAPTER 8**
Opener: © DLILLC/Corbis RF;
p. 131: © Ces'r Vera/Corbis RF;
p. 132: © Huntstock/age fotostock
RF; p. 138 (top): © BananaStock/
PunchStock RF; p. 138 (bottom):
© DLILLC/Corbis RF; p. 139:
© Huntstock/Getty Images RF;
p. 140: © Andersen Ross/Brand X
Corbis RF; p. 141: © John Giustina/
Getty Images RF; p. 145: © Jim
Arbogast/Getty Images RF; p. 148:
© Andersen Ross/Getty Images
RF; p. 150: © Chris Schmidt/Getty
Images RF; p. 151: © John Lund/
Drew Kelly/Blend Images LLC RF;
p. 155: © Erica Simone Leeds RF

## CHAPTER 9

Opener: © Spencer Grant/Science Source; p. 161: Copyright © FoodCollection RF; p. 163: Rob Simpson/USCG; p. 164: © Helen H. Richardson/The Denver Post via Getty Images; p. 166: © Heidi Orcino/Getty Images; p. 169: © McGraw-Hill Education/Kefover/Opatrany; p. 173: © Hero Images/Getty Images RF; p. 174: © Photo by Marvin Joseph/The Washington Post/Getty Images

## CHAPTER 10

Opener: © Hill Street Studios/Getty Images RF; p. 180: © Katrina Wittkamp/Getty Images RF; p. 183: © Dan Saleinger/Getty Images; p. 184: © Hill Street Studios/Getty Images RF; p. 188: © Roy Hsu/Getty Images RF; p. 189 (top): © Blend Images/SuperStock RF; p. 189 (bottom): © Hill Street Studios/Blend Images/Getty Images RF; p. 191: © SuperStock RF; p. 192: © BananaStock/PunchStock RF

## CHAPTER 11

Opener: © Aldo Murillo/Getty Images RF; p. 200: © Getty Images/Stockbyte RF; p. 201: U.S. Coast Guard Photo by Petty Officer 3rd Class Henry G. Dunphy; p. 206: © Hill Street Studios/Blend Images LLC RF; p. 207 (top): © Purestock/Alamy RF; p. 207 (bottom): © DreamPictures/Shannon Faulk/Blend Images/Corbis RF; p. 209: U.S. Census Bureau, Public Information Office (PIO); p. 210: © BananaStock/PictureQuest RF; p. 215 (top): © Realistic Reflections RF; p. 215 (bottom): © Steve Debenport/Getty Images RF

## CHAPTER 12

Opener: © Steve Hix/Somos Images/Corbis RF; p. 224: © Brand X Pictures/PunchStock RF; p. 225: © Image Source/Getty Images RF; p. 227: © Itstock/Jupiterimages RF; p. 229: © amana productions inc./Getty Images RF; p. 230: © Stock Connection/SuperStock; p. 231: © Purestock/Superstock RF; p. 232: © moorboard/Corbis RF; p. 233: © Tim Pannell/Corbis RF; p. 234: © Comstock RF; p. 239: © Doyle Harrell/Getty Images RF; p. 241: © Image Source/Getty Images RF

## CHAPTER 13

Opener: © Datacraft Co. Ltd./Getty Images RF; p. 250: © Chris Whitehead/Getty Images RF; p. 251: © Erproductions Ltd./Blend Images LLC RF; p. 253: © Design Pics/Don Hammond RF; p. 256: Photographs in the Carol M. Highsmith Archive, LOC, Prints and Photographs Division; p. 257 (top): © Douglas Mason/Getty Images; p. 257 (bottom): © Ralph Lee Hopkins/Getty Images RF; p. 258: © Roberto Westbrook/Getty Images; p. 259: © Andersen Ross/Blend Images LLC RF; p. 261: © Cris Bouroncle/Getty Images; p. 263: © Globe Turner, LLC/Getty Images RF

## CHAPTER 14

Opener: Library of Congress Prints and Photographs Division, Department of the Interior, National Park Service [3b48901u]; p. 271: © Mark Ralston/AFP/Getty Images; p. 272 (top): © Stockbyte/Getty Images RF; p. 272 (bottom): © Hill Street Studios/Getty RF; p. 273 (left): Courtesy Car Free Day, Metro, DC/car freemetrodc.org; p. 273 (right): U.S. Government website for distracted driving/www.distraction.gov; p. 274: © AP Photo/Amy Sancetta; p. 275: © Terry Vine/Stone/Getty Images; p. 279: © Purestock/SuperStock RF; p. 281: © Ian Hooton/Science Photo Library/Corbis

## CHAPTER 15

Opener: © Eric Audras/Getty Images RF; p. 294: © Ryan McVay/Photodisc/Getty Images RF; p. 296: © Comstock/Corbis RF; p. 300: © Oliver Hoslet/epa/Corbis; p. 303: © Spencer Grant/Photo Edit; p. 306: © MachineHeadz/Getty Images RF; p. 307: © Moment/cultura/Corbis RF; p. 309: © webphotographeer/Getty Images RF; p. 312: © Steven Debenport/Getty Images RF

# NAME INDEX

LePoire, B. A., 329
Letnic, A. K., 327
Levine, K. J., 332
Levine, S. L., 332
Levy, V. M., Jr., 329
Lewis, M., 327
Lim, J., 330
Lindset, E. W., 325
Linz, D., 330
Lipovsky, C., 335
Loots, G., 327
Lorenzo, G., 326
Louden, A., 325

**M**

MacGeorge, E. L., 329
Mackie, D. M., 329
Mann, Y. M., 335
Mark, A. Y., 330
Markman, B. S., 333
Marshall, L. J., 329
Martin, J., 327, 335
Martin, S. J., 335
Mather, M., 328
Mazer, J., 333
McCain, T. A., 328
McCroskey, J. C., 327, 328, 333, 334
McIntosh, A., 328
McKay, B., 325
McKay, K., 325
McKean, R. A., 325
McLean, A., 332
Mead, G. H., 15, 325
Mehrabian, A., 40, 326
Meier, Megan, 75–76
Mengis, J., 334
Merrier, P., 335
Messmer, M., 325
Miller, D. A., 329
Miller, G. A., 327
Miller, G. R., 328
Milliken, F. J., 332
Mize, J., 325
Moceanu, Dominique, 15
Monroe, A. H., 279, 280
Monteith, M. J., 330
Montgomery, B. M., 328
Morman, M. T., 329
Morrison, E. W., 332
Morrison, K., 328
Motley, M. T., 327
Mullen, B., 333
Murphy, G. L., 333

**N**

Nakayama, Thomas, 54, 327, 335
Nasson, T., 329
Nathanson, A. I., 330
Nett, W., 327
Nice, M. L., 328
Nichols, M., 325
Nikolaus, J., 326
Nisberg, J. N., 325

**O**

Oathout, H. A., 328
Obama, Barack, 86, 173, 274, 275, 284
O'Donnell-Trujillo, N., 332
O'Keefe, B., 329
Olson, E. A., 326
Ooms, T., 329

**P**

Paarvean, N., 326
Pacanowsky, M. E., 332
Parsons, Jim, 89
Pearson, J. C., 328, 329, 331, 334
Pempek, T. A., 331
Perse, E. M., 328
Petersen, T., 326
Peterson, Amanda, 188
Petrie, C. R., Jr., 335
Petronio, S., 331, 332, 336
Pierce, C. A., 327
Pierce, K. F., 329
Pitt, Brad, 70
Pittman, G., 328
Poeter, D., 332
Pomegranate, M., 328
Porter, R. E., 330
Potter, J., 331
Powell, Colin, 173
Power, T., 326
Price, Calla, 284, 285
Putnam, L. L., 332

**R**

Rancer, A. S., 328
Raven, B., 333
Ravi, Dharun, 127
Reamer, N. D., 330
Rihanna, 76
Rhode, D. L., 326
Richards, W. D., 332
Richmond, V. P., 327, 333
Riddle, B., 333
Ridley, A. J., 325
Righetti, F., 329

**R**

Roach, T., 335
Roberts, S. J., 335
Robinson, L., 334
Roessing, T., 326
Roloff, M. E., 329
Rubin, A. M., 330, 331
Rubin, J. E., 327
Rubin, R. B., 328
Rusbult, C. E., 329
Rytting, M., 327

**S**

Sablich, J., 332
Saeki, M., 329
Salas, E., 333
Sale, K., 327
Salopek, J., 327
Samovar, L. A., 330
Samter, W., 329
Sandusky, Jerry, 137
Sants, H., 328
Schellenberg, E. G., 327
Schneider, I. K., 329
Schoppe-Sullivan, S. J., 331
Schwartz, D. F., 332
Scott, E., 325
Selmer, J., 332
Severson, K., 333
Shackelford, T. K., 326
Shea, V., 331
Shellen, W., 328
Shumate, M., 333
Siefert, C. J., 329
Sillars, A., 328
Simkin, M. G., 325
Simonsen, M. M., 327
Sin, S. J., 334
Skenazy, L., 327
Sklare, A., 333
Sklare, G. B., 333
Sline, R., 328
Smith, E. R., 329
Smith, J., 327
Smith, M. W., 335
Soukhanov, A. H., 325
Spitzberg, B. H., 328
Springsteen, Bruce, 274, 284
Stansfield, S., 328
Stefani, L. A., 330
Stephens, W., 334
Strozier, A. L., 327
Sun, S., 332
Surra, C. A., 328
Susskind, A. M., 332

# SUBJECT INDEX

Attitudinal scale, 171
Attractiveness, relational
    development, 69
Attributes, wanted by employers,
    résumés, 302
Audience
    adapting to, nonverbal
      communication, 49
    conclusion of presentation,
      193–195
    confidence boost, and
      communication study, 4
    effective presentations, 250–255
    ethics, 282
    gain and maintain attention, in
      introduction, 179, 180–181
    informative presentations, 248–269
    involvement of, 255
    participation by, 180
    persuasive presentations, 270–292
    presentation delivery, 223–245
    respect for, 282
Audience analysis, 164–172
    adapt to audience, 49, 173–175
    attitudes, 165–166
    beliefs, 166–167
    captive vs. voluntary
      audience, 165
    chapter review, 176–177
    defined, 164–165
    demographics, 165
    levels of, 165–168
    methods for, 168–172
    values, 167–168
Audience analysis methods,
    168–172
    inference, 169
    Internet, 171–172
    observation, 168–169
    questionnaires, 169–171
    tips for, 172
Audience-centered visual aids, 260
Audio recordings, delivery by non-
    native speakers, 243
Authority, persuasion principle
    of, 283
Authority figures, rules of verbal
    communication, 25–26
Autocratic leaders, 149
Automatic attention, 56
Autonomy and connectedness,
    relational maintenance, 71
Avoidance, for conflict
    management, 153
Avoidance stage, relational
    deterioration, 73, 74

**B**
Bargaining
    defined, 78
    interpersonal communication
      behavior, 78–79
Barriers to listening, 58–61
Behavior
    defensive, small-group
      communication, 144
    interpersonal communication
      influence on, 78
    mass media influence on, 104,
      107–108
    supportive, small-group
      communication, 144
    violent, and media violence
      consumption, 108
Behavioral flexibility, maintaining,
    79–80
Behavioral role, 141
Behavioral-based interview
    questions, 308–310
Beliefs
    audience analysis, 166–167, 172
    conflict management to
      improve intercultural
      communication, 100
    defined, 166
    relationship with attitudes and
      values, 167
    strength of, 166–167
Bias
    ethnocentrism, 92–93
    intercultural communication,
      91–94
    physical attractiveness, 42
    prejudice, 94
    stereotyping, 93
    test, 94
Bibliographic reference, 218
Bing search engine, 211
Blocking self-centered function, small
    groups, 142
Blogs
    blogging rough outline draft
      sample, 186
    gatekeeping, 109
    origins, 112
    as social media platform, 113
BLS (U.S. Bureau of Labor Statistics)
    website, 210
Bodily aspects of delivery,
    238–242
    bodily movement, 241–242
    evaluation, 243
    eye contact, 240–241

    facial expressions, 240
    gestures, 238–240
Bodily movement
    categories of, 41
    defined, 241
    delivery, 241–242
    evaluation form, 243
    nonverbal codes, 40–41
Body image, mass media, 108
Body modifications, as artifact, 47
Body of presentation, 183–193
    defined, 183
    informative speech sample,
      262–264
    note card tips, 192–193
    organizational patterns, 189–191
    organize your thoughts, 196
    outline, 184–189
    persuasive speech sample,
      285–288
    samples, 262–264, 285–288
    signposts, 192
    transitions, 192
Bonding (stage), relational
    development, 69, 71
Books, gathering information from
    library, 204–207
Boolean operators, for Internet
    searching, 214
Boomerang effect, 273
Boston College Grouped Action
    Verbs List website, 296
Boundary-crossing media, 115
Brainstorming
    defined, 161
    topic selection process, 161–162
Brainy Quote website, 32
Bullying, 154

**C**
CA (communication apprehension),
    delivery, 225–227
Call to action
    to convey informative content, 254
    persuasive presentations, 272
    remind audience, with conclusion,
      193, 194–195
Capitalization
    computer-mediated
      communication (CMC), 119
    for outline subpoints, 184
Captive audience
    defined, 165
    persuasive presentations, 274
Cards for notes; *see* Note cards
Careers; *see* Workplace

Cause/effect pattern
  in body of presentation, 189, 190
  defined, 190
CBO (U.S. Congressional Budget
    Office) website, 210
Celebrity testimony, 284
Certainty
  creates defensiveness, 74, 75
  defensive behavior and
    statement, 144
Challenge Yourself box
  benefits of communication
    course, 7
  body language and appearance, 46
  choosing a topic, 176
  dating behavior and social
    media, 82
  effective listening, 60
  importance of using words
    carefully, 35
  job search, 313
  narrow a topic, 176
  nonverbal communication, 46
  organize your thoughts, 196
  persuasive methods, 283
  reducing fear of public
    speaking, 228
  selecting the highest-quality
    sources, 216
  social media privacy
    management, 126
  visual aids in informative
    presentations, 260
  when to stop gathering
    information, 216
Channel
  as communication component,
    6–7
  computer-mediated
    communication (CMC), 106
  defined, 6
  mass communication, 106
  models of communication, 9–11
Chat, online, 111, 306
*The Chicago Manual of Style*, 196
  website, 197
Children
  physical attractiveness, 42
  tactile communication, 44
Choice, listening and, 57
Chronemics
  defined, 43
  nonverbal codes, 43–44
Chronological organizational pattern,
    body, 189
Chronological résumés, 297, 300

Circumscribing stage, relational
    deterioration, 73, 74
Citations
  avoiding plagiarism, 218–220
  information gathering, 216–220
  Purdue University OWLs
    for, 218
City-data.com website, 172
Clarifying complex issues, with
    informative presentations, 249
Clarifying task function, small
    groups, 142
Claritas Segments website, 172
Clarity
  speak with, job interview, 307
  visual aids, 260
Cliché, 30
Closure, and perception, 11
Clothing
  dress code for interview, 306–307
  informative presentations, 252
  interview first impression, 306–307
  to involve audience, 180
  nonverbal codes, 45–47
CMC; *see* Computer-mediated
    communication
Co-cultural communication,
    strategies to improve, 98–101
Co-cultural groups, 88
Code sensitivity, 100
Code switching, 26
Codependency, 75
Codes
  as communication component, 8
  nonverbal, 39–48
  sensitivity to, 100
  switching, 26
  verbal communication, 8
Coercion, 148, 271
Cognitive restructuring, to reduce
    public speaking fear, 229–230
Cohesion, small-group
    communication, 143–144, 146
Cohesiveness, 142
Collaboration, for conflict
    management, 153
Collectivist cultures
  defined, 95
  intercultural communication,
    95–96, 99
College degree
  in résumés, 299
  value of communications degree,
    294–295
College students and healthcare
    concept map sample, 205

Comfort zone, expansion, and
    communication study, 4
Commitment
  and consistency, persuasion
    principle of, 283
  defined, 162
  to topic, assessing, 162
Commonalities with audience,
    audience analysis, 172
Communicating Globally box
  allowable information, 252
  audience analysis of values, 166
  eye contact and culture, 240
  focus on self, 25
  greetings, 47
  Hispanic vs. Latino, as label, 91
  listening, 54
  names of people, 8
  social media use, 104
  talking, 54
  work cohesively with diverse
    groups, 146
Communication; *see also specific topics*
  components of, 6–9
  and context, 5–6
  defined, 4
  described, 4–5
  interpersonal, 64–84
  how perception affects, 11–12
  models of, 9–11
  nonverbal, 38–50
  and perception, introduction, 319
  as a process, 4–5
  as résumé skill sought by
    employers, 302
  verbal, 19–37
Communication and Mass Media
    Complete and Communication
    Abstracts periodical index, 208
Communication and perception,
    introduction, 319
  chapter review, 17–19
  communication described, 4–5
  components of communication,
    6–9
  differences in perception,
    12–14
  errors in perception, 14–15
  how perception affects
    communication, 11–12
  models of communication, 9–11
  reasons to study communication,
    3–4, 7
  self-image, 15–17
Communication apprehension (CA),
  delivery, 225–227

Demonstration skills, informative presentations, 249, 259
Denotative meaning of words, 23–24
Describing skills, informative presentations, 256–257
Description
defined, 33
to improve verbal communication, 33
reduces defensiveness, 75
supportive behavior and statement, 144
Desensitization, to reduce public speaking fear, 227–229
Designated leader, 148
Desire, cover letter, 303
Deterioration in interpersonal relationships, 72–75
Development
forecasting in introduction, 179, 182–183
of interpersonal relationships, 71–72
Devices, social media advantages and disadvantages, 114
Dialectic theory, relational maintenance, 71
Dialogue, 15
Diary-based blogs, 112
Dictionary.com website, 236
Difference, in informative presentation, 250, 256
Differentiating stage, relational deterioration, 73–74
Differentiation and specialization
defined, 134
organizational structure, 134–135
Difficulties in interpersonal relationships, 75–76
Digital device, concept map on, 204
Digital media; see Online communication
Digital world, information gathering, 200–204
Direct inference, audience analysis, 169
Disclosure, relational development, 70; see also Self-disclosure
Discontinuance
defined, 274
persuasive presentations, 273, 274
Distance, proxemics as nonverbal communication, 42–43
Distinguish between things, informative presentations, 250

Distractions
hiding visual aids when not in use, 260
as listening barrier, 58–60
Diverse strategies usage, information gathering process, 203
*Diversity in America* (CNN story), 109
*Diversity Journal*, 91
Divorce, changes in interpersonal relationships, 67–68
Documenting your sources, information gathering, 216–220
Dogpile search engine, 211
Dogs, facial expressions, 41
Domestic violence, 76
Dominant culture
allowable information, 252
defined, 88
Downward communication flow, 136
Dramatizing maintenance function, small groups, 142

### E

Ease of communication, social media, 114
Economics, as reason to study intercultural communication, 90–91
Edraw Mindmap website, 204
Education Full Text periodical index, 208
Educational attainment
credentials in résumés, 299
value of communications degree, 294–295
EEOC (U.S. Equal Employment Opportunity Commission), 155
Effective interactions, small-group communication, 150–151
Effective listening, 60
Egocentrism, as listening barrier, 59
Electronic databases, gathering information, 207–208
Email
address on cover letter, 305
address on résumé, 298, 301
rules of verbal communication, 25–26
word-of-the-day, 33
Emblem, as bodily movement category, 41
Emergent leader, 148
Emergent small groups, 138–139
Emotional proof (pathos), 277, 279–280

Emotional regulation, deleting content from social media, 127
Empathic behavior, relational maintenance, 71
Empathic listening, 56
Empathy
interpersonal communication behavior, 77
in listening, 56
reduces defensiveness, 75
relational maintenance, 71
supportive behavior and statement, 144
Emphasis
defined, 39
verbal vs. nonverbal communication, 39, 40
Employment; see Workplace
Encoding
as communication component, 8–9
defined, 8
message interpretation process, 23
models of communication, 9–11
Encyclopedia Britannica Internet Guides search engine, 211
Endings; see Conclusion
Engagement, rules of, verbal communication, 26–27
English as a second language, 4
Enunciation
defined, 237
delivery, 237–238
evaluation form, 243
as vocal cue, 45
Equal Employment Opportunity Commission (EEOC), 155
Equality
reduces defensiveness, 75
supportive behavior and statement, 144
Errors, in perception, 14–15
Ethics
defined, 282
dilemmas in small-group communication, 153–156
persuasive presentations, 171
visual aids, 260
Ethnic and racial considerations
code switching, 26
intercultural communication, 86
racist language, 28–29
U.S. Census 2010 definitions of, 87
Ethnocentrism
avoiding, to improve intercultural communication, 100
defined, 92

as intercultural communication
bias, 92–93
Ethos (source credibility), proof, 277,
278–279
Euphemism
defined, 31
as words to use carefully, 31–32
Europe
cultural characteristics, 96,
97, 99
intercultural communication,
90–91
Latino or Hispanic, as term, 91
social media, 104
Evaluation
of alternatives, for problem
solving, 145–146
creates defensiveness, 74, 75
defensive behavior and
statement, 144
of outcomes, problem solving,
146–147
of sources, information gathering,
216, 217–218
of task function, small groups, 142
Evaluation form, delivery, 243
Evidence
defined, 275
persuasive presentations,
275–277
testimonial, 284
tests of, 276–277
Examples
defined, 282
factual vs. hypothetical, 282
Excite search engine, 211
Experience
in behavioral-based interview,
308, 309
inventory for, 308
past, perceptual differences, 13
*Experiencing Intercultural
Communication* (Nakayama), 54
Experiential superiority, as listening
barrier, 59
Experimentation stage, relational
development, 69, 70
Expert power, 149
Expert testimony, 215, 284
Explaining skills, informative
presentations, 257–258
Explanation, 257
Explicit-rule culture
defined, 97
intercultural communication,
97, 99

Extemporaneous mode
defined, 231
for delivery, 231–232, 233, 241
IMME, 60
Extending task function, small
groups, 142
Extrinsic motivation, 253
Extroversion
social media use, 116
tactile communication, 44
Eye contact
bodily movement, 242
culture and, 240
defined, 240
delivery, 240–241, 243
evaluation form, 243
by non-native speakers, 243

**F**

Facebook
online interaction analysis, 68
origins, 112
popularity, 113
social media, 116, 126
as social networking site, 113
survey information literacy
through user-generated
content, 170
Facetime, 306
Face-to-face interactions
action model of communication, 10
body movement and facial
expression, 40–41
computer-mediated
communication (CMC), 117,
118–119
conversational partners, 25
diminishing, 225
hearing vs. listening, 54
identity management, 16
interpersonal relationships, 68, 70,
81, 82, 121, 123
job interview, 303, 304, 306
open communications, 68
persuasion, 274
rules of engagement, 26
small group, 138
as synchronous
communication, 111
Facial distraction, as listening barrier,
59
Facial expression
defined, 240
delivery, 240
evaluation form, 243
nonverbal codes, 40–41

Fact
factual example, 282
persuasive presentations, 275
proposition of, 275
state striking, to involve
audience, 181
Factiva periodical index, 208
Factual example, 282
Family
changes in interpersonal
relationships, 67–68
as metaphor for organizational
structure, 134
FCC (U.S. Federal Communications
Commission), 28
Fear
cognitive restructuring, 229–230
communication apprehension
(CA), 225–227
pathos, 280
of public speaking, 225, 226, 227–231
skills training, 230
systematic desensitization,
227–229
Fear appeal, 279
Feedback
attention to, nonverbal
communication, 49
as communication component, 7–8
computer-mediated
communication (CMC), 106
defined, 7
to improve intercultural
communication, 100
mass communication, 106
models of communication, 10–11
Feelings
present, perceptual differences,
13–14
validating, in supportive
communication, 152
Feminine people, maintain
behavioral flexibility, 79
*50 Scientifically Proven Ways to Be
More Persuasive* (Cialdini), 283
Figures of speech, 35
Filtering, and gathering
information, 202
Financial problems, as common
fear, 226
First Amendment to U.S.
Constitution, 173–174, 252
First impressions
delivery, 224
informational interview, 314
job interview, 306–307

Protective social media user, 117
Provisionalism
    reduces defensiveness, 75
    supportive behavior and
        statement, 144
Proxemics, nonverbal codes, 42–43
Proximity
    and perception, 11
    relational development, 69
Pseudolistening, as listening barrier,
    59, 60
P-time (polychronic time schedule)
    defined, 97
    intercultural communication,
        97–98, 99
Public distance, range of, 43
Public presentations
    to inform, 248–269
    to persuade, 270–292
Public relations and social media,
    120, 122
Public service campaigns, 274,
    279–280
Public speaking
    audience analysis, 164–172
    fear of, 225, 226, 227–231
    improve nonverbal
        communication, 48–49
    information gathering, 199–222
    presentation delivery, 223–245
    presentation organization, 178–198
    reducing fear of, 225, 227–231
    rules of engagement, 26
    topic selection, 161–164
The Publication Manual of the American
    Psychological Association (APA),
    196, 197, 218, 219
    website, 197
Published summary of research,
    206–207
Punishment power, 148
Purpose
    for informative presentations, 250
    link to, outline, 184
    persuasive presentations, 272–273
    of speaking, adaptation to
        audience, 174, 175
    stating in introduction, 179,
        181–182

Q
Qualifications, establishing in
    introduction, 179, 182
Quality, as vocal cue, 45
Quantification of information,
    résumés, 298

Quantitative skills, as résumé skill
    sought by employers, 302
Quantity, information overload of, 254
Questionnaire
    audience analysis methods, 169–171
    defined, 169
Questions
    informational interview, 313, 314
    for investigating, organizational
        culture, 132
Quotation, to involve audience, 181

R
Race, 86; see also Ethnic and racial
    considerations
Racist language
    defined, 28
    as words to avoid, 28–29
Ranking values, 171
Rate
    of delivery, 234
    evaluation form, 243
    as vocal cue, 45
Readers' Guide to Periodical
    Literature periodical
    index, 208
Reasons for survey, 209–210
Reasons to persuade, 274
Reasons to study
    communication, 3–4, 7
    intercultural communication, 89–91
    mediated communication, 104–105
Receiver
    computer-mediated
        communication (CMC), 106
    defined, 6
    feedback, 7–8
    mass communication, 106
    models of communication, 9–11
    people as communication
        component, 6
Reciprocity, persuasion principle
    of, 283
Recognition seeking self-centered
    function, small groups, 142
Recommendations, to audience, and
    conclusion, 193, 194–195
Recording task function, small
    groups, 142
Recording your informational
    interview, 313
Reference librarians, 204
References
    defined, 196
    informative speech sample, 265
    persuasive speech sample, 288

in presentation, 196–197
    samples, 265, 288
Referent power, 149
Reflexivity
    defined, 100
    to improve intercultural
        communication, 100–101
Regionalism, 35
Regulation, verbal vs. nonverbal
    communication, 39, 40
Regulators, as bodily movement
    category, 41
Rehearsal; see also Practice
    delivery on YouTube, 239
    enunciation, 237–238
Reinforcing norm maintenance
    function, small groups, 142
Relating
    to convey informative content, 254
    listening for, 56
    small-group effective
        interactions, 150
Relational deterioration, 72–75
    avoidance stage, 73, 74
    circumscribing stage, 73, 74
    defensiveness, 73, 74
    deleting content from social
        media, 127
    differentiating stage, 73–74
    stagnation stage, 73, 74
    termination stage, 73, 74
Relational development, 71–72
    bonding stage, 69, 71
    experimentation stage, 69, 70
    initiating stage, 69
    integration stage, 69, 71
    intensifying stage, 69, 70
Relational maintenance, 71–72
Relational messages, supportive
    communication, 152
Relational model, Knapp's, 69–74
Relationship-oriented small
    groups, 139
Relationships
    behavioral-based interview, 308
    cultivating positive, small-group
        communication, 149–151
    informative presentations, 249
    interpersonal; see Interpersonal
        relationships
    sensitivity to, and communication
        study, 3
    soured, deleting content from
        social media, 127
Relaxation, systematic
    desensitization, 227–229

Relevance
    gathering information, 202
    visual aids, 260
Reliability, statistics, 210
Religious considerations, nonverbal
    communication, 46–47
Remembering, listening and, 57–58
Remind audience, with conclusion,
    193, 194
Repetition, verbal vs. nonverbal
    communication, 39, 40
Representative sample of survey, 209
Research
    for informational interview,
        312–313
    for presentation; *see* Information
        gathering
    research studies, 206–207
Resolution, for conflict
    management, 154
Resourcefulness, behavioral-based
    interview, 309
Response, call for, to convey
    informative content, 254
Responsibility, behavioral-based
    interview, 308
Responsiveness
    defined, 69
    kinesics of, 41
    relational development, 69
Résumés
    action verbs for, 298
    chronological, 297, 300
    content, 296, 298–300
    format, 300–302
    functional, 300–302
    online resources for
        improving, 296
    sample of chronological, 297
    sample of functional, 301
    style, 295–296, 297
    top 10 attributes wanted by
        employers, 302
    writing, 295–302
Reward power, 148
*Rhetoric* (Aristotle), 277
*Rhetoric ad Herennium* (Cicero), 238
Rhetorical questions, 252
Rich interaction medium, social
    media advantages and
    disadvantages, 114
Rituals, organizational culture,
    132, 133
Role
    defined, 13, 140
    perceptual differences, 13

small-group communication,
    140–141
Role-play, to involve audience, 180
Roman numerals, for outline main
    points, 184
Rough draft
    defined, 186
    outline of presentation, 185–187
    sample outline, 186
"Routine Body Shrinking" outline
    sample, 191
Routines, organizational culture,
    132, 133
Rules of engagement
    defined, 26
    verbal communication, 26–27
Rules of verbal communication,
    24–27
    conversational partners, 25–26
    engagement rules, 26–27
    place (location), 24–25
Russian children adoption
    outline, 185

S

Safety, deleting content from social
    media, 127
Sample size of survey, 209
Samples
    body of presentation, 262–264,
        285–288
    chronological résumés, 297
    conclusion, 195, 264–265, 288
    functional résumés, 301
    informative presentations, 261–265
    introduction, 261–262, 285
    outline; *see* Outline samples
    persuasive presentations, 285–291
    references, 265, 288
    of research, 212–213
Sampling method of survey, 209
Satisfaction stage, Monroe Motivated
    Sequence, 279, 281
Scale, attitudinal, 171
Scanning and choosing, 57
Scarcity, persuasion principle of, 283
Scholarly journals, gathering
    information from library,
    204–207
Search engine, 211
Secondary source, 206
*The Secret Life of the American Teenager*
    (TV show), 110
Sedentary lifestyle study, 277
Selection, and perception, 11
Selective attention, 57

Self, interpersonal communication, 65
Self-assessment, to improve
    intercultural communication, 99
Self-centered functions, small groups,
    141, 142
Self-centered social media user, 117
Self-concept, interpersonal
    communication behavior, 77
Self-consciousness and delivery, 239
Self-disclosure
    approaches to, 72
    defined, 70
    to involve audience, 181
    relational development, 70
Self-image, and communication,
    15–17
Self-presentation, manage online, 17
Self-talk, cognitive restructuring, 229
Semantic distraction, as listening
    barrier, 59
Seminal sources, 212
Sender, mass communication, 106
Sensitivity
    desensitization to reduce public
        speaking fear, 227–229
    to improve intercultural
        communication, 100
    improve nonverbal, 49
Sentence, as single idea in
    outline, 184
Sentence outline
    defined, 187
    eating breakfast sample, 187–188
    informative speech sample,
        261–265
    persuasive speech sample,
        285–288
    samples, 187–188, 261–265,
        285–288
    texting and driving sample,
        285–288
September 11, 2001 terrorist attacks,
    89–90
Setting
    body language and appearance, 46
    improve nonverbal
        communication, 49
    for presentation, audience
        analysis, 172
    regionalism, 35
    rules of engagement, 26
    rules of verbal communication,
        24–26
    self-image and communication, 16
    words to avoid, 27–29
    words to use carefully, 30–32

meaning, 23–24
simple, to convey informative
   content, 253
to use carefully, 30–32
in verbal communication, 22–24,
   27–32
Work attitudes, behavioral-based
   interview, 309
Work ethic, as résumé skill sought by
   employers, 302
Work experience, behavioral-based
   interview, 308
Workplace, 293–315
   body language and
      appearance, 46
   chapter review, 314–315
   communication jobs, 294–295
   connection building, 310–314

contemporary jobs using
   communication degree, 294–295
cover letter, 303, 304–305
deleting content from social
   media, 127
hostile work environment
   harassment, 28
internships, 311–312
jargon, 30–31
job interview, 303, 305–307
listening importance, 52, 56
M-time vs. P-time, 97, 98
networking, 310–314
professional success and
   communication study, 4
résumé writing, 295–302
sexual harassment, 155–156
social media, 126, 310–311

Written communication
   cover letter, 303
   informative presentations, 248–269
   persuasive presentations, 270–292
   résumés, 295–302
WWW Virtual Library website, 211

Y

Yahoo Libraries virtual library, 211
Yahoo search engine, 211
"You" language, for conflict
   management, 154
"The Youth Vote" outline (Peterson),
   188–189
YouTube
   origins, 112
   respond to speakers, 239
   social media use, 116